THE
ALPINE JOURNAL
2014

On the aproach to Ulvetanna, Queen Maud Land, Antarctica. Such stable conditions could change rapidly, turning this-hour long 'pleasure trek' into white-out struggle for survival. *(Alastair Lee)*

THE
ALPINE JOURNAL
2014

The Journal of the Alpine Club

A record of mountain adventure
and scientific observation

Edited and Produced by Bernard Newman

Volume 118

Number 362

Supported by the
MOUNT EVEREST FOUNDATION

Published by
THE ALPINE CLUB

© 2014 by the Alpine Club

THE ALPINE JOURNAL 2014
Volume 118 No 362

www.alpinejournal.org.uk

Address all editorial communication to the Hon Editor:
Alpine Club, 55 Charlotte Rd, London, EC2A 3QF
email: admin@alpine-club.org.uk

Address all sales and distribution communications to:
Cordée, 11 Jacknell Rd, Dodwells Bridge Ind Est, Hinckley, LE10 3BS

Back numbers:
Apply to the Alpine Club, 55 Charlotte Rd, London, EC2A 3QF or, for
1969 to date, apply to Cordée, as above.

First published in 2014 by The Alpine Club
Typeset by Bernard Newman
Photo production by Tom Prentice
Printed and bound by Novoprint SA, Barcelona

A CIP catalogue record for this book is available from The British Library

ISBN 978-0-9569309-3-4

Front cover: Dave MacLeod leading a strenuous Scottish grade VIII, 9
pitch during an attempt on a steep gully line on the east face of Aguja
Mermoz, Paine, Patagonia. *(Calum Muskett)*

Endpapers

Front: Aerial view looking west along the Orvinfjell mountains,
Antarctica. The south buttress of Ulvetanna catching the sun at bottom
right. *(Alastair Lee)*

Back: Annapurna III from Peak 6505m. *(Stéphane Benoist)*

Foreword

The 150th Anniversary of the first *Alpine Journal*, the 60th of the first ascent of Everest have come and gone, landmarks in the history of the Alpine Club and mountaineering and worthy of celebration. The 118th *Alpine Journal* marks a more sombre date, of course, the centenary of the outbreak of the First World War – The Great War, the War to End All Wars. . . I remember a conversation with a good friend of mine, the printer of my first climbing journal at Leeds University way back, the late Werner Trimmel, an Austrian who was born into the Second World War. I'd glibly commented how awful it was that so many climbers and mountaineers on both sides had been killed in the two wars – kindred spirits. He pulled me up sharp, saying that a great many non-climbers had died too along with all their hopes and dreams. Werner was right of course, but I think climbers might be forgiven for perhaps saving a little more reflection for those young men of our community who strode into oblivion at the end of that 'golden' summer of 1914.

But we climbers like to think that mountaineering celebrates the indestructibility if not the perversity of the human spirit and in the year since those celebrations the climbing community has not been idle.

Thus this year's *Journal* is packed out with tales of diverse achievements across the globe.

From the 'wastes' of Antarctica – that other planet on our doorstep, Alastair Lee and Leo Houlding relate the rewards of extreme rock climbing indulged at the edge of the physiological and logistical envelope. Stalwarts of the Alpine Club record their efforts from the Andes of Peru, the Alps and of course the high Himalaya. Piotr Szawarski describes the trials of a group of tetraplegics who manage to get themselves and their wheelchairs across the Tibetan plateau to Everest base camp, a mind-boggling achievement.

The *Alpine Journal* has a broad remit: Mike Searle continues his review of the current state of research into the geological origins of the Himalaya and Tim Pollard explores the motivations and techniques of the mountain artist. John Cleare recounts the fascinating history of making movies in the high mountains, from the mobile darkrooms of John Noel to the flash drives and 4K of today.

The political and environmental arenas are not neglected: Steve Goodwin reports from an international conference 'Mountaineering in the Future – challenges for alpine associations' in Pontresina and co-attendees Katharina Conradin and Dominik Siegrist provide a disturbing insight into the problems threatening mountain communities and environments.

With this issue several long-standing contributors have stepped down (perhaps it's something I've said. . .). Bill Ruthven has delivered his final expedition report round-up after 29 years as Secretary of the Mount Everest Foundation; I'm sure anyone who has been involved with the *AJ* over the years will join me in a heart-felt vote of thanks to Bill for providing one of of it's key foundations. Harish Kapadia retired from keeping the climbing world up to date regarding happenings in the Indian Himalaya after 25 years, another colossal contribution. Finally, due credit and gratitude to Paul Knott, who also stepped down after the last issue, for his essential work over the years as Assistant Editor and in collating the Area Notes – a vitally important department of the *Journal*.

I'd like to thank also those who gave so freely of their time and efforts to make this *Journal* possible, particularly: Steve Goodwin, who's decade-long stint as Hon. Editor must surely qualify him for sainthood, for his encouragement and sound advice; Margot Blyth for her calm and diligent proofing; John Cleare, the 'Godfather' of British mountaineering film and photography who always answers 'yes' before my endless requests for photos; and, of course, thanks to the many contributors who's only reward is posterity and glory!

Being given the opportunity to produce and edit this edition of the *AJ* has been a great personal honour, if not challenge it must be said, and could be seen to complete the circle begun with the *Leeds University Union Climbing Club Journal* of 1973.

Bernard Newman

Contents

HISTORY

AREA NOTES

REVIEWS

IN MEMORIAM

ALPINE CLUB NOTES

High Asia

Aiguille du Grépon, oil on canvas, 51x76cm. *(Tim Pollard)*

MICK FOWLER

Kishtwar Kailash

Kishtwar Kailash (6451m) from the north. *(Mick Fowler)*

There were four of us: Paul Ramsden, Mike Morrison, Rob Smith and me. Our objective was the first ascent of Kishtwar Kailash (6451m) the unclimbed highest peak in East Kishtwar and excitement levels were high. It was August 2013 and the troubles in Kashmir which had caused access problems for the last 20 years appeared to have subsided and Indian Home Office approval was expected any day now.

Then out of the blue:

12/8/2013 Srinagar News Report: *In a direct fallout of Friday's clashes in Kishtwar, all national highways leading to Jammu are now shut. Mobile and internet services were disconnected on Monday while schools and colleges remained shut.*

A stressful month followed, the end result being that we didn't get all the paperwork in place until the day before we left. With hindsight I like

Chenab Gorge approach road. No place to practice your three-point turns. *(Mick Fowler)*

to speak positively of these challenges as they keep the crowds away and leave plum objectives unclimbed. But somehow I have trouble enthusing in this way at the time.

It appeared that the valley beneath Kishtwar Kailash had not been visited since Andy MacNae and Shan Singh Mann crossed the Muni La and travelled beneath the west face nearly 25 years ago. They had described the mountain as 'a very challenging objective' and Paul and I already knew it to be an inspiring mountain having viewed it from Shiva the previous year and Cerro Kishtwar in 1993. Inspiring and challenging is a good combination we thought.

To avoid the troubles in Kashmir our approach was via the Rhotang La and down the Chenab gorge. The last 50km of road to the start of our walk-in proved to be the most exciting that any of us had ever experienced. Paul took a 3-minute video clip of one section which had 835,000 hits when posted on Facebook.

The walk-in to base camp shared the first part of the once well used Umasi-la crossing from Paddar to Zandskar. The troubles in Kashmir have hugely reduced the number of trekkers but conversely the 'Machail Yatra' pilgrimage in August, started only 40 years ago, now sees a remarkable 350,000 or so pilgrims covering the first two days to the small temple at Machail. The troubles in 2013 reduced that number by about half but even so that's a huge number of people to cater for, particularly on mountain mule tracks designed to link villages with no more than 200 inhabitants. But we were here in late September by which time the only evidence of the

The north face of Kishtwar Kailash, showing the line of the Fowler/Ramsden Route, and bivvys 3, 4 and 5. *(Mick Fowler)*

hordes' passing was a very significant amount of rubbish and a curiously large number of well-used portable toilets.

Beyond Machail our route entered the Darlang Nullah, a 70-mile-long valley at an altitude of above 3500m. It was immediately clear that we were on less travelled paths which had not been used by mules loaded with mountaineers' equipment for many years and several sections had to be built up before the mules could pass. It was eight days after leaving the UK that we established a base camp a few hours short of Kishtwar Kailash at about 4000m. What with the last minute permit stress and numerous uncertain moments with the mules it was a relief to arrive and be faced with just the challenge of climbing the mountain.

Four for Kishtwar: l-r Mike Morrison, Paul Ramsden, Mick Fowler, Rob Smith.

Bivvy site Day 2 – Ramsden surveys the way ahead. Rihoni Sikhar in background. *(Mick Fowler)*

'Establishing a base camp' is actually rather a grand way of putting it. In practice each pair of climbers had one tent and Rinku, our Liaison Officer, Pritam, our cook, and Devraj, the kitchen boy, had another tent between them which doubled up as the cook tent.

The weather was indifferent but as our time was restricted by full-time jobs, every day had to be used to the full to stand a chance of success on a 6400m peak in a 30-day trip from the UK. With such thoughts uppermost in our minds Paul and I left promptly to explore and acclimatise around Kishtwar Kailash while Mike and Rob decided to explore a side valley.

It felt excitingly adventurous to be heading up towards the peak that had been the focus of our attention for so many months. It would, however, have been more satisfying had we been able to see the mountain and thereby choose a line. Instead, a full day was spent clambering over a moraine covered glacier beneath low cloud in the drizzle, wondering exactly where we were.

On our third day out from base camp we reached a col at about 5700m, still without getting a good view of the mountain. The col had been spotted through clearings in the cloud and looked as if it would provide a suitable spot for relaxing, reading and acclimatising with maybe the possibility of ascending to a good viewpoint. In fact, though, it turned out to be a knife edge crest which, once flattened, gave a comfortable camping spot but little else. Fortunately, after over 10 years of Himalayan climbing together, Paul and I are pretty well used to this acclimatising business and the fact that we spent the next two days pinned down in a small tent with just a small flattened area in front to walk about on was not a problem. We relaxed, read books and breathed in lots of thin air. At one point we even had a good

'The millions of tons of snow that must have poured down here during the monsoon had left well compacted névé.' Mick Fowler, Day 3. *(Paul Ramsden)*

view of the mountain. We couldn't see the face we planned to climb but what we saw did at least convince us that our vague plan of descending the other side was a very bad one. If we were successful it was clear that we would have to descend by our line of ascent. After two nights perched on the little col we returned to base camp for a day's resting and eating before we were ready to go. Mike and Rob were there already, fattening up in preparation for a trip to the unexplored upper reaches of the glacier.

We don't tend to bother with gadgets that deliver things like weather forecasts, so it was a surprise and relief to see clear skies as we waded the river by our base camp and headed for the climb. Despite failing to get a really good look at the face, clearings in the weather during our return from the col had at least given us a good idea of the best line to follow. Our plan was to avoid the risk from icefall at the foot of the face by climbing a couloir leading to a possible entry point above the danger. Mind you, to get there involved a lot of uncertainty: steep loose ground to gain a glacier, an icefall and a couloir of uncertain angle. The icefall, which looked easy from a distance, sported an overhanging section which required a heel-hook for success. By the end of the second day, though, we had reached the edge of the face and were relieved to see that our hunch was right – we could easily access the face proper above the dangerous icefalls at its base.

It somehow feels more intimidating to step out onto a face and immediately be confronted with exposure than it does to build up to the same position from the bottom. The climbing very soon became memorably atmospheric with smooth icefields and huge monolithic walls soaring above us and no obvious way through. But from my photograph, taken from the summit of Cerro Kishtwar in 1993, we knew that a fault-line cleaved through the walls at one point and our hope was that this would provide the key to the lower part of the face.

Classic European north face climbs tend to include sections of steep icefield which succumb to calf-wrenching teetering on front-points, and initially the ground here was not dissimilar. As we gained height the ice became increasingly thin and the climbing increasingly precarious. By evening we were relieved to find a single spot on which to pitch our little tent – a small projecting prow just beneath the fault-line. The weather remained glorious, the mountains beyond 'our' valley were coming into view and, as we snuggled down in the evening sunshine, we sensed we were climbing in a very special place.

Above: Ramsden at the fourth bivvy and (opposite) on steep, difficult ground, Day 4 *(Mick Fowler)*

***

'Think I might have to come down.'

Paul had already been up and tried, removed his sack and tried again and now he was sounding uncharacteristically defeated.

'Round the corner might be better,' he offered.

I hung from my ice screw belay, sucking in the cold morning air and peering around. There was another possibility to the right but it didn't look any easier to me and to get there would require an abseil and a traverse that would take a couple of hours at least. And I really didn't want to do that. Losing upwards momentum can so easily lead to dithering and retreat. It looked to me that if we could just reach a point five metres or so above Paul's high point the difficulty would ease for a few more metres at least. Higher up we could see a clearly overhanging section of ice but that was not the immediate problem. The section causing difficulty was a loose and thinly iced bulge in the fault-line splitting the huge walls. It had looked to be standard Scottish Grade V but once Paul had set out I could see that it was much steeper than it looked and clearly loose and unprotected.

'Shall I have a look?'

I had no great confidence that I could get up if Paul couldn't but somehow it seemed the right thing to say. There was a long silence.

'I'll have one more go.'

As he inched higher and higher I felt a slight pang of guilt, wondering if I had indirectly encouraged him to push on against his better judgement. This was no place to fall, there was no further protection and the climbing

was obviously hard. I was almost as relieved as he was when he finally reached a belay and shouted for me to climb.

As I approached Paul was looking relaxed and his usual positive demeanour was restored.

'Hard pitch that. Brilliant position,' he enthused as I gasped my way inelegantly though the desperately insecure crux.

The climbing for the rest of the day was typical of the harder Scottish gullies – steep, sometimes thinly iced grooves interspersed with a couple of wild, overhanging sections. The millions of tons of snow that must have poured down here during the monsoon had left well compacted névé and conditions were generally very good. Much pleasure was had and as evening approached another solitary projecting prow to one side even allowed us to pitch the tent. Life was good. Usually on this kind of climb we end up bivouacked with one person wrapped in the tent fabric and another in a bivouac sack, or sometimes we cut a bum ledge and sit side by side inside the tent fabric. On this route we had managed to get the poles in the tent and actually pitch it, after a fashion, every night thus far. And that makes such a difference. . .

Above us our fault-line reared up vertically for a long, long way to reach the summit crest just north of the south summit. Back in the UK our initial

Ramsden (above) and Fowler (opposite) in the steep ice runnels, Day 4.

plan had been to climb the fault in its entirety, but close inspection of various photographs made it clear that the highest point was at the north end of what looked to be a potentially long and difficult knife-edge ridge. So with that in mind our intended route ahead now lay leftwards across ice slopes beneath more huge blank walls to a shallow groove-line leading up the headwall directly to the highest point.

We were now above most of the surrounding peaks and new horizons were opening: to the south the Prow of Shiva that Paul and I had climbed the previous year, whilst the 7000m peaks of Nun and Kun now reared their heads above the Cerro Kishtwar/Chomochior ridge on the far side of our base camp valley.

'Is that our tent?' Bivvy number 5.

That evening we ended up perched on two separate 30cm wide ledges hacked out of an ice patch on the headwall. Sitting there soaking up the last rays of evening sun high on an unclimbed peak and marvelling at the cloudless view was one of those 'it's great to be in the mountains' moments. I was using the tent fabric as a bivouac sack but Paul was in just his sleeping bag. I could hear Paul's slow and heavy breathing through the still night air but I was too excited to sleep. Away to the south a thunderstorm was brewing and gradually through the night it came our way. I lay there marvelling at the almost continuous lightning and wondering how close I should allow it to get before waking Paul and preparing ourselves for its arrival. But then it was 4am and our alarms were beeping so it was time to stir ourselves anyway.

On a bivouac like this it takes about two hours from the alarm sounding to get going. Normally the first thing to do is get the stove going but on this particular morning some water must somehow have frozen inside it and the day started with Paul thawing it out down his trousers for 15 minutes or so. There was much relief when the gas started to flow freely and we were able to start melting snow for a cup of the best quality Yorkshire Tea that Paul insists we have to have on these trips.

By the time we were ready to start climbing the thunderstorm had moved away but a front was clearly moving in. Our way up the headwall was not immediately obvious but after a false line we gained a slanting fault-line that gave some fine climbing leading directly to the summit. And what a wonderful summit it was. As I arrived Paul was sat on the knife edge crest with a leg on either side. The sun was still shining and with good visibility

Opposite: Mick Fowler crossing ice slopes to gain the headwall, Day 5. *(Paul Ramsden)*

'And what a summit it was. . .' Fowler and Ramsden triumphant.

we could soak up the scenery and see that we were higher than any of the other peaks in this area. It felt a great privilege to be able to make the first ascent of a mountain like this. We loitered for 30 minutes taking photographs, generally revelling in the achievement of something we'd dreamed about for many months.

The weather stayed fair, the descent was pleasingly uneventful and seven days after setting out we were back at base camp. Mike and Rob had enjoyed their exploratory trip to the upper glacier and Pritam had prepared a Kishtwar Kailash success cake. Relaxing felt particularly good and the enduring retrospective pleasure that goes with Himalayan success was beginning to flow – long may the exciting peaks of Kishtwar be accessible for mountaineering.

Next day our perfectly timed weather window closed and snow came to base camp. The mules arrived as planned and it was time to go home.

Summary: An account of the first ascent of Kishtwar Kailash in the Kishtwar Himalaya, India, by Mick Fowler and Paul Ramsden, 4 – 10 October 2013. Other team members were Mike Morrison and Rob Smith who explored the upper reaches of the Chomochior Glacier but were unable to climb their chosen objective due to difficult conditions on the glacier.

Acknowledgements: The team would like to thank Berghaus who helped make the climbs possible.

DEREK BUCKLE

An Invitation to Zanskar

Tributary glacier 1 and the north face of Z8. *(Derek Buckle)*

The decision to return to India in the autumn of 2013 was made much too late for us to apply for grant applications since it was April before we had really got the makings of an expedition together. Eventually four of us committed to the trip: Mike Pinney, Chris Storie, Tony Westcott and me – all seasoned Alpine Club members, some would say. The next decision, of course, was exactly where to go. Having been to the Indian Himalaya several times before, I for one was keen to visit somewhere different. Harish Kapadia's article *Zanskar Anyone?*[1] finally solved the dilemma, providing photographs of the mountains to the south-west of the road taken on his journey from Kargil to Padum. Our research rapidly established that several of these side valleys were infrequently visited, at least by Westerners. One valley, the Durung Drung, situated a little beyond the Pensi La watershed, has received much attention, but what attracted us was the neighbouring Pensilungpa Valley. Despite being adorned with some impressive peaks, this valley seemed considerably less well-known,

Peak 5641m

The peaks at the head and to the NW of the Pensilungpa Valley. *(Derek Buckle)*

with the potential for both exploration and unclimbed summits. On hearing of our plans Harish not only encouraged us to visit the Pensilungpa but readily supplied us with a number of high resolution photographs. From these and the aid of GoogleEarth we finally homed in on several peaks straddling the Pensilungpa-Durung Drung divide.

Our preferred objective did not feature on the 'approved list' of the Indian Mountaineering Federation (IMF) and we were assigned another, much harder, mountain situated at the head of the Pensilungpa Valley. We duly paid the appropriate peak fee for this otherwise unknown Peak 6048m, but in the knowledge that we had freedom to explore and climb virtually anywhere in the valley; including our primary objective. Things were looking up at last and we were set to go. To our knowledge only Z8, the peak at the head of the valley, had been climbed, by the Italian husband and wife team of Gino and Silvia Buscaini via its west-north-west ridge in July 1978[2].

The journey to the Pensilungpa Valley

At our obligatory IMF briefing in Delhi we were introduced to Suman (Happy) Kant, the Liaison Officer assigned to our expedition. Happy subsequently proved himself a true asset by facilitating our passage through multiple military check-points and by assuming a role as the team's surro-

gate Sirdar – not strictly necessary, but very useful in ensuring there was no confusion concerning our plans once we were established in the valley.

We soon left a sweltering Delhi to acclimatise at the cooler altitudes of Leh where Rimo Expeditions, who facilitated our trip, have their headquarters. There were many familiar faces from earlier visits: Dan Kumar, who was with us three years previously in the Jiwa Nala[3], would again be our base camp cook, ensuring excellent food, but the five additional support staff, Robin, Dawa, Karma, Ambir and Ajay were all new to us. They too did not disappoint, the young Sherpas could not have done more to help us establish assault camps higher in the valley.

After visiting the impressive 17th century Leh Palace – a mini replica of the Potala in Lhasa situated on a hill above the town – and the established monasteries of Shey and Hemis, we began the long drive along the Indus Valley, taking in the ancient 11th century Alchi Gompa and the impressive 8m high Maitreya statue, depicting the future Buddha, at Mulbekh – believed to have been carved into the rock in the 8th century – en route to an overnight stop in Kargil. From Kargil we followed a gradually deteriorating road beside the Suru River until it was possible to access the Pensilungpa a little north of the Pensi La. From here a 3km trek over easy ground led to our planned base camp at 4650m, only 0.6km short of the current glacial snout and the source of the Suru itself.

Above: Mike Pinney (front) and Tony Westcott on the ascent of Hidden Peak. Left: Tony Westcott descending from the summit block of Hidden Peak. *(Derek Buckle)*

Exploration of the Pensilungpa and its south-eastern glaciers

Like most glaciers worldwide, the Pensilungpa has contracted massively in recent years. At one time five subsidiary glaciers to the south-east flowed directly into the main glacier – but no longer. Today they are separated by excoriated ground and substantial boulder-fields which, though unstable, are relatively easily traversed. Remote sensing studies suggest that up to 38% of the Pensilungpa Glacier disappeared between 1962 and 2007[4] and that the snout has receded about 120m over the same period[5]. More recent ground surveys indicate that the process continued over the period 2008-2013 with an average annual recession of the snout of 11m[6].

Having established base camp on 9 September our first task was to establish the topography of the valley and to reconnoitre possible sites for higher camps. Thus, while Mike and I followed the medial moraine of the main glacier, Tony and Chris negotiated the more complex true right lateral moraine by traversing beneath both the second and third tributary glaciers. A combination of radio and clear visual contact between our two parties simplified the task and it was soon apparent where we needed to be, even if our primary objective was blocked by a prominent triangular peak that dominated the skyline of the third tributary glacier. This peak was subsequently named Pyramid Peak, although we made no attempt to climb it.

On 11 September we relocated to camp 1 at 4845m and the next day to camp 2 at 5223m situated close to the edge of the third side glacier (see map). Despite the excellent views afforded by this camp, Pyramid Peak continued to dominate the southern aspect to the extent that there were initial concerns we may have entered the wrong valley.

There was only one way to find out! Leaving Chris, who was not yet fully acclimatised, we set off early on 13 September roping up where the glacier markedly steepened and wound through a maze of crevasses as it steepened further. Eventually the angle eased and, to

Mike Pinney, Chris Storie and Tony Westcott low on the north Ridge of Peak 5641m. *(Derek Buckle)*

our relief, the snowy arête that we had identified from satellite pictures came into view. With hindsight we should have trusted the satellite images, but visual confirmation is immensely reassuring.

We then crossed two major bergschrunds to a small rocky col, south-east of Pyramid Peak, from where we climbed the steep north-north-west ridge via a snowy top to the rocky summit at 5802m (first ascent, Alpine PD+). We subsequently named this Hidden Peak on account of its relative invisibility from anywhere in the Pensilungpa Valley, although it did offer extensive panoramic views over the Durung Drung Glacier and its surrounding peaks. In deteriorating weather we retraced our steps to camp 2, arriving

Derek Buckle, Tony Westcott and Chris Storie descending from an attempt on Peak 5641m. *(Mike Pinney)*

just as the only significant snowfall of the trip set in. We returned to base camp the following day.

With our primary objective in the bag, our attention turned to Peak

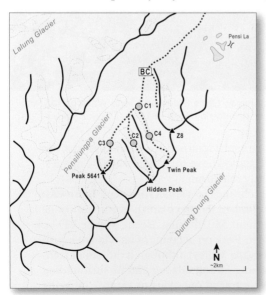

5641, situated at the foot of the fourth tributary glacier. We had looked long at its impressive north face from base camp and elsewhere and spotted what appeared to be a climbable line up the mixed north-northeast ridge. So two days later (16 September), all four of us established camp 3 at 4950m on the true left lateral moraine at the foot of this glacier.

It was not an ideal site as it still lay some way below the plateau by which we hoped to gain the ridge; but it was the only place that provided relatively flat, even ground that was objectively safe and with access

The sharp second pinnacle on Twin Peak. Hidden Peak is just visible at half height beyond. *(Derek Buckle)*

Tony Westcott nearing the summit of Twin Peak. *(Mike Pinney)*

to water. It would have to do.

We set out at sunrise next day in brilliant weather and continued up the moraine until it was possible to move right onto the rocky north-northeast ridge proper. Climbing relatively straightforward broken ground we made

Tributary glacier 3 with Pyramid Peak at centre. *(Derek Buckle)*

one or two forays onto the hard ice of the north face before returning to the relative security of the rocks. At 5576m, however, we reached an impasse. At this point a prominent rock finger projecting into the face forced us to choose between difficult rocky ground to our left and a threatening 65-70° ice face on our right. From here it was evident that the summit was still some way above (more than the 70m suggested by the map height) and that it was likely to prove a challenge. With a higher assault camp we may have made a different decision, but under the circumstances we chose not to continue and, having spent a further night at our high camp, returned to base camp the following day.

With Chris still not feeling on good form Mike, Tony and I established camp 4 at 5186m on the true right of tributary glacier 2 on 20 September with the intention of attempting a peak on the Pensilungpa – Durung Drung divide that we had seen from the main glacier. The weather remained clear the next day and we climbed the rough glacier left of centre until it visibly steepened and extensive crevasses forced a detour leftwards before we headed south to a snowy col around 5600m. Westwards from here lay the more easterly of two rock towers at 5825m (first ascent, East Summit, AD). We declined to attempt the second, more technical, isolated rocky spire even though it was the slightly higher of the two. Twin Peak, as we subsequently named it, commanded panoramic views towards Z3 and the Durung Drung Glacier to the south, Z8 immediately north and Hidden Peak to the south-west. Further north held distant views of Nun and Kun.

Next day, with our time in Zanskar coming to an end, we managed to scramble to 5118m along the north ridge of Z8 for a good view of its impressive north face before finally leaving the valley on our return journey to Leh, Delhi and home.

Z3 and the Durung Drung Glacier from Twin Peak. *(Derek Buckle)*

Summary: Expedition to Pensilungpa Glacier in the Zanskar region, Indian Himalaya, 3 September – 2 October 2013 by AC members Derek Buckle (leader), Mike Pinney, Chris Storie and Tony Westcott. The team explored four of the major subsidiary glaciers descending from the Pensilungpa – Durung Drung divide and made the first ascent of Peak 5802m 'Hidden Peak' (PD+) via the north-northwest ridge and Peak 5825m 'Twin Peak' (AD). They also reached a height of 5576m on the north-north east ridge of Peak 5641.

References
1. H. Kapadia, *Himalayan Journal*, 65, 151-163 (2009)
2. G. Buscaini, *American Alpine Journal*, 52, 614 (1978)
3. D. Buckle, *Alpine Journal*, 115, 31-38 (2010/11)
4. A. C. Pandey, S. Ghosh, M.S. Nathawat & R. K. Tiwari, *J. Indian Soc. Remote Sens.*,40, 245-255 (2012)
5. S. Schmidt, M. Nüsser, M. S. Nathawat, S. Ghosh & A. C. Pandey, *Geophysical Research Abstracts*, 12, EGU2010-13451 (2010)
6. Field studies carried out by the Birla Institute of Technology, Mesra, India over the period 2007-2009 as indicated by position markers and GPS measurements taken by A. Westcott during our 2013 visit.

Mike Pinney, Chris Storie, Tony Westcott and Derek Buckle in Leh. *(Derek Buckle coll.)*

YANNICK GRAZIANI

Life Wish

Ten days on the South Face of Annapurna

We left for Nepal on 15 August, feeling good to be starting our adventure at last – a scary prospect, of course, but we were in very good shape; we were ready. The previous summer had been tough in the Alps – as guides Stéphane and I had been kept very busy. This summer had been great too, with days and days of good weather, so we couldn't really stop climbing.

But now we were on our way – this would be my third time on Annapurna: the first was in 2000 with Christian Trommsdorff and Patrick Wagnon, the second in 2010 with Stéphane Benoist.

The massive south face of Annapurna. See page 296 for the route taken by Benoist and Graziani. *(Yannick Graziani)*

This time we decided not to set up a base camp but to use the lodge at the Annapurna Sanctuary, so the logistics in Kathmandu were easy and fast and after just two days of organisation we took the local bus to Pokhara, where we hired a jeep and five porters.

We soon became immersed in the wild and beautiful hills of Nepal. For us it was pure delight to trek into the Annapurna Sanctuary again. Our plan was simple. First we would camp in the valley that leads to Annapurna 3. Here on the eastern edge of the Sanctuary we found a fine un-named peak marked on the map at 6505m, which we would use to acclimatise. We climbed a prominent 700m couloir on the south-west flank and spent two nights on the summit.

After a month's training we left on 16 October and headed up to the huge South Face of Annapurna and set up camp at 5000m. For the past month we had talked endlessly about our route: which line to take, what equipment, how long would it take, but now, walking through the glacier, wrapped in fog on the five hour approach to the foot of the wall you had time alone with your thoughts.

Next day in the early morning darkness we ploughed our way through deep snow to the start of the climbing. Exhausting exercise. . . The South Face of Annapurna is very impressive, a massive, steep wall without even a square metre of level space. In the afternoon cloud we settled into our small but comfortable tent. We talked about the coming days – the forecast seemed to be a bit more unsettled than expected.

We decided to start early and climb to 6700m where we knew, from our previous attempt in 2010, we could dig a half-metre wide ledge in a cornice sheltered beneath the spur of the Japanese Pillar that dropped straight from the central summit. I was impatient; I wanted to climb fast to avoid the heat of the day with its stonefall and avalanches. We found our cornice

Yannick Graziani on the acclimatisation climb, Peak 6505m. *(Stéphane Benoist)*

and dug an uncomfortable but magical bivvy site – we would stay there for three nights. . .

The reason was simple: the weather had turned and moving onto that vertical face in those afternoon snow-squalls would have been pure suicide and no climber is suicidal – daring to climb is a life-wish not a death-wish. So it was early in the morning of the 20th before we set out again. Hours of very steep climbing brought us to the yellow rock band. It was 2pm when we reached the crux, Stéphane moving perfectly on unprotected, thin, vertical ice pitches, me looking on as if I were at the theatre! Stéphane, you are a great climber.

Darkness called a halt and forced us to improvise a bivouac on a small ledge at 7100m without the tent. I had a dead mattress, killed by a small hole. Hell, I would (literally) freeze my ass off for the rest of the climb.

Actually the night was OK, and the sun came onto us early that morning, so we melted some ice for tea and started to climb. October 22 was a perfect day, such a day you remember for a long time. A stick of ice in the yellow rock gave us a hard, natural line to follow. In the middle of the rock band there is a big black roof which we avoided by climbing vertical waterfall ice.

Then we carried on to what we thought should be our last bivouac, at

Above: Acclimatisation camp on Peak 6505m, looking over Gandarbha Chuli (6248m), climbed in Spring 2013, to Machapuchare (6993m). On this day Ueli Steck completed his remarkable solo on Annapurna's south face.
Left: A fine ice pitch in the 700m gully.
(Stéphane Benoist)

7450m, directly above the dihedral on the spur coming down from the summit.

Next morning we took for ever to get going – I almost lost my satellite phone and Stéphane lost a few hours finding the way. We realised we were too far left – a dead end. We moved back right and after a last, very technical pitch we reached our final bivouac at around 7600m. We were now at the top of the rock band and knew the most difficult climbing was behind us.

We stood on the summit of Annapurna at 11am on 24 October. It was my birthday and I was with

Setting out for the face on 16 October. *(Stéphane Benoist)*

my old friend from St. Jeannet (that magnificent limestone cliff above Nice) with whom I had started climbing at the age of 15!

We spent half-an-hour on the summit, anxiety growing with the realisation of our remoteness and vulnerability. We were exhausted, we had to descend – and quickly.

Back at our high

How it is done these days. Graziani at 7000m, Day 5. *(Stéphane Benoist)*

camp we spent the night trying to recover from the day, cooking soup and drinking water. The wind had picked up – 100kph and snow was forecast. I felt uneasy and went out into the night a few times to organize ropes, pitons, slings, ready for an early start next morning. I froze my ass off again, of course.

The idea was to abseil to our first bivouac at 6100m, a long way. Stéphane began to feel weak, moving slowly – nine days of continuous effort had begun to take its toll. I would have to manage the descent for both of us, it was a question of life or death. Everything I had planned and done the previous night was 'pre-organised' in my mind; I felt strange as if

Above and below: Graziani tackles the ice cascade, still two days from the summit.
(Stéphane Benoist)

Approaching the final bivouac. *(Stéphane Benoist)*

someone else was taking control of me, not due to altitude but just because I had switched into survival mode.

We decided not to stop at the foot of the rock band but continued down into the night. We were lucky; the bad weather did not materialise and at 2 or 3am we stopped to rest at our first bivouac site. Our headtorches had run out some time before and I had had to rig the abseils by the light of our stove, so now we had no gas. But I knew we would stay alive and reach safety the following day. What I didn't know was that my partner was suffering from severe pneumonia and frostbite.

Next day, 26 October, we reached our advanced base camp after a painfully slow descent from the bergschrund. I was in a bad way, but Stéphane was much worse. I realised we would need rescue. We were at 5000m, cold, down to half a cartridge of Gaz and a few biscuits, waiting for a helicopter to grab us from the foot of the face – damn! I hate helicopters. . .

Two days later, as we flew back to Kathmandu, I stared out of the window at the great Himalaya and in that noisy machine I gradually returned to a normal state of mind, dropped all my emotions, thought of myself, only of me, and all my natural feelings came back.

Returning to Europe after the climb was not a piece of cake. We were both suffering from frostbite: mine wasn't serious but Stéphane spent a lot of time in hospital recovering from serious frost injuries to his feet and the fingers of his right hand.

Climbing in the biggest mountains in the world is not without danger but the physical integrity of the climber must be respected, so our success was

Graziani approaches the summit. *(Stéphane Benoist)*

only half complete.

Annapurna, the goddess of fertility, is behind us now and life goes on; Stéphane is living in Nice and I am back in Chamonix. But the cold is over now, spring is here tomorrow and with it all the renewal that comes with the sun's warmth. Life is full of good things. . .

Acknowledgements: Many thanks to J. B. Gurung from the Annapurna Sanctuary Lodge and to the pilots of Simrik Air who brought us to safety.

Summary: A personal account of an alpine-style ascent of the South Face of Annapurna, by Yannick Graziani and Stéphane Benoist, 16 - 26 October 2013.

Left: Benoist, top, and Graziani on the summit of Annapurna, 11am, 24 October, 2013.

MARK THOMAS

Tharang I

Tharang I. The British Route takes the right-hand skyline. *(Mark Thomas)*

How beautiful, yet how worrying to emerge from my pit to a vista of snow covered valleys and the rocky peaks of yesterday now painted white with heavy windslab.

Our night at 3300m, in a charming farmstead, had been sleepless, filled with thunder, flashes of light through the bedroom window and the constant scuttling of resident rodents in the wall cavity next to my pillow. But worse than all this, the new snow would make reaching our objective, in this beautiful corner of the Indian Himalaya, all the more arduous and punishing.

We'd reached Urgos after a 26 kilometre hike with supplies from Udaipur (2700m), a beautiful journey through the river gorge and valley, with our brollies up and regular tea stops, a perfect acclimatisation day. Urgos welcomed us, as with all the places on our travels so far, with open arms, dry floor space in a friendly farmhouse, hot tea and homemade fodder.

The slog to high camp, Tharang beyond. *(Richie Mockler)*

The people here are so generous and caring, with nothing but smiles and curiosity.

We pack our kit and begin trail-breaking up to Sukto. The going is wet, marred by land-slides and torrents; the rain and snow continues through the morning toil. At Sukto we are ushered into a farm-house, where we dry our souls and warm our hearts on sweet tea and hospitality beyond all expectations.

After much debate about the approach up the valley to Base Camp, we decide to set off in the early afternoon and hope for a break in the weather. The mules make light work of the heavy loads and after just a few hours we arrive at our base for the next few weeks. What should be a lush oasis of green resembles an Arctic wilderness!

Too wet and too tired to set up individual tents, we pile into the mess tent and bed down for the night, buzzing with excitement. Daybreak brings blue skies, deep snow and a view up the valley towards our unclimbed peak, totally awesome!

After a brisk scoff and brew we pack extra gear to set up an advance camp. With a skip in our stride, we begin trail-breaking and load carrying and by midday are at a good site for camp 1 at 4300m. It hasn't been plain sailing – there was a bad gully, with a massive risk of stonefall, where two lateral moraines met. We named it the 'gully of doom' and fixed lines there to speed our passage. I leave the team to set up the tents and return to base, while I continue up to the snout of the glacier to recce and put a track into camp 2. The going is tough, hot and sweaty, breaking through the crust into the boulders beneath, snow up to my waist. I am rewarded with an excellent site for camp 2 and a clear view of the peak we would climb and name Tharang Fang (5490m). Slip-sliding and tumbling back down past camp 1, I arrive back at base camp late in the evening, damp and tired, but full of excitement while Navim, our chef, feeds me endless quantities of sweet tea and chapattis.

What an amazing existence. For the next five days life mainly consists of eating, sleeping and ferrying loads, establishing camps 1, 2 and 3 (5450m) on the glacier below the unclimbed Tharang 1 (6066m). Some of the crevasses en route are a little fragile and worrying in the afternoon heat, whilst the west face looks like it could shed its load of snow at any moment. Camp 3, Summit Camp, is in a remarkable location, but its surrounding slopes pose a threat from deep, fresh snow and most corridors are barred by hanging seracs.

On 24 September 2012, Robin, Simon, Steve, Richie, Jacob, Luke and myself, move up from camp 2 to camp 3 and prepare for summit day. The plan is for myself to attempt the west ridge of Tharang 1, with the two stronger and technically able climbers, Steve and Richie, whilst the others wait and rest for an attempt the following day. Our night at camp 3 is uncomfortable and sleepless. Robin becomes very ill and all night I worry for his wellbeing during the long, cold night. At 2am Simon, the expedition doctor, and I agree that Robin must be evacuated to the nearest hospital.

At 3am, Richie, Steve and I head off into the unknown. Not much is said. We climb towards the west col, casting thoughtful eyes on what seems a formidable peak. The night is still, the sky a canvas of stars, our feelings confused: excitement, fear, fascination. The desire for adventure drives us upwards, across the gaping jaws of the bergschrund and the next five pitches of ice climbing. At last, the sky glows a tint of red

Mark Thomas belays Steve Birch. *(Richie Mockler)*

and the rising sun burns away all anguish and doubt. After four hours of front-pointing and pitching, we reach the col and pause for a moment, the first stop in a long while, to take in the beauty of our views to the south, very cool!

The west ridge bristles with rocks and needles, but soon broadens out. A tiring and vulnerable ridge of deep snow sweeps up ahead of us– but will it actually hold us all onto the mountain, or slide off into the abyss of the South Face below us? We climb slowly and gingerly, the effects of altitude making our progress slow and lethargic. Suddenly our senses are sharpened by the terrifying sound of a 'whoof' beneath our feet. In a dizziness of confusion, it seems we are still attached to the ridge – a warning perhaps. The will to push on overwhelms us but after only a few more minutes,

Tharang I (left) and the unclimbed Tharang II. *(Richie Mockler)*

An avalanche wipes out the team's ascent tracks. *(Richie Mockler)*

another heart stopping movement of the snowpack alerts us to the acute danger we are in – the ridge is about to avalanche. I recommend the boys stay put while I quickly run out all the rope and head for the crest of the ridge in the hope that if the south face avalanches I could at least counterbalance the others by jumping down the north face. After what seems an eternity, I reach the haven of a rocky spur and with relief bang in a monster cam! At that point it becomes clear how close we'd been to disaster, as I glance beneath my feet to see not only a fracture line across the south side of the ridge, but a one metre high crown wall on the north side, with the whole of the north face snow pack strewn across the route we'd taken in at 3 o'clock this morning.

We tackle the upper rock band, the climbing tricky and the way not obvious, but at least we are off that gnarly snow ridge. After many

A panorama of unclimbed peaks unfolds. *(Richie Mockler)*

hours of mixed climbing, suddenly there is no more up! We all embrace on the tiny precipice, blown away with exhaustion and emotion.

All too soon I'm faced with the daunting task of descending the same, snowy ridge. The day is getting hot and we move slowly from fatigue. I keep the boys on the cam belay for as long as the rope allows and the ridge lets us off. I whisper a little 'thank you' to the mountain as we scramble down to the col. It's getting really hot now and avalanches are popping out all around us. Long abseils from Abalakovs lead down the north side of the col to the bergschrund.

Our approach track has been obliterated by the avalanche and we make our way over the debris as quickly as our physical state will allow. Summit camp is in sight and soon we are smothered by

On the loaded summit ridge which only just stayed put. *(Richie Mockler)*

welcoming man-hugs from Jacob and Luke. We slump onto our packs and glance up at our mountain. It had held our fate in its hands, allowed us to learn its secrets and touch its soul, blessed us with a summit and a safe passage, and provided memories to cherish for a lifetime.

The view from the summit of Tharang I. *(Richie Mockler)*

Summary: First ascent of Tharang I (6066m AD+) Mark Thomas, Steve Birch and Richie Mockler, 25 September 2012. The 'British Route' takes the west ridge from the west col.

On 28 September, Mark, Claire, Paul and Simon also made the FA of 'Tharang Fang' or 'Vishal Dant' (5490m) via the east ridge from camp 1.

First ascent of Jasminka (5401m), a peak to the NE of Tharang Fang, by Mark Thomas (solo) via SW ridge, 2 October. Thomas left base camp at 5 am and topped out at 12 noon. He describes the route as a beautiful climb on granite, PD+, III for the most part with a long pitch of AD, IV on the 'very airy' summit block, 1700m of ascent.

Acknowledgements: Thanks to Navim for his amazing cooking and warm smile. Thanks also to the high altitude porters: Hiro, Govind and Mangle and, of course, to Gajendra, the best liaison officer we could have wished for.

Summit team: Steve Birch, Richie Mockler, Mark Thomas. *(Richie Mockler)*

PIOTR SZAWARSKI

Across Tibet With a Broken Neck

Rob Creagh by Yamdruk Lake. *(Piotr Szawarski)*

Climbing is all about gambling. It's not about sure things. It's about
challenging the impossible. – Chris Bonington

The road spiralled down through the scrunched up geological Swiss roll.
The enormity of the landscape, barren and beautiful at the same time,
was difficult to encompass and to accept. Colours, shades and textures
folded into a canvas beyond comprehension. Small villages clung to the
sides of mountains where in honesty only yetis and trolls should reside.
Somewhere at the bottom of the valley, if you believed there was a bottom,
were small fields of millet and a flock of sheep, guarded by a lonely shepherd armed with a sling.

A forbidden alternative road towards the border, pointed out by our
leader, faded into the cloud. It seemed like a hell of a road, but today
excitement had faded.

A landscape out of myth. *(Piotr Szawarski)*

The bus trundled on, one tyre on the verge of blowing. Over nauseating high passes it took us down from the plateau towards Nylam, carving our way into a tectonic layer-cake. Nylam was an ugly little town, but a destination nonetheless. Tired but vaguely happy, the majority of our team sat numbly in uncomfortable seats. I kept gazing at the geological wonders, trying to appreciate a landscape straight out of myth. I was glad the mission was over. We had succeeded. Eyes filled with ruins of forts from untold legends, I tried to recall my previous visit here. Curiously, I couldn't.

***

I'd been overdue an expedition, but surely this would be a disaster? A cynical friend observed that disasters still make for good talks, but that was not what I had in mind when I signed up. Alternatively, it would be historical! Three ambitious tetraplegics from New Zealand were going to test human physiology to the extreme. You can't go any higher on a tricycle than Everest Base Camp, but that's high, more than high enough when your ventilatory capacity is reduced. It's hard to imagine how or why three wheelchair-bound people with broken necks would head to the base of this colossal mountain. Most in the community of medics thought it was folly, and so did I when I got the initial email. You've gotta be kidding me, I thought. This is mad. Then on reflection, remembering the recent London Paralympics, it occurred to me that while they do not know what they are in for, they will certainly go for it! I had the qualifications, I had the experience, I had the doubts. A forbidden land awaited. I wrote emails to experts,

The Big Cycle Expedition in Lhasa. *(Piotr Szawarski)*

set up meetings and listened to eminent opinions. Most people I spoke to were gently encouraging, but some were concerned. Are you sure it's not a suicide mission? What about oxygen? Eventually I packed my bags. My ticket arrived.

Tetraplegia is a medical term for the neurological consequences of a spinal cord injury following what is colloquially known as a broken neck. The degree of disability and dependence depends on the level of injury. The term implies that all four limbs are paralysed. That may be the case, but the more accurate description would be that all four limbs are affected. Individuals with tetraplegia universally lose all muscle power and all sensation below the neck, and their upper limbs may be partially or completely affected. In case of the three tetraplegics braving the ride to Everest BC muscle function was preserved in shoulder and biceps muscles. They could not grip and only one of them had function in the wrist. But the lack of limb function is but one of the problems to consider! A tetraplegic's blood pressure can be all over the place at times, threatening a stroke or a blackout, their bodies are unable to regulate temperature so heat illness or hypothermia is always just round the corner, and they need assistance with bathing. Travellers' diarrhoea spells disaster and the urinary catheters invite infection. Hard bedding brings pressure sores and the lack of oxygen... well, when we set out we were not sure, but respiratory reserve is diminished and a mere chest infection could be a herald of doom.

Heading into the mountains with a disability is not unheard of. Arthur

Yamdruk Lake, Tibet. *(Piotr Szawarski)*

Tarnowski, confined to a wheelchair by polio, writes about his remarkable travels across Asia, including a Himalayan ascent to 12,200 feet with him in a wheelchair strapped to a back of a pony[1]. Although he refers to living conditions in India: *'Unconsciously we place ourselves in their shoes. If conditions are crushing we assume their spirit will be crushed...'* one can not help but think about tetraplegia and the disability it confers. More recently, a similar ride to ours had been accomplished in a spectacular fashion by Paul Prichard (www.trikesrw.com), although his disability is different.

The Big Cycle expedition was conceived by Catriona Williams, the founder of New Zealand based CatWalk Spinal Cord Injury Trust, Catriona herself being tetraplegic following an equestrian accident. While the idea was born in New Zealand and that is where all the tetraplegic riders came from, the team included members from Australia and the UK. Those assembled included Sam Williams, Catriona's husband who would not leave her side and Anita Pomare her carer, Rob Creagh and Amy Shaw (carer), and Neil Cudby and carer Nicki Everton. In no particular order, others included Stephanie Williams, Kris Male, Penny Barnett, Michael Weston, Stuart Laughton, Scott Malcolm and Jack Hale. Ann Young, an experienced trek and biking expedition leader was drafted in to provide expertise in matters Nepali and Tibetan!

The epic adventure began in Kathmandu. Our team of cycle guides from a small but efficient outfit called Dawn Till Dusk, wanting to assess the team and in particular to see how the tetraplegics roll, organized a couple of rides. On the first ride to Bhaktapur, we found ourselves dodging the traffic and ripped power cables amidst cataclysmic monsoon downpours and with drains overflowing under our wheels. The guys found it exhilarating. I was understandably concerned that someone might go submarine and subterranean at the same time, but everyone survived! Then on a ride to Nagarkot, the 'tetras', as we called them, demonstrated their resilience and the power of their bikes.

Indeed the bikes they rode were technological wonders, with sensor-managed, battery-driven augmentation and multiple gears, but all were different. To begin with we did not appreciate the potential issues, but all had subtly different technology, different battery packs, different motors and different tyre sizes. This was to become an issue later in the Forbidden Land, with anxieties over burnt spare batteries and ripped tyres, where replacement was difficult if not impossible to secure. Those provided a constant headache for Sanjeev, our mechanic. But then while some things are priceless, for others, there is always duct tape.

Many things can be said about the group, but the Kiwis proved to be an enthusiastic bunch – driven, well-motivated, well-funded and just a touch

The famous pink cord. *(Piotr Szawarski)*

crazy! Folk from the other end of the world. Of course there were some tensions, but focus on the goal was maintained. While fragile logistics was looked after by an increasingly exasperated trek leader and cycling was supervised by bewildered, but very professional Nepali cycle guides, it was Cat, whose brainchild this trip was, who was the spiritual leader of the group. Soon, on her suped-up bike, she became *de facto* physical leader of the group too, as her tetraplegia would only become apparent when she was not cycling. It soon became apparent that she was addicted to cycling!

In fact the only one of us able to keep up with and support her was a cycling khan, former Nepali cross-country champion for four straight years, Mangal. Like a wind across the plateau, Cat would surge to the front and then on, beyond the horizon. To cycle or not to cycle was not the question. She was going to do it.

Soon it was time to head to Lhasa and get the trip underway. There were logistical hiccups, of course: visas, the equipment stuck at the border for lack of paperwork, hotel eating arrangements – rooftop terrace dining was not exactly wheelchair friendly, and we needed generators to re-charge the batteries. Even the flight to Lhasa was riddled with problems, with the pilot refusing to take off with three tetraplegics on board. A letter of support from New Zealand's Prime Minister came in handy to deal with that situation and to avert an international incident.

We had scorpions at the first camp site, exploding thermos flasks, some cracked bones and more traveller's diarrhoea than we bargained for. There were 40 medical incidents recorded, but thankfully nothing that was a threat to life. However, as with the Romans in Europe, the Chinese have stamped their mark upon Tibet by building roads, so at least riding was reasonably smooth.

In spite of adversities, broken necks and malfunctioning bodies, the three tetraplegics reached Everest Base Camp (North Side) on the 5th of July 2013. One of the tetra's bikes nearly disintegrated in the process, and the owner was towed the last few miles by another tetra – using a pink bathrobe cord (how on Earth did that end up on the equipment list?). They acclimatized well and coped with the drudgery of monsoon camping with great fortitude. Most importantly they coped with high altitude well, against my worries. Credit is due to the team who enabled this journey, to the carers and the cycle guides and the other members who helped with manual handling, repairs and a multitude of other small things.

The expedition was a success. It demonstrated that it is feasible for a tetraplegic to reach an altitude of 5200m and acclimatize. It highlighted a number of problems worth considering by anyone planning to repeat such a venture. Having three tetraplegics on the trip proved to be hard work for the support team and the cycle guides. Trying to mend three different models of bike along the way was not easy either. The team found Tibetan expedition cuisine difficult to enjoy and while able-bodied individuals could wash it down with Lhasa beer and laugh it off, the prospect of weight loss in the tetraplegics, threatening the integrity of the skin, remained a constant concern. The resilience of the carers not accustomed to travel in Asia and to the altitude was tested to the extreme as in addition to providing care while camping in the monsoon conditions they were cycling as well. In the future a greater ratio of carers, support team to tetraplegics would make the journey easier. Attention to detail needs to match the unpredictability of travels along Asian back roads. Burned battery, broken motor or indeed damaged sensor on the tetra's bike do prejudice their ability to perform. But, as the saying goes – 'where there is a will, there is a way'.

***

We did not cycle, but swam away from Nylam. Drenching rain and mist enveloped us as we descended into the chasm of the Bhote Kosi canyon. It was a cold and wet ride to the dirty frontier town of Zhangmo. It seemed like an endless spiral, a coiled snake of a road, punctuated by waterfalls that almost merged into the pouring rain. Eventually trucks, potholes and children filled the narrow road. We were swallowed by the border and its attendant formalities, checks, stamps, forms, payments, visas and so on.

A couple of days later, back in Kathmandu, I strolled through Durbar Square, getting lost and finding myself in a small temple courtyard. The ride, the battle, the conquest were over and peace reigned around that small temple. It is written that Buddha once said: 'it is better to conquer yourself than to win a thousand battles. Then victory is yours. It cannot be taken from you, not by angels or by demons, heaven or hell.'

Our battle to reach the foot of the greatest of mountains was also, perhaps, a battle with ourselves. Each one of us won, in some personal way, a victory that is ours to keep.

Neil Cudby, Catriona Williams and Rob Creagh at Everest base camp, 5200m.
(Piotr Szawarski)

Summary: Big Cycle Expedition, 14 June – 11 July 2013. The tetraplegics plus support team cycling from Lhasa to Kathmandu, via ten passes and Everest Base Camp. The Big Cycle team also used the opportunity to raise money for research into spinal cord injury, to bring about better outcomes for those who may suffer this terrible injury in the future.

The team: Catriona Williams (tetraplegic rider and Leader), Ann Young (logistics), Rob Creagh (tetraplegic rider), Neil Cudby (tetraplegic rider), Amy Shaw, Nicki Everton, Anita Pomare (Carers), Piotr Szawarski (Medical Officer), Sam Williams, Stephanie Williams, Kris Male, Penny Barnett, Michael Weston, Stuart Laughton, Scott Malcolm and Jack Hale (supporting riders). Anil Gurung (Cycling Guides Leader), Mangal Lama (cycling guide), Sanjeev Chhetri (cycling guide / mechanic) and Nima Sherpa (logistics support).

Acknowledgements
Thanks to our generous sponsors: DHL Global Forwarding, Trelawney Stud, Coolmore, Inglis, House of Travel, Cathay Pacific, Ben Falloon, Caroline Abbiss, Tessa Davenport, ElectricBikes.co.nz, Metalform Dannevirke, Keith Taylor Charitable Trust.

References
1. Arthur Tarnowski, *The Unbeaten Track*, Harvill Press, London 1971.

Commentary

Commentary

Aiguille des Grands Charmoz, oil on canvas, 51x76cm. *(Tim Pollard)*

STEPHEN GOODWIN

Snakes & Ladders

An Innocent at the UIAA General Assembly

The big picture-window of the Congress Centre Rondo in Pontresina looks straight up Val Roseg amid the western peaks of the Bernina group. It's a day of intermittent sunshine in October and the larches on the lower slopes are starting to turn from green to gold.

In the hall Phinjo Gombu, web editor of the International Mountaineering and Climbing Federation (UIAA), is giving a lengthy presentation of the wonders of the UIAA's upcoming new website. 'The UIAA is not using the simple tools that are available today for communications,' Phinjo regrets. (At least now the new website is up and running. Check it out: theuiaa.org)

Not everyone is paying rapt attention. As Phinjo tells us the UIAA is now ready to press the reset button on communications (even he admits it 'sounds cheesy') there is a low background mumble in many languages. Representatives from some 45 countries are in the hall. I'm drifting a bit myself: wouldn't I rather be out in that autumn sunshine? Will the good weather last 'til tomorrow when I'm free?

Next morning low cloud hangs just above the rooftops of Pontresina. But the day brightens for a while as I walk up the Morteratsch valley, clearing my head of the Babel babble and the after-effects of the Swiss Alpine Club's generous evening hospitality. A

'Pavilioned in splendour.' Hotel Walther, the UIAA's HQ in Pontresina. *(Stephen Goodwin)*

cold rain begins soon after I reach the Boval hut (2495m), obscuring the view of Piz Bernina and the peerless Biancograt.

Way below the hut the Morteratsch glacier is grey and disintegrating, torrents of water pouring over slabby cliffs from the subsidiary Pers glacier cliffs that were deep below 'perpetual' ice the first time I made the exciting

Shrinking ice. Bare rock now separates the Morteratsch glacier from the
subsidiary Pers glacier. *(Stephen Goodwin)*

ski descent of the Morteratsch from the col below Piz Zupo. That was in
1990. The Morteratsch was shrinking then, but today the effects of global
warming are more pronounced.

Here was the hard evidence of the climate change we had discussed at
a day-long conference preceding the UIAA meeting. The conference, entitled 'Mountaineering in the Future – challenges for alpine associations',
had been organised by the Swiss Alpine Club and the King Albert I Memorial Foundation (KAMF) as part the SAC's 150th anniversary programme.
Climate change is certainly an issue – glacier decay, for example, is threatening access to several alpine huts – but it is mainly one of dealing with
local consequences; actually curbing carbon emissions is for big politics.
What focused minds more sharply was our own impact on the mountain
environment, and in particular overcrowding on Mount Everest, an issue
that would spill over in the UIAA general assembly itself.

So there was plenty to think about as I wandered back down to the valley.
What follows are reflections on my first attendance at a UIAA general
assembly. I was there to represent the Alpine Club; the lead voice for the
UK is the British Mountaineering Council, represented at Pontresina by
Tut Braithwaite, Doug Scott, Anne Arran and David Hillebrandt, all AC
members. The issues addressed by the SAC conference are dealt with in
articles below by Dominik Siegrist, president of CIPRA International and
board member of KAMF, and Katharina Conradin, managing director of
Mountain Wilderness Switzerland.

The main work of the UIAA is done through Commissions: on training standards, ice climbing competitions, medical matters, mountaineering, and so forth. While the general assembly, as the UIAA's supreme body, rubber-stamps reports from the Commissions and on various matters such as the budget and membership, its most valuable function seems to be as an opportunity for associations from all over the world to get together, talk over matters of mutual concern and bend the ear of UIAA chiefs.

If that sounds rather vague, remember this was my first face-to-face encounter with the doings of the UIAA. If asked, what is the point of the UIAA? How is your trip to the crags or greater ranges actually enhanced by its existence? Well I cannot authoritatively give an answer yet. Head-quarters hotel for Pontresina was a turreted edifice in alpine-gothic style, special UIAA rates €185 double/€137 single per night. There seems almost a whiff of FIFA in such self-aggrandisement, but this apparently troubles few consciences. Ordinary climbers, who are by exten-sion footing the bills, may feel differently.

It is generally a good deal easier to influence an organi-sation by being on the inside rather than sulking on the sidelines; this must be true of the UIAA just as it is of the European Union. Certainly the Germans and Austrians think so. For Frits Vrijlandt, incoming UIAA president, the headline news of the meeting was the return to the UIAA fold of the Deutscher Alpenv-

The British are coming! BMC and AC representatives at the UIAA general assembly. L to r: David Hillebrandt, Stephen Goodwin, Anne Arran, Tut Braithwaite and Doug Scott. *(Goodwin coll.)*

erein (DAV) and the Österreichischer Alpenverein – the latter as the biggest component of an Austrian grouping VAVÖ.

With the DAV bringing a thumping 1.008 million members and the Austrians 626,925, the readmission of these powerful associations doubles the number of mountaineers, climbers and hikers under the UIAA umbrella.

Notwithstanding the diligent work of the Commissions, the test of an international body such as the UIAA must be its ability to find a common voice on issues of fundamental principle. And on this, the Pontresina assembly fell short. The issue it allowed to be fudged is that of whether a ladder should be fixed on the Hillary Step for the convenience of Everest 'climbers'.[1]

1. This report deals with issues at the 2013 UIAA general assembly. It was written soon after that meeting and several months before the tragedy on Everest on 18 April 2014. The death of 16 Sherpas and other high altitude workers that day totally eclipsed the ladder issue for the spring 2014 climbing season. However the proposal could well resurface, along with ideas such as lifting stores into the Western Cwm by helicopter if, in the wake of the tragedy, management of Everest traffic is raised at the next UIAA assembly in Flagstaff, USA, in October 2014.

When on 29 May 1953 Ed Hillary and Tenzing Norgay encountered the step on the ridge between the south and main peaks, they knew it spelt the difference between success and failure. Hillary described it thus:

I could see no way of turning it on the steep rock bluff on the west, but fortunately another possibility of tackling it still remained. On its east side was another great cornice, and running up the full forty feet of the step was a narrow crack between the cornice and the rock. Leaving Tenzing to belay me as best he could, I jammed my way into this crack, then kicking backwards with my crampons I sank their spikes deep into the frozen snow behind me and levered myself off the ground. Taking advantage of every little rock hold and all the force of knee, shoulder and arms I could muster, I literally cramponned backwards up the crack, with a fervent prayer that the cornice would remain attached to the rock. Despite the considerable effort involved, my progress although slow was steady, and as Tenzing paid out the rope I inched my way upwards until I could finally reach over the top of the rock and drag myself out of the crack and on to a wide ledge. For a few moments I lay regaining my breath and for the first time really felt the fierce determination that nothing could now stop us reaching the top.[2]

I have quoted Hillary at length here firstly to recall what a great piece of exploratory climbing it was and secondly as a reminder to UIAA officers and delegates (should any of them trouble to read this) of what 'alpinism' is really about. They are, in name at least, representing the alpine associations of the world. Alpinism should mean something to the UIAA; a ladder on the highest piece of climbable rock on the planet should surely be sacrilege?

Tut Braithwaite, Doug Scott and David Hillebrandt thought so; at the SAC conference Hillebrandt even managed to break through a ruling against hearing contributions from the floor, and make a spirited protest against any further defiling of the Hillary Step. Debate at the SAC event was otherwise restricted to the panellists; they too were concerned about the state of affairs on Everest; queues, the fracas on the Lhotse Face, combining with the shadow of a ladder to create an uneasy sense of 'something must be done'... but what?

Linda McMillan, president of the UIAA's mountain protection commission, said the UIAA had to try and change the 'tick list' approach to mountaineering; Martin Price of the University of the Highlands and Islands (and AC member) said mountaineers should remember where they came from, they did not always have to go to the Andes or Himalaya for adventure; Frank-Urs Müller, former SAC president, said Everest was a place 'where we, the real mountaineers, don't feel good any more... the personal goal of every person should not be to get to the top of Mount Everest. We know (those people) are not mountaineers. They are people who go with an expedition and stand on top of Mount Everest.'

Panellist Robert Bösch, a Swiss mountain guide, took a more pragmatic view: places that were untouched should stay that way, places with facili-

2. Edmund Hillary in the chapter 'The Summit' he contributed to *The Ascent of Everest* by John Hunt (1953)

ties should keep them. The fact was there were so many people on Everest because there was a good infrastructure; this was good business for the Sherpas in a land where there were so many things that didn't work.

The 'ladder' was a hot topic over dinner that evening, with Scott and others lobbying Frits Vrijlandt for a statement against any installation. The cheery UIAA president sounded emollient to me, however I was unaware at the time that he had already to some extent declared his position. In May 2013 Vrijlandt told *The Guardian* that a ladder could be a solution to increasing numbers on Everest.

'It's for the way down, so it won't change the climb,' Vrijlandt is quoted as saying. Did he really say that? Few nations are more observant of rules and codes than the Dutch, but it surely is naïve to think that a 'climber', already most likely on extra oxygen and drugs (Diamox etc) and assisted by Sherpas, isn't going to take advantage of a set of metal rungs. Come off it Frits!

Doug Scott preaches the old religion at the UIAA. *(Stephen Goodwin)*

And anyway, mountaineering is also about the art of getting yourself down safely too.

Dawa Steven Sherpa, a senior member of the Expedition Operators Association in Nepal had told *The Guardian*: 'We are discussing putting a ladder on the Hillary Step, but it is obviously controversial.' He said people could be waiting two or three hours at the Step, at risk of exposure. 'To make the climbing easier, that would be wrong. But this is a safety feature.'[3]

Nepal is represented at the UIAA by the Nepal Mountaineering Association. NMA representatives were clearly unhappy at all the 'don't go to Everest' talk at the SAC conference, but were unable to intervene. Next day, however, NMA president Ang Tschering was given a slot to make a statement to the UIAA general assembly. After regretting the 'incident' in spring 2013, which he hoped would not tarnish Nepal's image or the Sherpa's reputation, he moved on to commercial expeditions and 'rumours' about the ladder.

'Rumours' was an odd word to use given the very public statements of Dawa Steven Sherpa (Ang Tshering's son) and the UIAA president, but the Nepalis were clearly irked by the criticism at Pontresina. Ang Tschering pointed out to delegates that whereas in developed countries, mountaineering is perceived as a pleasure sport, a leisure activity and a source of additional income, in less developed countries it was fundamental, a bread

3. *The Guardian*, 27 May 2013. Report by Jason Burke in Khumjung.

and butter business where many were surviving hand to mouth.

No decision had been made to fix a ladder on the Hillary Step, Ang Tschering insisted. He said the NMA was reviewing Nepal's mountaineering and mountain tourism rules. Many suggestions had been received including the idea to fix a ladder at the Hillary step, 'just like at the Second Step on the China side'. 'We know very well that Mount Everest is an international icon and a natural world heritage site, so of course it goes without saying that we are very conscious and concerned about the impacts of our actions.'

The statement brought an almost audible sign of relief and temporarily laid the matter to rest. Doug Scott entered the debate later in the day, showing a selection of iconic Everest photos and endeavouring to remind delegates that they were climbers and it is a tradition of climbing that the way of the first ascent is respected.

'Our task now in the UIAA is to offer a few suggestions and recommendations to the countries concerned – mostly Nepal... We have to discuss how to protect a sacred mountain, and what is sacred to mountaineering... It is a future world heritage site, it isn't the Matterhorn and it isn't Mont Blanc. This is the roof of the world, the abode of the gods, and Miyolangsangma in particular.'

Given the numbers now attempting Everest, a limit on permits seemed almost inevitable, Doug said. Numbers would have to be capped, as on Denali. There could be checks on the experience of clients and the size of teams limited. Importantly, to compensate for any loss of income on Everest, he suggested that before anyone was allowed to attempt Everest they should have climbed one or two other peaks in Nepal, including perhaps one 8000er. This would spread the opportunity to make a living further afield from Everest.

To me, at least, this sounded a sensible way forward, but then so too do Doug's proposals for preservation of natural rock for adventure climbing – essentially a compromise between the bolt and trad – and they too have not been exactly seized on with both hands. Doug is chair of the Adventure Climbing Working Group but he has had the devil's own job getting the UIAA to adopt even the middle way he proposes as federation policy. Hopefully by the time this article is published, he will have succeeded – the recommendations were due to be discussed at a UIAA management committee in May – but the lack of enthusiasm within the UIAA for adventure climbing along with its apparent countenancing of a ladder on the Hillary Step make a worrying combination. There is an irony in the way Doug and his bold climbing style are revered at gatherings like Pontresina yet how little enthusiasm is evident to put adventure at the heart of UIAA policymaking.

Ang Tschering was correct when he pointed out that mountaineering is a leisure activity for westerners but a fundamental source of livelihood for Nepalis; however this distinction highlights a dilemma for the UIAA – whereas most of its member associations, such as the DAV or the BMC, represent thousands of 'amateur' mountaineers (I use the word in the French sense of pursuing an activity for the love of it), the NMA is in the mountain tourism business. There are few amateur mountaineers in Nepal, unlike, say, in its neighbour India. As with the Zermatt guides, whose ideas for equipping the Zmutt Ridge so upset adventure climbers, the visions of the two groups – amateurs and professionals – are not always the same. The UIAA must tread carefully here.

Back on the ladder, the NMA and the Operators' Association are likely to lean on the fact that one already exists on the Second Step. But surely the action of China in the dying days of Mao Zedong and the so-called Cultural Revolution is not the finest of precedents. Acts of vandalism were its hallmark. Indeed the existence of a ladder on the north side of Everest is all the more reason to keep the south side clean. But what leverage is the UIAA really likely to have? As Robert Bösch noted, the Sherpas have a new (and more assertive) self-confidence. 'They give the feeling they own this mountain in some way.'

DOMINIK SIEGRIST
Who Owns The Mountains?

The year 2013 saw the 150th anniversary of the Swiss Alpine Club (SAC). As a final event in a year of celebrations, the SAC, together with King Albert I Memorial Foundation organised a conference entitled: **Mountaineering in the future – challenges for alpine associations.** *It took place in Pontresina, Switzerland, on 4 October, the day before the UIAA General Assembly at the same venue. An international panel discussed a range of issues, notably free access, climate change and the protection of the mountain environment. The conference was opened by Dominik Siegrist, president of CIPRA International (campaigning to protect the environment of the Alps) and a board member of the King Albert I Memorial Foundation. The following article is based on his introductory speech.*

There's good news and bad news. First the good: climate change is standing still. So says the climate advisory board of the United Nations (IPCC) in its report published at the end of September 2013. May we now be delighted that the average temperature on Earth has hardly increased since the year 2000? Were all warnings of scientists and concerned organisations exaggerated, as in the past when they predicted that all forests in Europe would disappear within a few decades?

More precise study of the new climate report, however, leads to a different conclusion – and here comes the bad news. The IPCC states that the glaciers of Alaska, the Arctic, Greenland, the Andes, the Alps and the high mountains of Asia have all suffered big losses over the past 10 years.

Hotel Belvedere and the Rhone glacier – top: today and below: 100 years ago.
(Gesellschaft für ökologische Forschung, Munich)

These glaciers constitute a large part of the Earth's fresh water resources. So, in fact, this is not an 'all clear', the consequences of climate change are more tangible than ever. In fact the UN climate board has hardened its forecast of change for the end of the 21st century: sea levels will rise much more than anticipated; the amount of the greenhouse gas carbon dioxide (CO_2) in the atmosphere has reached its highest level for 800,000 years.

The challenges of climate change and free access to the mountains are two core issues for the future of mountaineering. One long-standing question connects both subjects: who owns the mountains? Is it just the people who live there and who cultivate them, or do those who travel to the mountains, explore and climb them also have a claim? The answer to this question is tightly bound to the future of mountaineering.

Climate change and mountaineering

As mountaineers we are familiar with the consequences of climate change; it can be clearly seen on every trip to the high mountains – each time we see glaciers they have retreated even more. Mountain slopes that in the past were covered with *firn* or corn snow until late summer are exposed earlier. Less obvious to the lay person is melting permafrost. Storms, heavy precipitation and floods seem to occur more often.

In the Alps alone there are more than 5000 glaciers. Since their peak level in the mid 19th century these glaciers have lost more than half their surface area and even more of their volume. The situation is similar in other high mountain regions of the world: in the eastern Himalaya, for example, about 2000 glaciers have already disappeared. In the United States the glaciers are disappearing from the very national park to which they gave a name – 'Glacier National Park'; Kilimanjaro, the highest mountain in Africa, has lost more than 80 percent of its snow and ice since records began 100 years ago. At least another half-metre of ice thickness disappears from Kili each year – the famous summit icefields of the volcano could be gone in 10 to 20 years. Glacier retreat is alarming in Patagonia too where, according to the calculations of Greenpeace, more than 40 cubic kilometres of ice are disappearing per year.

I asked a mountain guide friend of mine what is the biggest impact of climate change on his work. He said that there are no longer any specific tricky spots, but that nowadays he has to be ready for surprises on every mountain tour. It may be bergschrunds or cols that can hardly be crossed due to ice retreat; rockfall danger below the melted snowfields; or changes in the position and structure of crevasses. Many routes have become more difficult and dangerous, demanding more attention, experience and local knowledge. Literature for guides is slow to document such rapid changes. Sometimes the only source of information is the local hut guardian's website.

Two examples illustrate the consequences of global warming for mountaineering.

During the very hot summer of 2003 a large lake backed up at the snout of the Trift glacier in the Bernese Oberland and made access to the SAC's Trift hut impossible. Access was only restored by the construction of a long and expensive suspension bridge. In fact a second bridge had to be built, the first being destroyed by a storm shortly after it was opened.

Rockfall has become an increasing danger on the route from the SAC's Tschierva hut to the *Biancograt* on the Piz Bernina. A *via ferrata* had to be installed, with great effort, to avoid the dangerous section.

A recent study on behalf of the SAC has shown that in the medium

Stairway to heaven? Access
to the SAC Konkordia Hut.
*(Hansrudolf Keusen, geotest,
Berne)*

term access to every fifth
SAC hut will be endangered
due to climate change. The
most famous example is the
Konkordia hut on the Aletsch
glacier. The hut was originally constructed right at the
glacier's 'edge'; to reach it now,
mountaineers have to ascend
a metal staircase for almost
150 metres. If the Aletsch
glacier loses further thickness
or mass, the hut might have to
be moved or even closed due
to inaccessibility. Alternative
access routes to the new Monte
Rosa hut are also being examined. This hut is important for
tourism in Zermatt and costs
of up to one million Swiss
Francs for the work have been
mentioned, but the question
as to how such sums might be
raised remains unanswered.

An important aspect of
climate change is its effect on
water supplies. Where there is
too much water at one time,
there is not enough at another.
In some regions glacial lakes
are accumulating in a rapid and
dangerous manner. In order to
protect parts of Grindelwald
from flooding should a glacial
lake breach, a two kilometre drainage tunnel has been built at the Lower
Grindelwald glacier at a cost of SF15 million. Some years ago in the Upper
Engadine the river Flaz had to be diverted into a new riverbed at a cost of
almost SF30 million, in order to protect the village and airport of Samedan
from the consequences of heavy precipitation and high water levels in the
Bernina and Roseg valleys.

A study published in 2002 by the UN environmental organisation

(UNEP) for the Himalaya warned of potential flood disasters due to melting glaciers: 44 glacial lakes were identified as posing a threat to the valleys below due to high water levels. In the Himalaya, though, there is not the money to finance expensive protection measures.

And suddenly there is a lack of water: with the disappearance of glaciers the high mountains would no longer function as water reservoirs. In Europe, approximately 170 million people depend on rivers that rise in the Alps for drinking water; in countries fringing the Himalaya more than one billion people are similarly dependent. These perspectives are dramatic and of unimaginable extent. Where water supplies are drastically reduced or lost, the population loses its basis for existence and the valleys become wastelands. In such catastrophic circumstances there is not much likelihood of maintaining any infrastructure for mountaineering!

Free access to the mountains

Today, mountaineering, hiking and outdoor activities are booming worldwide. The big alpine clubs have seen a clear increase of members in recent years. Membership of the German alpine club (DAV) reached one million in summer 2013, and the SAC today has 140,000 members. At the same time, the number of non-organised mountaineers is constantly growing. One indicator of this is the strong increase in sales of outdoor equipment. Retailers such as Globetrotter in Germany, Transa in Switzerland or MEC in North America have reached the size of shopping centres. A survey by the DAV in 2009 revealed that its members alone accounted for more than 50 million person-days of mountain sport activities per year. These activities included hiking, mountain biking, mountaineering, sport climbing and ski-touring.

Big mountain-sport events have become very common: the Marmot Climbing Festival in the Frankenjura attracted about 20,000 visitors in 2012. A climbing event in the Val di Mello, which began 10 years ago with 400 participants, today attracts thousands of visitors and in mid-March the big North Face Climbing Festival returns to the Greek island of Kalymnos.

Our seemingly unlimited mobility is also a concern. The number of kilometres driven for leisure purposes in the small country of Switzerland totals 300 times the distance from Earth to the Moon. A survey by the DAV members' journal *Panorama* in 2010 provided a sobering result: almost 90 percent of German mountaineers mainly drive to the hills, often for distances of up to 1000km. In other countries the situation is probably quite similar, though the number of mountaineers using public transport in Switzerland is higher.

Mont Blanc is often in the news, not only for suffering the highest number of accidents in the Alps but also for visitor numbers. On some days way over 500 mountaineers are present on the roof of the Alps. Even the access routes to the huts are not harmless, with fatal accidents from time to time. The traverse of the Grand Couloir is infamous for heavy rockfall yet every summer it is crossed by about 20,000 people. There is now a proposal

Above: Albert I, King of the Belgians from 1909 to 1934, on the Albigna glacier, Bregaglia, July 1930. *(Walter Amstutz)*

King Albert Mountain Award

Established in 1993, the aim of King Albert I Memorial Foundation is to grant the King Albert Mountain Award to persons or institutions that have rendered exceptional, sustainable services with respect to the world's mountains.

Award winners have included outstanding mountaineers and rock climbers, geographers and geologists, photographers and writers, publishers of alpine literature, doctors specialising in high-altitude medicine and persons and institutions that have dedicated themselves to the protection of mountains. To date 52 persons and institutions have been granted the Award including British recipients Mick Fowler, John Hunt, Martin Price and Stephen Venables.

The award for 2014 goes to the Swiss National Park, celebrating its 100th anniversary. **DS**

See also: **king-albert.ch**

King Albert I on the Tannenspitze, Engelhörner range, 30 Sept. 1930. The Engelhörner, the 'Dolomites of the Bernese Oberland', are not far from the Haslihorn estate, summer residence of the Belgian Royal family on Lake Lucerne. *(Walter Amstutz)*

Mer de Glace, then and now. *(Gesellschaft für ökologische Forschung, Munich)*

to bore a 180 metre tunnel to avoid this accident black spot.

The Alps are both an Eldorado for mountaineers and the biodiversity hotspot of Europe, home to around 30,000 animal and 13,000 plant species according to the WWF. In order to preserve and promote this diversity, dozens of protected areas and parks have been established. This protection is important, but it requires a good balance with mountaineering. A positive example has been set in Switzerland in the case of ski-touring and snowshoeing maps. Furthermore the Swiss Alpine Club with the cantons examine the environmental impact of all publicised routes. Unfortunately, even in Switzerland there are still instances of conflicts of interest between wildlife protection and mountaineers; for example when the cantons disregard the need to involve the most important interested parties.

Whether nature and wildlife conservation in the Alps really is a serious handicap for mountaineering is judged differently according to one's particular interest. The numerous mountain railways and ski areas are, however, a real limitation. Many of the places where the masses are now having fun were once popular ski-touring areas. For sure tourism has brought economic wealth to the mountain regions, and the various infrastructures have improved access to the high mountains for mountaineers, however further ski industry developments in the Alps are planned that would have negative consequences for all who want to travel in peace through the natural environment – for example at Piz Val Gronda near Ischgl in Tyrol.

In the Himalaya organised mountaineering has become ever more popular; Mount Everest is breaking all records. According to figures from Elizabeth Hawley and Richard Salisbury, whereas in the first three decades after the first ascent of Everest 143 mountaineers reached the summit, since 1983 around 6000 have stood on top. On 19 May 2013, 150 persons stood on the summit on a single day. Most of today's ascents take place as part of commercially organised expeditions, with prices ranging from $20,000 up to one million US dollars for an ascent of the peak. Between 1953 and 1989 the ratio of non-commercial to commercially guided ascents was 1 to 1.5; between 1989 and 2009 this ratio changed to 1 to 22 – and there are many signs that this development is not over.

The issue of 'free' access by mountaineers to Mount Everest was further highlighted by the fracas on 27 April 2013 involving mountaineers Ueli Steck, Simone Moro and Jonathan Griffith and a group of Sherpas. (The incident was commented upon in *AJ* 2013.) Reporting went global, with rounds of discussion on TV and pages of print, often illustrated by images of long queues of mountaineers high on Everest.

Many uninvolved people seeing this reportage probably asked themselves what could be the sense of this happening on the roof of the world? Was the attack by the Sherpas the result of more than just a lapse by one party or other? Is free access to Everest for mountaineers now basically a point for discussion? There is, of course, an historical dimension that should be considered here: we easily forget that early ascents in the Himalaya and Karakoram were made in the spirit and practice of colonialism and are part of colonialist history.

But what of the future of mountaineering, and our initial question: who owns the mountains? In my opinion the mountains belong to all human beings, irrespective of race, religion or gender. Mountains constitute a natural and cultural heritage for all mankind and thus we all have a duty to protect them, be we residents, land managers, visitors – or mountaineers.

KATHARINA CONRADIN
Mountain Wilderness – Responsible Alpinism

Heli-skiing is allowed even in the Jungfrau-Aletsch UNESCO World Natural Heritage site. *(Mountain Wilderness)*

One of the panellists at the SAC conference on the future of mountaineering was Katharina Conradin, executive director of Mountain Wilderness Switzerland. In the following article Katharina gives an overview of the origins, activities and aims of the mountain campaigners.

From '*montes horribilis*' to 'The Playground of Europe'

The perception of mountains has changed greatly over time. For centuries mountains were a place where the forces of nature humbled humanity, a place where bad harvests, hunger and natural disasters dominated everyday life. Almost no one came to the mountains for pleasure.

This only changed in the 19th century, when industrialisation saw cities explode, their air darkened by soot and smoke. All of a sudden, glaciers and rugged peaks appeared in a different light, clean air became desirable – elegant ladies and cultivated men arrived, astonished at the impressive landscapes spread before their eyes. Tourism started to boom; the mountains became fascinating. But then it was no longer enough to simply look at the Mer de Glace in Chamonix or at the steep north face of the Eiger – the peaks were to be ascended. At first such endeavours were the preserve of brave mountaineers, but on their heels came the first cog railways, and

A new alpine leisure park, Madrisaland near Davos, Switzerland. Such developments are being built close to cable car stations in order to increase their usage during summer. *(Sam Kreuzer, Mountain Wilderness)*

comfortable hotels to serve them soon sprung up in what had been poor farming villages. Cable cars followed and soon everyone who had the necessary funds was able to enjoy breath-taking views from high mountain summits.

Yet this sufficed only for a short time. More tourists arrived. Ski-lifts were invented. Rock climbing became popular. Resorts were built in the middle of nowhere. Artificial snow made the skiing season almost independent of natural weather conditions. Technical innovations such as battery-powered drills made even the steepest rock walls accessible. So the story has gone on until hardly any blank spots remain on the maps of our planet.

A new organisation is born

For the men and women who founded Mountain Wilderness in 1987 these developments were alarming, because they are emblematic of our sense of entitlement and the domination of man over the natural environment. Many now take for granted the ascent of any given peak at any given point in time.

An ascent is too long for you, but you still want to be the first to ski its powder slope? Take a helicopter ride. The rock walls are too steep but you still want to call yourself a climber? Sure, you'll find enough *via ferrata*. You've never even seen crampons at close quarters? Don't worry, you'll learn how to put them on at base camp of the peak you've paid for. And what about all the traffic generated and the waste left behind? No worries, someone will take care of it.

Concerned at these developments, a number of renowned mountaineers, among them Chris Bonington, Yvon Chouinard, Reinhold Messner and Doug Scott, got together in the Italian city of Biella and signed the 'Theses of Biella', bringing Mountain Wilderness into being. The Biella conference attracted a large attendance of mountaineers and intellectuals from all over the world, several of whom were to become founding guarantors and founding members of Mountain Wilderness, including Haroun Tazieff, Kurt Diemberger, Jim Bridwell, John Hunt and Wanda Rutkiewicz.

From the very beginning, wilderness was not only understood as 'a place unaffected by man and his activities, a place where natural processes govern environmental change and man is at most a spectator or visitor', it was also clearly visualised in opposition to civilisation, as its antithesis and a complement to the physical and social structures of man (Henderson 1992). Mountain Wilderness hence views it as crucial that wilderness is preserved, that spaces remain where adventure can still be lived. Yet it is clear that this brings with it an obligation to respect mountains and to leave them as they were before we came.

In the following years, various MW national chapters were founded, dedicated to preserving wilderness and promoting a self-responsible, respectful and environmentally sustainable mountain sport.

Mountain Wilderness Switzerland

Mountain Wilderness hence shares some of the values of traditional alpine clubs as well as of environmental organisations; but is somehow distinct from both, placing a strong value on the human experience of wilderness. Some of its core activities include:

• From the very beginning, Mountain Wilderness lobbied against heli-skiing. Heli-skiing stands for fast, consumption-oriented mountaineering and is the complete opposite of the self-responsible alpinism that Mountain Wilderness advocates. While most European countries apply severe restrictions, heli-skiing is enormously popular in Switzerland, with more than 42 landing spots, half located either directly in or adjacent to protected areas. With demonstrations and political lobbying, MW Switzerland has tried for more than 20 years to reduce the number of landing spots – not an easy undertaking when the federal office responsible clearly adopts the position of the flight lobbyists – but we will definitely continue our struggle.

• Mountain Wilderness works together with other environmental organisations to preserve an intact mountain landscape, and is entitled to file legal complaints against infrastructure projects. MW Switzerland makes use of this with regard to new tourist infrastructure such as ski areas, cable cars and the like, but more and more over projects for the production of renewable energy, particularly so when the existence of the last remaining free-flowing rivers becomes problematic.

• Keepwild! climbs: In Switzerland, a heated debate is going on over where routes should be bolted, how 'historic' climbing routes should be improved or made safer, and where no bolting should take place. MW Switzerland sensitizes the climbing community on this issue and promotes peaceful co-existence between bolted and 'clean' routes.

Numerous other awareness-raising campaigns urging respectful sporting use of the mountains have been launched, not only by MW Switzerland but also by other chapters. In France, the national chapter encourages alpinists to travel to the mountains by public transport; German activists grant an ironic award for the 'best' tourism project of the year. Internationally, MW has become known for its clean-up campaign 'Free K2', which has seen large amounts of rubbish removed from that mountain.

The 'highest suspension bridge in Europe' was opened last year on Titlis in central Switzerland. The bridge has no function – it leads from the top station into an artificial tunnel and back. *(Sam Kreuzer, Mountain Wilderness)*

Where do we head?

The work of Mountain Wilderness is not that of romantic dreamers who live in the past and glorify a style of mountaineering popular 100 years ago. We value and respect recent great mountaineering accomplishments, many of which would not have been feasible decades ago. Nevertheless, it has become necessary to question whether much of today's mountaineering, as well as the current mountain-related tourism development is what we really want.

Is it justifiable that the province of the Tyrol produces so much artificial snow every year that a four-lane highway from Innsbruck to Madrid, more than 2000 km, could be covered by 1 metre of snow (ÖRF 2013) – for the sake of maintaining a form of tourism that is long beyond sustainability? Is it reasonable, that a tunnel should be built on Mont Blanc to protect mountaineers from potential rockfall on their ascent to a newly renovated Cabane Goûter? Should a ladder be installed on Hillary Step in order to prevent deadly congestion on the world's highest mountain? Is it desirable that alpinism become an Olympic sport?

These are questions that should concern all of us. As responsible mountaineers, we should not allow mountaineering to become a commodity. Mountain Wilderness has a clear take on this: it is in our hands whether we leave the joy of wild areas to future generations – or whether we subject mountain sports to total commercialisation.

References

Henderson N. 1992. *Wilderness and the nature conservation ideal: Britain, Canada, and the United States contrasted. Ambio* 21(6): 394-399.
Mountain Wilderness International. 2008. *The origin of Mountain Wilderness.* **mountainwilderness.org/mountainwilderness/origin/** accessed on 12.12.2013.
ORF. 2013. *Verblüffendes Zahlenspiel mit Kunstschnee.* **tirol.orf.at/news/stories/2613179/**; accessed on 13.12.2013.

PAUL SCHWEIZER

The Golden State Revisited

Climber on *Knob Job* (5.10b), Pat and Jack Pinnacle, Yosemite. *(Dan Moore)*

My jet landed in Fresno on a Friday night, close to midnight local time. Fortunately there was still one lone taxi loitering outside which conveyed me to the La Quinta Inn where I had a reservation for the night. I'd been invited by the American Alpine Club to participate in their week-long 2012 International Climbers' Meet (ICM), to be held in Yosemite in early October. The late night air was warm, dry and pleasingly fragrant with the scent of fruit trees wafting in from the vast tracts of agricultural land surrounding the city. A subtle wave of nostalgia followed on the fragrance – I was back in the Golden State after many years away.

The hotel looked a bit seedier than in their website photos, and there was a bunch of Harley choppers parked outside. In an exhausted and jet-lagged state I struggled to wedge myself, duffel bag and large rucksack through the narrow spring-loaded reception door. Two enormous black Hell's Angels were in the process of checking in and turned around to watch as I wrestled my bags through. Their Levi jackets bore the winged insignia of Black Hawks M.C. Each wore a large sheath knife at his belt, legal in California as long as it's plainly visible and doesn't constitute a 'concealed weapon'. In my youth I'd spent a lot of time in the Bay Area between trips to the Valley, and in those days there was an uneasy alliance between hippies and Hell's Angels, mainly because we had a few basics in common: drugs, long hair, choppers and rebellion. In general, gang members tended to be OK – as long as they thought you were on their side.

After coolly clocking me the two burly dudes returned to their check-in. Turned out that the whole gang was arriving that night and staying in the hotel for their annual reunion – great.

I awoke next morning from a surprisingly restful sleep and, after successfully if groggily negotiating a breakfast room packed tight with Hell's Angels, made the Amtrak train connection to Merced where a YARTS bus picked me up exactly on schedule.

Early that afternoon, as the bus climbed steadily through the Sierra Nevada foothills on the long and twisting approach to the Valley, the familiar scenery of sparsely wooded mountain sides and sparkling riverbeds beneath a sunny blue sky brought back wistful memories. My first encounter with Yosemite in the summer of 1972 was a revelation. Nothing can prepare you for your first sight of El Capitan – that impossibly sheer wall of gleaming rock, rising endlessly out of the forest, seems too vast to be real. The whole scale of the place was several orders of magnitude beyond anything I'd ever seen – gigantic waterfalls poured thousands of feet into empty space, serene meadows were surrounded by fragrant forests of towering pines – and everywhere you looked massive cliffs of shimmering white stone pierced a cobalt sky. Stunning natural beauty. The impact of Yosemite was so strong that I took up rock climbing the very next year.

I was lucky enough to undergo many of my formative climbing experiences in the Valley in the 1970s, during the 'Golden Age' of Yosemite free climbing. Life in the Valley was good: hanging out in Camp 4 and climbing every day on soaring, sundrenched cracks and immaculate slabs; swimming in the Merced River and sunbathing in the meadows; lounging in the shade at the deli drinking beers in the afternoon; smoking spliffs and drinking wine around a campfire at night, sleeping under the stars. In those days the counterculture was still strong, and the California Stone Masters were at the forefront of technical prowess. Dropouts, druggies and longhairs living in the dirt outside of society's grasp – hardened devotees of freedom. Climbing was still esoteric then – a rebel sport that hadn't yet sold its soul to gear manufacturers and the mass media.

When I first stayed at Camp 4 there was no time limit – you could remain as long as you wanted. The legendary Jim Bridwell was a fixture at the rescue site, and younger rock-stars like John Long and the two emerging *wunderkind* of the era, John Bachar and Ron Kauk, were habitual residents. Set up in the trees behind the rescue site was an elaborate outdoor gym – the Yosemite climbers' version of an Olympic training camp, replete with the original Bachar ladder, pull-up bars, finger tip pull-up boards, parallel bars, iron cross rings, knotted rope, as well as a slack chain set up between two

Ulrika on pitch 1 of *Commitment* (5.9), Five Open Books, Yosemite. *(Paul Schweizer)*

trees for honing your balance. The Valley was a mandatory pilgrimage site for dedicated climbers from around the world – people like Pete Livesey, Ron Fawcett, Reinhardt Karl, Bill Denz, Wolfgang Güllich, Kurt Albert. There was a very special vibe to Yosemite in the 70s. At that particular moment it was at the cutting edge of the possible, the place where the future was already happening.

That was many years ago. I'd been living in Edinburgh since 1989 and now, somewhat ironically, was returning to Yosemite as a representative of the Mountaineering Council of Scotland. Winding along the deeply forested entrance road to the Valley once again after so many years brought on a heady *déjà-vu*. The pines were still towering and the endless expanse of El Capitan still seemed too big to be real. I stepped down from the bus in Curry Village to meet Carol Kotchek, the ICM's organizer, and a few of the local hosts and participants who were already there, including Andrey from Brazil, and Ulrika and Susanne from Sweden. Spent a pleasant first evening sitting around the picnic table, drinking wine and chatting with new acquaintances. Then on Sunday before the meet began I went cragging with Ulrika and Susanne – they'd been out climbing the day before and thankfully had a rental car.

On Monday 8 October the meet officially began. It got off to an auspicious start with the Nepali team performing a blessing ceremony and bestowing a white prayer scarf and 'namaste' upon each participant. The

Offwidth. Ulrika on *Doggie Doo* (5.10a), Camp 4 Wall, Yosemite. *(Dan Moore)*

strategy for the first couple of days was to divide people into groups of six or seven with a local host, so the participants could mingle and meet each other. After a leisurely breakfast my group, along with three other gangs, headed off to the Pat and Jack Pinnacle area for a pleasant and sociable day on the rocks. Initial re-acquaintance with Yosemite 5.10s didn't seem too bad, with *Knob Job* and *Knuckleheads*. But I soon rediscovered the fact that Yosemite 5.11 flaring groove cracks can be damned hard, when I seconded Ted from Montana on *The Tube*, an old Bridwell testpiece from 1974. Just like Ted I fell off and had to rest on the rope before managing to crank through the technical and vicious crux section.

On day two of the Meet I was paired up with John Bragg, a renowned American climber from the old days. Amongst a number of other things, in 1973 he'd done the first free ascent of *Kansas City*, one of the earliest 5.12s in the Shawangunks, and in 1976 he'd done the first ascent of Torre Egger in Patagonia with Jim Donini and Jay Wilson. Now he was one of the head honchos in the AAC and the easy-going overseer of the ICM. We scrambled high up to left of the base of Middle Cathedral Rock and did the *Kor-Beck Route*, a six-pitch 5.9 classic that I hadn't previously ticked. It was great to be climbing once again with an old-school American. Like me and virtually no one else at the meet, John didn't wear a helmet. And he set up belays the same way I did – nothing was equalized, there was no clear directional, and not a cordelette or locking karabiner in sight. Sunshine rock climbing should be casual.

Wednesday provided another day of sociable climbing on Manure Pile Buttress. I was settled into the rhythm of the ICM and really enjoying a good spirited and well organized event. Then on Thursday the unthinkable happened – it rained. Spent the day puttering about on some short routes down the Valley and below the clouds at Reed's Pinnacle. As it transpired, ironically, one of the other climbers on the Reed's Pinnacle excursion, Dan Moore, was also from Scotland. Turns out he'd been living in Edinburgh for the past couple of years and we'd never stumbled into each other before.

The forecast was fluctuating, and initially Friday was supposed to be clear. So on Thursday evening Dan and I prepared for the *NE Buttress* of Higher Cathedral Rock, a long and committing 5-star route on one of the highest formations in the Valley. But rain began pattering on my tent wall as I drifted off to sleep. Got up in 5am darkness to take a look, but the sky was filled with low clouds and the ground still quite damp from overnight rain. So Friday turned into another soggy and low-key day, spent on short routes at Camp 4 Wall. Things were now getting critical – tomorrow was Saturday, the last day of the meet, and we were both flying back to Scotland on Sunday. Badly wanted to do a long, classic route before the precious week was over.

On Friday evening the forecast was announced at dinnertime – clearing weather on Saturday. So Dan and I re-racked for the *NE Buttress*. That night one of the planned activities was to attend a slide show by 'Hollywood' Hans Florine on El Cap speed records. I didn't really care about El Cap speed records, but at least it was something to do. As Dan and I ambled along the pathway to the lecture hall for Florine's talk, we encountered the entrance to a neighbouring theatre, with a table outside and a poster advertising a film featuring Ron Kauk. This made me stop and ponder. Kauk has to rank as one of the most gifted climbers ever, with a string of remarkable first ascents including *Astroman*, *Separate Reality* and *Tales of Power*, along with *Midnight Lightning*, probably the most famous boulder problem on the planet.

There was a very polite woman at the table, and a somewhat scruffy looking bloke, heavy-set with long oily black hair, standing in the shadows about five feet away. The woman went into a low pressure sales pitch, saying it was an award winning film about climbing as a way of life, and as an added bonus, the climber himself would introduce the film. I looked again at the bloke in the shadows. I hadn't seen Kauk since the 1986 California Bouldering Championships at Mount Woodson. He'd aged a fair bit and put on some weight, but that had to him. 'Hi, you're Ron, aren't you?' 'Hey Bro, how's it goin',' he replied as we shook hands.

Ron's talk and the film in which he featured were not mainstream climbing fare. The cinematography was expert and the images superb. But the images weren't primarily about climbing. Instead, they centred on the astonishing and ever transforming wild beauty of Yosemite Valley and Tuolumne Meadows. The soundtrack was supplied by the haunting Native

American cedar wood flute of Jeff Ball and his ensemble, and the music and scenery were in perfect accord. Sequences of Ron climbing in totally relaxed and masterful style were interspersed with footage of soaring birds, flowing steams, lush forests, rainbows and crashing waterfalls. Awesome climbing on glowing stone just blended in as an integral part of the scene.

After the film I went up and bought a copy of Kauk's book, *Spirit of the Rock*. While he was signing it I asked if there was any truth to the fabled story about how *Midnight Lightning* got its name. According to climbing folklore back in the day, Bridwell, Bachar, Kauk and some other Camp 4 locals were sitting beneath the overhanging Columbia boulder one stormy night, tripping on acid. A sudden bolt of lightning split the sky, illuminating the boulder, and in a flash of psychedelic inspiration the sequence was revealed to Bridwell. The next day they worked on the problem, following Bridwell's prophetic vision, and Kauk was the only one who could pull off the moves. Ron laughed in reply. 'Nah man, Bridwell had nuthin ta

Paul Schweizer on upper headwall, *NE Buttress*, Higher Cathedral Rock. *(Dan Moore)*

do with it. Yabo and Bachar were workin' on the problem so I started workin' on it too. I was the one who got it first.' 'So it's just named after the Hendrix track, like *Astroman?*' 'Yeah – it's a great song.'

Woke up again at 5am and this time the ground was dry. Got the MSR *Pocket Rocket* purring in the darkness and put on a pot of espresso. Ate breakfast and packed up my gear by headtorch. The *NE Buttress* was like a long rock route in the Dolomites or Swiss Alps and we had to get an early start. Motored up the steep and forested approach track in the dark – it was a weekend and we wanted to be first on the route. The initial four pitches were fun and the sky turned bright and blue – it was going to be a good day. A funky and exposed traverse after the fourth pitch gained the sustained and committing upper headwall, with pitch after unrelenting pitch of physical, old-school climbing in hand cracks, fist cracks, off-widths and flaring chimneys. Hadn't used that kind of technical body language for ages. On the summit we were rewarded with amazing views of the Valley, and especially El Cap – we were directly across from the Nose and at the same level as where it topped out. Then a bitter-sweet descent through a serene and ancient pine forest in the late afternoon. My lungs savoured once again that unique and evocative Valley fragrance of pine trees and bay leaves. It had been a great route and a perfect way to end the trip. But when would I return?

Campfire. *(Dan Moore)*

75

KELLY CORDES

Patagonia – Winds of Change

Maestri's infamous compressor, some 50 metres below Cerro Torre's summit. *(Kelly Cordes)*

Imagine yourself weary and worn, camped in the woods of Patagonia, just back from an attempt where a sucker-window of weather had slammed shut when you were three thousand feet up your climb. It was as if the fury of the gods had suddenly descended upon you, but somehow you'd survived. Your body went numb, the wind slammed you into the wall, and you couldn't hear your partner yelling at you from three feet away. Every second of every hour for the next twelve was laced with a primal fear. Then you staggered back to camp and crashed out, deep into a dreamless sleep. You hadn't slept in thirty-some hours and as the storm raged, you hoped for only one thing: that it would continue, so you wouldn't even have to think about going back out there. But in the middle of the night you'd had to piss. You'd rolled over and mumbled, unzipped the tent door, and stag-

76

The late Mauro Giovanazzi attempting a new route on the east face of Cerro Torre in 2001.
(Ermanno Salvaterra)

Colin Haley approaching Cerro Torre with a perfect forecast before his and the author's climb in early January 2007. *(Kelly Cordes)*

gered outside. Through bleary eyes your gaze strayed to the gaps between the lenga trees, and you'd seen stars shining bright. *Shit.*

In 1975, following one of his many Patagonian expeditions, Ben Campbell-Kelly wrote: 'An expedition should be prepared to be spending a minimum of three months in the mountains, particularly if they have chosen a difficult objective.'

In 1995 on *Infinito Sud*, an incredibly difficult new route up the centre of Cerro Torre's south face, Italians Ermanno Salvaterra, Roberto Manni and Piergiorgio Vidi hauled a 200kg aluminium box for shelter as they went, to wait-out storms. Salvaterra, Cerro Torre's all-time greatest climber, had been worried that regular portaledges would be destroyed by the wind.

In his 2000 book, *The Big Walls*, Reinhold Messner wrote: 'The big problem on Cerro Torre is the storms. Every big face there should really be measured twice.'

But that was then. Old Patagonia. Before the arrival of the single biggest change in the history of Patagonian climbing, which wasn't the bridge over the Río FitzRoy, or the airport in El Calafate, or the paved roads, or even the evolution of modern climbing gear. . .

Cerro Torre is home to one of history's most infamous and bizarre

A Polish team racing the wind and incoming storm on the *Compressor Route* in 1996. *(Gregory Crouch)*

assaults on a mountain. Over the course of two trips in 1970 (often mis-reported as 1971), Italian climber Cesare Maestri used a gasoline-powered air compressor to jackhammer some 400 bolts into the mountain's south-east ridge. In what became known as the *Compressor Route*, Maestri placed many of the bolts beside perfectly usable cracks, while elsewhere he

Old Patagonia. Slovenian hard men Francek Knez (left) Stane Klemenc (right) on the first ascent of *Devil's Dihedral*, FitzRoy, 1983. *(Silvo Karo)*

launched up blank stone, seemingly determined to avoid natural features.

Though Maestri returned home to terrific fanfare, the greater climbing world was less impressed. Most climbers considered his tactics an affront to the spirit of alpinism and to long-held notions of fair play. The September 1972 issue of *Mountain* magazine, the most influential English language periodical in the world at the time, had Cerro Torre on its cover and featured a now-famous article entitled *Cerro Torre: A Mountain Desecrated.*

But in the ensuing decades, something curious happened: The *Compressor Route* became the most popular route on Cerro Torre.

Few climbers even attempted other routes on the mountain. Until the mid-2000s the *Ragni Route*, the next most popular route and Cerro Torre's line of first ascent, was summitted only four times.

Even as more climbers came and tried, multiple years would pass, often consecutively, without Cerro Torre seeing a single ascent. Each summit-less season, each nightmarish attempt that ended in a hellacious storm, and each rare success further embedded the *Compressor Route* as part of Cerro Torre's lore. For many climbers, the moral affront of Maestri's prolific bolt ladders became easier to overlook.

Tales of terror were omnipresent. Since storms race in from the west, if you were high on the *Compressor Route*, you wouldn't know you were in trouble until it was too late. Eyelids froze shut. The wind would send ropes sailing horizontally into space before shifting and launching them back into the wall like wild, slithering snakes, twisting them irretrievably around flakes and forcing climbers to cut their ropes and make ever shorter rappels with what remained. Climbers would stagger down to the safety of the forest looking like battle-worn soldiers, their eyes fixed in thousand-yard stares.

In 1980 Kiwi climber Bill Denz made thirteen attempts to solo the route. He endured a seven-day bivouac trapped on a tiny ledge a thousand feet below the top on one attempt. Another time, his best attempt, Denz retreated only two hundred feet below the summit.

Each previous suitor validated the next, particularly when many were renowned figures—starting with Jim Bridwell's 1979 true first ascent of the route (Maestri, it was later learned, retreated from below the top in 1970), which effectively bestowed the blessing of climbing royalty.

As testament to Cerro Torre's inherent difficulty, aside from the four complete ascents of the *Ragni Route*, until 2005 every other climb to the summit depended upon using the bolts of the *Compressor Route* to get there. The three routes on the south face descended upon intersecting the southeast ridge, while the two routes on the east face summited via the *Compressor Route.*

By the time a nearly two-week-long stretch of clear skies hit the Chaltén Massif in late November and December 2008, the number of *Compressor Route* ascents had grown too many to count, but stood at well over one hundred.

That late 2008 weather window, however, was different. Not only because of its duration, but because everyone knew it was coming.

In his Chaltén Massif summary in the *American Alpine Journal*, Rolando Garibotti wrote: 'The big news was that the *Ragni di Lecco Route* on the west face of Cerro Torre had six ascents (nineteen climbers), more than all previous ascents of the route combined. In contrast, the season saw only one ascent of the *Compressor Route*. It is as if overnight everyone stopped climbing Everest with oxygen, fixed rope, and Sherpa support. While Maestri's hundreds of bolts remain in place, the climbing community appears to have finally given them a cold shoulder. The list of non-*Compressor Route* ascents of Cerro Torre has now grown to fourteen.'

Above: El Chaltén in January 1986, less than one year old, when the town had only one building (red roof is faintly visible). *(Sebastián Letemendia)*
Below: El Chaltén in January 2013. *(Kelly Cordes)*

Weather balloons had probably been going up around Patagonia long before anyone made forecasts, Jim Woodmencey told me. He's a climber, skier, and former Grand Teton National Park ranger who owns a forecasting company called MountainWeather. He says each country has weather service stations, and they launch balloons that gather data at various points in the atmosphere. There are other ways to gather data as well, like surface observation stations, ocean buoys, and satellite photos of clouds at different elevations and time intervals, which indicate things like wind speed and atmospheric moisture concentration. Even though data is comparatively sparse in less-populated places like Patagonia, virtually nothing stands between the storms brewing in the ocean and the Chaltén Massif. Thus, the data collected allows for accurate forecasts.

Data alone means nothing, though. It's computer models that actually analyze the data and make predictions – forecasts – and they've improved tremendously over the years. Data transformed into a forecast answers the key question: *Is it climbing weather, or not?*

In the 2004-05 season, German climber Thomas Huber decided to see if his weather guru, Karl Gabl, could provide forecasts from afar. Forecasts for the Chaltén Massif were unprecedented. 'We had no idea if it would work for Patagonia,' Thomas told me, 'but it worked, so everybody was looking at me to see if I'd go or stay, because the climbers thought I knew via Innsbruck the secret about the weather. I had a great first season. Not only for Patagonia but everywhere, weather reports changed a lot in alpinism.'

As Gabl's forecasts have shown over time, accurate mountain forecasts require specific knowledge. Even if you could teach yourself how to do it, you'd need the ability to access the information, which requires functional Internet access.

The Internet didn't come to El Chaltén until 2003. Even then, it was scarce, and it barely worked. The first *locutorio* (Internet cafe) arrived in 2004; climbers would come to check the weather on NOAA, but they'd struggle because the connection was so bad.

Local resident Adriana Estol recalls, 'I came here in 2006 and it was almost impossible to have Internet at the house, but some houses were lucky.' One of the lucky houses belonged to Bean Bowers.

Bowers, a tough-as-nails alpinist and full-on lifestyle climber from the USA, was always the do-it-yourself sort. For several consecutive years, he'd lived the entire season in El Chaltén, and he'd scraped together enough money to buy a small house there. In 2011, at age thirty-eight, Bean died of cancer, but several of his friends remember how he figured out the weather. He guided in the Tetons in the summers, where, one season, Climbing Ranger Ron Johnson showed him how to read weather models.

Doug Chabot, an accomplished alpinist and avalanche forecaster, also helped out. 'I gave Bean the weather

Good to go? Hayden Kennedy checks the met before his historic ascent of Cerro Torre with Jason Kruk in 2012. *(Jason Kruk)*

basics on forecasting in 2004 since he was keen to learn. In fact, during his first trip there [to El Chaltén], he would call me to check on a few weather models. I was avalanche forecasting; I'm used to looking at weather models every day.' He added, 'Most importantly, I had a real job and was reachable by phone.

Bowers also took a course from Woodmencey on mountain weather forecasting.

Climber Josh Wharton remembers well the first season of forecasts, as he and the late Jonny Copp were climbing together in the massif. Many

The late Charlie Fowler racing the wind and incoming storm on the *Compressor Route* in 1996. *(Gregory Crouch)*

climbers expressed gratitude to Huber for sharing his forecasts that season, and soon the gratitude would shift to Bowers. 'Bean was reading the navy maps a friend had showed him, but he was still pretty new to it, so it wasn't always that spot-on. Thomas Huber was using a satellite phone to call his Austrian meteorologist, and between the two I remember growing increasingly confident throughout the trip. In fact, when Jonny and I started down Poincenot [the final tower in their fifty-two-hour linkup of Agujas Saint-Exupéry, Rafael, and Poincenot], the wind came up harshly right on queue, almost to the hour Thomas's guy had predicted three days earlier. It was an 'ah-ha!' moment!'

As he was learning, Bowers kept his dirtbag forecasting knowledge close to his chest, mostly sharing it with friends. In 2006 he taught it to Rolando Garibotti, and soon climbers were knocking on their doors asking for forecasts and how-to instructions. After all, knowing the weather in Patagonia was like having a golden ticket – and it was especially good because it was free.

Climbers literally lined up at Garibotti's house wanting to learn, so he typed up a 'how-to' email (now he has a weather forecasting section on his **pataclimb.com** website). Before long, everyone could get a spot forecast for the massif. Just follow the steps, punch in the data on the right websites – the location coordinates for Cerro Torre, by the way, are -49.3° and -73.1° – and you get frighteningly accurate projections for precipitation, temperature and, most importantly, wind speed. It was as if the walls had shrunk.

Within a few years of that 2004-05 season, the forecasts had become so accurate that climbers could confidently leave behind most of the storm gear they used to carry, making for lighter loads and faster climbing. Around the same time, interest in the *Compressor Route* rapidly subsided –

climbing the *Compressor Route* in Old Patagonia meant something different from getting up it in New Patagonia. Maybe it took the clarity of blue skies to bring to the fore what most climbers objectively knew: with the entirety of difficult climbing covered in bolt ladders, the *Compressor Route* was so compromised that it was hard to consider it a valid climbing route.

Remove the crippling fear of being caught in one of those legendary storms, and the change in Patagonian climbing is impossible to overstate.

Nowadays in El Chaltén (nobody camps in the woods anymore), climbers can be heard saying things like, 'Yeah, looks like sixes and eights tomorrow, then dropping to twos on Wednesday.' They are talking knots of wind speed at the lower, forecast elevation, which translates into nay or yay for climbing at the higher mountain elevations.

In early 2007, I remember staring over Bean Bowers's shoulder as he pulled up the weather map on his computer: the mother of all high-pressure systems was coming our way. The skies were clearing from there to Australia for four days, and so Colin Haley and I headed for Cerro Torre, where we completed an oft-attempted link up of François Marsigny and Andy Parkin's 1994 route *Los Tiempos Perdidos* to the summit via the *Ragni Route*. Despite the exposure to the ice cap, and the harrowing story of Marsigny and Parkin's epic retreat from high on the route, Colin and I climbed with ten-pound backpacks. Our only concern was whether or not we could climb the route; the storms were of no concern, and we were playing a different game to the climbers of Old Patagonia.

When I visited El Chaltén in 2013, a friend had been monitoring the forecasts from the US. He saw a window coming, took advantage of today's increased accessibility, hopped on a plane and a few days later climbed the *Ragni Route*. Around the same time, a pair of young Slovenians arrived, dropped their bags at their hostel – the forecast was perfect – and, without sleep, ran up the trail to FitzRoy and established a hard new route.

Practically overnight, climbers had been given the means to avoid the most horrifying and brutal component of Patagonian climbing.

The place would never be the same.

Some things never change: Tomas Franchini during an attempt on a difficult new big wall line on Torre Egger in 2013. *(Ermanno Salvaterra)*

Surveys

Nantillons Glacier, acrylic on canvas, 51x61cm. *(Tim Pollard)*

MATTHEW TRAVER

Exploring The Alichursky Mountains

Peak 5384m and the rock ridge leading to Peak 5361m lie undisturbed within the Koluchkol Valley. *(Matthew Traver)*

I came to the Pamirs in September 2013 with British writer Jamie Bunchuk to produce a film, in association with the Murghab Ecotourism Association, about a Kyrgyzstani-Tajik hunter and herder named Orozbek who lives in a small settlement just off the notoriously beautiful Pamir Highway and overlooking the verdant Alichur Plains of Eastern Tajikistan.

During the month we spent with Orozbek we had a rare and unforeseen opportunity to explore and document the unclimbed North and South Alichursky Mountains which overlook the Wakhan Corridor. Although this was not a climbing trip, I felt the first ascent and exploration potential we inadvertently encountered during this film project was worth sharing with others.

Our journey into the Alichursky Mountains involved a lengthy two-day overland hitch-hike and taxi share from Almaty in Kazakhstan, where we had been resting up after completing a two month crossing of Eastern Kazakhstan on horseback.

Our first day in Tajikistan saw us bumping and grinding our way down the Pamir Highway in a decrepit Lada driven by two young soldiers from

Dushanbe. As I peered through tinted windows at the Chinese border fence cutting an arbitrary line through this expansive wilderness, I thought it comical how, amidst the pristine snow-capped peaks and uninhabited plateau, our little car was an absurd microcosm of the modern world – the stench of tobacco smoke and vodka breath mixing with ear-splitting Uzbek techno and the soldiers' conversations of missing their girlfriends in the capital.

This somewhat surreal journey turned farcical when the Lada snapped an axle whilst descending the Ak-Baital Pass (4655m), resulting in four grown men screaming wildly, vainly clutching the dashboard, seats, hair and each other in the irrational and futile hope it might stop the truck rolling over into the ditch.

Eventually, after an overnight car-nap in the middle of the highway and the axle repaired with salvaged wire and zip-ties, we spluttered our way

Hidden walls and countless multi-pitch routes await visitors to the Orozbek Massif. *(Matthew Traver)*

into Orozbek's farmstead and yurt approximately five kilometres north of the Kyrgyz settlement of Bash-Gumbez.

The first prominent area we spotted of interest for climbing was a series of 500m-high compact rock walls in the North Alichursky range over-looking Orozbek's place. We affectionately nick-named it the Orozbek Massif (Peak 4984m) in honour of our host. Intriguingly there were also extensive fracture caves throughout the massif, some accessible from the base, but others requiring technical climbing to access. During our reconnaissance along the base of these cliffs I would speculate that 600-800m-long rock routes could be possible for future parties in the region. It also has the distinct advantage of being only an hour's walk from the highway.

The longer we spent exploring this small pocket of eastern Tajikistan, the greater the secrets the land seemed to reveal to us; both in terms of its history and potential for first ascents. Already in our first two weeks we had made small archaeological discoveries in the caves of the Orozbek Massif, stumbled upon a Tsarist-era mine, sampled a cave-growing organic painkiller known as *mumya* and accidently ventured in to the uranium polluted Baz-Terek Valley.

The second region encountered with considerable potential was presented to us on a visit to the ancient caravanserai and long abandoned silver mining settlement of Bazar-Dara. Accessing this area requires a UAZ/4WD at a cost of $250 - $500 from Murghab. The entry point to start the off-road jaunt is via a northerly running road up an unnamed valley located near to the distinct hilly mound of An-Balik (4196m). Two hours up

After hunting marmots, Orozbek finishes off the day collecting teresken grass for firewood. *(Matthew Traver)*

this valley saw us at the top of the 4864m Bazar-Dara Pass and another three hours winding our way down a valley of the same name towards the caravanserai.

According to Soviet maps the nearest peaks to this region that may have been climbed are Peak Trezubets (5845m) and Peak Skahssmy (5781m) which are located 10km to the east within the Uzengyu-Niazek Mountains.

Within the Bazar-Dara sector of the North Alichursky Mountains we encountered five valleys rolling outwards in a north-easterly direction. The first two valleys were up to three kilometres long and feeding a glacial lake that would be ideal for a base camp. Following either of these will lead to four to five unclimbed peaks, the highest in the region being Peak 5617. The three valleys to the north are somewhat drier, shorter and much

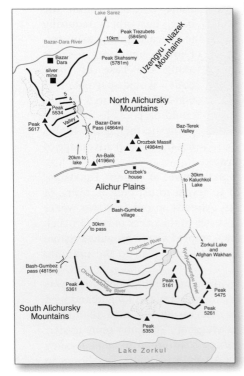

less prominent, although there are significant granite slabs up to 500m high at the head of these valleys, which could make for great multi-pitch alpine rock routes. Alternatively these valleys would provide ideal access to approximately four unclimbed ridges and summits over 5000m. It would also be possible to site a camp near to the caravanserai itself and access these peaks via two short glaciated valleys, one of which leads up to the ancient silver mine!

Our final week with Orozbek saw us head in to the South Alichursky mountains five kilometres from Zorkul, a lake which separates Tajikistan from Afghanistan. Our primary goal was to film the endangered argali sheep of which he and many other Kyrgyz in the region are avid hunters, both for sport and to sell the meat on the black market. Our own jaunt took us down a turn

Jamie Bunchuk beneath one of the many big walls in the Orozbek Massif. *(Matthew Traver)*

off south from the highway from Chamyr-Tash following the mostly dry Iri-Yak River up towards Koluchkol Lake.

The most prominent feature in the Koluchkol region was the magnificent and unclimbed Peak 5384 and an appealing granite ridge line snaking its way for 9km towards Peak 5361 which was out of view up the Chonkaradzhilga river valley. Aside from these two prime objectives, numerous other unclimbed peaks abound, I estimate eight primary summits sprouting in the vicinity of these two peaks, as well as within the Chokman and Kyulyuchsurdyu river valleys.

Whilst it was somewhat frustrating as a climber to be visiting these virgin realms without a rack or rope, it felt a real privilege to be able to document these regions, spend time with Orozbek and share my findings with like-minded individuals. Should you ever wish to plan your own expedition to the Alichursky Mountains, I strongly recommend paying a visit to Orozbek and liaising with the Murghab Ecotourism Association (META).

Acknowledgements: Thanks to Malgosia Skowronska for checking the Russian to English translation, Gulnara Apandieva and Tony Nelson of the META for their support and the other twenty-two sponsors of the wider *One Steppe Ahead* documentary film project.

Summary: A description of three virgin climbing regions within the North and South Alichursky Mountains of Eastern Tajikistan which were encountered by Matt Traver during a visit to the area to produce a documentary film about the life of a local hunter and herder.

TAMOTSU NAKAMURA

Nyainbo Yuze

A future climbing paradise?

*[Editor's note: what follows is an abridged version of a tantalising article
published in the recent **Japanese Alpine News** – Vol. 15 (2014), page 98]*

When you stand on Longgeshanyaku (4398m), the high pass *en route*
to Nyainbo Yuze, you can't fail to be overwhelmed by the gran-
deur of range upon range of granite peaks and pinnacles that reach into the
distance and cut the sky like the teeth of a saw.

Nyainbo Yuze is the local Tibetan name for the Golok Mountains,
which form the easternmost rim of the east Bayan Har Shan, and may be
compared to the rock peaks of Siguniang in the Qionglai Mountains in
Sichuan.

The massif measures about 40km north to south and 25km east to west
with deep valleys and many glacial lakes therein.

Apart from the main peak, which is relatively easy to climb, there are
countless more alluring rock peaks that will undoubtedly attract climbers
in the near future.

panorama of the west wall of just the northern half of the Nyainbo range viewed from the
nggeshanyaku pass (4398m), detail below. *(Tamotsu Nakamura)*

West face of peaks c.5000m in the southern half of the Nyainbo range.
(Tamotsu Nakamura)

Nyainbo Yuze, a brief history

The Kyoto Alpine Club made the first ascent of Peak II of the main peak group in August of 1989. Peak II is slightly lower than the main peak at 5396m. The party set up a base camp near the southern end of the Ximen Co lake and followed a route via a glacier.

In 2009, a Chinese party attempted the main peak (5369m) but was unsuccessful. In July of 2011 they returned to the mountain and three members of the team succeeded in making the first recorded ascent of the main peak (5396m) via the north-east face. They followed the glacier from camp 1 and then a 60 degree rock buttress to the top.

In August of 2013 all 8 members of another Chinese party, from Chengdu, made the second recorded ascent of the main peak also via the north-east face, encountering few difficulties.

Note: Both the China Mountaineering Association (Beijing) and the Qinghai Mountaineering Association (Xining) have no climbing records for Nyainbo Yuze. Details of the two Chinese ascents described above were gathered from web-sites in China.

Nyainbo Yuze, an overview

A Guide to Mountaineering in China (jointly edited and published by the China Mountaineering Association and Chengdu Cartographic Publishing

West wall of the main peak (5396m), highest in the Nyainbo Yuze massif.
(Tamotsu Nakamura)

House, 1999) describes Nyainbo Yuze, as follows *[paraphrased]*:

'On the Tibetan Plateau, the vast Kunlun Shan comprises west and east sections. The south satellite of East Kunlun Shan is Bayan Har Shan, the main peak of which, Nyainbo Yuze, stands in Jigzhi County of Qinghai Province on the east section of Bayan Har Shan.

Rising to 5369m above sea level, Nyainbo Yuze lies at 101.1°E and 33.3°N. The main summit group is composed of seven peaks, which are capped with snow in the shape of petals all the year around.

Steep ridges and gorges are common features of the Nyainbo Yuze massif. The gorges contain hanging glaciers and valley glaciers in their upper parts. The magnificent and fascinating natural scenery includes over 160 valley lakes of various sizes, surrounded by snowy and lofty rock pinnacles with forests at their foot.

This solemn and graceful beauty is most probably the reason local herdsmen admire and worship the Nyainbo Yuze massif as divine mountains.

The Nyainbo Yuze area, located in the fringe of the subtropical monsoon zone and the highlands is home to various animals and plants, the latter including herbal medicines. Ancient forests of dragon spruce and pine soar into the sky. Mountain slopes abound with precious traditional herbal medicines such as caterpillar fungus, fritillary and wild rhubarb. The lower reaches of the mountains proves to be the haunt of such rare

Detail of West wall of c.5000m peaks south of the main peak. The walls are estimated to be c.600m high. *(Tamotsu Nakamura)*

animals as wild asses, wild yaks, *Pantholop hodgsoni*, bharal, white-lipped deer and asiatic black bears. More than twenty species of fish, peculiar to the plateaus, live in the lakes. Jigzhi is 875km from Xining, a capital of Qinghai Province, by road.'

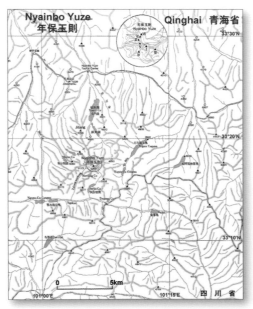

Climate

In July and August the average temperature is around 10 degrees, but daytime temperatures can reach 27°C.

Meconopsis sp. – yellow poppy. *(Tamotsu Nakamura)*

The Alps & Beyond

Petit Dru, acrylic on canvas, 40x50cm. *(Tim Pollard)*

DES RUBENS

Key Moments on The Peuterey Ridge

or

The Tale of an Elderly Partnership on the Longest Ridge
in the Alps, in the Fervent Hope of Being of Use to
Others of a Similar Vintage

Geoff Cohen a few pitches above the Bivouac des Dames Anglaises. *(Des Rubens)*

*'I know of no scene more dominating, more damning to hope and optimism,
than the Peuterey Ridge viewed from the Col de l'Innominata.'*
– Frank Smythe, *Climbs and Ski Runs* (1929)

[deleted expletive. . .]
I should not be sliding down here towards the Col de Peuterey. Sheer.
Bloody. Utter. Stupidity. What would the hi' heid yins o' the Alpine Club
– that prestigious body of which I'd recently become a member – think
of this demonstration of incompetence? *(And Was Not the Current President*

103

Particularly Severe on Raw Recruits bringing The Club's Name into Disrepute?) More worryingly, what would be the immediate outcome, for the moment beyond my control?

I experienced a short flight over the bergschrund and decelerated gently to a halt, courtesy of the ropework of my lifelong friend and fellow martyr to unrelenting masochism, Geoff Cohen.

He carefully descended to join me and we continued quietly to the col. Although Geoff could justifiably have given way to some degree of emotion, he was tolerance personified.

The author at the Dames Anglaises Bivouac Hut, Brenva Glacier and Géant in distance. *(Geoff Cohen)*

To go back a few days: I eventually reckoned five key moments of our ascent. The first was that in scrutinising the long term forecast from the comfort of Geoff's base in the Ecrins, we realised the unsettled weather was improving to give six fine days.

'What do you fancy?' asked my worthy friend of forty years' standing.

'The Peuterey Ridge', I replied instantly.

And that was more or less it. No further discussion necessary. We packed, drove to the Val Veni and walked up to the Monzino Hut.

Next day, shortly after dawn, we were examining the Peuterey Ridge from the Col de l'Innominata, a powerfully atmospheric place adorned with plaques commemorating the disastrous retreat of Walter Bonatti's party in 1961. This was a second critical point in the climb – my confidence of the brief decision-making process much diminished. We'd had an awkward moment during the ascent when one of us took a short tumble, indicative of a lack of 'flow' or sympathy with the environment. Although I had passed this way about 30 years earlier, approaching the *Gervasutti Route* on the Gugliermina, the monumental scale of the south flank of Mont Blanc had faded from memory. Just regarding the massive architecture of the Peuterey Ridge was enough to arouse a swarm of butterflies in the stomach. With a combined age of 127, it had to be acknowledged that Geoff and I were hardly the honed athletes of our youth (the assumption inherent in this statement has been questioned by a few 'friends') and such a long route was a daunting prospect.

An aside to growing old: hesitant though I am to play the 'old man' card,

Geoff Cohen approaching main summit of the Aiguille Blanche; south-east summit (Pt. Seymour King) 4107m and North Face of the Aiguille Blanche in background. *(Des Rubens)*

it is nevertheless difficult to ignore the fact that age does begin to restrict your ability to achieve on the mountains. More exasperatingly, a problem (at least if you are competitive, which, of course, I'm certainly not) is that however old you are, there'll always be someone doing better than you. If, say, you're on an indoor wall, happy on F6b at sixty, it's guaranteed there'll be someone of seventy gracefully flexing on F7a. I don't doubt my own father, going to the local gym at 95, encounters even more aged veterans who both inspire and enrage him.

So with a number of excuses to hand, had my companion suggested backtracking, I would probably have acquiesced with little comment and subsequently remained mute about the whole stupid idea. However, no offer of retreat was forthcoming so we tacitly agreed to continue.

Even the short descent to the Freney Glacier, which I had recalled as a loose scramble, maintained its capacity to alarm: we teetered around exposed, unattached blocks to find abseil slings – the lack of 'flow' continued with a dropped belay plate. However, we then crossed the Freney Glacier without difficulty and moved up the Schneider Ledges. Although the ground is not difficult, you are constantly confronted with rounded holds and ball-bearing gravel underfoot. A combination of misreading the guide

Geoff Cohen on the lower rocks of the Grand Pilier d'Angle.(A more direct line was taken due to poor snow conditions above the Col de Peuterey.) *(Des Rubens)*

and wrong information meant a delayed arrival at the Bivouac des Dames Anglaises. (Tradition holds that the shelter is named due to its difficulty of access.)

Still, a fabled spot! And what an outlook over the Freney and Brenva Glaciers! We were the first visitors to the shelter that year (12 July), supporting the statement by the guardian of the Monzino Hut that we were the first team to attempt the Peuterey this season. The hut book also showed a few familiar names from ascents of the Peuterey Integrale from previous years. We had not seriously considered the Integrale, put off by the description of the alarming abseils off the Aiguille Noire. Anyway, we had both previously ascended the Noire's classic South Ridge, in Geoff's case forty-five years previously. Also there were

Geoff Cohen on bivouac at the foot of the large gendarme, Grand Pilier d'Angle. *(Des Rubens)*

Geoff Cohen approaching the upper part of the Peuterey Ridge (above the Grand Pilier d'Angle); Central Pillar of Freney in background. *(Des Rubens)*

limits as to how far we should test the patience of our guardian angels, who throughout our climbing careers have been unwaveringly loyal regarding our best interests.

Daringly, we did decide to spend a day acclimatising at the Dames Anglaises, as we had only been in the Alps for a week. Respite from the mental strain of the route was balanced by faith in the accuracy of the weather forecast – a very modern benefit. We spent a couple of hours of our rest day clarifying the route back up to the Schneider Couloir , and then passed a delightful day in this historic spot.

The following day we set off before dawn and made steady progress up the broken rocks to the snows of the Aiguille Blanche, supposedly the most difficult of access of the Alpine 4000m peaks. We travelled unroped and, as the snow conditions were excellent, continued so over the arête above the North Face to the main summit. Nevertheless, I felt uneasy looking back at my companion negotiating the arête. This was exacerbated by dropping my ancient and beloved water bottle down the face. (Dropping personal items into a huge abyss often gives rise to uncomfortable feelings in me.)

The view from the summit of the Aiguille Blanche across the south flank of Mont Blanc is without parallel. It's easy to see why the Central Pillar of Freney was the big prize of the '60s. The Chandelle is well named and the

The Freney Pillar from the final pitches of the Peuterey Ridge. *(Des Rubens)*

detachment of the Pillar makes it the outstanding feature on the Freney Face. However, looking across towards Col Eccles, supposedly an escape route from the Upper Freney Glacier, I didn't like the look of the ground at all. No gentle snow slopes but steep, exposed glacier and rubble, possibly made more hazardous in recent years by climate change. Nowhere in the Alps would I less like to be in poor weather. History has shown it to be a desperate place in heavy snowfall. My respect for the pioneers of the Freney Face grew. So the certainty that there was no obvious escape other than over the summit of the Blanc was the third key moment during our climb.

We climbed and roped down towards the Col du Peuterey. The fourth key moment was soon upon us: with a concern to keep moving quickly, I said to Geoff I didn't need belaying as I set off down the final snow slopes to the Col de Peuterey. Unfortunately, the snow gave way to harder ice, I misjudged the holding power of my lightweight axe and I was soon flying. I beat myself up for a while regarding this fundamental error, but soon realised there was no alternative but just to get on with the route.

Having not fully absorbed the guidebook description, I hadn't quite realised the Grand Pilier d'Angle had so much mixed ground below it. Rotten snow forced us to take to the rocks earlier than we would have liked, climbing two difficult pitches of about HVS before laborious slopes led to the cold and exposed arête of the peak. Evening was drawing in. We eventually found the bivvy at the foot of the Grand Gendarme, a noted feature hereabouts, and what a grand bivvy spot it was too! Slightly worryingly, a little snow drifted down as we settled into our bags, but we dismissed it as an evening *averse*.

I started brewing about 3am. Yet another perfect morning and the near certainty of the weather holding with success only dependent on our own efforts was the fifth and final key moment. My mood was much improved from the previous day – the Freney Face was flushed with the morning sun and we absorbed the remoteness. Regaining the ridge, we negotiated some mixed ground beyond the gendarme to reach the wonderful snow arêtes of the upper part of the route, with terrific views of the Freney and Major faces on either side. Higher up, we hit hard ice and pitched it to the top of the climb at the junction with the Brouillard Ridge.

For mile upon mile, peak after peak, pinnacle after pinnacle, the Peuterey now lay below us – the finest and longest ridge in the whole of the Alps. A

Geoff Cohen on the final pitches of the Peuterey Ridge, just before its junction with the Brouillard Ridge. *(Des Rubens)*

lifetime's ambition had been achieved.

This was worth more than a handshake. An emotional hug was in order and I confess to shedding some tears. Geoff was similarly moved. It was as fine a moment as any in our long partnership.

A few figures could be seen on the summit, the first humans we had seen since leaving the Monzino Hut three and a half days before.

We headed over the summit to the Gonella Hut on the Italian side. The mountain, which so far had been benign, was becoming hostile, as if regretting its previous tolerance. Firstly, a substantial rockfall raked the line of descent onto the Glacier du Dôme. We had anticipated this possibility by taking a more circuitous line. However, shortly after, we were not spared an hour-long crevasse incident when one of us failed to leap sufficiently far over the covered bergschrund (probably also age-related – the gazelle-like sinews of youth having atrophied).

After the tension of extrication from the crevasse, which was not particularly straightforward given the rotten snow, the mountain relented and we were no more inconvenienced.

We reached the modern and comfortable Gonella Hut around sunset, four days after leaving the Monzino Hut. The transition from exterior to interior and the kindly welcome of the Italian guardian could not have

Geoff Cohen descending the Bosses Ridge with the Aiguille de Bionnassay beyond. A plan to continue over this peak was abandoned due to lack of time (or, perhaps more accurately, speed) and snow conditions. *(Des Rubens)*

been more marked. We relaxed into food, beers and chat, continuing to marvel at the shift to the luxuries of modern living.

The following day, we descended through the Himalayan-scale scenery surrounding the Miage Glacier to a wonderful green meadow. The following morning, the rain came as predicted. It was the end of our Alpine holiday.

Summary: An account of an ascent of the Peuterey Ridge of Mont Blanc via the Dames Anglaises (Craveri) Bivouac Hut, by Geoff Cohen and Des Rubens, 11 – 16 July 2013, round trip from Val Veni.

Geoff Cohen (left) and Des Rubens on the summit of Mont Blanc. *(Rubens coll.)*

STEPHEN GOODWIN

Dent d'Hérens

Saluting The Pioneers

Raising the Alpine Convention flag on the Dent d'Hérens. L-r: Stephen Goodwin, Maurizio Gaillard, Daniela Formica and Andrea Celesia. *(Claudio Rosset)*

When Montagu Woodmass gained the summit of the Dent d'Hérens on 12 August 1863, he immediately danced a Highland fling. Well bully for him. One hundred and fifty years later to the day, on reaching the same spot, I sat down for a rest; well earned, I thought, and much needed. My excuse? Woodmass, at 29 years old, was less than half my age, and he was match fit. I had driven pretty well non-stop from Cumbria to the Aosta valley and gone straight on the mountain next day. But I guess we shared a certain satisfaction, even if mine was less exuberantly expressed.

Neither of us was alone. Woodmass had made the first ascent of the 4171m peak with fellow Alpine Club members William Hall, Florence Crauford Grove and Reginald Macdonald, accompanied by guides Melchior Anderegg, Peter Perren and Jean-Pierre Cachat. The AC men had planned the expedition and 'Le Grand Melchior' led the way throughout.

I was in similarly safe hands. The guides of Valpelline had extended an invitation to the Alpine Club to join an anniversary ascent of the mountain

Dent d'Hérens: left is the sunlit north face, the right hand skyline is the West Ridge. *(John Cleare)*

and I was their grateful guest. Maurizio Galliard, president of the guides, took charge and with us were his colleagues Claudio Rosset and Andrea Celesia, plus Daniela Formica, president of Club 4000 and the first Italian woman to climb all the 4000ers of the Alps. We'd been brought together by my friend Marco Onida, former secretary general of Alpine Convention, who has roots in the Aosta valley. Marco accompanied us to the Aosta hut, then disappeared to another mountain but left us the Convention's banner – campaigning for a greener Alps – to take to the summit.

Hall's somewhat verbose account of the first ascent was published in

On the West Ridge of the Dent d'Hérens. *(Stephen Goodwin)*

the first volume of the *Alpine Journal* (1863-64). He'd read it before the AC on 2 February 1864 and perhaps his wit worked better live than it does in print today.

What impresses on re-reading Hall after actually being on the Dent d'Hérens is what a determined effort it must have taken to locate a route onto the mountain. The party crossed the Col de la Valpelline from Zermatt, dossed in a hay shed for two nights, making an abortive foray on the intervening day, set off from Prarayer at 2.30am, ascended the lower Tsa de Tsan glacier and on to the Grandes Murailles glacier and picked a way up the mountain's South-west Flank to join the West Ridge to the top.

Unbeknownst to them, Edward Whymper had been on the mountain just days earlier with Jean-Antoine Carrel and Luc Meynet. They had opted for the full West Ridge – a serrated rock crest – but turned back,

The Matterhorn from the summit of the Dent d'Hérens. *(Stephen Goodwin)*

finding it difficult and unjustifiably loose. Whymper was not best pleased. 'This was the only mountain in the Alps which I have essayed to ascend, that has not, sooner or later, fallen to me. Our failure was mortifying,' he wrote.

Times change: today the lower part of the Tsa de Tsan glacier has melted away, a huge reservoir fills the upper Valpelline below Prarayer and there is no more sleeping in hay sheds. Instead the comfortable Aosta hut at 2781m more than halves the effort our forebears must have put in. We left the hut at 4am and were back on the terrace eight hours later enjoying a celebratory beer.

Hall summed up their 1863 route as 'a very pretty scramble', which seems something of an understatement given the melodrama of his earlier paragraphs. Today the South-west Flank-West Ridge is graded AD and remains the easiest way up provided the snow is well frozen. More entertaining is to ascend, as we did, via the West Ridge (AD III-) and return down the SW Flank. Conditions were perfect, early morning sun on dry rock as we negotiated the gendarmes along the crest. The *coup de théâtre* comes as you pull on to the summit rocks and ahead, almost within touching distance it seems, bursts the west face of the Matterhorn and the Italian Ridge. Memory's chocolate box image of the mountain from Zermatt melts away under the intensity of it all.

We raised Marco's banner and took the obligatory photographs. An ascent of the Dent d'Hérens from Valpelline had suited the aims of both the Alpine Convention and the local guides. A key part of a greener, yet economically sustainable Alps is the promotion of 'soft tourism' – that is low impact pursuits like hiking and climbing. And Valpelline has plenty of scope.

Contrary to expectations, the great reservoir has quite a natural feel to it, once, that is, you're out of sight of the soaring dam wall. Old larches along the shoreline give way to flower-rich pasture then the wild upper valley; there is no public road beyond the dam, just a track to Refugio Prarayer at the head of the reservoir, and no ski infrastructure of any sort. The contrast to the Zermatt or Chamonix areas could hardly be starker – but wildness and a dearth of visitors hardly make for a vibrant tourist economy. The Valpelline guides' association has only 18 members and of these only one is close to working full time as a guide and instructor (and then often out of the area); the rest have day jobs as electricians, firemen and so on. Not only would the guides welcome more business; its effect would percolate through hotels, B&Bs and restaurants to the valley in general.

Celebrating success at the Aosta hut: Claudio Rosset, Andrea Celesia, Stephen Goodwin and Daniela Formica. *(Maurizio Gaillard)*

Mountain anniversaries come thick and fast these days. Often, due to weather or perhaps the age of the participants, there is a good deal more wining and dining than climbing. Our ascent of the Dent d'Hérens was something of an exception: dining was mostly pasta, a hearty evening meal at the Aosta hut and a few Birra Morettis, wine and fontina cheese when the job was done. We raised a glass to the AC pioneers and their guides and went on our way.

*Great thanks are due: firstly to Maurizio and Marilia Gaillard for warm hospitality at their lovely pension at Fénis in Valle d'Aosta (**chezgaillard.bb@libero.it**); to guides Maurizio, Claudio Rosset and Andrea Celesia for their care and company on the mountain; also to Daniela Formica of Club 4000 (open to all who have climbed 30 alpine 4000ers and crave more: **club4000.it**), to Gigi Vignone, guardian of the Aosta hut, and not least to our 'facilitator', Marco Onida.*

DEREK BUCKLE

Four Valleys, Five Summits

The 2014 AC Expedition to The Peruvian Andes

Dedicated to our late Honorary Treasurer, Mike Pinney

Huandoy Sur (6160m), Oeste (6356m) and Norte (6395m), with Pisco (5752m) on the far right, from the upper Llanganuco Valley. *(Derek Buckle)*

Late in 2013 Mike Pinney and I started to think seriously about a suitable expedition to the greater ranges in 2014 and Peru's Cordillera Blanca came high on the list of possibilities. Having been there seven years ago with Stuart Worsfold we easily identified some key objectives, with the iconic Alpamayo – arguably one of the world's most attractive mountains and a coveted summit – dominating the programme. Not long after advertising the expedition we had a full team. Indeed, more than a full team as it was hugely oversubscribed. Eventually eleven participants were enrolled, although Mike's untimely death in a climbing accident in Wales in March ultimately reduced this to ten.

Team members from various parts of Britain eventually converged on Paris at the start of June for the long flight to Lima. With everything going

117

to plan we then travelled northwards to Huaraz, the climbing capital of Peru, taking advantage of a luxury limousine for the 8-hour journey.

Huaraz (3100m) was the base to which we regularly returned, a town devastated like much of central Peru by the Great Peruvian Earthquake of 1970 which measured 7.7 on the Richter Scale and killed an estimated 70,000 people. Over forty years later the place still looks like a project under construction, but it is nevertheless a vibrant centre of activity that provides a stupendous panorama of Huascaran, Peru's highest peak, and other stunning mountains.

After two days of acclimatisation, including the classic walk up to Laguna Churup, we left for Pashpa where, assisted by *arrieros* and donkeys, we trekked for five hours to our first base camp at 4400m in the Quebrada Ishinca. Despite the popularity of this valley, it was not crowded and base camp offered magnificent easterly views towards Tocllaraju (6032m) and Palcaraju (6274m).

Two days later John, Nick, Richard and I traversed Ishinca (5530m), ascending by its north-west slopes (PD) and descending to base camp via the south-west ridge (PD-). The next day Andy and Yvonne collected Mel from her bivvi at an intermediate camp to make a second traverse of Ishinca.

On 9 June Richard and I set off early to climb the south slopes and east ridge of Urus Este (5495m, PD-) while John and Nick, who had set off some while later, galloped past high on the route with a group of Canadians in hot pursuit. Despite a marked cloud inversion in the valley the compact summit offered great views of Tocllaraju, Ishinca and other peaks and is an attractive acclimatisation peak.

Meanwhile, Kate, Keith and Adele contented themselves with an exploratory walk up the valley to the Tocllaraju high camp while the other three took advantage of the fine *almuerzo* provided by our cook Antonio and his

The team: Richard Toon, Andy Stratford, Adele Long, John Kentish, Keith Lambley, Yvonne Holland, Kate Ross, Mel Michon and Nick Berry. *(Derek Buckle)*

John Kentish on the descent from Peak 5368m. *(Andy Stratford)*

assistant Chrisaldo after their climb on Ishinca.

The following day we decamped for the return to Huaraz accompanied to the road-head by our *arrieros* and donkeys. It was only an overnight stay as we planned to walk into Yanapaccha base camp on 11 June. Taking advantage of four porters, Adele, Andy, John, Nick, Richard, Yvonne and I were driven up the Quebrada Llanguno until we reached '*curva* 42' at 4580m from where a two-hour straightforward traverse led to the scenic moraine camp nestling beside a small lake at 4817m. The views from this camp were stunning too, with the multiple summits of Chacraraju (6112m)

Yanapaccha moraine camp, Huandoy massif beyond. *(Derek Buckle)*

dominating the extensive panorama.

The whole team bar Andy, who was still suffering from altitude head-aches, climbed the west face (AD-) of Yanapaccha (5460m) the next day in the company of two other parties by what must be considered as one of the classic non-technical routes in the area, surpassing Pisco (5752m) – which I climbed with Stuart Worsfold in 2007 – by some margin. Many parties make two abseils from *in situ* snow stakes on the steep final pyramid leading to the summit, but down-climbing is not at all difficult. There was some excitement early on when Richard dislodged a fridge-sized boulder on the short moraine traverse to the glacier in the dark, but fortunately he deftly avoided any unpleasant consequences. Back at camp a quick brew was called for before we decamped for the return to the road-head and another short sojourn in Huaraz.

June 13 was a rest day on which Adele, Kate, Keith and I sampled the delights of the hot springs at Monterray. Unusually, the water here is dark brown and there is the expectation of emerging a darker colour than on entry. Fortunately this is not the case. Others in the party spent the day exploring Huaraz or shopping, but the opportunity to use the cheap local *collectivos* with their colourful occupants is not one that I would have missed.

It was now time to move on to Alpamayo base camp in the Quebrada

Richard Toon on summit slopes of Yanapaccha. *(Derek Buckle)*

Santa Cruz for an attempt on the major objectives. Leaving Kate and Keith to do some exploring at Caraz the remaining party continued to the road-head at Cashapampa (2900m) where we met up with a new group of *arrieros*. Initially the trail followed the true left bank of the steep-sided Santa Cruz gorge until it broadened out before reaching the intermediate Llamacorral camp at 3787m, some way before Laguna Ichicocha.

Continuing past the two lakes the next day the trail then crossed the desiccated plain caused by the 1997 rupture of the Quebrada Arteson moraine lake, before a series of zig-zags led steeply to the base camp at 4345m. From the comfort of armchairs at home we had then planned to ascend directly to the Alpamayo col camp on June 16, but Andy, Mel, Nick, Richard and I eventually settled for a night at the intermediate moraine camp at 4973m. A guided party pressed on towards the higher camp, but even assisted by high altitude porters they made very slow progress up the steeper section of the glacier. As if to vindicate our decision several centimetres of snow fell that night and we chose to stay put the next morning.

Once again this decision was fortuitous as around midday the guided party descended with news of the dangerous state of both Alpamayo (5947m) and our alternative objective, Quitaraju (6036m). Apparently some 60-70 cm of new snow had fallen to the east of the col and both mountains were avalanching and treacherous. Conditions were so bad

Richard Toon approaching the summit of Urus Este. *(Derek Buckle)*

that they had been forced to camp on the col itself rather than reach the customary plateau camp area some 100m lower. It would be several days before conditions stabilised; time that neither they, nor we, had. Keen to see the classic faces of both Alpamayo and Quitaraju we spent a second night at the intermediate camp before making an attempt to reach the col and returning to base camp. Richard abandoned the attempt very early on but Mel and I continued to within 200m of the col before heading back to camp.

The Author on Yanapaccha summit. *(John Kentish)*

Only Nick and Andy carried on to the 5520m col, climbing two short pitches of seventy degree ice, to confirm that the conditions were indeed dire, although they did get some impressive photos of Alpamayo.

Back at base camp John had been hatching a back-up plan which involved crossing the Quebrada Santa Cruz to the Sentilo valley from where he hoped that we could attempt Millis(h)raju

Mel, Nick & Andy on the glacier above Alpamayo moraine camp with Laguna Arhueycocha and the Pulajirca group behind. *(Derek Buckle)*

II (5420m), the northernmost peak of Pyramide (5885m). Despite its distance from base camp Andy, Nick and I enthusiastically signed up for the venture. Meanwhile Adele, Mel and Richard had set their sights on traversing the Punta Unión col to complete the classic Santa Cruz trek while Yvonne decided to rest and enjoy the delights of base camp cooking.

Setting off on June 19 the four of us followed the easy traverse along and across the Quebrada Santa Cruz until we were forced to slog up the undulating and boggy Sentilo side valley to camp on a grassy knoll at 4584m. Evidently the path marked on the map no longer exists, presumably being overgrown through disuse as there was little sign of recent activity in the valley. Rather disappointingly while sitting comfortably in camp John and I failed to see an obvious route through the glaciated buttress leading to the NNE ridge of Millis(h)raju II and we were expecting to return empty-handed the next day. Andy and Nick, on the other hand, spent some considerable time on a closer inspection of the wall and just as they were about to give up eventually found a sequence of cairns following a natural line of weakness. The climb was on after all!

Clambering over a complex boulder-field in the dark, we followed cairns left by Andy and Nick, and easily located the older cairned route leading up from the left of the buttress and followed this easily to the sharp NNE ridge where we geared up just as a brilliant dawn broke to reveal the magnificent south-west face of Taulliraju (5830m).

John (left), Andy and Nick starting the descent of the NNE ridge of Millisraju II (5420m). *(Derek Buckle)*

Climbing on perfect snow, we skirted a number of large crevasses on the corniced ridge to reach the small summit of Millis(h)raju II (PD) – on the morning of my 70th birthday – five hours after leaving camp. Returning by the route of ascent we then decamped for the long trek back to Alpamayo base camp ready for our return to Huaraz.

With the *arrieros* having arrived the same evening we departed for Cashapampa early the following morning in blisteringly hot weather and continued by bus to Huaraz to allow Nick to return home and the remaining team to recoup.

On Monday 23 June we left Huaraz for Olleros and our fourth and last valley. At 3800m and a little beyond Olleros we were met by our third group of *arrieros* with horses and donkeys to begin the trek to base camp at 4300m in the Quebrada Rurec. Having been to the Rurec valley previously the plan was to attempt Cashan (5716m) from a high camp on the moraine to its south, but since this is not a frequented peak little information exists on the optimal route.

Starting from the prominent sub-valley just north of base camp it was possible to access the narrow, unstable true right lateral moraine which led inexorably towards the glaciated south face of Cashan but after three hours we could locate only one small area at 4820m that was deemed suitable for one tent. Moreover, the southern aspect of Cashan did not look appealing and the approach suggested by our agents, the Morales brothers, had distinctly deteriorated in the intervening eight years since they had made the climb. Not only had a substantial rockfall exposed a major section of the traverse line to the south-west ridge to unnecessary risk, but a line of impending séracs compounded the objective danger. As a result all bar Richard and I retreated back to base camp to rethink alternatives.

Although we too had no intention of running the gauntlet across the face, Richard thought that he could see a direct alternative to the summit that we could investigate the following day and the views of Uruashraju (5722m) were stunning. Continuing up the moraine, however, soon suggested that the direct alternative was more technical than we were prepared for, but that Cashan Norte to our left might be a viable option. Ultimately this was not to be as we became entrenched in deep, unstable snow and gradually ground to a halt near 5240m. Invoking the maxim 'discretion is the better part of valour' we retreated and returned to base camp.

Andy and John meanwhile had relocated further up the valley, intent on climbing one of the subsidiary summits on the south ridge leading to Rurec (5700m). In this they were successful, managing to gain the summit of Peak 5368m (PD) before returning to base camp.

With little time left three of the party climbed to the narrow col at the head of the sub-valley south of base camp at approx. 4940m before having to return to Huaraz for the journey to Lima and the flight home.

Summary: In June 2014 ten members of the Alpine Club: Nick Berry, Derek Buckle (leader), Yvonne Holland, John Kentish, Keith Lambley, Adele Long, Mel Michon, Kate Ross, Andy Stratford and Richard Toon, visited four separate valleys in the Cordillera Blanca region of Peru, from which various parties successfully climbed Ishinca, Urus, Yanapaccha, Millis(h)raju and Peak 5368m. Attempts on Alpamayo, Quitaraju and Cashan were thwarted due to poor, unstable conditions.

John Kentish at the start of Millisraju's NNE ridge. *(Derek Buckle)*

Cold Climes

Ben Nevis North Face, oil on canvas, 61x76cm. *(Tim Pollard)*

ALASTAIR LEE & LEO HOULDING

The Last Great Climb

North-east Ridge of Ulvetanna, Queen Maud Land, Antarctica

The mile-long north-east ridge of Ulvetanna divides the sunlit north face (right) and shaded east face (greatly foreshortened). ABC was sited on the small promontory at the foot of the ridge. *(Alastair Lee)*

A lastair Lee – I've often wondered what it must have been like to be a pioneer in the golden age of mountaineering, to be the first to stand at the foot of a mountain and wonder at its possibilities.

But as we climb on into the 21st century there are seemingly few areas in the world that remain unexplored and even fewer mountain ranges with significant unclimbed peaks – the politically inaccessible five and six thousand metre peaks of Eastern Tibet perhaps an exception.

So the modern adventurer must find new ways to explore boundaries, find new ground and push limits. Combining speed ascents, purer and purer style, solo or multi-day ascents, with emerging disciplines like para-

Aerial photo looking north to the west faces of Holtanna (r) and Kintanna with the south buttress of Ulvetanna catching the sun at left. The crash site of the DC3 is just visible, the aircraft was subsequently rebuilt *in situ* and flown back to Canada. *(Alastair Lee)*

alpinism (climbing and BASE jumping) does create the most mind-blowing adventures imaginable, all fantastic stuff but a long way from the simplicity of the early pioneers where the task was simple, the goal and motivation clear.

In this context, the Fenriskjeften mountains of northern Queen Maud Land, Antarctica perhaps represent the last chance saloon for today's adventure climber. They are so remote and inaccessible that they remained unexplored, and one of the planet's best kept mountaineering secrets, until

1994 when Ivar Tollefsen lead an eclectic 13-man Norwegian expedition to the area aboard a Russian icebreaker.

The Fenriskjeften were first sighted and photographed from the air in 1939 by the Nazi Antarctic Expedition. Conspiracy theory variously speculates that they were looking for a secret base to hide the Third Reich should they lose the war, or a location from which to run top-secret projects – an Antarctic Atlantis. Their whale-spotting planes overflew Queen Maud Land dropping iron crosses with swastikas on them to usurp the territory originally claimed in 1938 by the Norwegians; Queen Maud Land, named after the Queen of Norway.

After WWII the Norwegians re-claimed the territory and in the late

1950s conducted a photographic survey of this unexplored area revealing a striking collection of peaks including a large triangular summit poking clear of the horizon. It would be this photograph, which lay unseen for 35 years in the Norwegian Polar Institute's archives, that would light the fire for Ivar Tollefsen to organize an expedition of climbers to find out just how big that peak might be. His motive was to find 'the highest peak in Norway' recognizing that Queen Maud Land was Norwegian territory.

In 1997 Ivar, with just the climbers from the original trip, explored an area further to the east to climb the Ronde Spire. They were accompanied to the Russian science base Novolazarevskaya (a.k.a. Novo, the veritable launch pad for expeditions to Queen Maud Land) by an American 'dream team' including Alex Lowe, Conrad Anker, Gordon Whistler and Jon Krakauer. The ensuing *National Geographic* magazine article describing their ascent of Rakekniven Peak was my first exposure to the possibilities of climbing in Antarctica and the baffling visuals of the peaks of northern Queen Maud Land. Like every mountaineer I was simply blown away by the photos – this was a different planet and certainly somewhere I would never get to, no way. Besides I'd never be a good enough climber with the skills required to operate in such an environment.

Quite how I ended up on the first ascent of one of the planet's outstanding rock features is unclear – perhaps the wild ambition of my mountain film making had paid off, that and a fruitful filming partnership with a world class climber: Leo Houlding. However, just being there on the mile-long north-east ridge of Ulvetanna, a combination of a 600m knife-edge ridge, steep cracks, perfect corners, roofs and overhanging off-widths; would rank as the ultimate 'perk of the job' for any adventure film maker.

The team was dropped off by ski plane 5km from the wall with 1700kg of equipment. *(Alastair Lee)*

We touched down at this wildest of places in a giant Russian Antonov, on a blue ice runway, at 4am on 16 December 2012. Novo was even more desolate than I was prepared for, with no permanent structures or population and no sign of Western development or comfort. We were met by the news that a DC3 aircraft picking up a team from their camp at Holtanna Peak (also in the Fenriskjeften range) had crashed on take off. The plane was a write-off with propellers and undercarriage strewn across the ice but fortunately no one was seriously hurt. With one aircraft down the ALCI scheduling was put under extra strain and our flight into Ulvetanna was

Leo Houlding halfway up the crumbly 'Dinosaurs Spine' (XS 5b), which involved full rope length run-outs between hand-drilled bolt belays. *(Alastair Lee)*

now in doubt – at one point rescheduled by a week.

Luck was on our side, though, and as we flew into the Fenriskjeften range next day, on schedule but in 50/50 conditions, I tried to imagine what it must have been like for the Norwegians in their Russian helicopter approaching Ulvetanna that first time. Robert Casperson, the lead climber on the 1994 expedition, described to me how the mountain just grew bigger and bigger as did their excitement at what such a peak might provide in terms of climbing. Cliffs of 1000m or more are rare jewels on Planet Earth, so rare that you can name most of them on one hand. It seems the world's geological processes have resulted in a plethora of walls between 500 and 800m, there are hundreds of these with umpteen still unexplored and unclimbed but a magic 1000m wall, unbroken by significant ledge systems, is rare indeed. When it became apparent that the north face of Ulvetanna is comparable with El Cap and the east face even bigger, the Norwegians knew they had found a very special mountain, 'the masterpiece of the range' with the unclimbed north-east ridge being 'the' line of the mountain.

We were almost three weeks into our expedition before finally being in a position to start climbing. It had been an arduous time ferrying loads across 5km of white desert from base camp to advance base camp at the foot of the face. Leo had spent the morning 'faffing' with the enormous amount of climbing gear then, like an overburdened ironmonger he stepped towards the massive wall and declared: 'I'm exhausted, I feel terrible and there's ice in my boots, let's do it.' With our champion climber demonstrating his ruthless determination to succeed, it was time to step into the unknown.

There I was hanging on the fixed lines en route to the ridge, totally out of shape, intoxicated by adrenalin and awe. Few things in life can be as terrifying as jumaring on a single line on a huge cliff and I spent a lot of the time convinced that the rope was about to snap and I'd soon be in freefall along with my heavily laden sack of glass and camera bodies. Add to that the sheer physical exhaustion of jumaring twelve consecutive rope-lengths, complex knot-passing manoeuvres and moments of total amazement at your situation. Indeed if Antarctica's jaws were to snap me up, this would be an easy opportunity – I was a sitting duck.

Filming did offer a window of relief from my own personal terror: getting just the right shot often involved being in the most exposed position and then pushing out on your toes that inch or two more to get the frame looking just right. My first action sequence on Ulvetanna was of Stanley on the fourth pitch, a dream splitter crack on the first headwall cutting into the ridge proper. This followed my first session of jumaring in almost eight months and by the time I was in position to film my arms were totally shot. I couldn't unclip a karabiner or unzip my jacket; this is the reality of big wall filming. Hopefully the shots look well executed and considered – the reality is they were bloody desperate occasions, usually a case of get in position, shoot one take and get the hell out of there.

The remoteness of this location is really hard to convey. There's no prospect of rescue and you're a long way from anything edible (bar expedition members). Working-class hero Jason Pickles's surreal quip summed up the situation: 'I've just realized I've never been this far away from a policeman.' This was during lavish New Year's Eve celebrations at our deluxe base camp, all courtesy of meticulous organization by expedition master Leo Houlding. Perhaps the fear of what could go wrong on this most serious of extreme camping holidays had put Leo's preparations into overdrive. Every eventuality had to be thought through and accounted for, from 100mph blizzards to New Year's Eve celebrations. So there we were on the ice, cracking open the champagne wearing party hats and down suits, momentarily in shadow as the midnight sun dipped behind Ulvetanna.

At 12am on the 25th day of the trip I found myself on the 'dinosaur's back', the most exposed section of the north-east ridge, alone. The rest of the team was lower down the wall hauling 300kg of gear to the ledge camp below the final headwall. I looked up at the ridge, the wind blowing a hoolie as the fixed line lay draped down the more exposed northern side. The unusual angle of the ridge and crazy exposure had me a little stumped on how to proceed. I decided to wait on the hanging belay for a bit of moral support from the rest of the crew. That didn't work as hanging around just increased my anxiety so I climbed onto the ridge, shunting my jumars on the sagging line, unsure whether if I weighted it I'd just pendulum down one side of the face. I berated myself yet again for putting myself in such a position – I was not a big wall climber and really had no business to be there. I'm no pioneer; I just don't have the mental construction to deal with it all. I will, however, put myself through what is necessary to get the

Sean 'Stanley' Leary on pitch 5, *California Crack* (5.11d / E4 6a), a splitter hand crack running 60m from ledge to ledge, vertical to slightly overhanging. *(Alastair Lee)*

Sean Leary leading the first pitch (E4 6a / A2) of the 600m headwall from the spacious 'plateau of great expectations' camp. Already 1000m up, this pitch required the only two lead bolts of the route and a few aid moves. *(Alastair Lee)*

shots I need, sticking my neck out yet again for the film I'm making. Not for the first time in my career I pondered whether this would, one day, be the end of me.

The next 40 minutes was one of the most blood-curdling experiences of my life as I climbed the ridge with just jumars on the fixed line as back-up. This was, of course, completely the wrong technique – if I'd just had faith and weighted the rope I'd have found it okay. But shock of the exposure on either side made me instinctively stay close to the rock. Familiarity breeds contempt and a couple of days ferrying loads and shooting Leo re-leading some stunning pitches had me moving with ease. I take my hat off, though, to the lead climbers Leo and Stanley – true adventurers stepping into the unknown with each pitch, 5.12 corners, overhanging cracks, off-widths and chimneys.

We were confident, despite the deepening cold and increasing wind as we gained height, that if we just kept pushing the rope a couple of pitches higher each day without overextending ourselves, we would eventually reach the top.

Leo was sat on the summit block, a classic pointy top, looking relaxed but eager to keep moving. Time was of the essence and it was cold, like really effing cold. For almost a month we'd been treated to blue skies and almost no wind. Then just a few hundred metres below the summit the weather started to turn. But Leo knew the crucial importance of good summit shots, not only for the film's visual narrative and historical perspective but also to appease the sponsors who had written the cheques to get us here.

Alastair Lee, extreme adventure cameraman. *(Leo Houlding)*

This is how I came to be the twelfth person to stand on the summit of Ulvetanna and the second behind Leo to complete the north-east ridge. Seems my film making has made me an accidental big wall alpinist.

The film depicts a perfect summit scene in less than perfect weather – a delirious team high-fiving and hugging in well composed technically sound shots. But at a cost: in the process of capturing stills and footage from two or three positions in close to minus 30° my right hand had lost all feeling. A mild panic came over me. I removed my glove and shoved my hand between Chris's legs groaning in pain as he massaged my digits back to life. Leo and Jason were discussing how this poor weather rated amongst their library of poor weather experiences, all the while Stanley cursing his way through another lighter as he failed to light up. This was the more realistic summit scene but one that might confuse the audience and certainly put broadcasters off, but more to the point the one that was impossible to capture.

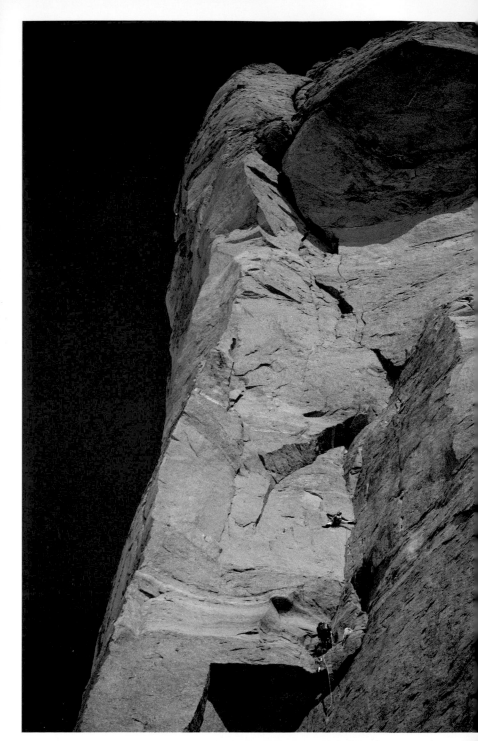

Leo Houlding leading pitch 3 of the headwall (E5 6b, A1) with Jason Pickles belaying – one of several pitches subsequently re-climbed for stills and video photography. *(Alastair Lee)*

Thanks to Leo's superb leadership and guidance and after eight days on the wall and 17 climbing days in total we were all back on the glacier, exhausted, elated, accomplished and just glad to be alive. There was still a mammoth amount of work to do but at least no more hanging on 10mm lines. We had survived the double suffer fest of big wall climbing and polar exploration and succeeded in a stunning first ascent. I also had that warm feeling inside that once again we had succeeded in capturing some unique alpine footage.

Flying out over this surreal mountain range in piercing light we could see it was one hell of an impressive line. There will always be a 'last great problem' and maybe there are still some otherworldly mountains to be discovered on some overlooked map. I wrote in my diary as I waited on the ice to be airlifted out:

'. . . somewhere out there, in somebody's mind is the last great climb.'

Leo Houlding – It was just after I left school that I first laid eyes on Ivar Tollefsen's inspirational book describing the first climbing expedition to the mythical Fenriskjeften mountains. My soul was instantly captivated by the other-wordly landscape, the mile-high granite spires penetrating an endless white desert in that most romantic last great wilderness – Antarctica. I was particularly struck by the immaculate perfection of Ulvetanna, the fang of the Fenris wolf, a beast of Norse legend so fierce it almost destroyed the world, that dominates the most remarkable mountain range on earth. From then on I'd dreamed of amassing the skill, strength and support necessary to get me there.

Back then, of course, I'd never climbed a big wall, had no expedition experience and was only just beginning to flirt with sponsorship. As ambitious as I was naïve, 'One day,' I thought, 'I'm going to climb that.' On 19 January 2013 that dream became reality, as Sean 'Stanley' Leary, Jason 'Manly' Pickles, Chris Rabone, Alastair Lee and I stood atop that lonely spire so very far from home.

Ulvetanna is simply magnificent – like Cerro Torre only 3000 miles from the nearest town and, save for the farthest reaches of the ocean, as remote as anywhere on earth.

During the mammoth task of organisation and research for the trip, apart from the obvious issues of extreme cold and hurricane force

A blizzard pins down the team above the Dinosaur's Spine. *(Alastair Lee)*

winds, my key concern was reports of rotten rock, often described as 'kitty litter' granite. That and the fact the trip would cost twice as much as my first house. . .

Antarctic logistics are a vastly complex and costly business, which no doubt explains why our magnificent north-east ridge of Ulvetanna, surely one of the most impressive, compelling and aesthetic lines on Earth, had remained unclimbed. Although around a dozen climbing expeditions had had the good fortune to observe this rock masterpiece at first hand, only once had it been attempted, by the seasoned polar wall climbers Ivar Tollefsen, Robert Casperson and Trond Hilde whose ambitious alpine-style attempt in poor conditions the previous season had been abandoned after just a couple of pitches.

Encountering the feature in the flesh for the first time I could immediately see why. The scale is indescribably immense, the setting extremely intimidating, very much 'the big scary mountain' as it became un-affectionately known.

Our objectives for our time in the Fenriskjeften were threefold: first and foremost, for everyone to return home alive, in one piece and frostbite free. Second to make the first ascent of the mighty north-east ridge and thirdly, of equal importance, to make a film of our expedition encompassing the highest production values ever achieved during such an endeavour. This was no small ambition. The filming would be just as challenging as the climbing, effectively doubling an already monstrous task and requiring the whole team to work together with this specific goal constantly in mind.

We discussed our ascent tactics at length. In our hearts, Stanley, Jase and I were keen to attempt the route in alpine style over a week or so. But in our heads was the overwhelming fear of failing in our primary objective i.e. dying – that, coupled with the epic scale of the route and not being able to shoot a film of the quality we wanted, meant we opted for an all-out siege assault.

After establishing a base camp citadel and advanced base fort we began the arduous task of fixing rope up the initial 300m vertical wall. The architecture of the north-east ridge, whilst making it so striking, presents some major complications to any form of ascent.

The climbing, however, was of fantastic quality, the conditions better than we had dared hope for: clear skies, no wind and temperatures in single negative figures which enabled free-climbing in rock shoes and, incredibly, without gloves. Stanley and I shared all the leading partnered by Chris and Jase respectively. Our teams alternated between pushing the rope higher up the face and re-climbing sections for Al with his camera.

The lower angled initial section of the ridge fell to Stanley and Chris and proved more taxing than anticipated, with unconsolidated snow covering surprisingly sparsely featured rock. The rock quality, though sufficiently crumbly on the surface to create an uncomfortable sense of insecurity was certainly not as bad as we had feared.

The main section of the ridge is a feature unlike anything I have ever

'Just let me know when you've had enough.' Jason Pickles cleaning the second headwall as the weather deteriorates. *(Alastair Lee)*

seen: a 45 degree edge about 400m long, less than a metre wide and with a 500m drop on either side. How such an unusual shape formed or how it remains standing I do not know. What I do know is that leading up it into the abyss, with clouds swirling in the cauldron of the north face, for entire rope-lengths with out any protection, facing certain death should I slip, on terrain that was only just easy enough, with one of my best friends, was a rare privilege indeed.

Arriving at the large ledge at the base of the headwall, already a thousand metres up our line and having just completed a spacewalk of mind numbing exposure, I felt for the first time that we might actually reach the summit.

Next we had to haul some 450kg of equipment, food, fuel and cameras up 500m of vertical wall and 300m of 45 degree, one-metre-wide Dinosaur's Spine to this, the Expectant Plateau. It took four whole days of ball-breaking effort and endless gargantuan faffs to pack, carry, repack, haul, repack again, jumar loads, pull up ropes and finally establish a safe haven stocked for ten days with sufficient supplies, hardware, software and rope to face anything this big scary headwall in this harshest corner of the Earth could throw at us.

The headwall above the Expectant Plateau delivered the goods for which

Sean Leary re-climbs the Immaculate Corner, pitch 2, of the headwall (E4 6a)
for the camera during improved conditions on the descent. *(Alastair Lee)*

we'd travelled so far to sample. Steep corners and splitter cracks enticed us upwards with much but managed strain, without need for hammer nor piton save two bolts on the initial blank slab. True free-climbing gave way to French free as temperatures plunged before declining further to all-out aid as shade and searching wind put paid to any ideas of freeing the beast.

When Stanley slayed the Slot of Despair – a flared off-width through a huge roof halfway up the headwall – our shadowed glimpse of success was made real. Of course next day a storm broke, but without time to wait it out we pushed cautiously up into the gathering clouds.

Jase and I reached 'Snow Petrel Pillar', a great ledge, perched directly on the ridge. The blizzard intensified: in the shade, in the wind, the anemometer read minus 27°C and dropping. I massaged sensation back into Jase's feet, ignoring the trace of fear on his brow; my own urge to run away.

The summit group, jubilant even at minus 35°C. Top left to bottom right: Leo Houlding, Jason Pickles, Chris Rabone, Sean Leary, Alastair Lee. *(Alastair Lee)*

'We really need to bag another pitch, but let's not expire ourselves,' I encouraged.

'Just let me know when you've had enough!' replied Jase, his manly tone wavering as he realized that dropping the gauntlet can lead to frostbite.

'It's like that, is it? Right then pass me the sharp ends.'

Dry humour, controlled denial, essential assets for polar wall-climbing.

The storm raged all night and into the next day. Nobody was keen to leave the relative comfort and safety of camp. But time was desperately tight and in the lulls of the tempest we could hear the faintest whispers of the summit calling. Chris and Stanley gallantly set off up the ropes for their turn at the cold coal face.

Some hours later we all convened on Cold Ledge. The second headwall lay desperately close to the summit but the terrain had become complex and convoluted. On the east face, in the full force of the wind, the anemometer read minus 35°C. Upper lips frozen stiff, chins held high but buried deep in layers of hood and scarf, it was a great relief when Stanley radioed down that the line was fixed and the ground above looked better.

Crowded stances, the crawl of a five man pace, the relentless gale and shade-cold, ice-caked eyelashes and beards testing the sternest determination, a pitch below the top the assault on us unexpectedly ceased. The unmistakable summit was just 50m further on – a pinnacle no larger than a coffee table that was barely big enough for the five of us to stand on together. A outburst of emotion was greeted by a momentary break in the cloud and bath of golden light. Dave could actually see us with the 600mm lens from ABC a mile below. Howling to the moon like the Fenris wolf itself, Al fought desperately frozen fingers to capture that ephemeral moment, before we began the massive descent.

At Snow Petrel Pillar we paused to consider the state of play. Stanley and I were equipped with wing-suits and BASE rigs, ready to fly the entire line of the ridge back to ABC. It would be impossible in the current storm, but we had the option of leaving lines fixed and praying for better weather the next day. Conversely, should the weather deteriorate further we would still have to jumar some 600m up to the exit point to clean the ropes before we could even begin a more conventional and now greatly extended descent. This prospect, combined with the serious complications involved in descending the Dinosaur's spine with our masses of kit, taxing even in fine conditions, close to critical in the current blizzard, convinced us that we could not leave our friends in such a predicament and that our climactic flight would have to wait for another day.

Five days later we all stumbled back into base camp exhausted but safe. We had achieved our three objectives and all trace of our presence in that pristine wilderness would be erased.

Summary: Personal accounts of climbing and filming the first ascent of the north-east ridge of Ulvetanna, (E6 6b, 5.12a, A2, 33 pitches, 1750m), Queen Maud Land, Antarctica, January 2013. Leo Houlding, Sean 'Stanley' Leary, Jason Pickles, Chris Rabone and Alastair Lee (David Reeves ground support). Lee's film, *The Last Great Climb* won the Best Climbing Film category at Banff Mountain Festival and the Judges' Special Prize at the Kendal Mountain Festival.

Sean 'Stanley' Leary 1975 - 2014.

Postscript: A little over a year after our return from Antarctica 'Stanley' was killed proximity flying his wing-suit on a BASE jump in Zion, Utah.

The unsung hero of modern Yosemite climbing, Sean Leary was a true big wall master, highly skilled in hard aid, high speed and long free climbs. With his broad smile and laid-back demeanour he was the finest and fittest partner you could hope for and one of my best friends. *Leo Houlding*

CALUM MUSKETT

Wall of Paine

In Patagonia. Twid Turner battles the elements on the approach to advance base camp in the Bader Valley. *(All photos: Calum Muskett)*

Like many Welsh students, I first learnt about Patagonia at secondary school. The history of the Welsh migration to the area was interesting but it wasn't until I read Paul Pritchard's seminal first autobiography *Deep Play*, with its photos of hulking granite monoliths and tales of epic ascents and ferocious storms, that the area really caught my interest. Patagonia sounded truly wild and of all its mountains the ominously named Towers of Paine seemed to me some of the most aesthetically pleasing and inspiring summits I had ever seen.

In late spring 2013 I received an email from Jerry Gore inquiring as to whether I'd be interested in joining him on an expedition to climb the south face of the South Tower of Paine – the biggest unclimbed wall in Patagonia. Given Jerry's enthusiastic sales pitch on top of my own desire to visit the area I readily committed to the expedition without pausing to check my diary: it's not every day you get the opportunity to visit one of

Sunrise on the Cuernos del Paine, the west wall of the Bader Valley.

the world's foremost mountaineering destinations with a team intent on such an awe-inspiring objective. Flights were booked the following day and many evenings were spent ruminating over the forthcoming trip whilst gazing at pictures of the unclimbed face.

On a midsummer day out in the Alps I was enthusing about our perfect, sunny, south facing wall on Paine to British climbing star Hazel Findlay, when she pointed out that Patagonia was in the southern hemisphere. My response was something like, 'Yeah obviously' but then she further pointed out that a south face in the southern hemisphere would be akin to a north face in the Alps. Thoughts of sun cream and shorts were suddenly replaced with down jackets and goggles; we'd be in Patagonia during its early spring – a time of year not renowned for warm weather. . .

Following this extraordinary revelation I travelled to Grindelwald and spent a week on the north face of the Eiger experiencing cold bivvies and

Bader Valley peaks: 1. Cuernos Oest,
2. Cuernos Norte, 3. Mascara, 4. Thumb,
5. Blade, 6. Sword, 7. Paine Grande.

Right: Advance base camp.

Above: the 900m south face of the South Tower of Paine, and right: showing
the route. The central and left hand sections are yet to be attempted.

difficult rock climbing; surely perfect preparation for a Patagonian south
face? On my return home from the Alps I maintained my fitness for the
forthcoming trip by spending evenings at the climbing wall and going for
night time runs. Despite a busy work schedule I was feeling fit and couldn't
wait for the opportunity to be climbing on the pristine granite walls of
Patagonia.

By mid-September our team was finally sorted. I would be heading out with Mike 'Twid' Turner, a mountain guide with perhaps the greatest track record of first ascents of big walls of any climber in Britain, Jerry Gore, an ever enthusiastic ex-Marine, climber and Type One diabetic, and Raphael

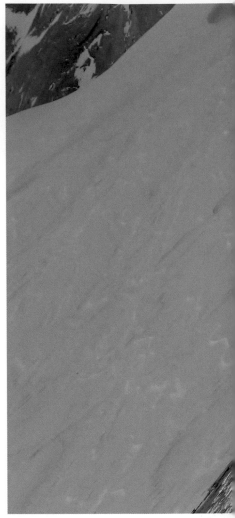

Twid Turner on the apron slabs.
(Calum Muskett)

Jochaud, a lively and witty French cameraman who would be filming the expedition.

The wall we had our sights set on had been attempted once before by Twid and Stu McAleese in 2006. After many days on the wall, inching their way up through the complex and dangerous loose rock of the central section, they began to think that they'd broken through the most difficult ground when they were hit by a savage storm. On the descent, the updraft was so strong on the steepest part of the wall, they had to pull themselves down the fixed lines! The ropes ran out at the ridge leaving them stranded 250m above the glacier. After enduring several days of storm the pair were nearly hypothermic and starving when the weather abated just enough to allow them to recover a rope and complete the descent. For Twid, this wall was clearly unfinished business, but this time he was better prepared and ready to face the Patagonian weather once more.

After several flights we arrived at the small Chilean airport of Punta Arenas – but we were one Frenchman short. Having received a message from Raphael that he would be a couple of days late we decided to make our way to Torres del Paine and wait for him at base camp. In Puerto Natales, three hours' drive from Paine, we did a huge food shop to cater for the three and a half weeks' camping in the remote Bader Valley. Unfortunately the supermarket offered only meagre supplies so for breakfast we'd be eating porridge and all evening meals would consist of either noodles or Smash. To supplement this varied diet we had cereal bars to feed a small army and enough chocolates to stop Jerry going hypo for a whole year!

The bus journey into the park crosses plains and lowland hills on a dirt

track until you finally round a hillside and the majestic Paine massif swings into view: granite spires and snowy summits above large lakes. Guanacos graze the side of the road, condors glide overhead and the lakes support a colony of flamingos. Despite ever increasing visitor numbers, the park has maintained its wilderness feel, due to careful management by the national park service that limits development of the area rather than pushing a clearly profitable tourist trade.

From the roadhead we faced a pleasant trek into the Bader Valley along the spectacular 'W' trail, which attracts thousands of trekkers every year. It was nightfall and the ground was covered with a thin layer of freshly fallen snow when we finally reached our base camp in a small wood beside a river. The infamous Patagonian wind had already picked up and we hastily

Raphael Jochaud jumaring; the apron slabs below and right.

settled down to a cold and noisy night in the tents.

Next morning I was confronted by a valley like nothing I had ever seen. Granite towers and rock walls lined the left side whilst on the right were a series of huge moraine slopes capped by a massive red-tinged wall. At the head of the valley, gradually coming into sight as we stumbled upwards under the weight of our heavy sacks, was the biggest wall of them all – the south face of the South Tower of Paine.

We set up camp just an hour's walk from the base of the cliff and got to work preparing the area. This proved more problematical than we had anticipated due to a fierce wind that left us cowering behind boulders during the stronger gusts. After banking up walls of snow against an over-hung boulder we thought we'd created a fairly sheltered spot to pitch a tent. I started erecting the tent from the inside but before Twid and Jerry could tie it down, an almighty gust lifted the tent with me inside, blowing it over into the boulder field. Bruised and disorientated I hung on for dear life – to the tent with one hand and a boulder with the other, until the wind abated enough for us to flip the tent back into its alcove with me still inside! We hastily weighed the tent down with bags of rocks and were soon inside the meek and now highly ventilated fabric shelter trying to light the stove.

By this point Raphael had made it into camp and after another day of ferrying gear in exceptionally strong winds we decided to walk up to the base of the wall for a closer inspection. From a distance the cliff looks featureless, unusually blank for something this size – it's only when you get up close you begin to notice small corner lines and cracks weaving their way upwards. As we gazed up at the wall Raphael asked: 'Where do the other routes go?' He hadn't quite grasped that there could be an unclimbed wall as big as this left in Patagonia.

After weighing up the alternatives we decided to attempt a line up the right-hand side of the face and Twid and I returned the following day to begin the route.

The apron of slabs at the foot of the wall are surprisingly tricky given their amenable angle. There are few cracks or features of any kind to take protection and snow collects on any ledges, be they fingertip edges or wide enough to sit down on and the granite is bald enough to require tight fitting rock shoes. Given the sub-zero temperatures this was pretty inconvenient, if not uncomfortable, to say the least. So I pulled on my cold rock shoes and headed upwards, brushing snow off little ledges as I went. Although the climbing was relatively easy, care had to be taken placing your feet to avoid verglas and cold fingers felt unreliable on the smaller edges. I reached the first belay just as the sun briefly hit the crag and I was able to enjoy a little bit of warmth as I removed my tight rock shoes – shooting pains of pins and needles a brief torture as the blood rushed back to my toes. Twid jumared up behind me and we were soon making good progress up to the ridge.

Reaching the ridge opened up an impressive new vista for us over to the Central Tower of Paine and the large glacier and lake beneath it. The ridgeline was, however, very exposed to the wind and after another couple of pitches we retreated to ABC to ravenously consume a packet of noodles and a tortilla. . .

Over the following few days, bad weather kept us stuck in our tent. My holiday read was *Moby Dick* and it seemed somewhat ironic to be reading about ships being caught in huge storms off the coast of Patagonia. The wind was relentless and the noise of flapping fabric so loud you could barely sleep. In fact the wind beat on the tent so hard we thought it was in danger of being ripped apart. Toilet breaks were quite problematic. I recall leaving the tent bleary-eyed one morning and being hit by such a strong gust of wind whilst taking a leak that I was pinned against a boulder for twenty seconds. . . messy!

The problem with the wind is that when it finally does die down and you're left with some semblance of peace and tranquillity, all you feel like doing is sleeping and

The weather closes in – again.

Twid Turner aid climbing a loose A3+ pitch low down on the face. This pitch would later go free, with a couple of rests due to numb hands, at F7b+.

recovering. In Patagonia, though, any bit of good weather needs to be quickly seized upon as time spent relaxing is time wasted. Conditions were significantly colder when we headed back up, a southerly wind whipping the wall. Whoever was belaying would soon be freezing cold despite layers of down and synthetic jackets. After some moderately difficult pitches we reached a narrow groove line, steep and loose. Twid went for the lead, aid climbing on insecure short pegs in expanding flakes. After a nerve racking five hours and a short fall Twid was much of the way up the pitch but short of gear and freezing cold he decided to return to the belay and leave the pitch for the next day.

We were keen to free climb as much of the route as possible although given the dreadful, cold weather this was often impossible, but I did manage to free climb to Twid's high point, albeit with a couple of rests due to cold, unfeeling hands. From there I could see that another ten metres would put me on easier ground, but with poor gear and clearly difficult climbing, I was trepidatious about setting off. I warmed my fingertips, went for it and, moving as quickly as possible between the small edges, reached bigger holds just as my fingers were uncurling from the cold. At the top of the pitch I suffered a severe bout of hot-aches but was content with the effort I'd put in; free climbing this trip might be impossible at times but I felt we couldn't have tried much harder given the conditions.

Progress over the following week was slow. Jerry, Raphael, Twid and I all put in plenty of effort but the weather limited the amount of time we were able to stay on the wall. On one particularly miserable day we were caught in a blizzard which briefly lifted the air temperature above freezing, melting the snow all over the face before it re-froze, covering the rock in a treacherous layer of verglas.

Twid Turner in typical Patagonian conditions, high on the route.

After days of bad weather Raphael and I were finally treated to blue skies and almost no wind for the first time of the trip. A tiring 500m jumar gained our high point but once there we got straight to work. The quality of the rock had finally improved and the climbing was really enjoyable. I free climbed as much as possible, pulling on gear occasionally when my fingers became too cold or the climbing looked particularly difficult. After several more pitches we had overcome a black band of rock high up on the face and for the first time felt that success was near, with perhaps three more pitches before we could scramble to the summit.

The weather had other plans. Four days of ferocious storms dumped snow on the wall and the wind was stronger than ever. After an enforced rest Twid and I were chomping at the bit and we headed out the moment the wind dropped. I was first up the ropes but after 500m realised I'd made a mistake several days before. I'd failed to tighten the fixed lines on my descent and the wind had whipped one horizontally from the belay over a flake and now it hung straight down to the belay I was on. After ten minutes of flicking and pulling I realised the rope wasn't going to budge. All our gear was at the top of these ropes so after shock testing it I decided to jumar the stuck line and attempt to release it whilst Twid belayed me with another rope. Nerve racking fails to describe the few minutes I spent jumaring this rope but eventually it was freed and I vowed never to make such a blunder again.

I led on from the top of the fixed ropes into the teeth of a blizzard. Snow streamed down the rock, filling my eyes and the neck of my jacket but having started the pitch I felt compelled to finish it and gain at least some height after all the effort to get to our high point. I was rewarded with the first good ledge for 500m and at last a view of the top of the wall. A swift retreat followed as the weather rapidly worsened but we felt optimistic about our chances of success with the summit so close.

With three days remaining before our flights home we were rapidly running out of time. Storms were still preventing us from getting on the face but on our final day we headed up despite the weather. At the top of the ropes Twid took over the lead and reached a wide and easy-angled corner; the final pitch of the wall before a scramble to the summit. But now the winds had picked up again, blowing spindrift across the face and by the time I had joined Twid the only sensible decision was to descend – if the wind grew stronger it would become nearly impossible to abseil. It was a good call – the wind increased the further we descended and as we neared the ridge we were being blown sideways. The final abseil to the glacier was in a complete white-out and descending to ABC was both hard work and demoralising after putting in so much effort over the previous month.

We were close but we hadn't reached the summit of the South Tower of Paine. Months of preparation and effort were poured into the fulfilment of this dream and defeat, so near the summit, was a bitter pill to swallow. At the same time, the decision to descend was an easy one: no summit is worth risking your life for and the objective dangers were totally out of our hands. Climbing isn't just about making it to the summit but more about the experiences you have whilst trying to get there and returning safely is an imperative of a successful expedition.

Overall we'd spent eighteen days at ABC with only two days of good weather. Temperatures were consistently sub-zero and our diet of smash and noodles left us constantly hungry throughout the expedition. Despite these drawbacks we'd climbed 900 metres up one of the biggest unclimbed walls in South America. The climbing was amongst the best of its kind in the world, the area truly stunning and I won't hesitate to return to Torres del Paine if the opportunity presents itself again.

Summary: *Wall of Paine* (A3+ & F7b+, 900m to high point – estimated to go free at approx F7c+ or E7 in suitable conditions), south-east face of the South Tower of Paine, Torres del Paine National Park, Patagonia. First ascent to end of hard climbing: Jerry Gore, Raphael Jochaud, Calum Muskett and Mike 'Twid' Turner. October/November 2013.

DICK TURNBULL

Ice Cold in Canada

Fabulous, 'big league' ice-lines on Mount Howse, seen from the Parkway.

The onset of age and the increasing desire to avoid pain, struggle, major discomfort and unknown unknowns had prompted my abandonment of 'proper' winter climbing – alpine grande courses etc, etc – for more modest 'ice cragging,' the winter equivalent of giving up trad (proper?) rock climbing for the more hedonistic but enjoyable and safer antics on bolt encrusted crags! Where to this winter? Canada, home of modern icefall climbing and long hoped for destination, won the day.

We – a breakaway team of AC worthies jumping ship from the annual AC Ice Meet included Pete Holden, Bill Church, 'young' Nick Donahue and myself flew in to Calgary in late January (apparently this is known as the 'dark' season!) to hear that the weather had been unseasonally mild for the last two weeks. Luckily the forecast was for colder but dryer and more settled weather.

Nick Donahue attempting the final pitch, (WI5), of *Polar Circus*.
(All photos: Dick Turnbull)

An hour out of Calgary in our large 4-wheel drive SUV hire-monster,[1] we pulled up outside the Alpine Club of Canada's HQ in Canmore. Now this is what I call a Clubhouse – one that any self-respecting Alpine Club could (should?) aspire too! A beautiful wooden building, warm, comfortable, with reasonably cheap self-catering accommodation and open to all comers. Being well placed and reasonably priced it was full of climbers who were happy to bring us up to speed on conditions and what routes were in nick. We were raring to go.

As usual fear made us opt for easy days to get us in the swing (geddit?) of things. After a bad day in Johnson Canyon where Bill's trip abruptly ended with a ruptured Achilles Tendon and a better half-day at a local ice kindergarten known as the Junk Yard we were ready for something more meaty.

We chose *Moonlight* (100m WI4) – top of the Grade 4 list (hubris?) – a three-pitch route that has a 3.5km approach along a frozen river through the ubiquitous all-covering Canadian pine forest. After an hour's meandering up the creek we rounded a bend to see a thick column of blue ice cascading down a 100m rock wall. We were there and we had it to ourselves.[2] The route turned out to be a bit harder than we expected. These Canadian grades were at least half a grade up on European ones! Being a three we climbed it 'arrowhead'[3] which is pretty efficient for three in ascent but, naturally, abbing is significantly slower.

The next day we took advantage of the stable snow conditions and climbed the elegant and very public, but usually avalanche threatened, *Cascade* (300m WI3). Then we moved on to a Banff hostel and set about. *Professor Falls* (210m WI4), one of the must-do climbs of the area. Everything went well as we romped up a succession of lovely WI3-4 cascade pitches culminating in a spectacular final pitch elegantly led by Nick. *Professor Falls* was good for our morale as it is, in essence, a mini, more do-able version of our ultimate objective, *Polar Circus*.

After that we rested, but not for long, and a day later Nick and I ventured out to try our luck on *Kidd Falls* (55m WI4). This was a short-ish route, somewhat compromised by the two-hour uphill thrash to get there, of great quality on a high, rock-flanked ribbon of ice in a wild setting. No queues here. Our apprenticeship was over and it was time to bite the bullet, seize the day, face the facts, or whatever, and get to grips with 'proper' routes!

Our kick-off point was the Rampart Creek hostel 150km north up the Jasper-Banff Parkway. Rampart Creek is a lovely but remote hostel stuck in the snow surrounded by massive crags and peaks and well positioned to access some of Canada's most iconic ice routes. Life there is hardy with freezing outdoor pit-loos, designated male-only peeing sites, no water for body washing and the nearest facilities 125km away! It was run by a really enthusiastic and helpful warden, Ken Wood. By now it was getting seriously cold. Minus 30°C was the everyday temperature although with no wind it was just bearable. However, such extreme cold imparts a palpable frisson of danger – make one mistake and things could go badly wrong very

Nick Donahue on first pitch (WI3+) of *Moonlight*.

quickly.

Our final test of competence would be *Weeping Wall RH* (160m WI5). The famous Weeping Wall is a massive sheet of ice draped over a vertical 160m band of limestone. Its southerly aspect provides a deceptively sunny, friendly appearance but it was steep and, for us, cold! Three pitches of beautiful flowing ever-steepening ice towered above us. Nick led the elegant 2nd pitch while Pete and I got decidedly chilly, despite being in the sunshine which just reinforced how cold it was becoming. I was half-way up the final pitch when I realised that I had broken a front point on my new-ish Lynx crampons![4] After a brief moment of panic all I could think of was how in the hell I was going to fix them before going on *Polar Circus* the next day. The descent brought it home to us just how steep the *Weeping Wall* was as we swung down the bolted descent line in three 55m abseils, half the time floating free! A brilliant route and we had done a WI5! Now we were ready for the big one.

With *Weeping Wall* in the bag we had passed our final test for *Polar Circus* (800m WI5). All I needed was another pair of crampons or new front points. The nearest decent climbing shop was a 350km round trip away in Canmore so it was in desperation that I asked Ken at the hostel if he had any suitable crampons I could borrow. His instant and generous reply was 'Sure, I've got some BD rigids that will fit your boot size.' Ten minutes later I was re-equipped and ready to go.

Polar Circus had become, overnight, the 'must-do' route of the area after the Burgess Twins, Bugs McKeith and Charlie Porter had fought their way up the line over four days in 1975. Remember this was long before modern axes and screws; in fact only just into the advent of curved gear! The name came from Charlie's comment somewhere on the route that the mess of ropes was 'more like a Polish Circus than anything else!'

Next morning we were up at 5am, and drawing on our experience of the day before, dressed in ALL our warm clothing. Then, out of the hut at 5.30 and walking by 6am. The car thermometer read minus 32°C! The air was still and the snow beneath our feet squeaked so loud we couldn't hear each other unless we stopped. Despite the tracks it took us an hour to stomp up the deep-ish snow to the base of the route where Nick stepped up to set off up the first (WI4) vertical pitch. This was a relief to Pete and I (older and wiser?) who hung back unashamedly! It was a good lead on steep organ-pipe/chandeliered ice in the dark and bitter cold of a February morning. After that Nick and I swung leads up the next two pitches (WI3/4) pitches until we were beneath a hanging ice-boss that occasionally grows into a dramatic pillar called *The Pencil*. Luckily for us it hadn't formed this year – of course, we were really disappointed not to have a vertical WI6 pillar to relish (!) so we followed the big rightward diagonal traverse line until an exposed snow slope led us back left into the vertical heart of the route.

Nick took the lead on the 80m WI4 pitch above, via a great tongue of ice cascading from a narrowing high above. We were in impressive scenery now following the only weakness up a succession of vertical waterfalls and surrounded by huge vertical walls of rock. Nick belayed on screws and our first Abalakov whilst we came up arrowhead and I led straight on through to the bolts beneath the final three pitches. I led the next winding pitch (WI4) too, up

Nick Donahue on second pitch (WI4) of *Kidd Falls*.

deceptively steep ice to a small bowl tucked beneath the final 100m vertical cascade pouring out from the huge snow bowl above. I continued; 'up and at it' being my credo as the 50m pitch (WI5) seemed endlessly steep. It was getting on in the day by now and although the sun was on us we felt no warmth. Nick had checked his fingers earlier and was shocked to see the tips white and lifeless. We momentarily panicked, thinking the worst, and I gave him my final spare set of 'heat pads'[5] which seemed to save the day – and his fingers!

Once we were all assembled at the perfect cave stance below the final vertical pitch Nick set off up the alternately cruddy then concrete ice,

Nick Donahue and Pete Holden on
1st pitch (WI4) of *Weeping Wall*

complete with dripping water –
how does that happen at minus
30°C? He was finding it desperate
to place screws and get decent
axe placements, faltering after
six metres as discretion overcame
valour. I was volunteered and
swung up to his high point, grateful
for his hard-won screws, put my
head down and battered my way to
the top. Once past the initial, dripping section and a bad moment
when both my feet popped off, the
ice improved somewhat and after
40m the angle eased and I was up.

Elation! We had done it. The
great snow bowl looming above
me amply illustrated why the
route is considered so potentially
dangerous. Today it was solid and
benign. All I had to do now was
stride across the icy platform and
clip the final bolts and bring them
both up.

As I stepped across right the ice
broke under me and a geyser of
freezing water spouted thigh-high
up my leg and cascaded down
the ice in a great wave. I stood
appalled. It flowed over the top of
the pitch but more crucially all over the ropes! We had been told that some
parties had had trouble with jammed ropes from the top belay and now
I could see why. The cold was palpable so I immediately shouted to the
others not to come up as we had to get down NOW before everything froze
completely solid. I clipped the ropes in and started down. It's lucky that I
weigh a lot! The ropes had become rigid tubes of ice and I had to hammer
them through my belay brake to make downward progress. Eventually I
reached the others and we instantly set about pulling the ropes down.

Nothing. No movement. Desperation burst through as the prospect of
a forced bivi at less than minus 30°C was something we couldn't even
contemplate. I jumped and pulled, using my weight again. Nick literally
said 'pull the other one!' and we set up a see-saw motion which magically
seemed to loosen the ropes and gave us hope. Then it was free – after a
fashion – and down it came – reluctantly. Never was there a more relieved
team than us three on that belay. Laughter broke out, albeit briefly, as time
was flying and we had 750m to go. (There were two Abalakov belay threads

right at the back of the cave – was this a sign of some poor unfortunates having to spend a night shivering in the tiny cave in similar circumstances?)

By 6pm we were at the foot of the climb. Climbing as a three is fairly efficient in ascent but time consuming when abbing, even from good stances and bolts and our previously placed Abalakov. Luckily it all went smoothly – the last ab is always a breeze as you really don't care about the ropes jamming – you know you're down! Then, after an hour of tripping and floundering down in the cold and dark, we flopped into the car at 7pm after a 14-hour round trip. Not bad for a rope of three, especially as of one of us was 70! We'd done it – a great classic route with the crux right at the top and the descent. . . phew!

Back at Rampart Creek we were greeted with enthusiastic congratulations – 'awesome, dudes!' This was more likely relief as, despite 'young' Nick, they had obviously been concerned at our combined age! In fact whilst we were relaxing and bullshitting to some friendly guys up to do the route the next day, we received a visit from Ken's partner who talked us

Above: Dick Turnbull starting pitch 6 (WI4) of *Polar Circus*. *Below:* Pete Holden's mouth fortuitously sealed by icicles at minus 32°C on *Polar Circus*!

through the climb perhaps to see if we had been genuinely in control or just lucky! She pointedly told us that locals mostly don't bother to go out when it's below minus 25°C. We took the point, agreeing we'd had our wrists, very politely, slapped!

We had earned a day off. Our drive south down the Parkway the next day to the Lake Louise hostel started with our car thermometer registering minus 38°C! (Thank God we had been able to pull those ropes!) The 150km drive is another 'must-do' trip in winter. I had done it in summer when the pine-fringed mountains, without a covering of snow, boringly resemble giant rubble heaps. In winter they become magnificent and the drive is a fabulous journey through an archetypal mountain landscape with tantalising ice lines on every peak.

Pete decided to rest on his laurels after his efforts on *Polar Circus*. His right thumb was slightly frost-nipped and he maintained that being 70 was a good enough excuse for anyone. Nick and I decided that we had one more route in us despite being a bit jaded after two weeks of steep ice. Our first aim was to do *Carlsberg Column* (WI5) but as I was lumbered with my broken crampon again we opted for the easier *Guinness Gully* (160m WI4) just outside the small village of Field.

After doing what the guide-book[6] said you couldn't do – get lost in Field – we set off up the approach trench to the route with more of a sense of duty than desire. The cold had the last word as Nick broke the pick of his Grivel axe on the final steep move! The route was good but we (and our gear!) had had enough[7].

Home beckoned but we still had one outstanding 'must-do' – a trip to the Banff Hot Springs baths to swim in the hot spring-water outdoor pool! It was great – lying in (plus) 40°C water with your hair freezing white on your head in minus 20°C air is a bizarre experience, especially as you gaze up at snow-clad peaks surrounding the pool. Now we could relax and enjoy the mountains without having to go back into them again – well, not until next year anyway!

Polar Circus from the Parkway road.

Summary: A personal account by Dick Turnbull of an ice-climbing trip to the Canmore area of the Canadian Rockies with AC members Bill Church, Nick Donahue and Pete Holden, 24 Jan – 8 Feb 2014.

Notes

1. 4-wheel drive car – essential to ensure getting into many areas (particularly the *Ghost* area) – make sure your car has snow tyres/chains and a 'cold-start' cable for helping starting in temps below minus 20°C.

2. It is customary for climbers to write the names of the route they are walking in to do on the dirt on the rear window of their car so that you don't walk in for miles only be second on an ice route – and we all know what that means!

3. Arrowhead: when two seconds climb simultaneously, one on each of the leader's double ropes (easier on ice as you don't have to climb on the same line), the main learning curve seems to be not to smack your tools into the heels of your mates when they are just above you! (Pete managed this but decided to plant his nice new BD Viper straight through my rope instead!) Arrowhead is probably the quickest way for a team of three to climb and is made much easier if the leader has a self-locking Reverso-style belay plate and the belays are bolted! Swapping leaders does mean that you have to untie and retie the ropes on stances – so decent stances/belays help a lot!

Weeping Wall from the Parkway. *RH Route* takes the ramp,corner and wall on the right.

4. Luckily I was using twin front points or I would have been in big trouble. I use twin points on steep ice as my experience of using mono-points on chandeliered ice is that you can't always get your mono- point to reach into the back of the grooves formed by the vertical corrugations in the ice. For mixed ground mono-points rule! (NB Petzl has since upgraded the front points of the early Lynx crampons as they have experienced a small incidence of breakage.)

5. Heat pads or hand warmers (Hothands) are potential finger-savers in extreme conditions. I climbed most of *Polar Circus* with one in each glove and I still got cold fingers especially when seconding. One of the team who climbed the route next day got bad frostbite in his thumb – he didn't have any heat pads! They last for as long as 10 hours but take at least two packs in case you are caught out. You can get 'Hotfeet' but I am told that they do not work as well as there is less oxygen available in your boot!

6. The new selected climbs guidebook to the area *Icelines* £16.95 – now imported to the UK by Cordee – is a welcome arrival as the old guide is long out of print and reputedly fetches $250 on the internet!

7. Extreme cold is fairly simple to deal with as most of what you do is common sense.

- Wear more but beware of 'membrane' gear (Gore-tex etc) as keeping dry is essential and you don't need waterproof covering when it is -20°C. Membrane garments, whilst breathable, will impede moisture movement more than un-membraned clothing.
- Make sure your boots are up to it as reheating feet is difficult.
- Eat and drink regularly. Keep some water/isotonic drink in a robust bottle inside your clothing to ensure it doesn't freeze.
- Carry plenty of 'Hot pads' to keep your hands warm. (plus spare gloves, Buffs etc)
- DON'T PUT METAL IN YOUR MOUTH or if you do find you have done it without thinking, bite it in your teeth and don't let your lips touch any metal.
- Try and choose routes where you can keep moving reasonably quickly as long technical slow pitches will badly chill your second!
- Be careful with placing the picks of your axes as v cold ice is rock hard and more likely to damage and cold stress over-driven picks.
- Above all be aware that epics/accidents in extreme cold conditions will be more difficult to control/survive!

JIM GREGSON

The Really Northern Playground

North Liverpool Land, East Greenland

Looking north from Varmtind. *(Jim Gregson)*

During the twenty-plus years of my own expedition visits to Greenland, narrated in my book *Exploring Greenland* (Vertebrate Publishing 2012), I have seen, climbed, trekked and skied in some amazingly spectacular landscapes. There have always been far more mountains than there has been time to attempt or climb. Even now, East Greenland is still one of the largest reservoirs of unclimbed, unvisited terrain anywhere on Earth and for the determined adventurous alpinist it holds many treasures waiting to be enjoyed.

Some of these treasures lie in areas that are not the remotest to reach but being largely unvisited they are not well documented. Liverpool Land, in the Scoresby Sund region is a case in point. The maps of the area, for all of their imprecision, show any number of names in English, Danish and Greenlandic, but not many are on individual mountains. The area was 'discovered' by whaling ship captain William Scoresby who in the early

Tony Hoare arrives at the rough location of base camp. *(Alexandre Buisse)*

19th Century mapped the coast and bestowed names on many islands, capes and headlands, plus the gigantic fjord system that bears his father's name. Originally called the Liverpool Coast by Scoresby in 1822 – some of the place names commemorate Scoresby's Merseyside friends – it was changed to Liverpool Land by Nordenskjold in 1907, and extends from N 70° 27' to N 71° 31', a mountainous area bounded to the west by Hurry Inlet, Klitdal and Carlsberg Fjord.

There is evidence of ancient Inuit occupation in the area, but the village of Scoresbysund (Ittoqqortoormiit) was only founded in 1925 and settled by a group of about 70 Greenlanders who moved from the Ammassalik area. Nowadays there are about 500 permanent residents, many of whom are still traditional hunters who take seal, walrus, narwhals, musk ox, arctic fox and polar bears (annual quota for polar bears is 30 specimens, but may not be females with cubs). Access to the area can be by sea for a limited summer period, but more usually is by air, flying into the airport at Constable Pynt / Nerlerit Inaat, built in 1985 on a low peninsula / delta on the west side of Hurry Inlet to serve gas and oil exploration centred on Jameson Land.

The mountains of Liverpool Land, although modest in height, have a very alpine character, rising directly from the sea in narrow fjords or projecting above many glaciers. The southern reaches have had large numbers of visitors and many ascents have been made. Numerous ski-touring and trekking groups have also been active here. Records are however somewhat incomplete and details of ascents are sketchy. The absence of a cairn on the summits is a very unreliable guide as to a peak's status. Few mountains carry official names, but there are many striking and spectacular peaks.

The rock quality is variable – the best is good, the worst demands care. Summertime melt-out is considerable, especially in recent years as climate change has accelerated. There are several hunters' cabins in the area and a number of warm springs. The most northerly part of Liverpool Land has had far fewer visits. A few parties, intent on a north to south ski traverse, have started from or near to Kap Greville. Climbing groups, to the best of my knowledge, have only numbered three – two of them my own.

My eye was drawn to the map of North Liverpool Land where a small icecap feeds a system of glaciers radiating west, east and north. On the west side, above Carlsberg Fjord, the mountains are relatively gentle but in the rest of the area there are chains of superb alpine peaks whose flanks fall steeply onto glaciers or directly into the sea. For many months of the year the fjords and inlets are frozen over and snow cloaks the mountains. Once the winter darkness abates the sun begins to work on the snow cover and conditions change rapidly.

My first chance to see North Liverpool Land came at Easter 2007 when I led a ski-touring group for Tangent Expeditions. When we landed at Constable Pynt the thermometer read minus 20°C and we wrapped up carefully to go by skidoo through Klitdal and over Carlsberg Fjord to get up onto the icecap. From a camp towards the west side my group spent two weeks in ski exploration, making a number of non-technical mountain ascents. Two things registered with me – firstly the extended period of sunshine hours even in April, and secondly that this area held a great trove of fantastic mountains. I'd have to return.

In 2011, despite my attempts to stay below radar, I was contacted for information by two Australian women alpinists. They were planning their own visit to North Liverpool Land which they duly carried out in early 2012. Gemma Woldendorp and Natasha Sebire arrived in Constable Pynt, rented some kit from Tangent Expeditions then went north by dog-sled before setting up camp on the icecap further east where they explored on ski and climbed several good peaks, including Mount Mighty and Longridge Peak. They even made parapente descents from some of their summits.

Tony Hoare helping to dig out the tents on day 4 of the storm. *(Alexandre Buisse)*

Gemma and Natasha made a must-see short film of their adventures, *Resounding Silence*, before rounding off the 5-6 week trip by skiing all the way back to Constable Pynt. Watching their film renewed my own interest in returning to North Liverpool Land.

I had a nucleus for a group: myself, my wife Sandy and old pal Geoff

Mount Mighty Group, North Liverpool Land, East Greenland. **A.** Mount Mighty (FA Australians 2012, parapente descent), **B.** Kuldefjeld, FA via *Charlotte Road* (Gregson, Gregson, Bonney 2014), **B*** descent,

Bonney were all Greenland regulars spanning many years. However, when a further keen friend had to drop out, the economics didn't work. ALPINET to the rescue – surely there would be other AC members who could be recruited? Soon enough I was receiving lots of inquiries, particularly about costs and dates. Eventually, to my relief, signatures on the dotted line came from the above three plus Yorkshiremen Michael Smith and Peter Chadwick, Alexandre Buisse from France and Tony Hoare from Canada.

Of the seven, five are AC members – this helped to access grant aid from the AC Climbing Fund and First Ascent which was very helpful, as one thing you can be sure of is that expeditions to Greenland do not come cheap. As this was a group of experienced independent alpinists I would not be acting as a formal leader but as an organiser/coordinator. Using my own long-standing links with Tangent Expeditions I was able to secure a very good deal for the party in terms of logistics, food and fuel, specialist kit, advance freight, insurance, charter flights, transit accommodation and snowmobile transport, so we soon had flights to Iceland fixed up and were eager to go.

Alex, being the Benjamin of what would be a fairly greybeard bunch (apologies to Sandy!) contrived to be involved in a small avalanche incident above Courmayeur just a few weeks before departure and suffered a ruptured knee ligament. After a scan and consulting his surgeon he was fitted with a bionic knee brace and bravely joined the trip. We expected him to be a bit of a greyhound in any case, so now we more 'mature' gents might stand a bit of a chance.

C. Snow White Col North face (Buisse, Hoare 2014), **D1-7.** The Seven Dwarfs
(all unclimbed): Grumpy, Sneezy, Bashful, Happy, Dopey, Doc, Sleepy, **E.** Tower
of Silence (unclimbed, Australian attempt 2012). *(Alexandre Buisse)*

Thus we all buzzed into Reykjavik, pitching up at our favoured transit
spot, Snorri's Guesthouse. On the next day we flew by charter flight
over the ice-pocked ocean to Constable Pynt and a night under cover in
'Tangentville', the forward base of Tangent Expeditions. Kit, food and fuel
all gathered, we were good to go.

Next morning, we loaded up Tangent's Snow Dragons snowmobile
sledge train, donned multiple layers of clothing and set off. Riding pillion
on a snowmobile is fine, albeit cold, but riding in a box-sledge is a bone-
jarring, teeth-rattling bumpfest, to be endured but not really enjoyed. We
were looking at 80 kilometres of it, first over frozen Hurry Inlet, then
through Klitdal (a zone of sand and riverbeds in summer), down by Paselv,
over icebound Carlsberg Fjord and with luck right up onto the northerly
icecap of Liverpool Land.

At about halfway, Michael exclaimed and pointed 'A bear!' A gaze was
caught by a rapidly retreating dark shape which suddenly burst into three
– a mother polar bear and two fair-sized cubs. These were the first live
polar bears I had seen in more than twenty years of Greenland expeditions,
and a salutary reminder of why we had firearms, flares, pepper spray and
tripwires with us.

At last we were dropped off with all of our stuff – high enough on the
icecap, but a few kilometres short of our ideal spot. There remained an
abrupt bout of heavy pulk-hauling for a few hours to get further up and
across the ice to an elevated but level glacier shelf at c.525m, just 1500m
from our pre-chosen location. Camping where you are vulnerable to deep
shade is to be avoided in the Arctic.

Tony Hoare passing the Seven Dwarfs, on the way to Mount Hulya. The unclimbed Tower of Silence in profile. *(Alexandre Buisse)*

Next day the cloud cleared. We organised base camp: latrine, trip-wired perimeter, kit allocated and distributed. Firearms drill followed; the rifle was good and reliable but the pump-action shotgun kept jamming (worrying), flares and pepper spray shared out. Now it was time to go out and do so we split into two teams of two and one of three.

Alex and Tony, both pro photographers, had a few obligations to one or two equipment sponsors so they were looking for a mix of skiing and climbing outings. They opened with a move off south where they skied up the north-east glacier face of Mount Thistle (1040m), with an option on a steeper descent. Icy conditions led them to ski back down their ascent line. Their next excursion was a ski traverse north-east from base, over Bird Bone Peak and along the ridge as far as Kagoo Peak and then back. A good first ascent followed on Mount Hulya 1 where they climbed the Marmotte Ridge (NW) at PD sup and decided against pushing on for a further traverse which would have had a lot of ups and downs. In pursuit of photographs they went to the top of 3pm Attack Nunatak, 528m, and skied down its west face. (3pm should have been 'Noon Attack' Nunatak but Tony and Alex started too late from camp!). On another day they also set out for the Seven Dwarfs, a row of summits across the glacier. They climbed the Snow White Col by its 200m 60° north face to access the ridge but later retreated due to mistrust of the rock. The Dwarfs as a full traverse would be a major undertaking, needing warmer weather (and maybe a few bolts for rappel anchors, according to Alex, due to compactness of the rock). They had spied other peaks and lines, among them an interesting mini-Matterhorn, but like all of us ran out of good weather days.

Michael and Peter, revelling in being in the pristine Arctic, wanted to focus on seeing as much of it as possible in available time rather than seeking out overly technical climbing. After an early ascent of Bird Bone Point and Bird Bone Peak right above base camp they used their Nordic

Tony Hoare on the lower slopes of the small Birdbone Peak, during the second ascent and first ski descent. *(Alexandre Buisse)*

ski gear to whiz about on a long excursion southwards taking in several tops on Old Men's Peak and ending in a view over into the lake-studded non-glacial transverse valley which runs east-west right across Liverpool Land from Pasfjord to Carlsberg Fjord. They returned by a more westerly glacier arm. After this they decided to make a move off to the north so packed up and hauled away for a few kilometres to a new campsite with a wide vista across ocean and mountain. From this location they made a few first ascents but also accessed the ridge bearing Kagoo, Diamond and

High on Kuldefjeld. Geoff Bonney and Sandy Gregson arrive at the summit on the first ascent of *Charlotte Road*. Longridge Peak and more unclimbed mountains away to the north-east. *(Jim Gregson)*

Icecream Peaks (Aus 2012). When the weather turned they moved back to base camp.

Jim, Sandy and Geoff opened their account with a very good first ascent on the big mountain between Mount Mighty and the Seven Dwarfs, which they called Kuldefjeld (Cold Mountain, 980m). Their route up the north-west spur Charlotte Road went at AD inf / PD sup for c.450m with fine positions. A descent was made by the ridge leading towards Mount Mighty then down the north-east face. For the next outing Geoff (75) elected to take a rain check so Sandy and Jim skied out east towards Neild Bugt aiming for a possible ridge traverse starting up Hvithorn (White Horn). After a nice arête climb they were very surprised to reach an unexpected small summit cut off from Hvithorn by an almost vertical drop of a rope length, with steep goulottes to north and south. This was not obvious from below and in reality a start point for Hvithorn would need to be made further along the glacier, so this small top was named Varmtind (Warm Peak 750m). Geoff rejoined the active list for a day of ski ascents reached by going north from base then up to the top of Carlsberg Dome (845m) from the north-west with a continuation ski ascent onto Kagoo Peak before a return as all the lower fjords and valleys filled with inversion fog as pressure fell.

From all the summits reached we realised that there were many more stunning peaks than we would have time for in just this one trip. Many would not be pushovers as the ridge crests of Hulya and the Seven Dwarfs showed. There is also the still virgin big Tower of Silence just west of the Dwarfs. During our visit there was still a lot of winter or recent storm snow on the mountains and quite a lot of avalanche evidence as the sun got to work. Perhaps a slightly later visit would reduce the risk of slides, but the onset of melt in the Arctic can be very rapid and seasons vary. 2014 was

The upper ridge of
Hvithorn from Varmtind.
(Jim Gregson)

definitely colder than 2007 but the snow was more unstable.

When the fog came it brought a very chilly whiteout and our activities were limited to short outings from base to nearby tops like Bird Peak and 3pm Attack Nunatak which had a fascinating icicle-fringed glacier moat on three sides. Itching to do more we realised we had run out of time, but our summit days showed a whole range of possible future targets and good reasons to return. Then we had a day and night of knifingly cold north winds which blasted us with spindrift to emphasise that we must finish.

A satphone call fixed our snowmobile pickup. We needed the wind to drop and whiteout to lift as safe motorised glacier travel needs good visibility. We agreed to haul down off the icecap to make a rendezvous. The weather co-operated as we broke camp and the collar-work was for just an hour or two before the Snow Dragons drove up onto the ice to meet us. We gratefully loaded up the sledge-train to descend to Carlsberg Fjord, from where the bump and bang through Klitdal began. The discomfort eased as we re-entered Hurry Inlet but we were still glad to see Constable Pynt.

After a final night in 'Tangentville' we flew the next day by Twin Otter to Akureyri in northern Iceland for hot showers, clean clothes, eating at tables, sitting on chairs, sleeping in beds. Then there was a 5-6 hour drive through the mountains of Iceland back to Reykjavik for more R&R at Snorri's Guesthouse. Good memories, good company, some good climbing and skiing, no major differences of opinion, lots of smiles. No real gripes – except maybe a bit too much chocolate in the ration packs and a mysteriously severe shortage of tea bags.

Looking south-east from Varmtind, across frozen Neild Bugt to unclimbed peaks on the coast of Liverpool Land. *(Jim Gregson)*

Summary: Independent expedition to North Liverpool Land, East Greenland April/May 2014. Geoff Bonney, Alexandre Buisse, Peter Chadwick, Jim Gregson, Sandy Gregson, Tony Hoare, Michael Smith – 5 of these are AC members. Thanks go to the AC Climbing Fund/First Ascent for grant aid and to Tangent Expeditions Ltd who were also very helpful in handling so much of our arrangement.

References:
Exploring Greenland: Twenty Years of adventure mountaineering in the great Arctic wilderness by Jim Gregson, Vertebrate Publishing 2012.
AAJ 2009 pp 154-155.
AAJ 2013 pp 184-185.
Geol. Surv. Den. Green. Bull. 21 *Exploration history and place names of northern East Greenland* by Anthony K Higgins, Copenhagen 2010.

North Liverpool Land First Ascents

3pm Attack. . . (528m)	N71° 22.038'	W22° 03.295'	(Buisse, Hoare)
Bird Bone Peak (853m)	N71° 22.736'	W22° 5.251'	(FA? Smith, Chadwick)
Bird Bone Point (726m)	N71° 22.214'	W22° 06.350'	(FA? Smith, Chadwick)
Carlsberg Dome (845m)	N71° 22.929'	W22° 04.851'	(Gregson, Gregson, Bonney)
Consolation Point (808m)	N71° 22.921'	W21° 59.699'	(Smith, Chadwick)
Kuldefjeld (980m)	N71° 21.219'	W21° 59.522'	(Gregson, Gregson, Bonney)
Mount Hulya 1 (830m)	N71° 21.732'	W 21° 56.564'	(Buisse, Hoare)
Mount Thistle (1040m)	N71° 19.00'	W22° 03.00'	(Buisse, Hoare)
Old Men's Peak (707m)	N71° 19.024'	W22° 6.795'	(Smith, Chadwick)
Pt. 810 (810m)	N71° 25.871'	W22° 6.037'	(2nd A? Smith, Chadwick)
Snow Dome (816m)	N71° 25.442'	W22° 6.218'	(FA? Smith, Chadwick)
Snow Knoll (722m)	N71° 25.118'	W22° 5.967'	(2nd A Smith, Chadwick)
The Wedge (708m)	N71° 25.734'	W22° 1.530'	(FA? Smith, Chadwick)
Varmtind (750m)	N71° 23.036'	W21° 56.156'	(Gregson, Gregson)
Snow White Col (788m)	N71° 21.126'	W22° 00.003'	(Buisse, Hoare)

Science

Chamonix Aiguilles, oil on canvas, 61x91cm. *(Tim Pollard)*

MIKE SEARLE

The Rise of Tibet

Aerial view of the Gongga Shan (7556 m) granite massif along the eastern margin of the Tibetan plateau. *(Mike Searle)*

The Tibetan Plateau region is the largest area of high elevation (averaging just over 5000 metres above sea-level) and thick crust (70-90 km compared to 30-40 km thickness for normal continental crust) anywhere in the world (Fig. 1). It is bounded by mountain ranges on all sides: the Himalaya to the south, Karakoram and Pamir to the west, Kun Lun and Altyn Tagh ranges along the north and the Longmen Shan in the east[1]. The internally drained part of the plateau interior is extremely flat but in the southeastern part, where rivers drain off the high plateau into Burma, Thailand and Yunnan, deep gorges have been carved into the plateau. Tibet lies in the rain shadow of the Himalaya so the strong monsoon winds that blow from the south during the summer months only usually reach up to the crest of the high Himalayan peaks.

Tibet comprises several major tectonic plates that have been progressively accreted onto the stable Siberian – Mongolian craton over the last 400 million years. Tethys, an east-west aligned, world-wide ocean during Permian to Mesozoic times, separated the Gondwana supercontinents of

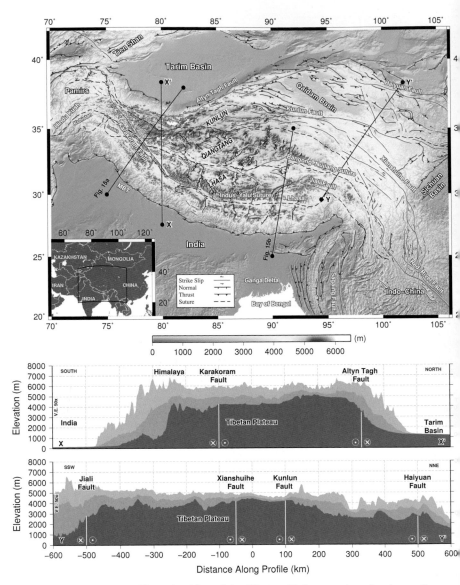

Fig. 1. Top: Digital Elevation Map of the Tibetan Plateau region showing active and recent thrust faults (red), normal faults (blue) and strike-slip faults (grey), together with major suture zones. Lines of sections in Fig. 2 shown.
Below: topographic profiles for Eastern and Western Tibet: X-X' and Y-Y'.

the southern hemisphere from central Asia and Europe. The closing of this ocean due to subduction along its northern rim led to the collision of these southern continents, Africa, Arabia and India, with Eurasia forming the Alpine – Zagros – Himalayan mountain ranges. The Indian plate collided with Asia approximately 50 million years ago.

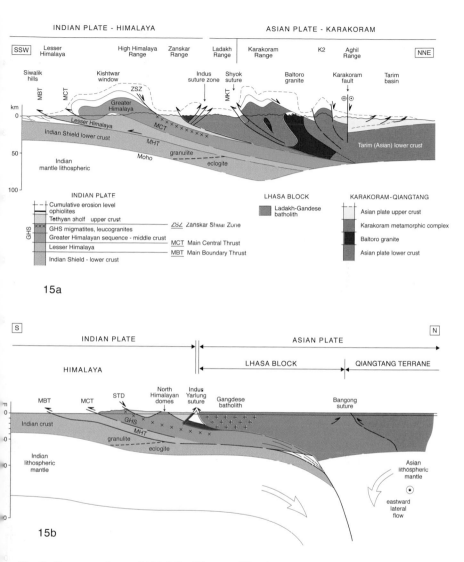

Fig. 2. Cross-sections of (15a) the Western Himalaya – Karakoram – Tarim ranges, far west Tibet, and (15b) Nepal – central Tibet regions showing the large-scale interpreted structure of the Tibetan Plateau. *(After Searle et al 2011)*

In Asia the trapped remnants of the Tethyan ocean floor are preserved along the Indus-Tsangpo suture, the zone of collision that runs along the northern boundary of the Indian plate through Waziristan and Kohistan, across Ladakh and southern Tibet before swinging around the Eastern Himalayan syntaxis and running south through Burma.

These rocks can only have been formed in the oceans: deep-sea sediments, oceanic volcanics and ophiolites, the latter comprising segments of oceanic crust and upper mantle. The youngest marine sediments, both in the suture zone and along the northern margin of the Indian plate, are shallow marine limestones that contain small planktonic foraminifera that have been precisely dated at 50.5 million years old. After that time the two continents had collided, closing the ocean and resulting in mountain building and uplift both along the Indian plate to the south in the Himalaya and along the Asian margin to the north in Tibet (Fig. 2).

Subduction of the oceanic plate under the south Tibetan margin also resulted in the intrusion of Andean-type granites along the Kohistan, Ladakh and Gangdese ranges of Tibet and eruption of voluminous andesitic lavas similar to those of the Andes today.

For the 50 million years since collision, India has continued to penetrate northwards, pushing into Asia and causing uplift of the Himalaya and the Tibetan plateau. The mechanisms and timing of crustal thickening and uplift of Tibet have been the cause of much controversy in geological circles. Ninety years ago, long before the plate tectonic revolution of the 1960s, a Swiss geologist Emile Argand embraced Alfred Wegener's theory of continental drift and proposed that India had underthrust the whole of Tibet resulting in the double thickness crust and high topography[2]. If this model were correct then the geology of Tibet, notably the deformation and metamorphism would have to be generally older than 50 million years.

Another model proposed the opposite, in that Tibet has formed by horizontal shortening and thickening after the India-Asia collision[3]. If this was correct then most of the folding and metamorphism should be younger than 50 million years.

A third popular model, termed continental extrusion, proposed that the thickened crust of Tibet was pushed sideways to the east and southeast out of the way of the rigid Indian plate 'indentor'[4]. Huge strike-slip faults bound this extruding block, the Karakoram fault in the SW, the Kun Lun and Altyn Tagh faults along north Tibet and the Xianshui-he and Jiale faults in east and SE Tibet. If this model were correct then the faults would

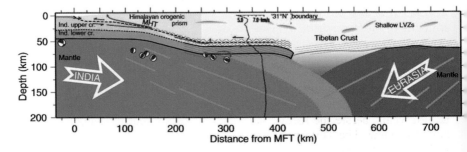

Fig. 3. Cross-section of the Tibetan Plateau showing the geophysical constraints derived from deep crustal seismic experiments. MTF – Main Frontal Thrust. *(After Nabelek et al, 2009).*

Fig. 4. Outcrop north of Lhasa showing folded Cretaceous Takena Formation red-beds truncated by a prominent unconformity (dashed line), above which are flat-lying volcanic rocks dated at 60 million years. *(Mike Searle)*

display hundreds of kilometres of lateral offset and would need to reach down into the lithospheric mantle.

Since the opening of Tibet to foreign geologists in the 1980s, a large amount of geological mapping has been carried out across the plateau. Unlike the Himalaya, where deep crustal metamorphic and granitic rocks are exposed and exhumation – erosion rates are extremely high, the Tibetan plateau has low relief and low exhumation – erosion rates and very few lower crustal rocks are exposed. We are therefore reliant on geophysical methods, notably seismic, gravity and magnetic studies to interpret the structure of the lower crust in Tibet.

One such study (Fig. 3) shows that southern Tibet is underlain by relatively cold lithospheric mantle as far north as about 32°N, suggesting that Argand's model was partially correct, with India underthrusting at least the southern half of the plateau[5]. Geological fieldwork revealed that most of the folding and crustal shortening in southern Tibet occurred prior to 60-70 million years, before the India – Asia collision (Fig. 4), again supporting Argand's view. The Tibetan plateau is also riddled with small volcanoes and intrusive igneous rocks that have a very unusual alkaline geochemistry. These volcanics require a very hot mantle source and their ages, which show a progressive northward younging from 50-13 million years in the south to 4-1 million years along the Kun Lun in the north, again

Fig. 5. A view of western Tibet from the Space Shuttle, towards the south-east. The two prominent faults forming an arrowhead are the Karakoram and Altyn Tagh faults and bound the eastward extruding Tibetan crust. *(NASA)*

support the model of underthrusting of Indian lower crust and cold mantle northwards.

The prominent strike-slip faults that cross the Tibetan plateau region are among the largest and most active such faults in the world (Fig. 5). Large destructive earthquakes regularly occur along actively moving faults such as the San Andreas in California or the North Anatolian Fault in Turkey. The Karakoram fault running from the northern Pamirs along the Tashkurgan (Xinjiang), Shaksgam, Siachen and Nubra (India) valleys south-west to Pangong Lake and the Kailas region of south-west Tibet is one of the most prominent strike-slip faults in Asia. It runs along the northern flanks of the K2 – Broad Peak – Gasherbrum ranges in the central Karakoram and appears to partially control the uplift of these extremely high peaks that are aligned along the south-west side of the fault. Along the Siachen glacier and Nubra valley in Ladakh, the highest uplifted peaks of the Saser Kangri range are aligned along the north-east side of the fault. The Karakoram fault cuts obliquely across the Baltoro granites and offset markers show that there is only about 25 km of total offset (Fig. 6).

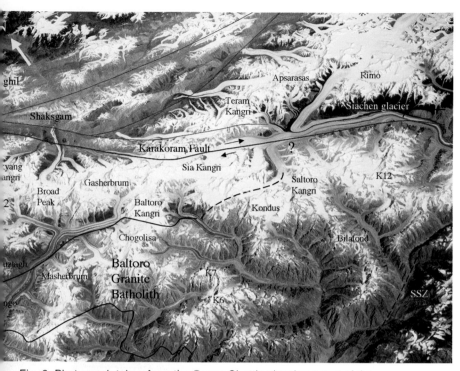

Fig. 6. Photograph taken from the Space Shuttle showing a part of the Karakoram ranges on the borders of Pakistan (west), India (east) and China (north). The trace of the Karakoram fault is marked along the Siachen glacier and Shaksgam valley offsetting the vertical northern margin of the Baltoro granite batholith by only 17-25 km. *(NASA)*

These Tibetan strike-slip faults appear to be extremely large but do not show a great amount of offset. Furthermore, there is, surprisingly, very little seismic activity along the Karakoram fault. Either the fault is now tectonically dead or the recurrence time between very large earthquakes is of the order of several hundred years and the strain is building up for a huge earthquake. Only time will tell.

In eastern Tibet the Xianshui-he fault in the eastern plateau appears to be the most active, recording at least eight Magnitude 7+ earthquakes along its trace since 1725. River channels of the Yangtse river tributaries in the high plateau show abrupt offsets, pulled apart by motion along the fault of up to 30 km laterally. The Xianshui-he strike-slip fault also cuts across the huge Gongga Shan granite batholith in eastern Tibet. Uranium-lead dating of minute radioactive zircon crystals show that these granites are mainly old, of Jurassic age but have an interesting much younger component dated as Miocene. By dating the youngest granites in the 7556m high Gongga Shan (Minya Konkka) massif (~4 million years old) that are cut by the fault we can provide a maximum age constraint on initiation of the

Fig 7: The stunning array of mountains around the Namche Barwa – Gyala Peri
ranges of the Eastern Himalayan Syntaxis. *(Mike Searle)*

Fig 8: The Eastern Nyenchen Tanglha ranges in SE Tibet taken from the Lhasa
to Chengdu flight. *(Mike Searle)*

fault and a long-term average slip rate. Global Positioning System satellite measurements suggest the fault is presently slipping at a rate of ~10 mm/year, extremely fast in geological terms.

The Tibetan Plateau is a unique feature on the Earth's surface. Its uplift has affected global climate and the plateau is thought to be a major factor in the strengthening of the Indian monsoon system. A high-pressure system sits over the plateau in summer heating up the atmosphere over Tibet. This sucks in the tropical, moisture laden air from the Indian Ocean to the south which releases vast quantities of rain over the Indian sub-continent during the summer monsoon – in the Assam and Meghalaya regions of north-east India an incredible 18 metres of rain has been recorded in a single year, almost all of it falling in the three months of the summer monsoon.

The Tibetan plateau even affects the northern hemisphere high-altitude jet stream, causing it to divert around the plateau to the north and south – where it produces the characteristic snow plumes that stream from the summit of Everest.

Much has been written and surmised about the geology of Tibet, but more than half the plateau remains unmapped and unsurveyed especially in the myriad of mountains than occupy the southeastern part (Fig. 7). We know more about the geology of the Moon than we know about the geology of the eastern Nyenchen Tanglha mountains (Fig. 8).

So next time you stand on a Himalayan summit, look north across the vast 'plateau' of Tibet and reflect on 50 million years of geological history.

References

1. Searle, M P, Elliott, J R, Phillips, R J & Chung, S-L. 2011. Crustal – lithospheric structure and continental extrusion of Tibet. *Journal of the Geological Society London*, **168**, 633-672.
2. Argand, E. 1924. Le tectonique de l'Asie. *Proc. 13th Int. Geol. Cong.* **7**, 171-372
3. Dewey, J & Burke, K. 1973. Tibetan, Variscan and Precambrian basement reactivation: Products of a continental collision. *Journal of Geology*, **81**, 683-692.
4. Tapponnier, P, Zhiqin, X, Roger, F, Meyer, B, Arnaud, N, Wittlinger, G & Yang, J. 2001. Oblique stepwise rise and growth of the Tibet Plateau. *Science*, **294**, 1671-1677.
5. Nábelek, J, Hetényi, G & the Hi-CLIMB team. 2009. Underplating in the Himalaya-Tibet collision zone revealed by the Hi-CLIMB experiment. *Science*, **325**, 1371-1374.

See also Mike Searle's book *Colliding Continents*, reviewed in *AJ* 2013.

EVELIO ECHEVARRÍA

Summit Archaeology

Prehistoric Ascents in The World's Highest Mountains

Mountaineering in the past found itself associated with diverse branches of knowledge – with geology, botany, meteorology, history. Why should it not come to the help of archaeology? – (Douglas Freshfield, *Alpine Journal* **38**, 1926).

Douglas Freshfield wrote these lines when he noted that the ruins of the ancient city of Petra were to be explored mostly by practiced cragsmen. Before this, in 1905, he had found the remains of a cell of unknown origin on the summit of Taiyetos (2407m), Sparta's highest mountain. Earlier still, in his Algerian travels of 1886, he had learned about daring hillmen who, traditionally, had climbed rock summits hunting wild sheep. He guessed rightly that some day, though not in his time, mountaineering would become associated with archaeology.

It was mountaineers who first drew the attention of archaeologists to traces of ancient visits to important summits. But it was archaeologists who, enlisting the aid of mountaineers, were to uncover and study such finds. This peculiar alliance between climbers and scientists nowadays goes by a variety of names. Andean South Americans call it *arqueologia de cumbres* (summit archaeology), central Europeans prefer the term *pre-Alpinism*. Other titles include *orolatric* mountaineering, high altitude archaeology and pre-Columbian mountain ascents.

However, this branch of our sport is seldom acknowledged by mountaineers themselves, who tend to view it as just plain science. Perhaps such indifference is due to the fact that a comprehensive survey of the extent of prehistoric ascents in the world's mountains simply does not exist. True, there have been attempts by a few studious souls to remedy this, but their rare contributions have concentrated on limited geographical areas and are, by now, outdated.

Albeit in a very summarized form, this article may be an early if not the first attempt at an updated review of the number and nature of verified prehistoric ascents worldwide.

Two basic facts to be placed squarely before the mountaineers of today: firstly, some 260 mountain peaks, between 2500m and 6700m+, unevenly distributed across five continents, were ascended in prehistoric times; secondly such unrecorded ascents go back 8000 or even 18,000 years and may have continued to as recently as AD 1850.

When reviewing the achievements of the ancients, a sense of proportion must be kept in mind at all times. This incredible activity began in

Volcán Llullaillaco (6739m), northern Chile-Argentine Andes, highest altitude archaeological site in the world. This photograph was taken during the 'first modern ascent' in 1952. *(Bión González)*

the late Mesolithic or early Neolithic . Another simple fact to note: a leaf arrow point was found in 1963 near the summit of Ben Macdui (1309m), proof that prehistoric men hunted the red deer in the Grampians. But what protective clothing did they have? What did they wear on their feet? What were the weather and terrain like at that time, during the last glacial recession?

The Finds

This survey deals exclusively with proven summit, or summit ground findings. To date, the oldest ancient summit evidence is of obsidian quarries high on volcanoes where this glassy rock was worked for tools and weapons from 18,000 to 8000 years ago. This implies that the hunt for obsidian was the ultimate origin of mountaineering! However, every summit find left by the ancients points in one direction – survival. Even after nomadism, orolatry or the adoration of mountains enshrined sources of water – survival again.

A geographical distribution of important mountain summits with proven archaeological remains compiled by the author is listed below.

North and Central America
57 mountain tops in the Rocky Mountains and in the Sierra Nevada of California, ranging from Chief Mountain (2767m) to Blanca Peak (4373m). In Mexico, 12 such summits so far known, ranging in height from Cerro Wishi (3997m) to Pico de Orizaba (5620m). Several Central American volcanoes (3700m to 4220m) have yielded ancient remains or proof of previously unrecorded human occupancy.

South America (Andes)
Some 30 peaks, 4000m to 5220m, with Neolithic (non Inca) structures in Ecuador and northern Peru.

Over 130 peaks, from 3700m to Llullaillaco (6739m), the highest archaeological site in the world, with proven remains of Inca origin (incidentally, 19 among such peaks rise to 6000m and above).

Europe
10 summits crowned with Christian and pre-Christian remains, including remnants of cells and others with cairns erected by game hunters.

Middle East
10 high peaks ranging from Mount Hermon (2814m) to Damavand (5671m) in Iran, the latter showing sulphur diggings of unknown date and origin, described by the then British ambassador to Persia, W. T. Thompson in 1837.

Asia
Just 5 lesser heights, such as Musaka Musala (4068m) and Takht i Suleiman (3374m), in the Kaghan district, exhibit ziarets (altars) on their summits, which are usually covered with snow.

In the much higher Himalaya and Karakoram, a handful of peaks, some 5200m high, have summits adorned with the ubiquitous Tibetan prayer-wheels.

Summit craters of volcanoes in Japan and South-east Asia have, for centuries, been sites for religious offerings and ceremonies.

Africa
Only 5 proven ascents by game hunters, with Toubkal (4165m) in the Atlas, showing what could have been a hunter's shelter and/or an altar to Kaumhauc, a benign spirit, according to the Koran.

Australasia
Less than a handful of volcanic heights have yielded traces of native or ancient occupancy.

Thus, the inventory comprises: 160 in South America, 63 in North and Central America, 10 in Europe, 10 in the Middle East, 12 in Asia, 5 in

The Inca ceremonial platform built on the summit ground of Volcán Copiapó (6052m). Drawn from a photo taken on the 1937 Polish expedition to northern Chile-Argentina. *(Witold Paryski)*

Africa and 2 in Australasia. A total of 262 so far. Only mountains recognized as actual peaks are considered in this survey. Lesser, forested hills and flanks of hills that have yielded traces of ancient activity, as well as mythical ascents, have been disregarded.

It should be noted that a number of important mountains in this inventory did offer technical obstacles to climbing. For example beneath the summit of Nevado Huanac Paccha (5920m) in southern Peru, Italian climbers found to their admiration evidence of technical aids, used by their Inca predecessors. On the steep walls of the Enchanted Mesa (2025m) in New Mexico, American late-comers in 1895 used the holes drilled by the ancient Acoma Indians to insert their own pegs, which enabled them to reach the summit ridge, where they found strewn pottery and ancient relics.

Tangible or visible proofs that we recognize today, or recognized as such in the past include: mummified human remains and buried human skeletons; monuments, megaliths or rock constructions believed by hill peoples to be or to represent the graves of saints or sages; cairns erected by local people; platforms constructed for ceremonial use.

Referring to the construction of one such platform on the summit of Cerro de las Tórtolas (6160m), Chilean mountaineers wrote (translated):

'The Incas erected a *pirca* or retaining wall on the summit, oval in shape, measuring 8 x 4 metres and with walls 1 metre high, constructed of rocks up to 25 kilos in weight, which were carried there from a place some 100m below the top. The whole work represents 30 cubic metres and, with the filling, a total of 90 tonnes, which [must have required] some 4500 ascents, braving adverse conditions and lack of equipment at an elevation of 6160m.'[1]

Other diverse objects: obsidian pieces or chips, arrow points, bows, sherds, statuettes, no doubt with symbolic meaning; prayer-sticks, feather-sticks, feathers, *kachina* dolls (these last four types common to the southern Rocky Mountains) and prayer-wheels (purely Asiatic).

There are diverse forms of altar (*huacas* in the central Andes, *ziarets* in Asia and the Middle East), butts or trenches for game hunters, crom-lechs, dolmens, icons or dressed stones, cells; remnants of walls of religious chapels (finds peculiar to European and Middle Eastern summits), enclosures and walls of dwellings, at times containing remains and objects abandoned by hill peoples.

Interestingly, enclosures in the northern Rockies, particularly of the Crow tribe, indicated ascents to important summits in order to invoke the Great Spirit. Warriors would inhabit such lofty places for extended periods of time so as to receive a revelation which would grant them success in war or in the hunt. They called this experience 'medicine'; in archaeology it is known as vision quest.[2]

Blanca Peak (4373m), Colorado Rocky Mountains. The masonry is of unknown origin, and was found on the summit by surveyors in 1873. It constitutes the highest archaeological site in the United States. (*Evelio Echevarría*)

The list continues: caves or shelters for hermits, excavated on rock summit ground; tools and sticks for digging or excavating; petroglyphs, hand-paintings; quarries (obsidian); diverse stone artifacts – marbles, rounded stones at times perforated for some unknown use, stone paths and staircases (as those found on the summit ridge of Picchu Picchu (5642m), in southern Peru); animal corpses, usually rodents, perhaps indicating a sacrificial offering.

Incidentally, regarding offerings, was the celebrated body of a leopard, found in the 1920s on the summit ground of Kilimanjaro, an offering or was it just an unfortunate animal that strayed 3000m above his native environment? Likewise, why was the carcass of a *guanaco* to be found beneath the summit ridge of Aconcagua, some 4000m above its habitat?

The Finders

The first mountaineers to come across such evidence were understandably bewildered as to its origin. Alpine Club member G. P. Baker, visiting Turkey's Ulu Dagh (2493m) in 1904 was undecided about the nature of the summit ruins: '. . .perhaps a chapel or a monastery. . . or a signal station or an altar . . .'[3]

Some summit visitors did not stop to reflect, simply seeking artifacts that would bring them monetary reward. At times finds were deliberately destroyed, as in the case of Malinche (4461m), a dormant Mexican volcano, in 1550. Upon learning that the summit was crowned with Aztec idols, angry colonial authorities ordered their destruction and replaced them with a Christian chapel.

Initially, the very few mountaineers and archaeologists who tried to rationalize such summit phenomena wrongly concluded that they represented watchtowers or stations for smoke signals, clearly not a sensible interpretation for sites some 3000-4000m above human habitation. Others opined that stone walls were fortifications, again a strange opinion, since there were no parapets nor water supply to sustain a garrison.

It was left to Chilean explorer and surveyor Francisco J. San Román, who had ascended several peaks that yielded Inca relics in the northern reaches of his country, to offer a reasonable conclusion, in 1885 (translated):

'In the great heights of the Andes... one always finds evident testimonies of human existence: wood and coal remains, copper artifacts and even small sculptures, which attest to the inclination of the prehistoric Indians for the ascent of summits, undoubtedly for some utilitarian purpose, for some purpose of public convenience.[4]

San Román then correctly surmised that his findings were proof of sustained mountain ascents, probably for political or religious reasons.

Once their curiosity had been aroused, mountaineers well versed in historical research began to make valuable contributions (see bibliography).

The German alpinist Walter Smidkunz published a first inventory of human activity in the high mountains of the world in 1931. He was followed by several expeditioners: Witold Paryski (Poland), who had discovered Inca shrines on two 6000m Andean volcanoes, Italian traveller-alpinist-author Mario Fantin, and the expert Chilean *andinista* Bion González. All three published early listings and descriptive analyses of the Andean remains. It was González who discovered the highest archaeological site on the planet on the summit of Llullaillaco in 1952.

In 1954 an Inca mummy was uncovered from the summit of Cerro El Plomo (5432m), Chile, the ice dome visible from the streets of the capital, Santiago. This well publicised event prompted several international expeditions intent not on making first ascents, but rather more humbly following in the footsteps of prehistoric mountaineers. Thus summit archaeology began to be recognized by mountaineers, although in the early days it was thought only to be found in the Andes.

A major step was undertaken by the Argentinian Antonio Beorchia (San Juan), who had experienced many such discoveries, some over 6000m, including that of the well-preserved mummy of Cerro El Toro (6168m). In 1972 he founded the CIADAM, (*Centro de Investigaciones Arqueológicas de Alta Montaña*), and began to publish the *Revista* (review) of the institution. This organization and its publication brought much international recognition. Beorchia was assisted by Juan Schobinger (Mendoza), Constanza Ceruti and Christian Vitry (Salta), all Argentinian professors who have made numerous discoveries and have published papers on this topic.

American University archaeologists James Benedict and Johan Reinhard devoted their studies to the Rocky Mountains and the Andes respectively. Benedict also founded the Center for Mountain Archaeology, in Ward, Colorado. Mexican university professor Ismael Montero, also with a large number of findings and publications in this field to his credit has, with Benedict, helped to expand the scope of summit archaeology by proving that it is not solely Andean.

Such academic professionals were ably assisted by mountaineers who became eager practitioners of this sport-plus-science: Rick Baugher, Joseph Kramarsic and Winston Crausaz from the US, Marcelo Scanu (Argentina), Javier and Queralt Sánchez (Spain), plus Sergio Kunstmann and Pedro Rosende from Chile.

Summit archaeology will remain unfinished business – who knows what further secrets are hidden on peaks untrodden by modern climbers? Further discoveries will certainly be made, either by climbing mountains or by delving deeply into written records – a task whose end is hard to visualize.

Enough is known already for us to recognize that prehistoric mountain ascents represent the core of a new and unavoidable 'Chapter One' in the history of world mountaineering.

Acknowledgements

With the exception of Walter Smidkunz, I have exchanged correspondence or been personally acquainted with all persons mentioned in the final paragraphs covering recent work.

With pleasure I also acknowledge the help rendered by fellow members of the Alpine Club, who responded to my request for information. Trevor Graham supplied data on the *ziarets* on Asia's mountains. The late Sydney Nowill went over the lists of Turkish mountain ascents I submitted to him in order to verify which were, or were not, properly prehistoric. Readers will also recall Johanna Merz's contribution, *Prayer in Stone*, in the *Alpine Journal* 111, 2006. In it, there was information about possible prehistoric ascents of Mont Bego above the French Riviera, that needed to be confirmed. Through Johanna's help and her contacts in the local *Musée des Merveilles* those possible ascents were ultimately disproved – a typical result that any researcher in this field has to face. I gratefully acknowledge the help of all these individuals and institutions.

Selected Bibliography

There exist several standard works that concentrate on findings pertaining to a single mountain (i.e. Aconcagua). Entries below were selected for containing surveys covering findings over wider geographical areas.

James Benedict, *Archaeologists above timberline: the early years,* in *Southwestern Lore* (Denver) **67**, 2, 1-16, 2001.

Antonio Beorchia, *El enigma de los santuarios indígenas de alta montana.* (San Juan: CIADAM, 1987).

Constanza Ceruti, *Cumbres sagradas del noroeste argentino.* (Buenos Aires: Eudeba, 1999).

_____, *Llullaillaco. Sacrificios y ofrendas en un santuario indígena de alta montaña.* (Salta :Universidad Católica de Salta, 2003).

Evelio Echevarría, *The South American Indian as a pioneer alpinist,* in *Alpine Journal* **73**, 81-88, 1968.

_____, *The Inca mountaineers: 1400-1800,* in Harold Drasdo *et al,* Editors, *The Mountain Spirit* (Woodstock, New York: Overlook Press, 1979), 117-124.

_____, *Chile andinista: su historia* (Santiago: Talleres von Plate, 1999).

_____, *Prehistoric mountain ascents in North America,* in *Appalachia* **LIII**, 4, 80-95, 2001.

Mario Fantin, *A settemila metri gli Inca precursori díalpinismo* (Bologna: Tamari, 1969).

Bión González, *Un poco sobre arqueológia de alta montaña,* in *Anuario de Montaña* **9**, 90-93, 1983.

Milenco Jurcich, *Arqueología de las cumbres* (Salta: Ediciones Culturales, 1974).

H. F. B. Lynch, *Armenia: travels and studies* (London: Longmans & Green, 1901), vol. II.

Ismael Montero, *Atlas Arqueológico de la Montaña Mexicana* (Mexico City: Estirpe, 2004).

Witold Paryski, *Indianie na szczytach Ameryki,* in *Taternik* **3-4**, 165-175, 1956.

Edward Pyatt, *The Guinness Book of Mountains & Mountaineering. Facts & Feats* (Enfield, Middlesex: Guinness Superlatives Limited, 1980).

Johan Reinhard, *High altitude archaeology and Andean mountain gods,* in *American Alpine Journal* **25**, 54-67, 1983.

_____, *The Ice Maiden. Inca Mummies, Mountain Gods and Sacred Sites in the Andes* (Washington: National Geographic Society, 2005).

Marcelo Scanu, *Santuarios de altura de los Andes* (Lima: Industrial Gráfica, 1987).

Juan Schobinger, *Arqueología de alta montaña. Santuarios incaicos en los Andes*

A cover of *Revista del CIADAM*, the review issued by the *Centro de Investigaciones Arqueológicas de Alta Montaña*, San Juan, Argentina. Pictured is a statuette typical of those found on Andean summits. *(Evelio Echevarría)*

centro- meridionales, in *Beitrage zur Allgemeinen und Vergleichenden Archaeologie*, Band **18**, 363-400, 1998.

_____, Editor, *El santuario incaico del Cerro Aconcagua* (Mendoza: Editorial de la Universidad de Cuyo, 2001).

Walter Smidkunz, *Alpine Geschichte in Einzeldaten*, in *D.u.O.A.V.*, Editors, *Alpine Handbuch* (Leipzig: F. Brockhaus, 1931), 310-349.

Herbert Ungnade, *Guide to the New Mexico Mountains* (Albuquerque: University of New Mexico Press, 1972).

References

1. Humberto Barrera, Editor, *Arqueología de alta montaña*, in *Revista Andina* **90**, 8-9, 1968.

2. Dale Fredlund, *Vision quest sites and structures*, in *Archaeology in Montana* **1-2**, 14-20, 1969.

3. G.P.Baker, *The Mysian Olympus*, in *Alpine Journal* **22**, 124-9, 1904.

4. Francisco J. San Román, *Desierto y cordilleras de Atacama* (Santiago: Imprenta Nacional, 1896), vol. **I**, 40.

Arts

Sgùrr Dubh Beag and Sgùrr Dubh Mòr across Loch Coruisk, oil on canvas, 40x50cm. *(Tim Pollard)*

TIM POLLARD

Painting Mountains

Aiguille Verte. Acrylic on canvas, 40x50cm. *(Tim Pollard)*

Painting can be really addictive. It's highly involving. Sometimes it can be very frustrating. However, when it goes well, it is ultimately hugely satisfying.

Fleeting views of mountains are drawn, photographed and remembered. In the studio, a canvas is stretched drum-tight and tubes of elaborately named oil paint wait to be worked together to produce a mountain composition. A blank canvas poses a unique and challenging starting point: a quest; a beginning. As a climber I recognise similar feelings of anticipation. Just as at the beginning of a route, you can imagine some of what might be ahead but you can't be sure of the outcome.

A fine brush held at the very end works across the canvas to create a basic outline in ultramarine. Depth of field is determined by scale and lighter tones. The light of the sun is cast to produce shadows and show warm

Triple Buttress, Ben Eighe, oil on canvas, 50x76cm. *(Tim Pollard)*

Langdale Pikes, oil on canvas, 50x76cm. *(Tim Pollard)*

rock and brightened snow and ice. In the shadows darker tones reveal the hidden topography of the mountain.

Rock and snow are darker but not as in a photograph when things are darkened into oblivion. Ridges and pinnacles are painted to show them

Pavey Ark, oil on canvas, 45x60cm. *(Tim Pollard)*

projecting from the glaciers and glacial debris which surround them. It is important to continually contrast rocky silhouettes with the sky that lies behind them: at times the rock is darker than the sky; at others the roles are reversed.

Managing light and dark is of particular importance whilst developing the composition. Bergschrunds and icefalls are painted to show depth and shadows and subtle colour changes. Where snow fields gradually fade, colours change. Mountain debris and moraines are painted in both warm and cool tones. Vegetation is hinted at with subtle blends of reds, greens and ochre. The blues within the painted landscape need to be different that of the mountain sky.

A carpet-like veneer of landscape should hint at the rock structure beneath.

Above all, I try to show mountains as powerful

Langdale Pikes, oil on canvas, 61x91cm. *(Tim Pollard)*

Above Ailefroide, oil on canvas, 71x91cm. *(Tim Pollard)*

elementary structures pushing their way skyward through the surrounding landscape. I want them to be quite gothic yet detailed enough for a climber to recognise and follow the significant routes. As a young climber, I remember sitting in the Old Dungeon Ghyll pub looking at Heaton Cooper's illustrations of the rock climbs in Langdale. I'd be checking out routes while admiring his artistic prowess. His drawings showed through shading the block-like structure of the mountains and crags. This is something I always wanted to embody in my work.

The process is continual and developmental. I'd like to think I'm getting better. Being self-critical is vital to the process. It is still difficult to predict how a painting will turn out but that is all part of the all-consuming fascination.

All the original paintings used to illustrate the section headings and this article are for sale from Tim Pollard. Email: **tjpvp@hotmail.co.uk**

JOHN CLEARE

Filming Mountains

John Noel at work with his 20 inch Cooke telephoto lens high on Everest, his sherpa assistant acting as focus puller.(© *Royal Geographical Society*)

By gum! They were men in those days. We all know the story of the pre-war Everest attempts, especially the 1924 epic from which Mallory and Irvine failed to return, and we will probably have seen, at some time or another, snatches of the original film which recorded the expedition. The film, shown quite widely in Britain, Europe and America in the aftermath of the attempt, was made by Captain John Noel, the expedition's official photographer, described as 'a soldier by profession, an artist in spirit and a brilliant camera technician by necessity' – and undoubtedly also a talented entrepreneur.

Noel working at his 'eyrie' on the rocky slopes above Camp III with his 20 inch Cooke telephoto lens trained on the North Col some 2½ miles distant. The snowy peak is Point 6862m. *(Alpine Club Photo Library)*

Shot on unstable nitrate, long-gone negative stock, the original projection prints deteriorated badly and five years before he died in 1989, Noel suggested to the BFI that his film might warrant restoration and be 'worthy of a place in the National Archive. . . I would welcome this destiny for my picture.' The film restored by the BFI over three years was premiered in October 2013.

Born in 1890, John Noel studied art in Florence, entering the ambit of the great mountain photographer Vittorio Sella, before passing into Sandhurst. Commissioned in 1908, he joined the East Yorkshire Regiment and while serving in India was able to indulge his passions for exploration and photography. In 1913 he made a remarkable journey into forbidden Tibet, using the 1881 reports produced by the pundit Chandra Das to plan his route. Travelling in disguise with three native companions and secreting cameras and basic surveying equipment in their sparse gear – plus a rifle and revolver – they crossed into Tibet from Sikkim and traversed formidable, unexplored country to within just 40 miles of Everest, before being arrested. Now joining the handful of Europeans who had seen Everest from the north, Noel befriended Dr Alexander Kellas, the doyen of Himalayan pioneers, and together they lobbied the British authorities for an official expedition to explore, map and climb the mountain. But the Great War intervened, and during the retreat from Mons and later at Ypres, Noel found himself in the thick of the fighting. Eventually withdrawn from the front suffering from shell-shock, he survived the war as a small-arms instructor. It was the lecture he gave to the Royal Geographical Society in 1919, recounting his 1913 journey, that proved one of the catalysts for the eventual convening of the Mount Everest Committee. This was formed jointly by the AC and the RGS in January 1921, chaired by Sir Francis Younghusband and charged with mounting the subsequent Everest expeditions.

Although not a technical climber per se, Noel was a tough and experienced wilderness traveller, and after military commitments had prevented him joining the 1921 reconnaissance expedition, he resigned his commission to become an important member, as support climber and photographer, of the full-blown 1922 attempt. His initial film – *Climbing Mount Everest* – the first movie footage ever shot in Tibet, documented the expedition during which he reached Camp IV (6990m) on the North Col. Cinematography was barely 20 years old and although he was guided by the Antarctic work of Herbert Ponting, there were many techniques to be developed and lessons to be learnt. For instance he rigged up a darkroom at base camp in which, working only at night, he managed to process hundreds of still photographs and 17,000 feet of cine film. But frozen developer and blowing dust almost jeopardised the entire exercise. There must be another way.

The 1924 expedition was expected to succeed and Noel was fully prepared to record it. He had floated a company,

1924 Everest Expedition: John Noel filming departing porters watched by their relatives, Darjeeling.
(Alpine Club Photo Libary)

Explorer Films Ltd, with Younghusband as chairman, which purchased the film rights to the entire trip for the princely sum of £8,000 – crucial funding for the Everest Committee. He built a proper film laboratory in Darjeeling, complete with electric generator, in which he installed two technicians to process the exposed film negative that would be returned regularly by runner from Base Camp. He even invented and produced the Base Camp Post Cards which would be signed by the climbers and posted

John Cleare in action driving the 16mm Eclair camera in the Khumbu Icefall during the International Expedition to the SW Face, 1971. *(John Cleare / Mountain Camera Picture Library)*

back to children and collectors at home in return for a small donation. Thus was produced *The Epic of Everest*.

Only two original 35mm nitrate prints had survived, though in poor condition, and at the BFI these were scanned at high resolution and a digital master reconstructed, selecting the best quality sequences from either. Scratches and mould were eliminated, while fading and the original colour toning of several rushes were repaired using new digital techniques. Finally many sequences were interpolated, a process in which – in this case every third frame – is duplicated to minimise the characteristic jerky movement displayed when the original 18 fps is run at the 24 fps required for digital cinema projection.

The original film was silent and used 'intertitles' – often lengthy fullscreen captions – which have been retained. However, if Noel was presenting the film himself he would add appropriate commentary and an accompaniment of live music composed by Somervell, and sometimes even a display and chanting by the 'Dancing Lamas' troupe he had bought over from Tibet – in so doing provoking a 'religio-diplomatic' incident. For the reconstructed film a modern sound track was specially commissioned from the film music composer Simon Fisher Turner 'made from found and

stolen life sounds, alongside new music and fake foleys,' he wrote – and
was played live at the London premiere, unfortunately very loudly, by a
five piece ensemble. It was, to my mind, a harsh cacophony entirely out of
keeping with the subject, though others may feel differently.

For those younger climbers accustomed to the gripping climbing footage
shot by the likes of Leo Dickinson and Alastair Lee or seen at the Kendal
Mountain Festival, this film may appear tame, naïve even. But it should
be viewed in the context, not only of 1924 and history, but of the mountain itself, at the time virtually unknown and its hinterland unexplored. It
was, after all, unique footage. The extensive coverage of the people and
their habits, their villages, of lamas and landscapes and of the expedition's
huge logistic train, would surely have been an eye-opener when seen in
flickering black and white some eighty years ago. After a lengthy and well
documented approach march, the mountain eventually appears in the
distance – the classic view of the northern flank from Rongbuk Monastery
– but then of course the camera follows the route to the North Col, located
by Wheeler in 1921 and explored only in 1922 by Mallory and Bullock,
which diverts up the tributary East Rongbuk Glacier. The North-east Ridge
itself, where we know in retrospect that the crucial action was played out,
is hardly seen again until the closing sequences, and that in enfilade at a
distance of some 2½ miles. And there are no diagrams, dotted lines or
named features to explain it all.

Thus we view charming footage of climbers and sherpas threading their
way through forests of imposing penitentes and crossing snowfields via 'Ice
Lake Camp' to 'Snow Field Camp' (Camps II and III respectively) while
many viewers might conclude that the savage North-east Ridge Pinnacles
towering over the head of the East Rongbuk Glacier are the actual summit.
Noel did reach the North Col himself (Camp IV – 'Ice Cliff Camp') but after
one short sequence at the camp, the coverage runs out apart from some
hazy, foreshortened, extreme telephoto images of the summit pyramid.
Knowing something of the politics of the expedition, and the logistic snarl-
ups in the face of fickle weather, I feel that though keen to do so, Noel was
restrained from going higher, although he is recorded as playing a valuable
part as a support climber. But with Mallory and Irvine now obviously dead
and the appropriate signals laid out in the snow, the film rapidly concludes
with an image of the memorial chorten and the final 'intertitle' bearing the
words:

'If you had lived as they had lived and died in the heart of nature, would
you yourself wish for any better grave?'

Words which were doubtless considered appropriate in the aftermath of
WW1.

Certainly the BFI have done an excellent job and the film is well worth
seeing, despite the incongruous sound track. As an intriguing, historical,
mountain travelogue it is a great tribute both to its maker and to the bold
expeditioners of 1924. They were indeed men in those days.

Dubbed by Bruce 'St Noel of the Cameras', and with no professional

John Cleare (camera) and John Peacock (actor) at work on the Zermatt
Breithorn filming BBC's *Last Blue Mountain*, March 1970. 16mm silent Arriflex
with a 400 foot magazine. *(John Cleare / Mountain Camera Picture Library)*

help, Noel had trained up two dedicated and extremely efficient Sherpa
assistants. His equipment included 14 cameras, both movie and still, his
work-horse being a Newman Sinclair 'Auto-kiné' which while normally
clockwork operated, used an electric motor for time-lapse shots. Essentially
an 18 x 12 inches polished duralumin box, padded with non-freeze rubber,
the Auto-kiné weighed nearly 20 lbs loaded with 400 feet of panchromatic
35mm film, which running at 16 frames per second was just enough for
six minutes shooting – all being well – before the precise yet fiddly process
of reloading became necessary, probably with numb fingers. The nitrate-
based film stock itself was fragile and in low temperatures would snap
under even slight stress.

Then there were various lenses and filters for each, both yellow and red,
to accentuate clouds and diminish the extreme UV content of high altitude
light. Noel's special lens was a 20 inch (500mm) Cooke telephoto with
a clip-on, six-power telescopic viewfinder synchronised with the optical
axis of the lens, a crucial lens for the distances at which he was forced to
work. The camera demanded a sturdy tripod, itself weighing at least 20
lbs. Cameras would gather the ubiquitous Tibetan dust blowing below the
snow-line, while lenses would fog with sudden changes of temperature,
such as struggling from the open air into a warm tent. To shoot anything at
all required a major physical effort besides mental stamina and dedicated
artistic and technical application.

Leo Dickinson at work with his Sony Digital Betacam on Everest's North Col in 1995. It was revolutionary to be able to view the rushes instantly.
(Leo Dickinson / Mountain Camera Picture Library)

Much of the 1924 action footage is concentrated on the steep face of the North Col, to observe which Noel established a camera platform – his 'eyrie' – on the craggy slopes above Camp III from where he could follow the action with his telephoto lens from a distance of a mile and half.

It is fascinating to compare the daunting problems which Noel overcame with those we faced filming on Everest almost 50 years later. The International Expedition of 1971 had two objectives: firstly, to make the first ascents of the South Face and of the West Ridge Integral; secondly, to film them. Cinematography had developed out of all recognition by then – Noel had worked of course in black/white, a process in which the cameraman must visualise his subject in terms of shape and texture, translating rather than copying nature, while we would be working entirely in colour, and the BBC hoped (against hope) that we would shoot 'sync' sound from Kathmandu all the way to the summit. Now we had an all professional camera team of seven, of which two cameramen and a sound man were experienced climbers technically capable of reaching the top, and we had dedicated sherpas to assist us.

Our main cameras, by now all 16mm, were three shoulder-balanced, sync-sound Éclairs, each weighing some 13 lbs with a loaded 400 foot magazine and carried in a neat, sherpa-able back-pack that we'd designed, and two Arriflexes, rugged, smaller, slightly lighter and designed in Germany in WW2 as a combat camera, again using a 400 foot magazine allowing just over ten minutes of shooting. Both were powered by batteries, each weighing a further 3lbs or so and giving a very limited run in cold conditions. We also had a couple of small Canon Scoopics, a brilliant and revolutionary camera with a fitted 6:1 zoom lens, weighting around 6lbs, similar to an amateur Super-8 though frustratingly using only 100 foot / 2½ minute film rolls. Crucial back-up was provided by two small, go-anywhere, unbreakable clockwork Bell & Howell 16mm 70 DLs, also taking 100ft loads, and a couple of tiny clockwork B & H Autoloads with 50ft magazines.

Although technically our gear was light-years in advance of 1924, the basic principles were the same: our equipment was still heavy and awkward to climb with at altitude when every ounce feels like a pound, but at least our cameras were ergonomically designed, well balanced and we could frequently dispense with the tripods which had hardly changed from Noel's day, still weighing well over 20lbs when fitted with a decent precision head. Although in theory each 100 feet of film gave about 2½ minutes shooting time, our cameras had to be started at slow speed to avoid film snapping in the cold, and were bastards to reload with numb fingers or in driving snow. During an alpine winter shake-down session we'd discovered that when reloading, valuable feet of every hundred foot film roll were fogged by glacial glare, and at the higher Himalayan altitudes I had to reload actually inside a specially designed 'changing bag' which covered both camera and me down to waist-level.

Solar cells were still in the future, and all discharged camera batteries were carried by runner to Lukla and flown to Kathmandu for recharging, a major drain on logistical resources. Exposed film, both still and movie, was periodically flown to London and reports cabled back to Nepal. Patience and persistence were essential.

Life was still tough enough three year later, when I found myself driving a 70mm Super Panavision camera on the Eiger with Clint Eastwood. Both technically and creatively it was a joy to use, a Rolls Royce among cameras; there were LCD readouts in the viewfinder for the controls and the two separate power sources, one of them solely to maintain the camera at the correct operating temperature. But not surprisingly it was large and very heavy and I suffered a hernia hauling one up the Difficult Crack on jumars.

Fast-forward another 40 years. Although Imax had reached the summit of Everest using 65mm film and vast resources in '96, the digital revolution was already happening. By the mid-80s video sound cameras had appeared with many feet of tape replacing film and creating new problems.

Leo Dickinson filmed on Everest's North Col in 1995 using the Sony Digital Betacam which was state of the art, weighed under 5 kgs, ran for 40 minutes per loading and recorded synch sound. Images contained 2k pixels – by 2012 much smaller cameras contained four times as many. Leo recalls that it was revolutionary to be able to play back the rushes instantly, one less headache at high altitude.

State of the art 2013 – but for how long? Alastair Lee with one of his two Canon EOS C300 digital cinema cameras in Queen Maud Land, Antarctica. See also page 137. *(Alastair Lee)*

By the early 2000s solid state 'flash drives' or memory cards had replaced tape, minimising moving parts. Indeed, technology is advancing so fast that there are many different cameras to choose from, each liable to be obsolete within a year or two. Typically they'll weight 6 or 7 lbs in running order, while the cameraman can expect to shoot sync-sound for a couple of hours before reloading. In fact broadcast quality movie (though the BBC are reluctant to acknowledge it) can even be shot on what is essentially a DSLR stills camera weighing little more than a couple of pounds, accepting a wide range of lenses and allowing about 30 minutes recording on a 4GB card: viewfinding and focusing can present problems in the movie mode and naturally it eats batteries, but solar cells can provide on-location recharging.

Truly go-anywhere filming may be easy these days, but however sophisticated the equipment, it is still the man or woman behind the camera who creates the pictures.

The Epic of Everest - The official record of Mallory and Irvine's 1924 Expedition, (87 mins).
A film by Captain John Noel, restoration by the British Film Institute. Available from **bfi.org.uk/shop**

TERRY GIFFORD

Painting Rock

A review of Julian Cooper's exhibition, **Natural Forces,** *at the Art Space Gallery, London, 14 March – 11 April 2014*

Mountain landscapes are the family's traditional subjects, but Julian Cooper's subject is now firmly, but not necessarily finally, established as rock. That Julian can still paint mountains was eloquently evident in the Alpine Club show that ran concurrently with his latest major show at the Art Space Gallery. At the AC a fascinating fugue of mountain portraits was played across peaks ascended by AC members that demonstrated an 'order in variety' of Alpine forms as much as the underlying unity of vision and technique in the voice of the artist.

In the Art Space show there were mostly large paintings from three locations of very different rock qualities in colours, forms, weathers and processes of change at work before our eyes. Yet all zoomed in on the essential drama taking place. This is Julian's preferred word for his subject: 'I'm struck by the wordless drama going on in these rock forms, such intense tension but also coherence. Perhaps an example of a subject for which painting can be the best medium.' What exactly does this mean? In the painting 'Cave Michaelangelo' the spiral stepped structure left by the quarrying of blocks of white marble at Carrara gives the immediate impression of vast industrial control. Here is the result of plundering perfect marble for the making of art since before Roman times. Green grass can only reclaim a hem at the bottom of the canvas. But through it leads a thin path to a cave of darkness. This could be the painting's subject and purpose – the cave of the imagination, the unknown underworld, the Freudian source or the Earth's source, Plato's Cave on the walls of which the shadows of reality were perceived as reality itself. But for the length of the left edge of the painting there falls a blur of dust: uncertainty undermining order, danger in industrial complacency, rockfall challenging artful structure and the artist himself perhaps – his imaginative enterprise up against material natural forces still alive and dangerous.

This drama of living rock is also caught in the rich ochre mineral mines of Tasmania where the lip of the quarry would give way from time to time as the artist was working on these brightly coloured, whitely lit, strongly painted canvases. The titles reveal the paradoxes: 'Philosophers' Ridge', 'Undermining'. As always in this work it is the vigour of the brush strokes and the plays with perspective in foregrounding/backgrounding, overhang/ undercut and crack/wall that justify the claim for paint as the medium for exploring the drama of rock.

Rock Steps 2, oil on canvas 116x76cm. *(Julian Cooper)*

But it is the new discoveries in the Lake District that provide the most subtle claims for the medium. In giving large-scale attention to the smallest of outcrops above the Naddle Beck, below and south of Castle Rigg stone circle, Julian has been trying, in his words, to 'get more out of less', painting the same outcrop in different lights and seasons (there are three pairs of paintings in this show) and deploying a greater range of effects in one canvas: 'I have more balls in the air, more techniques available in one canvas than before'. Now, in Julian's paintings we have sky – weather, even – and a tree rooted down into a crack that splits lit rock steps. *Rock Steps 1* is a stalking of light, 'skittering off rock and hitting a tree stem above momentarily', as Julian puts it. At the same time – and time, geological, evolutionary and immediate, might be a theme of this show – one is not sure whether this is a crack that sprouts a tree, or a tree that makes a crack. Again, the crack holds the darkness of mystery, the ancient interlocking of growth and decay.

Low Rigg 1, oil on canvas, 172x157cm. *(Julian Cooper)*

But it is *Low Rig 1* that is most breathtaking in revealing the painter's juggling and Michael Richardson cleverly placed it opposite the entrance to the gallery to maximum effect. The variety of brushwork in this large canvas suggests the full range of processes this small outcrop is undergoing: a thinly worked wash of running paint below overhangs of finely striated planes that catch the light, rough shadowed walls, gleaming wet rounded rocks, walled by blocks of lichened yellows and damp browns. The backdrop is a simple sky of speechless cobalt blue. Out of a dark central crack a thin silver tree manages an astonishingly healthy burst of spring greens. I felt I was in the presence of new textures, new combinations, new insights. As in several of these paintings, the artist's guidelines had been left visible, as if to remind the viewer that it is a painting after all; the thoughtfully worked shadows on the cave wall actually reveal the richly complex and simple natural forces and living processes that we call 'rock'.

History

Gervasutti Pillar, acrylic on canvas, 51x61cm. *(Tim Pollard)*

PETER FOSTER & GARETH JONES

The Brenva Feud

Graham Brown vs Frank Smythe

The Brenva face of Mont Blanc by Basil Goodfellow.
(Alpine Club Photo Library)

'Smythe is a great man!' wrote Graham Brown in September 1927 after their successful ascent of the Sentinelle route, the first to be made on the Brenva Face of Mont Blanc.[1] The following year they climbed the Route Major, another new route on the face. These climbs were amongst the leading achievements of British mountaineers in the Alps between the Wars. But they never climbed together again and twenty-two years later Graham Brown would write to Smythe, saying: 'I hope you perish'[2]. Soon

Left: Frank Smythe, Everest expedition, 1933.
(© *Royal Geographical Society*)

Below: T Graham Brown studying the Promontoire Hut logbook before traversing the Meije, 1933.
(*Basil Goodfellow, Alpine Club Photo Library*)

after, Smythe left on a trip to India where he contracted cerebral malaria from which he died some weeks later. What occurred to rupture their partnership and fuel such rancour?

In August 1927, Graham Brown, 45, professor of physiology, recently distinguished by election to the fellowship of the Royal Society and in possession of a mountaineering dream, met Smythe, twenty years younger, discharged earlier in the year from the RAF as medically unfit, with a reputation to make and career to establish. Both men were at Montenvers and without climbing partners. Graham Brown's alpine experience was limited to standard routes, mainly with guides, whereas Smythe was already an accomplished alpinist who climbed without guides, but they agreed to join forces. Graham Brown had a burning desire to fulfil his dream of making a new route on Mont Blanc via the Brenva face, which he had cherished since his time on the Salonika front during the First World War. For Smythe, a new route on Mont Blanc would provide a noteworthy climax to the book which he was planning to write based on his own exploits.

When they set out for the Brenva face, on 31 August, Graham Brown had the line of the Route Major in mind but Smythe, who had climbed the

Brenva spur some weeks earlier, was concerned about the risk of crossing the Great Couloir and the uncertainty of finding a way through the seracs above the final buttress and rejected it. Instead, they climbed the Sentinelle, the line of which Graham Brown had put forward as a via media, between the Route Major and Smythe's suggestion of the rock and snow rib, to the left of the Brenva Spur.

Smythe led the climb from their bivouac beneath the conspicuous red buttress which they named the Red Sentinel. Graham Brown wrote frankly concerning his ability to have led the climb, referring to himself as 'too much of a rabbit at the game for that.'[3] They celebrated their success with vintage wine and champagne in sufficient quantity that Graham Brown could not remember all the details of the latter part of the evening! During the succeeding months they maintained friendly relations but there were signs of the mutual antipathy that would fuel their later feud. They disagreed over the writing-up of their new route – Graham Brown proposed joint authorship but Smythe felt their styles were incompatible. Privately, Smythe was critical of Graham Brown's climbing abilities although he was more generous publicly, and wrote that 'the thought of a slip on the part of Graham Brown never entered my head.'[4] Smythe's light-hearted signing-off to a letter to Graham Brown reveals the undercurrent of feelings: 'Looking forward to our next scrap. My turn to draw blood next time.'[5]

On 6 and 7 August 1928 they climbed the Route Major. Although the cause of their subsequent feud was rooted in their personalities, it was the events that occurred on this route which provided the casus belli. But establishing what actually happened is problematical, since it was exactly these details that were the subject of their feud and each man made claims and counter-claims to support his version of events. Smythe was first into print with an article for *The Times* on 18 August in which, oddly, he completely omitted to name Graham Brown, referring to him anonymously, as 'a friend'. His subsequent, impressionistic account was also aimed at a general audience and appeared months later in Blackwood's Magazine. However, Graham Brown wrote a detailed letter to his friend and fellow Alpine Club member Professor Gask just two days after the ascent which, having the advantage of immediacy and antedating any public discord, provides the most reliable source. The extracts quoted below are taken from this letter.[6]

The approach to the bivouac site beneath the Red Sentinel involved crossing a series of snow couloirs which proved more difficult than the previous year and caused Graham Brown some anxiety:

'. . . the avalanche run in the second couloir after passing over 'Moore's Col' was nearly impassable. It was about thirteen-and-a-half feet deep and the whole of the near side overhung. I let Smythe down into it on the rope. He cut the few steps across it and then up the other side. He then climbed well up on the other side and I had one of the worst ordeals of my life before me. He kept the rope tight and I lowered myself as best I could over the edge and then dropped onto the ice – 6 or 7 feet – which fortunately was somewhat melted. I then hung by the rope on it until I could cut a step and so get up to Smythe's steps – then it was all over.'

They quit their bivouac just before 5am the following morning. Smythe led across the Great Couloir without incident and they climbed up over rocks and a series of snow and ice arêtes. The top of the upper ice ridge:

'. . . was exceedingly steep and involved a good deal of step cutting . . . Smythe cut the steps. . . the cutting must have occupied at least 45 minutes . . . (He cuts for long strides and then I come along cutting intermediate steps for my shorter legs! We were climbing in crampons).'

They reached the foot of the final buttress beneath the wall of seracs at 13.40. Their progress had been slow. They were carrying heavy loads but crucially they found it necessary to move one at a time for long stretches. The key to climbing the buttress appeared to be a short corner:

'. . . Smythe again cut across . . . into the corner which terminated in a 12-foot chimney. I came across to him (cutting additional steps in the brittle ice – I have never met anything like it before). Smythe tried the chimney and failed. I tried the chimney and failed. We thought this was the only way up and that the position was desperate. Smythe talked about retreat or an attempt to descend to the Great Couloir (under the seracs!) and gain the Sentinel route – I offered him a shoulder (in crampons!) he tried again and failed – coming down heavily on me and tearing my windjacket. He then gave me his shoulder, and I failed. . . I then suggested cutting round the descending rock rib . . . and did so.'

Smythe followed. Above, the lead changed hands as they prospected the route to the top of the buttress. Smythe led through the seracs which fortunately proved relatively straightforward. On the summit slopes they encountered strong winds which, according to Smythe, 'sent us staggering'[7] and Graham Brown wrote:

'. . . the gusts were terrific and I was blown over two or three times – and Smythe twice.'

They finally arrived at the summit of Mont Blanc at 20.20, fifteen hours after setting out from their bivouac. These, then, are the bare facts of the expedition. In a matter of weeks the opening shots of the feud were fired.

Smythe sent a letter to Graham Brown which was inflammatory in content and vitriolic in tone. Amongst other things, he accused Graham Brown of spreading lies, in particular, that Smythe had wanted to turn back on the climb and that it was Graham Brown's 'example and leadership [which] saved the situation'. Smythe countered:

'That I suggested retreat at any point on the climb is utterly untrue. . . [and] you have . . . had the honour of being taken up two of the greatest climbs in the Alps – an honour which would not have occurred had you not met me . . .'[8]

Was Smythe traduced by Graham Brown or did he have something to hide? According to T S Blakeney, a friend of Smythe's who had joined him and Graham Brown for an attempt on Route Major some days before the successful ascent, Smythe had a premonition of death in 1928 and consequently was in a 'funny mood'[10]. He was 'highly-strung' and prone to tantrums; additionally, he almost certainly had doubts about Graham Brown's competence and hence their safety. He was probably severely shaken after what was an uncontrolled slither from the corner onto Graham Brown's back, which could have knocked both of them from the stance and precipitated them to their deaths. Despite his repeated denials, Smythe had considered the possibility of retreat.[9] It would have been lengthy and risky. But Smythe had extricated himself from difficulties on big mountains before. Only the previous year, he and Macphee had retreated from the Peutery ridge, in appalling weather,

T Graham Brown at the cornice on the Red Sentinel route, Mont Blanc, 1927. *(Frank Smythe)*

by descending from the Col de Peuterey via the Rochers Gruber. (Forty years later the incomparable Walter Bonatti would be stretched to his limit over the same ground – albeit after enduring a storm lasting several days on the Freney Pillar above.) For Smythe, given their predicament after failing to climb the corner and the uncertainties of what lay ahead, retreat may simply have seemed the correct mountaineering decision but Graham Brown's remarks also carried the implication that he had lost his nerve. That Smythe argued the case for retreat vehemently and, faced with Graham Brown's obstinacy, even 'hysterically', as Graham Brown alleged later, is credible.

Smythe would never accept that Graham Brown had made a significant contribution to their success and years later would describe Graham Brown as 'virtually a passenger'[11] on the climb. But Graham Brown's two attempts to climb the corner were not the actions of a passive second and in dismissing his lead down and around the rock rib as 'some half-dozen steps'[12], Smythe did Graham Brown an injustice. Graham Brown downclimbed, cutting steps for 50 – 60ft to the toe of the rib, then led around its base and up the far side. The ice was steep, the exposure great and the belay precarious. This passage was committing and decisive.

In September 1932 Graham Brown learned for the first time that Smythe

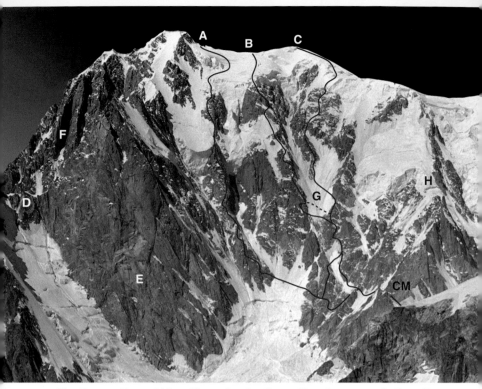

The Brenva Face of Mont Blanc showing Brown/Smythe routes: **A.** Pear Route (1933), **B.** Route Major (1928), **C.** Red Sentinel (1927), **D.** Col de Peuterey, **E.** Eckpfeiler Buttress, **F.** Freney Pillars, **G.** Great Couloir, **H.** Old Brenva Ridge, **CM.** Col Moore. *(John Cleare / Mountain Camera Picture Library)*

had recounted a story about Graham Brown having fallen on the Route Major and that he had saved his life. Graham Brown was flabbergasted and pressed his friend Col. E.L. Strutt, editor of the Alpine Journal, for detail:

'Yes I do remember S[mythe] saying you fell off and both of you fell 100ft. before the rope hitched. . . . S[mythe] told me such a lot of b.lls that I was bored to death and paid little attention.'[13]

It seems Strutt kept the tale to himself and Smythe did not circulate it widely although within months of their ascent of the Route Major, he had written to Geoffrey Winthrop Young describing his version of what had occurred on the ridge leading to the summit of Mont Blanc de Courmayeur:

'. . . when 10[ft.] up he came off, fell past me and flew off down the hard ice slope . . . I had no belay at all, and it was only a miracle that saved us. I managed to take in the rope as he slid down the rocks and somehow got it round a knob as big as my thumb. The fall was so bad that a wisp of rope was left on the knob but the rope (a Beale) held. For this I got not a word of thanks in apology though I flatter myself that it was the quickest bit of work I've ever done in my life . . .'[14]

Graham Brown flatly denied the story and it seems incredible that such a dramatic incident would have escaped reference in either man's accounts.

Did Smythe embellish events to discredit Graham Brown for his own advantage? Graham Brown certainly thought so. The gloves were now off and he chose his moment to retaliate.

On Christmas Eve 1932, he wrote to Smythe, with a distinct lack of seasonal cheer:

'You cannot have forgotten the scene you made at the ice-run on our 1928 Brenva ascent, and how you screamed as I lowered you down on the rope. You cannot have forgotten how you screamed in the corner when we tried to climb on that route, and then fell on me in crampons; nor how you behaved after that, and wished to give up the climb. You cannot have forgotten many other similar incidents.'[15]

Smythe replied:

'. . . Your letter contains statements about me which are untrue and which are merely intended to wound. It takes two to make a quarrel, but I am perfectly prepared to admit that my original letter began it.'[16]

And then continued by revisiting the details of the climb, inaccurately attributing the leading of the pitch down and around the rock rib to himself. But recognising that he and Graham Brown were going to serve together on the committee of the Alpine Club, offered an olive branch, saying that he was prepared to meet Graham Brown 'on the friendliest possible footing.'

Graham Brown was implacable. He made insulting and derogatory remarks about Smythe in his journals and notebooks, which may have been for his eyes only, and in private letters. Publicly, he dismissed the achievements of Smythe and his expedition on Kamet as 'a mere record'[17] and when Smythe's selection for the proposed expedition to Everest in 1933 became known, Graham Brown set out to discredit him. Over lunch at the Athenaeum, he told Hugh Ruttledge, the appointed leader, that:

'. . . I regarded Smythe as a fraud. . . I said he funked . . . I said he would probably have no 'guts' at high elevation. . . I told him that Smythe told lies . . .'[18]

and noted self-righteously:

'I must say that the fact that the leader of the Everest expedition has been properly warned of the possible danger which Smythe may be to the expedition is a great relief to me. I have always been afraid for my own conscience should there be a disaster; and now feel acquitted of any personal responsibility'[19]

In the early drafts of his book Brenva, eventually published in 1944, Graham Brown subjected Smythe's accounts of their climbs to forensic examination. The interventions of friends, his publisher and eventually Smythe's solicitor resulted in excisions and a moderation of tone but still Smythe felt slighted and maintained in letters that he had led 90% of the Route Major and that Graham Brown had been a passenger. At the end of 1948 Smythe sent a Christmas card to Graham Brown; just over six months later Smythe was dead.

Smythe, temperamental and quick to take offence, had, in an attempt to protect his reputation, unwisely ignited the feud. Each time he tried to justify himself, his version of events became more contradictory and exacerbated matters. But over the years, Smythe made numerous apologies for his part in their feud and repeatedly asked to restore friendly relations. Graham Brown was unwavering. What was at the root of his implacability? He was naturally combative; his obituarist, Lord Adrian, described him as 'a formidable opponent' who 'did not always conceal his pleasure in the fight and the victory'[20]. Graham Brown had a highly developed sense of self-esteem. He caused difficulties for Bill Tilman and James Waller over their respective accounts of the expeditions to Nanda Devi and Masherbrum because he felt his contribution had not received sufficient recognition. Although capable of friendship he did not hesitate to sever relations if he considered himself wronged and forgiveness did not come easily to him but eventually he relented, except in the case of Smythe, who, in his view, had feet of clay. As he observed Smythe's ascent to celebrity, he could not forget that Smythe had wanted to retreat from high up on the Route Major and that their success on the climb, which was the spring-board for Smythe's later achievements and fame, was due to him.

Acknowledgements: The authors would like to thank the Alpine Club and National Library of Scotland for permission to reproduce quotations from material in their possession.

References

1. TGB to Gask; 4/9/27; Alpine Club (A.C.) archives: Tracts T442
2. Thompson, S. *Unjustifiable Risk*; Cicerone 2010 page 161
3. TGB to Gask; 4/9/27; A.C. archives: Tracts T442
4. Smythe F.S. The Red Sentinel of Mont Blanc; *Blackwood's Magazine* 1928 224: 1-23
5. FSS to TGB 13/2/28; National Library of Scotland (N.L.S) Acc 4338/164
6. TGB to G. Gask 9/8/28; A.C. archives: Tracts T442
7. Smythe F, *Climbs & Ski Runs*; 1930 Blackwood p 297
8. FSS to TGB 12/9/28; N.L.S. Acc 4338/164
9. Smythe F, *Climbs & Ski Runs*; 1930 Blackwood p 285
10. T.S. Blakeney to A. Lunn 11/8/49; Arnold Lunn papers, Georgetown University, Washington Box1/folder57
11. T.S. Blakeney to Nona Smythe 24/10/50; A.C. archives 1922/B63
12. Smythe F, A New route up Mont Blanc without guides; *Blackwood's Magazine* 1928 224: 719-742
13. Strutt to TGB 25/9/32; N.L.S. Acc 4338/164
14. FSS to Geoffrey Winthrop Young (undated) A.C Archives 1922/B46
15. TGB to FSS 24/12/32; N.L.S. Acc 4338/164
16. FSS to TGB 28/12/32; N.L.S. Acc 4338/164
17. Graham Brown, T. The Alpine Club: 1920-32; *AJ* **45**: 120-32
18. Graham Brown T, Notes of Conversations at the Athenaeum and Alpine Club; N.L.S Acc 4338/191 (7)
19. Ibid
20. Adrian ED, Thomas Graham Brown 1882 – 1965; *Biogr. Mem. Fellows R. Soc* 1966 12: 22-33

DENNIS GRAY

The Pocket Hercules

A Portrait of Leo Amery

Leo Amery. *(Alpine Club Photo Library)*

'Swift as the wind my pursuer overtook me, seized me in a ferocious grip and hurled me into the deepest part of the pool. My fellow form members then advised me, 'It's Amery. He is head of his house; he is champion at gym, he has got his football colours'. 'A being of enormous strength.'

Winston Churchill. *My Early Life* (p 18).

This incident occurred at Harrow School where Churchill and Leo Amery were contemporaries in the 1890s. Winston had had the temerity to push the unsuspecting Leo into the swimming pool and Amery

231

delivered swift retribution.

There was a keen interest in mountaineering at Harrow in the late 19th Century, and Edward Whymper had given a lantern slide lecture at the school which inspired both Amery and Churchill. In 1894, during his time at Sandhurst, Churchill visited Switzerland and with Christian Kauffman as guide climbed the Wetterhorn and Monte Rosa. He wrote about his experiences to his former headmaster at Harrow, J E C Welldon, in enthusiastic terms. Welldon duly responded: 'You have got the figure of a mountaineer, and you ought to make yourself a name.' Although Churchill did that in many other fields, he never returned to the sport – though he remained fascinated by mountain scenery all his life.

Leo Amery's introduction was to be on an entirely different plane. Besides being the outstanding scholar in the school, Amery was keen on boxing and cross-country running and was the top gymnast. His nickname was 'The Pocket Hercules' – short in stature but renowned for his strength. At Christmas/New Year 1891/92 R C Gilson, a teacher at the school, took Amery to Wasdale Head and introduced him to rock climbing. His first route was Deep Ghyll, followed by some easier routes on Pillar Rock. At Wasdale O G Jones invited Amery to accompany him in an attempt on *Oblique Chimney* on the Ennerdale face of Great Gable. It turned out to be a baptism of fire – they started late, the crag was plastered with ice and coated with fresh snow. Traversing the slopes at the foot of the face to reach the chimney, Amery slipped and fell, cutting his hand badly. It was bitterly cold and already growing dark when they began to climb. As Amery recalls in the first volume of his autobiography, *Days of Fresh Air* :

'At last we found our gully, a slanting cleft, 20 feet deep perhaps, in a great bulging overhang of the cliff. We clambered up into the heart of this and then Glynne Jones, placing his feet on one side and back on the other, began with amazing skill to wriggle himself ever upwards and outwards for the best part of, I suppose 100 feet. At the end of which a powerful kick and straddle enabled him to transfer himself to face the rock on one side of the chimney and climb out of it'.

They finally reached the summit in darkness and a blizzard and, misreading the compass, came down via Windy Gap and Sty Head with an icy descent.

'How we managed to avoid broken limbs has ever been a mystery.'

Such an outing would have put most off a climbing career, but not Amery.

Leo Amery was born in Gorakhpur, British India, where his father worked for the Indian Forest Department. His mother was Hungarian and he was bilingual in English and Hindi by the age of three – perhaps this explains his amazing facility at languages in later life, speaking French, German, Italian, Bulgarian, Turkish, Serbian, Hungarian, and Arabic whilst still at Oxford. He left Harrow in 1892, loaded with prizes and three scholarships. He needed the latter, his father having abandoned his family, leaving for America with a mistress, never to be heard from again. From then on money was a serious problem.

He entered Balliol College, Oxford in the autumn of 1892 to read Classics and finished with a first in 'Mods' and 'Greats'. He continued cross-country running, rock climbing and boxing, on the latter commenting: 'My chief merit being unlimited wind, indifference to blows, and a very strong punch when my short arms did eventually reach.' He certainly lived up to his 'Pocket Hercules' sobriquet: with several pugilistic highlights in his life he remains the only member of the Privy Council to floor a fellow MP in the House of Commons over a point of honour.

Amery, right, with David Lloyd George at Criccieth during WW1. *(From In The Rain and The Sun)*

Amery's first alpine season was in 1894, climbing the Rothorn, Weisshorn, Dent Blanche and Matterhorn. The following season found him in the Göschener Alpen, ascending several summits and making a high level traverse of a part of the range. Thereafter he climbed at nearly every possible opportunity up to the Great War, visiting Zermatt, Arolla, the Dolomites, the Drakensberg, Canada, New Zealand and the North Albanian Alps, climbing such classics as the Zmutt Ridge on the Matterhorn, the Cima Grande, the Gletschorn, Aiguille de la Za, the Vajolet Towers and others too numerous to mention. He took up skiing in 1904 at Montana and eventually became President of the Ski Club of Great Britain.

In Albania he caused a minor 'international' incident when an official sent by the King to where he was staying took a dislike to Amery for some reason and started physically pushing him about. Inevitably Leo responded, sending the guy on his way with a large lump on his head, the result of a blow via an umbrella.

Such were Amery's diplomatic, political and linguistic skills that he managed to extract an official apology for the bad behaviour of the bureaucrat!

In 1907 Amery was invited by Tom Longstaff to join the first planned expedition to Everest. The India Office opposed the expedition and although the party eventually climbed Trisul, by then Amery was unable to take part.

After Balliol, Amery became a Fellow of Old Souls, but moved on to journalism, first with the *Manchester Guardian*, and then the *Times*, making his name (like Churchill) in the second Boer War (1899 – 1902). He made such a good impression that he was offered the editorship of the *Observer* in 1908, and the *Times* in 1912, though he refused them both, having decided that his future lay in politics.

Leo Amery in the Dachstein in 1937. *(From Days of Fresh Air)*

Amery still found time for some climbing, and in 1909 he was back in Canada for an attempt on Mount Robson. Whilst there he made friends with A O Wheeler, the 1906 founder of the Alpine Club of Canada and one of the leading authorities on the mountains of that country. Amery's future wife Bryddie was a Canadian, daughter of an eminent lawyer.

Back home it took Amery some time to break into the political hierarchy. He joined the Conservative Party and stood as candidate for a Wolverhampton constituency at the General Election of 1906. Here again Amery's robust character came to the fore. At election meetings a local councillor and businessman would regularly heckle him, eventually calling out for all to hear that Amery was a liar. This was too much for Leo – instead of resorting to legal action he visited the man's office next morning. Bursting in, to the amazement of the businessman's secretary, he demanded an apology and, when the man refused Amery, in his own words, 'boxed his ears soundly'. This led to a summons for assault and he was fined two Guineas and costs in the Magistrate's Court. When this was reported in the local paper, a collection was raised which not only covered the fines, but also paid for a gold watch and chain for Amery to remember the event by. I guess the councillor must have been unpopular!

In May 1911 he finally managed to get elected as MP for Birmingham South, which later became the Sparkbrook constituency, a seat he would hold until 1945.

Leo took off for the Dolomites again in 1912, climbing on the Punta Fiammes, the Cinque Torre, Croda da Lago, Tofana and Vajolet Towers, ascending the Winkler, Stabeler and Delago in turn.

During the Great War Amery served as an intelligence officer, returning in 1917 to become a political secretary to the War Cabinet. He was author of the final draft of the Balfour Declaration, which committed Britain to establishing a 'Jewish National Home' in Palestine. He became First Lord of The Admiralty in 1922 and Secretary of State for The Colonies and Dominions in 1924, which included the Palestine mandate. Amery was immensely significant in bringing about the Zionist enterprise which eventually led to the setting up of the State of Israel.

Amery lost his Cabinet seat when the Conservatives were defeated at the 1929 General Election, but found some solace in another trip to Canada where, with the Swiss guide Ed Feuz and Brian Meridith, he made the first ascent of what was to become Mount Amery (3329m) on 20 August.

Out of government during the 1930s Amery held many directorships, a necessity as he had no independent means. Several of these directorships were on the boards of German metal fabrication companies. During his time in Germany he had a lengthy meeting with Hitler, and gained a good understanding of German military potential. Along with Churchill and a few others he began to warn about the danger this might present in the future to Britain and her allies. Amery also met Mussolini, believed that Italy could be prised away from the German axis, but became convinced that confrontation with these fascist dictators was inevitable.

Amery was in Germany on business in 1938 and, despite the gathering war clouds, included a visit to the Julian Alps where, at the age of 64, he managed climbs such as the Slovene Route on the North Face of Triglav, and Kugy's Route on the North Face of Skrlatica.

Amery was a prominent backbencher at this time but as the conflict situation developed he came more and more to the fore. He is most famous as a Parliamentarian for two moments of high drama in the House of Commons. At the fall of Poland in 1939 when Chamberlain reported that he was not declaring war on Germany immediately, Amery called on Arthur Greenwood, who had stood to speak for the Labour opposition, to 'Speak for England'. This was to be the title of a biography of Amery and his two sons, John and Julian, by David Faber in 2005. The second occurred during the notorious Norway debate in 1940. After a string of military and naval disasters were announced, Amery attacked Chamberlain's government, quoting Oliver Cromwell:

'You have sat too long here for any good you have been doing. Depart, I say, and let us have done with you. In the name of God, go!'

This debate led to the downfall of the Conservative administration and the formation of a National Government under Churchill.

During the war Amery was Secretary of State for India. In some ways this was a surprise appointment for, although he spoke Hindi fluently, he had been in keen dispute with Churchill for years about Indian Independence, which the latter opposed. Amery declared that Churchill knew as much about the Indian problem as George III did of the American colonies! When Churchill was appointed Chancellor of the Exchequer in 1926, Amery publicly declared 'he would be a disaster', and history shows this may have been the case! Given these observations his long-term relationship with Churchill was remarkable. Somehow they stayed friends and even as late as 1945 the latter wrote to Amery in very warm terms whilst he was President of the Alpine Club.

Amery became Alpine Club President in 1944, following Geoffrey Winthrop Young. He wrote to Tom Longstaff on 15 November 1943 at his nomination: 'I have always thought the Prime Minister-ship and the Presidency of the AC as the two highest honours attainable.'

Leo Amery's private papers are held in the archives at Churchill College Cambridge, and amongst them are bulky files of personal letters, which are in some cases amusing and others shocking to read. Before Leo had even been elected AC President, the indomitable Colonel Edward Strutt had written to warn him that the Committee was made up of both sound and dangerous members! Amongst the latter were the Secretary, Donkin, a Vice President, Bartrum, along with Warren and MacPhee.

Amery was prominent in the machinations to form the BMC in 1944, which was very much an Alpine Club initiative. Although Geoffrey Winthrop Young is now credited with being the Council's main originator, the papers at Cambridge show that it was also the work of several other AC figures, including Barford, Donkin and Amery. It seems in mountaineering politics that nothing ever runs smoothly, and some prominent AC members were unhappy about the way the BMC had been formed and its objectives and felt that the Alpine Club should have taken on the role of the national voice for British climbing. Eleven members supported this in a letter to Amery, and inevitably Colonel Strutt was involved. Eaton and Unna put a motion of censure to an AC Meeting on 10 April 1945 to that effect, but were roundly defeated as the meeting overwhelmingly supported Amery and the Committee in its actions.

With the war coming to an end and a successful conclusion in sight, the Alpine Club started planning for a further attempt on Mount Everest in 1947. Of course Amery was in a special position to try to obtain permission for this and in 1945 he started writing to Wavell, Viceroy of India, outlining the Club's plans for a small, lightweight expedition to be led by Eric Shipton. Unfortunately the plans were stymied when, after making discreet enquiries, Wavell advised,

'The idea of making an attempt on Everest through Tibet in 1947 will have to be abandoned. The Religious authorities there are busy working out the young Dalai Lama's horoscope, and they are not willing for the spirits to be disturbed on any of their mountains at that time.'

It is interesting to note that for Amery and his colleagues, Shipton was the mountaineer that they identified so keenly with Mount Everest. After the mountain was climbed in 1953 they felt that despite the fact he was not on the successful expedition, he should be knighted for the part he had played in exploring the way to the summit. Overtures were made behind the scenes as to the possibility of such an award, but to no avail.

Two letters to Amery from R W Lloyd (a former AC Vice President) indicate how class-ridden the Club was at that time. The first reads: 'It was a great mistake to elect that shopkeeper G D Abraham as an Hon Member, after always refusing to admit him to the Club as an ordinary member.'

The second letter, regarding the proposed membership of Richard Cook, a Turf Accountant, reads as follows: 'I think it would be a great pity to have people like that going about as Alpine Club members. Remember we are a social club, not a climbing club.'

Amery disagreed in both cases and wrote back diplomatically, but firmly supporting the decision of the Committee for taking such action. Amongst the more amusing letters in Amery's files is the idea for a pressurized suit to be developed, rather like a deep-sea diver, to avoid the need to carry oxygen up the slopes of Mount Everest. And a wonderful letter from Frank Smythe in December 1947, advising

Leo Amery in the New Zealand Alps, 1927. *(From Days of Fresh Air)*

Amery about how to keep fit, '. . . apart from climbing and walking the only exercise I've ever regularly practised is deep breathing and you ought to practise that'.

In retrospect it is surprising that Amery could be so focussed as the AC President, as in his personal life a major tragedy had developed due to the activities of his eldest son John. Their relationship is now the subject of a fine play by the Oscar winning playwright, Ronald Harwood, *An English Tragedy* (2008). John Amery had a troubled early life both at school and then trying to pursue a career as a film producer in Paris. At the Fall of France he became an open Nazi sympathiser, and subsequently made propaganda broadcasts to Britain from Germany. He also toured POW camps trying to induce British prisoners to join a German-controlled, anti-communist 'Legion of St George', who would fight with Nazi Germany against the Soviet Union. He was captured in April 1945 by Italian partisans and handed over to British intelligence. John Amery was put on trial for treason at the Old Bailey in late November 1945, pleading guilty to eight counts of high treason and sentenced to death by hanging. He did this in order to spare his family any more embarrassment, but the papers at Cambridge show how Amery and his younger son Julian tried every way they could to save his life. Despite a psychiatric report by an eminent practitioner, Dr Edward Glover, that he was definitely abnormal with a psychopathic disorder and schizoid tendencies, and the intervention of the South African Field Marshall General Jan Smuts, an AC member, who pleaded directly for clemency with the UK Prime Minister Clement Atlee, it was to no avail. Albert Pierrepoint, the public hangman, described John Amery in his autobiography as the bravest man he had to execute. However, germane to this tragedy, considered by Ronald Harwood as significant to John Amery's story, is that his father had concealed his part-Jewish ancestry. His mother, Elizabeth Leitner, was actually from a family of well-known Jewish scholars.

Leo Amery lost his seat in Parliament in the Labour landslide victory in the General Election of 1945, and refused the offer of a peerage. He was however made a Companion of Honour.

Leo kept active in climbing circles almost to the end of his life, ignoring the advice of his old Canadian friend, Wheeler, who, quoting Whymper, advised him in a letter that, 'a man does not climb mountains after his 60th year'. He continued to visit Switzerland, particularly the Valais, climbing lower peaks and finally just walking in the mountains. He died in September 1955. I believe that we were lucky that such a man, burdened with all the problems posed by the war, austerity and family tragedy, and hard decision making in smoke-filled rooms at Westminster and Downing Street, gave up so much of his valuable time to support the sport he loved. Like all politicians he had his critics. Stanley Baldwin observed, 'if he had been two inches taller, and his speeches half as long he might have been PM,' and Field Marshall Alexander, who became Governor General of Canada, stated that 'Amery always got hold of the right stick on an issue, but usually by the wrong end'. However, the huge number of letters from when he was Alpine Club President reveal a very kind, considerate and humane person, who managed to keep friends with everyone from Colonel Strutt, to Arnold Lunn, Graham Brown and Winston Churchill, no mean feat of diplomacy for any AC President.

Concluding his valedictory address to the Club in 1947, Leo reflected:

'Farewell, yet still remain those shining ranges. Above the vale on high, where we're still free, despite all other changes, to climb the golden peaks of memory.'

TED NORRISH

Mount Robson – 1961

The team at Jasper after the Robson climb: l-r Olaf Soot, Ted Norrish, Willie Pfisterer, Bill Roberts and Michael Keen. *(Chris McCartney)*

The hardest successful climb of my life was without doubt an ascent of Mount Robson (3954m) in the Canadian Rockies in July 1961. It was my Oxford University climbing friend and companion on Saraghrar in 1958, Bill Roberts, who suggested this trip to me and I did not need much persuasion. A small but diverse team was gathered: Mike Keen, a geologist from University College, and two fine mountaineers from the American Alpine Club – Olaf Soot, a Latvian American from New York, and Cleve McCartney, a dentist from Denver.

Robson is certainly one of the great mountains of the world, perhaps not in height, but certainly in steepness, difficulty and unique character. The first known attempt on the peak was in 1907 by Arthur Wheeler, founding president of the Alpine Club of Canada, with Arthur Coleman, his brother Quincy and Alpine Club founder member George Kinney. Kinney developed something of an obsession with Mount Robson and came, at least, very close to the summit at his twelfth attempt in 1909 with non-climber Donald 'Curly' Phillips as second. They reached the summit ridge in storm and white-out and controversy still abounds as to whether they actually topped out.

Robson was unequivocally climbed on 13 July 1913 by William Foster and Albert MacCarthy with their Austrian guide Conrad Kain, who proclaimed as they reached the summit: 'Gentlemen, that's so far as I can take you.' Perhaps because of exhaustion the party failed to give a description of their climb. Kain went on to achieve 60 first ascents in the Rockies, detailed in his famous autobiography, *Where The Clouds Can Go*.

We travelled to New York on the liner *Statendam*, about a week's voyage from Southampton. At dawn I came on deck to see the great city from the Hudson River for the first time. A most spectacular sight – I had never seen skyscrapers before! Our American friends collected us from the dock in their huge car and drove us, along with their two wives, out to the Rockies, finally arriving in Banff after long days on the road. Here we stayed for two nights at the house of that great Canadian lady mountaineer, Phyllis Munday.

Phyl's husband Don, author of the book *The Unknown Mountain*, recounts that he and his wife were the first to sight Mount Waddington, (4019m), the highest peak of the Coastal Range, which they described as 'Mystery Mountain'. Together with their good friend and guide, the very same Conrad Kain, they made several first ascents in this range and were most deservedly honoured when the Canadian Geographic Board named the highest of their first ascents Mount Munday (3356m).

Phyl Munday was a very brave and strong lady. In Don's book there is a picture of her carrying a sixty pound pack across a single log bridge above a raging river and on one occasion she fought off a grizzly bear with her bare hands and saved her husband's life. Eventually the Mundays and Conrad Kain made an early ascent of Robson in 1924, Phyl being the first woman to climb the mountain.

Phyl gave us all the information we needed, but warned us that Robson was a serious mountain that we could not attempt without a reliable guide, so she introduced us to Willie Pfisterer, an Austrian guide who was about ten years older than me. Willie advised us that Robson could only be attempted in one out of every five or six years, as conditions allowed. So we were all delighted when Willie informed us the mountain was climbable that year.

Before our attempt on Robson we decided to warm up on two other fine peaks: Mount Assiniboine (3618m) and Mount Victoria (3464m). Assiniboine, 'the Matterhorn of the Rockies', is a steep mountain with a fine sharp, rocky summit. The peak was first climbed on 1 September 1901 by the Rev. James Outram and two Swiss guides, Christian Bohren and Christian Hasler, part of a group brought to the Rockies by Edward Whymper. Outram's party discovered that Assiniboine has a steep double summit. Not content with this first ascent, Outram decided to traverse the moun-

Cleve McCartney on the summit of Mount Victoria. *(Norrish Coll.)*

tain, descending by the steep North face and North-east Ridge – a very fine achievement considering Assiniboine had previously repulsed several strong parties.

We found Assiniboine quite easy in the event – an exciting steep scramble, but we did not attempt to traverse the mountain. That night we bivouacked beside a small, beautiful green lake. In the middle of the night a huge moose jumped over me as I lay in my sleeping bag – quite a shock! It was grizzlies that Bill and I were always a little wary of, although we didn't mention this to our American friends, and were extremely glad never to have encountered one.

Mount Robson, and (inset) the line of the SSW Ridge:
1. Emperor Ridge, 2. The Roof,
3. West Bowl, 4. Wishbone Arête,
5. Little Robson, 6. hut, 7. Great Couloir. *(Gregory Horne)*

Further up the mountain highway lies Lake Louise from where we had sight of our second objective, Mount Victoria (3464m), which rises grandly above the Plain of The Six Glaciers. Victoria was first climbed in 1897 by that fine British mountaineer, Professor J. Norman Collie, and American climber Charles Fay along with two guides. In Collie's account he writes that a typical rocky scramble on loose rock leads to a superb summit ridge. We enjoyed our climb enormously; it must be one of the best Alpine routes in the Rockies, with memorable views from its sharp snow summit.

We drove on to the Jasper, about 100 miles north of Banff, picked up Willie Pfisterer and continued on some 60 miles to the foot of Mount Robson.

There are two main approaches to Robson: from Berg Lake in the north and the South-South-west Ridge from Kinney Lake to the south, the route that Willie had chosen for us. From our camp beside the lake at 1000m, the mountain looked extremely steep and formidable. We set off early next morning and were soon faced with a 700 metre struggle, cutting our way up steep cliffs through dense undergrowth.

At length, after a further exhausting thousand metres of boulders and scree, we pitched our two small tents on a narrow rocky ledge, at about 3000m. That night we could hear Canadian National trains hooting as they sped beside the river – a very eerie sound in the darkness.

We set out at dawn as two ropes. The first section of about 350m was steep and difficult, followed by a 200m traverse along the very narrow Black Ledges, exposed to sérac fall. Willie cut steps for us on the 50 degree ice that followed; but despite the steepness and the exposure, I was able to hold my nerve and my fitness gave me confidence.

After six hours' climbing we reached a narrow band of overhanging rock and ice which Willie called 'the mushroom' and then, to our great relief, there was just a 200m walk to the summit.

There followed a much more testing descent. We abseiled endlessly, off small piles of ice and snow, for over a thousand metres; there was no rock to secure our belays. Willie carefully explained this unique method, describing it as 'hasties'. We had to reach our camp before dark – benightment might have proved fatal.

Two days later back in Jasper, we thanked Willie for the experience of a lifetime but he would accept little payment – he had enjoyed the mountain, he said, and our enjoyment was sufficient reward.

From Jasper I decided to hitch-hike back through Canada to Montreal, and from there to work my passage by ship to Scotland. The crossing was delayed by rough weather and I was late back for the autumn term at King Henry VIII School where I was teaching. I apologised profusely to the Head and Mr Walker, being the fine gentleman that he was, said that it had been, in the end, well worthwhile for the experience of climbing Mount Robson. His Deputy was less understanding and docked me a week's pay!

C A RUSSELL

One Hundred Years Ago

The settled conditions experienced in the principal Alpine regions during the first week of January 1914 enabled the Italian brothers Angelo and Romano Calegari, accompanied by G Scotti, to complete a successful expedition on New Year's Day. Climbing on foot from a bivouac above the Simplon Pass they made the first winter ascent of the Fletschhorn, reaching the summit by way of the Fletschjoch and descending the same route by moonlight. In the following month Marcel Kurz and the guide Théophile Theytaz completed the first winter and ski ascents of the Zinalrothorn and Grand Cornier.

The spring and early summer were notable for the heavy snowfalls which delayed the start of the climbing season for some weeks; R W Lloyd, who completed a route on the Liskamm at the end of July, found 'more snow everywhere than can be remembered'. Although conditions on many high peaks were unfavourable several strong parties were in the field. In July Geoffrey Winthrop Young, accompanied as in previous years by Josef Knubel, joined forces with Siegfried Herford and the guide Hans Brantschen to complete the first ascent of a famous route in the Bernese Alps: the south-west, *Rote Zähne* ridge of the Gspaltenhorn. Moving to Zermatt the party traversed the Matterhorn after ascending the north-west, Zmutt ridge, with Herford making only his second big Alpine climb. In the Mont Blanc range V J E Ryan returned to the Chamonix Aiguilles with Franz and Josef Lochmatter, completing a number of notable expeditions including a new route to the south peak of the Aiguille de Blaitière.

Later in the year, in October, an Italian party led by Franco Grottanelli completed the first guideless ascent of the steep north-east face of Monte Viso, following the route established by W A B Coolidge and his guides who had made the first ascent.

During the summer the first section of the Furka-Oberalp railway from Brig to Gletsch was completed, the original tunnel below the Furka Pass being then still under construction.

The Furka Railway was formally opened at Brig with a curious ceremony of blessing of the line, and sprinkling the locomotive with holy water. This was performed by the Dean of Brig in the unavoidable absence of the Bishop of Sion. There were great rejoicings all along the line as far as Gletsch.

In the Caucasus exploration was continued by several guideless parties and many new routes were completed. In July Harold Raeburn returned to the Adai Khokh region where his party was joined by Rembert Martinson,

Siegfried Herford on the Great Flake, Central Buttress, Scafell, April 1914.
(George Sansom, FRCC Archive)

the young Russian climber who as in the previous year acted as interpreter. Although the weather was unsettled Raeburn and his companions ascended several unclimbed peaks including Karagom East (4513m) and Vologata (4175m) before moving west to make the first ascent of Laboda (4320m). The Swiss climbers Carl Egger and Guido Miescher completed a number of successful expeditions including the first ascent of Jailik (4533m) in the Adyrsu region in addition to reaching the west, higher summit (5633m) of Elbrus. A Russian party led by M S Golubev was also active, climbing peaks in the Adyrsu and Elbrus regions.

In August, on learning of the outbreak of hostilities Martinson left Raeburn and his companions who, like the Swiss party, managed with difficulty to return to their home country. Other foreign mountaineers climbing in the range were less fortunate: Walter Fischer and Oscar Schuster, who made the first ascent of Dombai Ulgen (4040m) to the west of Elbrus, were arrested and interned.

Further afield the principal undertaking during the year was the expedition led by Filippo De Filippi to carry out scientific research and exploration at the eastern end of the Karakoram – an area which was largely unknown at that time. The expedition, which had been planned in great detail, was supported by the Italian and Indian governments and by numerous scientific bodies.

After spending the winter at Skardu with a number of scientists and the Courmayeur guide Joseph Petigax, De Filippi was joined at Leh by a detachment from the Survey of India. From a base on the Depsang plateau the survey party triangulated the whole of the Rimo glacier system and fixed the heights of neighbouring peaks in addition to exploring and mapping the area between the Rimo glacier and the Karakoram Pass.

Following this exploration De Filippi was able to determine the true position of the eastern watershed of the range and to confirm the Rimo glacier and its northern branch as the source of two important rivers flowing in opposite directions: the Shyok to the Indus in the south and the Yarkand to the north into Asia. Important scientific data and a comprehensive photographic record resulted from the work of the expedition and later in the year De Filippi was able to explore to the north as far as Kashgar before returning to Europe.

During the summer Dr Alexander Kellas returned to Garhwal to pursue his scientific work in connection with the use of oxygen at high altitude and to continue his exploration of the approaches to Kamet (7756m). This expedition was cut short in August when Kellas returned home after learning of the outbreak of war.

In South Africa climbing standards were raised following a number of notable ascents on Table Mountain (1087m) by members of the Mountain Club. During the year parties led by W T Cobern established *Africa Face*, *Erica Buttress* and other difficult routes.

In New Zealand Conrad Kain of Mount Robson fame commenced his first season in the Southern Alps after being engaged to accompany the Canadian climber Otto Frind. In addition to traversing Mount Cook (3764m) and opening a new route on Mount Sefton (3159m) they made the first ascents of Mount Bannie (2547m), Mount Maunga Ma (2486m) and other unclimbed peaks. Kain then returned to Canada where in August, with Albert and Elizabeth MacCarthy he made the first ascent of Mount Farnham (3468m), the highest peak in the Purcell range.

At home in April a famous climb was completed in the Lake District when a party led by Siegfried Herford and George Sansom made the first ascent of the *Central Buttress* route on Scafell – an outstanding achievement for the period.

In December the death occurred of the great guide Melchior Anderegg. The companion and friend of Leslie Stephen, members of the Walker family and other Alpine pioneers, he had taken part in many notable expeditions including the first ascent of the Brenva face on Mont Blanc.

By the end of the year the war, which it had been hoped would be over before Christmas, had already claimed the life of one Alpine Club member, J B Corry, and left two other members, L C F Oppenheim and E L Strutt severely wounded. At the Annual General Meeting in December the President, Lord Justice Pickford, announced that the Winter Dinner would not be held owing to the 'circumstances which I am sure we all hope may never again exist as long as the Club shall last'.

Area Notes

Dent du Géant, acrylic on canvas, 40x50cm. *(Tim Pollard)*

LINDSAY GRIFFIN

Alps & Dolomites 2013

East face of the Grandes Jorasses, showing line of *Borat* (F7b, 750m). *(Antonio Giani)*

Proportionally, the number of climbers graduating towards alpinism continues to decline. Yet there remains much to be discovered in the Alps and seemingly plenty of alpinists operating at the highest levels. This is highlighted by the following ascents, which represent some of the more innovative during 2013.

Dave MacLeod contemplates the Rote Fluh and Czech Pillar *en route* to *Paciencia. (Calum Muskett)*

Mont Blanc Range

On the east face of the **Grandes Jorasses** (4208m), two of today's most active French alpinists, Max Bionnet and Sebastien Ratel, put up *Borat* between *Groucho Marx* (Delisi-Delisi, 1983, 750m, ED2/3, F6b, A3) and the 1981 *Boivin-Diafferia* (TD, F5c, A1) to its right. The pair spent two days in July completing the 750m route, the third pitch led free at F7b, while the fourth was led at F7a with some aid, but followed free at F7b. They were surprised to find several old 8mm bolts on the lower pitches, the last having an old weathered sling. Above, where the difficulties were no more than F6b easing to F5+, they found no previous sign of passage.

On the south side of the Jorasses, British climber Tony Penning made a solo ascent of a previously virgin rock tower on the east side of the remote Pra Sec basin. In 2006 Penning had climbed a tower south of this, which he named Punta Giancarlo Grassi in honour of the legendary Italian alpinist. He returned in 2012, and with Mike Mitchell traversed the east flank of Punta Grassi to a col on the far side. From there the pair ascended another higher tower to the north. This gave a total of 750m of climbing up to HVS. In August 2013 Penning repeated this route solo and then followed the ridge north to the base of yet another, but this time smaller, tower. He soloed the 100m south face via an obvious chimney/groove system at HVS. The descent from the summit involved 350m of down-climbing and a few frustrating sessions with jammed abseil ropes.

Bernese Oberland

Robert Jasper and Roger Schäli made a rare repeat and first free ascent of the *Ghilini-Piola Direttissima*, on the north face of the **Eiger** (3970m), the third major first free ascent for this duo on the Eigerwand. This climb takes the very steep pillar rising to the west ridge above the right side of the Rote Fluh, and right of the 1976 *Czech Pillar*. On the first ascent René Ghilini and Michel Piola took five days to climb 32 pitches involving difficult protection, poor bivouacs and a grade quoted at the time as ABO- (Piola coined the grade Abominable), F6b and A3/4 (halfway through their ascent a then largely unknown Austrian, Thomas Bubendorfer, soloed the *1938 Route* in a record time of 4h 50m). Only eight of the pitches involved aid. Jasper and Schäli first climbed the route in 2006 and from 2007-09 invested much time re-equipping a number of pitches. Their final ascent, completed in 14 hours, involved difficulties of UIAA IX or F7b/7c with the 17th, 18th and 20th pitches (F7b, F7b/c, F7b/c) being the hardest.

Low down on the very far right side of the north face, a via ferrata leads through an area of rock left of the Eiger Rotstock. On the Rotstock itself Roger Schäli finally made a continuous, no-falls redpoint of his 2006 route *Emergency Exit* (climbed with the late Stephan Eder). The crux of this 10-pitch offering is F7c+/F8a and Schäli states it's the steepest rock he's ever climbed in an alpine environment.

Elsewhere in the Oberland David Hefti and Roger Schäli made a one-day ascent of what is dubbed the *Jungfrau Marathon*. From near Stechelberg in the Lauterbrunnen Valley, a huge ridge rises southeast to the summit of the **Jungfrau** (4158m). The lower section crosses the steep pillars of the Stelliflue, after which a long quasi-horizontal section of generally loose ground leads to the base of the Rottbrett, a 500m rock triangle below the summit of the Silberhorn (3695m). Above the summit of the Silberhorn glaciated terrain leads to the Wengen Jungfrau (4089m), and from there to the main summit. The main pillar of the Stelliflue has been climbed by the 11-pitch *Stägers Bürtblätz* (F7a+), while the steep west face of the Rottbrett ridge is breached by *Fätze und Bitze* (11 pitches up to F7a). Linking the two and continuing to the summit would give an ascent of 3383m and had been completed over two days in 1997. Starting from the valley at 3:30am, Hefti and Schäli reached the summit 16 hours later, though admit that it was 'the limit in terms of length and difficulty of any route we can climb in one day.'

Dolomites

Probably the most innovative ascents in recent years have taken place in the **Dolomites**, where talented parties are now seeking out ephemeral ice/mixed lines on the great walls. One such coveted winter line forms on the north face of **Sassolungo** (3181m), which finally succumbed to Adam Holzknecht and Hubert Morodor over two days in early January. *La Legrima*, climbed entirely with natural gear, gave 1000m of difficulties up to WI6 M6 UIAA V+, with two sections of A0.

Staying in the **Sella Group**, Chamonix based mixed masters Jeff Mercier and Korra Pesce made a fleeting visit to see if they could use their talents to similar effect. The result was *Ghost Dogs*, a line based around the classic 1929 *Fedele Route* on the north-west face of the **Saas Pordoi** (2952m) and clearly visible from Sella Pass. Pesce, on his first visit to the Dolomites, and Mercier climbed 150m up the *Fedele* to check conditions, cached some gear and abseiled, leaving their ropes in place. Next day they overcame the two crux pitches, the first having been climbed by a previous party, which had placed two bolt runners in the rock on the right. The pair climbed to

Top: Dave Macleod leading off on the second F7c pitch of *Paciencia* in 'atmospheric' north face conditions. *(Calum Muskett)*

Below: Dave MacLeod redpointing the crux F8a pitch of *Paciencia*. *(Alexandre Buisse)*

the huge terrace at 550m, then as the sun was hitting the upper wall, escaped to the right. Next morning they returned and finished off the route via a large left-facing corner. The 750m line weighs in at an impressive WI6 X R M5 F5+/F6a.

In the **Civetta Group** another big mixed route was established on the north face of **Piccola Civetta** (3207m) over four days in May. Stefano Angelini, Alessandro Beber and Fabrizio Dellai named their new 1200m line *Argento Vivo* (WI6+ M8 A2 F5+).

Relatively difficult but notably bold new rock routes continue to be done with trad gear only. Perennial activists Ivo Rabanser and Adam Holzknecht have been putting up hard routes in the Dolomites for over three decades in this way, establishing fine natural lines.

On the **Croz dell'Altissimo**, Heinz Grill, Franz Heiss, Florian Kluckner and Rabanser took two days to complete *Samuele Scalet* (1000m, VII and A1) on the vast south-west face. The route climbs the left wall of the huge dièdre taken by the 1932 *Corra-Detassis* but well right of better known classic *Detassis-Giordani* of 1936. The four climbed the line in 31 pitches with one bivouac and placed a bolt at each belay. Other than this the route relies on trad gear, with some sections needing very large cams.

Rabanser had attempted this line twice in 1995 with Scalet and Lino

Dave MacLeod redpointing the crux F8a pitch of *Paciencia*, Rote Fluh, Eiger Nordwand. *(Alexandre Buisse)*

The Peuterey Ridge of Mont Blanc with Supercouloir de Peuterey marked. Left of centre is the Aiguille Noire, while Mont Noir is the flat-topped rock tower close to the left of the picture. *(Lindsay Griffin)*

Celva. Almost 20 years later it is complete and dedicated to Rabanser's old friend Scalet, something of a legend in Dolomite climbing, who died in 2010 after a long illness, aged 70. Scalet created many routes in the Pale di San Martino, though it is his lines on the Saas Maor that are considered the most significant, with *Masada* commonly rated one of the best in the Dolomites.

Matt Helliker in the Supercouloir de Peuterey. *(Jon Bracey)*

Tod und das Mädchen (*Death and The Maiden*) is a well-known string quartet by Schubert. It is also the name of the route on the north-east face of **Torre Occidentale delle Mesules de la Biesces** (2336m) in the **Sella Group**, put up in 1986 by Dieter Demetz and Adam Holzknecht. In August Rabanser and Stefan Comploi climbed the relatively short, but beautiful, *Götterdämmerung* (*Twilight of The Gods*), keeping with the classical music theme. The pair climbed this eight-pitch, 250m route at VII

Matt Helliker in the Supercouloir de Peuterey. *(Jon Bracey)*

and A1, but later the same month Rabanser returned with Holzknecht and the latter freed it at VIII.

A week later Holzknecht and Rabanser were at the base of the north-west face of **Cima Immink** (2855m) in the **Pale di San Martino**, where they proceeded to put up *Fraulein Else* (460m, 10 pitches, VIII-), following a fine, logical crack system. As with the preceding route, the pair used only trad gear and a few pegs.

On the west face of the **Sasso della Croce** (2825m), Josef Hilpold and Ulrich Viertler climbed *Wüstenblume* (400m, VIII+). Although it was completed in sections and with some fixed rope, the pair only used trad gear, which led to several challenging pitches. This celebrated wall has a number of famous routes, though it was the first ascent of the *Central Pillar* that became legendary, involving two young brothers – Gunther and Reinhold Messner. The crux is variously rated from VII to VIII-, is very poorly protected and badly positioned above an ankle snapping (or worse) ledge. It marked a breakthrough in standards, as it now seems likely that Reinhold Messner not only broke through to the 'Seventh Grade', but also could have climbed the first 'Grade Eight' in Europe's high mountains.

Austria

David Lama made two interesting ascents in the **Zillertal**. Over two days in March, with Hansjorg Auer and Peter Ortner, he made the first winter ascent of the steep *Sagwand* on the **Sagzahn** via the 800m *Schiefer*

The west face of the Grands Charmoz showing the line of *Birthright*. *(Lindsay Griffin)*

Riss. Difficulties were rated as VI, M7, 80°. Later, in December, Lama soloed a new route on the north face of the **Hohe Kirche** (2634m). *Nordverscheidung* (400m, UIAA VI/VII, WI4, M4/5, 90°) was completed in temperatures down to minus 10°C.

Pyrenees

Finally, mention should be made of an innovative traverse of the entire Pyrenees. In a single odyssey, Spanish alpinist Elio Callado spent 67 days completing the 1200km trip, during which he climbed 55 routes, among them *Spigolo d'Ansabère* (F7a+), *Embarradère* on the **Ossau** (F6c+), several hard and classic routes in **Gavarnie** and the north face of **Vignemale**: a total of 25,000m of climbing, with most routes graded between F5c and F6b.

Alpine Club Ascents

Alpine Club members also made noteworthy repeats and first ascents. Calum Muskett (climbing with Dave Macleod), made the third free ascent of the 2008 Siegrist-Steck route, *Paciencia* (F8a) on the north face of the **Eiger**. After an inspection of the first few hard pitches, the pair climbed the route in three days, with the objective – which they both achieved – of freeing all 24 pitches either on lead or seconding, with no falls. They

Above: Matt Helliker during the first free ascent of *Birthright*. *(Jon Bracey)*

on-sighted every pitch up to and including F7a+. The crux seventh pitch, which both redpointed, is on the Rote Fluh, climbing through the main roof at its apex. But several 'easier' pitches were considered undergraded, and the one that gave them most trouble was pitch 14 (originally graded F7b+ but thought to be F7c+).

Matt Helliker and fellow Chamonix-based guide Jon Bracey made the third known – but first free – ascent of *Birthright* on the west face of the **Grands Charmoz** (3445m) in the **Mont Blanc Range**. This is the line of an old, wet, Desmaison rock route, which was climbed in 10 pitches as an ephemeral ice route in 1992 by Scott Backes and Mark Twight at ED/ ED+, 90°, 5.9, A2. In 2008 it was repeated by the talented Italian alpinist Rossano Libera, who quoted a grade of WI6, V, A2.

Bracey and Helliker approached on ski from the Plan de l'Aiguille and reached the foot of the route at 11am. Three hours and 45 minutes later they had reached the middle terraces, where the route finishes, having climbed every pitch free at an overall grade of approximately V/6 and F4c. A ski back to the Plan enabled them to catch the cable car down to Chamonix that afternoon.

Bracey and Helliker also made the first complete ascent of the **Supercouloir de Peuterey**, a relatively low-lying ephemeral ice couloir, which lies on the northeast flank of **Mont Noir de Peuterey** (2928m), a small

Above: Mont Vert de Greuvettaz and (below) *Casa dei Gracchi.(Tom Prentice)*

summit at the end of the east ridge of the Aiguille Noire de Peuterey. In March 1983 local activist and guide, the late Hans Margherettaz, with Gianfranco Sappa, climbed a steep, narrow goulotte on the lower flanks of the face, and after 350m, where the angle eased, traversed left c.200m to snow slopes and descended. With sections of 90° the so-named *Supercouloir de Peuterey* was graded ED1 and as far as is known remained unrepeated. Bracey and Helliker left the Val Veni at 6am in mid December and,

Simon Richardson, pitch four of the *Pilier Alphonse Couttet*, Aiguille du Chardonnet. *(Tom Prentice)*

starting up the line, found the near vertical snow/ice to be perfect styrofoam. Passing two old hand-drilled bolts (protection was sparse) they followed easier ground to reach steep mixed towers that bar access to the ridge. Helliker opted for an open groove full of turf and moss, which gave good placements: this was just as well, as the groove offered nothing in the way of protection. A snow couloir led to a prominent notch on the ridge just right

Pte. 3660m

Piller du Cairn
1979

Pilier Alphonse Couttet (350m, TD, F6a+) on Gendarme 3660m. (Tom Prentice)

of Mont Noir's summit. The pair rappelled the line, which they graded TD (650m, 90°).

During their 2012 exploration of **Mont Vert de Greuvettaz** on the Italian side of the Mont Blanc Range, Tom Prentice and Simon Richardson spotted a prominent left-slanting corner system on the vertical granite wall rising toward the top of **Punta 3469m**, a point on the south-south-east ridge of **Mont Greuvettaz** that is sometimes referred to as **Punta Bosio**. Believing it to be unclimbed and noting the lower section to be loose, in August 2013 they climbed four pitches up the left side before traversing into the corner, whereupon they were surprised to discover ancient rappel slings and a peg. They finished the route, following a right-slanting ramp at the top, to reach the summit ridge, from which point they abseiled.

They later discovered this was the rarely repeated 1982 *Grassi-Lang-Meneghin Route* (originally graded D; the British four-pitch variant was F6b). Richardson had always assumed this route followed a well-defined corner system on the left side of a prominent pillar that falls from a point north of Punta Bosio, closer to **Punta 3557m**. The result of this error meant that the prominent pillar was unclimbed, and the pair returned to rectify this with a series of excellent pitches that led to the completion of *Casa dei Gracchi* (500m, 11 pitches, TD+, F6b).

On the French side of the range this pair was also able to add a route to the south face of the **Aiguille du Chardonnet**. The first main rock pillar left of the Col du Chardonnet was climbed in 1971 by Jérome Belin and Jean-Franck Charlet at TD-. Between this and the *Pilier du Cairn* (Charlet-Ducroz, 1979) to the left lies another major pillar rising to **Gendarme 3660m**, aka **Pointe Alphonse Couttet**. Prentice and Richardson climbed this line, naming their nine-pitch new route *Pilier Alphonse Couttet* (350m, TD, F6a+). The climb was felt to be similar in scale and difficulty to the *Bonatti Route* on the Red Pillar of Brouillard, though not as sustained in the upper section.

SIMON RICHARDSON

Scottish Winter 2012-14

Editor's note: In the 2013 edition of the Journal the Scottish winter notes were labelled as 2012-13 when in actual fact the report covered the 2011-12 season. What follows is a bumper fun-sized round-up of the two seasons since. . .

Greg Boswell, pitch 2 *Vapouriser* (VIII,8), Creag an Dubh Loch. *(Guy Robertson)*

2012-2013 SEASON

2012-13 was a winter of two halves. The weather until January was characterised by periods of extreme bad weather with gales so ferocious that mountain travel was sometimes impossible. By contrast, the months of February and March will be long remembered for their superb winter climbing. A settled high-pressure system following a brief thaw resulted in easy going across hard snow slopes, iced up crags and scores of classic routes in perfect condition. Some of the finest climbing was found on Ben Nevis where many of Scotland's most prized winter climbs, from *Orion Direct* to *Galactic Hitchhiker*, and *Hadrian's Wall* to *Minus One Gully*, were enjoyed by many teams.

Four climbers dominated the season. Greg Boswell was quick off the

263

Iain Small, crux pitch of *Deadly Presence* (VIII,7), Ben Nevis. *(Doug Hawthorn)*

mark with outstanding new routes such as *Tomahawk Crack* on Ben Nevis and *Vapouriser* on Creag an Dubh Loch, and concluded his season with the highly significant second ascents of *Mort* and *The Cathedral*. Guy Robertson had an exceptional winter that included four new routes graded IX or harder. Robertson's ability to consistently find routes in condition, and maintain momentum climbing at the highest level throughout the season, was nothing short of extraordinary. By contrast, Iain Small had a slower build up, but his collection of testing new routes to Ben Nevis stands out – especially as they involved both technical mixed and bold thin ice. Finally, Nick Bullock was a late arrival on the scene in March, but he soon left his mark with a jaw-dropping series of routes culminating in his magnificent lead of *Nevermore* on Lochnagar.

The long, cold and snowy winter, extending from October through to May, led to a high level of activity across all grades. Predictably, Andy Nisbet stands out as the most prolific activist with an incredible tally of 74 new routes, but many other climbers delighted in discovering new ground.

Ben Nevis

Cold and snowy conditions at the end of November resulted in some excellent ascents in Coire na Ciste. Many of the modern classics were climbed such as *Sioux Wall* (VIII,8) on Number Three Gully Buttress, and *Darth Vader* (VII,7) on Creag Coire na Ciste. Over on Pinnacle Buttress of the Tower, *Smooth Operator* (VI,7) also had an early repeat. The pace increased at the end of the month when Guy Robertson and Greg Boswell made the third ascent of The *Knuckleduster* (VIII,9) on Number Three Gully Buttress. Boswell had repeated this route the previous season with Will

Sim (adding a more direct finish), but this time they took a more direct winter version of the summer crux pitch. Their ascent was remarkably fast as they only started climbing at 11.30am after being halted by unstable snow conditions approaching a new line in Observatory Gully earlier in the day.

For Boswell this was only a forerunner of things to come, as he returned to Number Three Gully Buttress three days later with Adam Russell and made the first ascent of *Tomahawk Crack* (VIII,9), which takes a line straight up the centre of Sioux Wall. This imposing wall is cut by a number of thin cracks and is ideally suited to modern mixed climbing, but even so, Boswell described the climb as 'a funky route with some surprisingly steep and tricky sections.' This section of cliff was already home to the eponymous *Sioux Wall* (the most popular Grade VIII in Scotland) and *Apache* (VIII,9), so the Boswell-Russell addition now gives it one of the highest concentrations of top end winter routes in the country. *Tomahawk Crack* was climbed in perfect style – on sight at the first attempt – and does not follow an existing summer line.

In early February, Iain Small upped the ante another notch with the first ascent of *No Success Like Failure* (IX,8) with Simon Richardson. This bold and compelling line takes the shallow roofed groove running up the front face of Rogue's Rib in Coire na Ciste. Small had previously attempted the route just after Christmas with Blair Fyffe, hence the evocative name. The following weekend Small was back on Ben Nevis with Tony Stone. In a vain effort to seek some shelter from the high winds they climbed the impending corner between *Fat Boy Slim* and *Rogue's Rib*. New route enthusiasts were well aware of this prominent unclimbed feature, but close up it is an imposing and unfeasible-looking

Iain Small arranging protection below the crux overhang on the first ascent of *No Success Like Failure* (IX,8), Rogue's Rib, Ben Nevis. *(Simon Richardson)*

line. Small was typically modest in his assessment after the climb: 'The route was pretty bold and delicate for the first two pitches, and Tony really pushed the comfort levels on the first pitch, even though he appeared consummately in control

Iain Small climbing through a storm on the crux pitch of *The Wolves Are Running* (VII,7) on Ben Nevis.
(Simon Richardson)

throughout.' In common with the majority of Iain Small's Nevis winter routes, it is unlikely that *Migranya Profunda* (VIII,8) will see more than a slow trickle of potential suitors in coming seasons.

Further left, Simon Yearsley and Helen Rennard climbed *Beggars Belief* (VII,7), a winter version of *Beggar's Groove*, and higher up in Coire na Ciste, Jim Higgins and Neil Adams linked the start of *Angels With Dirty Faces* with the finish of *Avenging Angel*, to produce *Avenging Angel Direct* (VIII,8) – the first route to fully meet the challenge of the compelling line of overhanging corners on the left side of Creag Coire na Ciste.

As ice conditions moved from good to excellent at the end of February, Robin Clothier and Richard Bentley scored one of the biggest coups of the season with the first ascent of *Shooting Star* (VI,6). This 500m-long expedition links together nine existing routes with two pitches of new ground resulting in the longest climb on the Orion Face. Equally impressive was the forbiddingly steep *Deadly Presence* (VIII,7) on Observatory Buttress by Iain Small and Doug Hawthorn, which forces its way up the vertical headwall above *Appointment With Fear*. Small, who is renowned for his delicate touch on ice, remarked afterwards that this was probably the leanest ice pitch he has ever climbed.

Observatory Buttress saw more attention in March when Clothier teamed up with the father and son team of Doug and Uisdean Hawthorn to make the third ascent of the fabled *Point Blank* (VII,7), which takes the imposing rib bounding the right side of *Point Five Gully*. They were closely followed by Tim Neill and Donald King later that day, whilst next door, Small and Richardson added *The Wolves Are Running* (VII,7), a bold icy mixed climb taking the vertical headwall to the right of *Rubicon Wall*. More mixed in nature was *Angry Chair* (VII,7) on the steep wall right of Tower Cleft by Dave MacLeod and Helen Rennard.

Small and Hawthorn had a superb run of routes on Ben Nevis at the end of March with ascents of *Pointless* (VII,6), *Space Invaders* (VI,5), and *Journey Into Space* (VII,5). On 30 March they were joined by Clothier for the second ascent (via a new start) of *Urban Spaceman* (VII,6), a mythical line that was first climbed by Arthur Paul and a young Doug Hawthorn way back in 1983. A week later Small was back again, this time with Murdoch Jamieson and Nick Bullock, to added *Spaced Out* (VII,7), a new direct route between *Space Invaders* and *Journey Into Space* on the Orion headwall.

The dramatic contrast in climbing conditions over the season, from the perfectly sublime to the absolute impossible, was captured in a route name given by Blair Fyffe and Helen Rennard to a new addition in December. *The Copenhagen Interpretation* (VI,7) takes the prominent ramp, cracks and corners between *The Minge* and *Joyful Chimneys* on South Trident Buttress. 'The name refers to the unusual mathematics of quantum mechanics,' Blair (a PhD astrophysicist) explained. 'The ephemeral and uncertain world of the sub-atomic particles shows similarities to the transient and uncertain world of Scottish winter climbing conditions. Both worlds, although challenging, and in some ways always alien to us, have an other-worldly beauty.'

Exploration of Old Haunts

The cold and snowy season allowed a reappraisal of several well-known venues such as Arrochar, Arran and Glen Clova. On **Beinn Ime**, Stuart McFarlane and Stuart Burns found the five-pitch *Gangnam Style* (V,7), which takes the right-facing corner system to the left of *Ben's Fault* on Fan Gully Buttress. A few days later McFarlane visited **The Cobbler** with John Williams and made the first winter ascent of *Echo Crack* (VI,7). The south-facing routes on the North Peak are notoriously hard to find in winter condition as they strip fast in the sun, but McFarlane circumvented this by making a very early start following heavy snowfall the day before.

Also of note was the first winter ascent of *Hangover* (VI,6) on **Creag Tharsuinn** in Arrochar by Dafydd Morris and Matt Buchanan, and *Silence of The Rams* (V,6) on The Cobbler by Dougie Beck, Andy Bain and Jake Thackrey. Bain and Thackrey continued their Arrochar explorations with three new long routes on nearby **Beinn Narnain**.

A major snowstorm in late March brought the mountains on Arran into good condition. Stuart McFarlane and Simon Richardson visited the island soon after and added a couple of new routes to **Beinn Nuis**, including *After The Storm* (VI,5) that tackles the face right of Nuis Chimney. During the same period, Andrew Fraser, Nigel Marshall and Ian Magill added *Power*

Malcolm Bass, on FA of
Twisted (VII,7), Stob Coire
nan Lochan.
(Simon Yearsley)

Outage (II/III) and *White
Witch* (IV,4) to the 250m-
high north face of **Ceum na
Caillich**.

Glen Clova is under-
going something of a
renaissance, with a steady
stream of quality winter
routes added over the
past few seasons. Winter
Corrie, long regarded as a
venue for easy to middle
grades, with only one route
graded harder than Grade
IV, now sports several
excellent technical routes
including *Wildcat Wall,
The Tiger Finish, Waterfall
Buttress Direct* and *Moon Ice
Jazz.* The 2012-13 season
saw more additions such as
Stalingrad (VI,6) and *Gram-
pian Club Buttress* (IV,5) by
Forrest Templeton, Brian
Duthie and Kevin Murphy.
Henning Wackerhage
has been at the forefront
of the Clova developments with new routes in Corrie Fee, exploration
of Glen Prosen's Bawhelps and the development of Coire Farchal. This
easily accessible coire now sports ten routes with pride of place going to
the superb *Silver Threads Among the Gold* (IV,5) which takes the prominent
central buttress.

Cairngorms

The first major new route of the season in the Cairngorms fell to Guy
Robertson and Greg Boswell on 11 December when they added *Vapouriser*
(VIII,8), a stunning five-pitch icy mixed line cutting up directly through
Vertigo Wall on **Creag an Dubh Loch**. The route uses a spectacular finish
first attempted by Henning Wackerhage a couple of seasons before, but
as is so often the case, the real crux of the route was being in position at
the right time and finding the lower grooves sufficiently iced. Robertson
commented afterwards that it is transitory climbs like this, which rely on
ice rather than snowed up rock, that result in the most memorable Scottish
winter routes. 'The climbing was an exquisite combination of thin ice and
steep rock, with a distinctly cerebral element throughout,' he wrote later on

his blog. 'There simply are not enough adjectives to describe how good this route is – the exposure on the top pitch was quite ludicrous!'

The following day Pete Macpherson and Martin Moran made the third winter ascent of *Steeple* (IX,9) on the Shelter Stone. This team are no strangers to high standard routes on the **Shelter Stone**. Two seasons earlier Macpherson made the first ascent of *Stone Temple Pilots* (X,9), and the previous December Moran made a winter ascent of *The Needle* (VIII,8). The first winter ascent of *Steeple* was a landmark ascent climbed in a 24-hour push by Alan Mullin and Steve Paget in November 1999. It set a new standard for Scottish routes of such sustained difficulty, and deliberately climbing through the night redefined the approach to climbing long Scottish winter routes.

Heavy snow conditions from February onwards effectively curtailed Cairngorms pioneering activity through the rest of the season, however Guy Robertson nipped into **Lochnagar** with Greg Boswell and Pete Benson, just before the mid February thaw, to snatch *Fancy Free* (VII,9), the prominent groove-line left of *Footloose* on Central Buttress.

Glen Coe

Early in December, Andy Nisbet and Brian Davison visited the West Top of **Bidean nam Bian** in Glen Coe to put a long-standing project to rest – the steep unclimbed rib to the right of *The Gash*. Arriving at the foot of the route, Nisbet couldn't resist climbing the wall to its left, which provided a deceptively difficult VI,7 called *The Pash*. Davison then led the rib resulting in the steep and serious *Incision* (VI,7). Later in the month, Donald King and Mike Pescod made the first winter ascent of the impressively steep *Engineer's Crack* (VIII,9) on **Buachaille Etive Mor**. This steep two-pitch route on the North side of Crowberry Ridge is rarely in winter condition, but it fell to a well-timed and determined ascent just before the late January high-pressure weather system broke.

In March, Malcolm Bass and Simon Yearsley made the first ascent of *Twisted* (VII,7) on **Stob Coire nan Lochan**. This superb three-pitch addition, takes a central line up the broad buttress between *Moonshadow* and *Chimney Route*. The most significant winter ascent in the Coe fell to Guy Robertson and Nick Bullock at the end of March when they made the first ascent of *Cold Revenge* (IX,8) on Buachaille Etive Mor. This serious and committing climb, which is based on the summer routes of *Bludger's Revelation* and *Bloody Crack*, is only the second winter route on Slime Wall.

Northern Highlands

In early December, Andy Nisbet and Brian Davison teamed up with Pat Ingram to visit **An Teallach**. A recent snowfall and short thaw had worked their magic, and the trio found a line of ice dribbling down a shallow corner-line on the gully face of Goblach Buttress. The 350m-long *Tweener* was graded V,6, but is likely to be significantly harder in powder conditions. A couple of days later, Guy Robertson and Andy Inglis made an enterprising visit to Coire Ghranda's Upper Cliff on **Beinn Dearg**. *The Rebirth of Cool* (VII,7) takes the easiest line up the steep and complex area of overhanging grooves and bulges immediately right of *Tickled Rib*, another Robertson route from way back in 2001.

The lead up to Christmas was characterised by a combination of gales, sharp thaws and occasional good days, but this period was dominated by Andy Nisbet, who demonstrated his years of experience by consistently outwitting the weather forecast and being in the right place at the right time. On 18 December he joined forces with Jonathan Preston and Dave McGimpsey for the first ascent of *Rongbuk* (IV,4) on Toll an Lochain on An Teallach. 'This buttress is arguably the second biggest cliff in Scotland, and although there are steeper contenders, it is a surprisingly intimidating face and I love climbing there,' Nisbet enthused afterwards. Their 500m-long route makes a fine companion to *Potala Buttress,* first climbed by Des Rubens and Dave Broadhead in January 1987.

In the middle of January, Guy Robertson and Greg Boswell made the first winter ascent of *Shoot The Breeze* on **Beinn Eighe's** West Central Wall. This spectacular summer E2, first climbed in 1992, is described in the current guidebook as 'a stunning route, one of the wildest in Scotland, with a well protected crux and a Troll Wall ambiance.' Robertson and Boswell's winter version is a sustained IX,8 destined to become a future testpiece. 'Every move was Tech 8 after the first few metres, and the protection was generally superb,' Robertson explained afterwards. Two weeks later, Robertson was back on Beinn Eighe with Jason Currie to climb the prominent line between *Colgarra* and *King of The Swingers*. This was untouched in summer and resulted in the sustained and technical *Immortal Memory* (IX,9).

Other highlights in the Northern Highlands include the first ascent of *Haigha* by Malcolm Bass and Simon Yearsley, a new 340m-long VI,7 in Coire na Poite on **Beinn Bhan**. This route joins *Realisation* and *Wonderland* as the third Bass-Yearsley addition to the impressive Realisation Wall between *March Hare's* and *Mad Hatter's* gullies. Also on Beinn Bhan, Martin Moran and Pete Macpherson found the bold *Suspended Animation* (VIII,9), a new four-pitch mixed adventure on Suspense Wall in the neighbouring Coire na Feola. Nearby on Beinn Eighe, Michael Barnard and James Duthie struck it lucky on Beinn Eighe with *Lightning Strike* (VI,6), the weakness left of *Achilles*, and Roger Webb and Simon Richardson made the long trek in to **Beinn Dearg Mor** for the first winter ascent of the superbly proportioned *Flake Buttress* (VI,6).

Towards the end of the season Guy Robertson and Roger Webb made the first ascent of *Morgane* (VII,8), a prominent corner-line on Atlantic Wall on **Slioch**, and Webb later returned with Pete Macpherson to add *Yggdrasil* (VIII,8) up the right side of the wall. Over the last 20 years Webb has authored over a dozen new routes on this remote face, which has a total height of over 400m and can lay claim to being one of the highest cliffs in Scotland.

Right: Greg Boswell seconding the big arête on pitch 2, FWA *Shoot The Breeze* (IX,8), Beinn Eighe. *(Guy Robertson)* Below: Iain Small, pitch 3 of *Jib* (VIII,8), Blaven. *(Simon Richardson)*

Skye

The Cuillin Ridge came into excellent condition during the second week in December and four teams made the winter traverse. The most impressive was a solo outing by Barry Smyth with one bivouac. The Cuillin Ridge has been traversed solo in winter several times before, but to do it early in the season, with precious little daylight and long lonely nights, takes a very special resolve.

Cuillin guidebook author Mike Lates organised a highly successful winter meet based at the BMC Hut in Glen Brittle in late January. Conditions were close to perfect, and five new routes were climbed including the first winter ascents of *Dyke Gully and Buttress* (V,6) and *Vixen Groove* (V,5) on **Sgurr a'Mhadaidh's** North Face. The same weekend, Iain Small and Simon Richardson made the first winter ascent of *Jib* (VIII,8), the spectacular E1 corner system left of *The Great Prow* on **Blaven**. Small returned a few days later with Doug Hawthorn to make the first complete winter ascent of *Slanting Gully* (VI,7) on Sgurr a'Mhadaidh's North Face. Lates also returned to Mhadaidh with Andy Huntington in mid April to make the long-awaited second ascent of *The Smear*, an undercut Grade V ice route first climbed in 1979 by Doug Scott and Jim Duff.

Pete Benson on pitch 2 of *Nevermore* (X,10), Lochnagar during an attempt in March 2013. *(Guy Robertson)*

Repeats

In a seemingly never-ending world of harder and harder new routes, second ascents and early repeats are important to reset the gauge. The most impressive run of repeats fell to Fort William based mountaineering instructor Guy Steven. In early November, he made the third ascent of *Archangel* (VII,7) on Ben Nevis with Kenny Grant, and he continued his run of hard Nevis routes with ascents of *Strident Edge* (VII,7) and *Sidewinder* (VII,8) on South Trident Buttress. On 2 December Steven made the second ascent of *The Survivor* (VII,8) on Number Three Gully Buttress with Keith Ball and Ewan Rodgers, and then as the snow level dropped, he turned his attention to Glen Coe with a series of excellent repeats. First off was the second ascent of *Nirvana Wall* with Ball and Grant. This sustained VI,8 takes the striking crack on the Far Eastern Buttress of **Aonach Dubh** and was first climbed by Donald King and Mike Pescod in December 2003. The following day the same trio made the second ascent of *The Twarf* (VI,7) on Aonach Dubh – an excellent chimney-groove cutting deep into the North Face that was first climbed in winter by Sam Chinnery and Muir Morton in February 2002.

Steven and Ball concluded an intense four days with the second ascent of *June Crack* on Great Gully Buttress on Buachaille Etive Mor. This route was so little known that it had escaped a modern two-tier rating and is given a traditional grade of V in the current Glen Coe guide. It was first climbed in winter by the formidable team of Robin Clothier and Doug Hawthorn way back in January 1984, which for the cognoscenti may provide a clue to its potential difficulty. 'We all found it very hard and agreed that it was somewhere around VIII,8,' Steven wrote later. 'It's harder than anything I've tried in the past... a cracking route in a fantastic setting!'

Other noteworthy repeats include second ascents of *Scrabble* (VIII,7) in Stob Coire nan Lochan by Adam Hughes, Matt Stygall and Blair Fyffe, *Mistral* (VII,8) on Beinn Eighe by Jim Higgins and Malcolm Bass, and *Steam Train* (VII,7) on Ben Nevis by Guy Robertson and Pete Macpherson. Greg Boswell made the third ascent of Dave MacLeod's *Cathedral* (X,11) on The Cobbler, earning multiple bonus points for climbing the route in spectacularly rimed conditions.

The biggest repeat of the winter however, was the long-awaited second ascent of *Mort* (IX,9) on Lochnagar's Tough-Brown Face, by the all-conquering team of Greg Boswell, Guy Robertson and Nick Bullock. This seminal route was first climbed by Brian Davison, Andy Nisbet and Dave McGimpsey in January 2000, and had a reputation for great seriousness and only being possible in icy conditions. The second ascent team confirmed the highly serious tag, but dispelled the notion that unusually icy conditions are required.

Nevermore

At the end of the season, Nick Bullock and Guy Robertson put to bed one of the last great problems on Lochnagar with the first winter ascent of *Nevermore* on the Tough-Brown Face. This rarely repeated summer E2 was first climbed by Dougie Dinwoodie and Bob Smith in August 1981 and takes a direct line up the face between *Post Mortem* and *Mort*.

Pete Benson and Guy Robertson were the inspiration behind this climb. Over the past two seasons they made several attempts with Pete Macpherson, but were repeatedly turned back by the extreme difficulty of

Scottish winter men of the moment: Iain Small, Nick Bullock, Guy Robertson.
(Simon Richardson)

the second pitch. When Benson finally succeeded on climbing this clean during their third attempt in March 2012 (a pitch thought to be worth IX,10 in its own right), they were shut down by a rapid thaw on the fifth and final pitch.

For their fourth attempt in March, the pair roped in Nick Bullock, but ferocious cold and dwindling daylight forced another retreat from high on the climb. Robertson and Bullock probed the fifth pitch, but both climbed back down unwilling to commit to the difficult initial roof.

On their fifth attempt on 8 April, Benson was unable to join the team, but Robertson and Bullock were highly focused on their goal. Bullock led the challenging second pitch leaving Robertson the crucial fifth pitch. After some hesitation, Robertson pulled over the roof, but then with his last protection below the roof, he fell. With the on-sight lost, he handed over the ropes to Bullock who soon passed Robertson's highpoint and pushed on into the unknown.

'The climbing difficulties above the second overlap increased,' Bullock wrote later. 'There was no more gear until the pitch and the angle eased. I took a long time as the technicalities were brain-ache inducing, stomach churning – the prospect of falling now slowed me – terror was the tang of battery terminals licked.' Incredibly Bullock kept his cool together and a winter ascent of *Nevermore* was finally a reality.

The significance of *Nevermore* goes far beyond Lochnagar and the Tough-Brown Face. The route was graded X,10 – a significant step up from the dozen or so Grade IX first ascents that have been climbed on-sight. Of course, with the prior attempts, *Nevermore* was not the perfect on-sight, and although there are a handful of higher graded winter routes in Scotland, they have typically benefitted from pre-inspection, multiple attempts on the crux pitch or knowledge from summer ascents. In a season that stands out for its superlatives, *Nevermore* was undoubtedly the ascent of the winter. Not only is it technically difficult, bold and committing, but it opens the door to the chilling prospect of on-sight Scottish winter Grade X.

Guy Robertson, Nick Bullock, Greg Boswell, Will Sim, Uisdean Hawthorn, Iain Small and Callum Johnson after making first ascents of *Defence of The Realm* (VII,7), *The Cure* (VIII,8), *Hustle* (VII,7) and *Take The Throne* (VII,6) on Creag and Dubh Loch's Broad Terrace Wall. *(Simon Richardson)*

2013-2014 SEASON

The 2013-14 winter season was an unusual one. Higher than average temperatures and almost continuous south-easterly gales led to huge depths of snow across the Highlands, but a lack of freeze-thaw meant that ice formation was limited. The last months of 2013 brought an almost continuous series of storms and calm days were few and far between. The atrocious weather peaked over the Christmas and New Year period, but during January and February the strong winds continued. Huge cornices were formed from vast amounts of wind-blown plateau snow, and dangerous full depth avalanches occurred in many corries. The result was that few cliffs came into good climbing condition, but those that did – namely Creag an Dubh Loch, Stob Coire nan Lochan in Glen Coe, Coire Mhic Fearchair on Beinn Eighe, and the Minus Face on Ben Nevis – yielded a rich series of routes for those fortunate enough to be in position at the right time.

The BMC International Meet, which fortuitously was held in the last week in January (one of the coldest spells of the winter) was the most productive period of the season. Throw together 44 talented international climbers from 26 countries with an equal number of highly motivated and experienced Scottish climbers, feed and water them at Glenmore Lodge, and let them loose in the Highlands for a week, and you have a recipe for success regardless of weather. Despite continuous gale force easterly winds, the 2014 Meet was the finest ever, with over a dozen new routes and a significant number of repeats.

Will Sim on the first ascent of *The Cure* (VIII,8), Broad Terrace Wall, Creag an Dubh Loch. *(Simon Richardson)*

Creag an Dubh Loch

The early winter storms were not all bad news because at an altitude of 750m or so, the rapid temperature fluctuations were perfect for ice formation. The finest example was on the great cliff of Creag an Dubh Loch in the Eastern Cairngorms, which came into the best ice climbing condition in living memory.

Callum Johnson teetering up the bold second pitch on the first ascent of *Take The Throne* (VII,6), Creag an Dubh Loch. *(Doug Hawthorn)*

The 300m-high Dubh Loch cliffs have the highest concentration of summer E-grade mountain climbs in the country, however it is notoriously difficult to find the crag in good winter condition. The smooth fine-grained granite needs a very specific weather pattern to create a coating of ice to render it climbable. In late December however, continuous gale force southerlies transported snow on the plateau to the more northerly

Iain Small climbing the crucial second pitch on the FWA of *Scansor* (IX,9), Stob Coire nan Lochan, Glen Coe. At least four prior attempts had ground to a halt near this point. *(Tony Stone)*

aspects of the cliff, and a rapid series of freeze-thaws around Christmas time allowed ice to ooze down the main drainage lines.

The first indication that the cliff was in condition came when news broke of the first winter ascent of *The Giant* (VII,7). This 200m-high summer E3 had been admired as a futuristic possibility by winter climbers for over three decades, but ice had never formed down the full length of the corner. Incredibly, the father and son team of Doug and Uisdean Hawthorn were in the right place at the right time to make the coveted first winter ascent on 29 December. Photos of their ascent on the internet attracted several strong teams to Central Gully Wall at the next weather window a few days later. Unfortunately, an overnight thaw softened the ice, and none were successful, except for Team Hawthorn who bided their time and then made a matter-of-fact second winter ascent of *Sword of Damocles* (VIII,9) the following day when the temperatures dropped again. *The Giant* collapsed a few days later as the freezing level rose, but this was the perfect ice-making scenario for the higher altitude routes on the neighbouring Broad Terrace Wall.

The 120m-high upper tier of Broad Terrace wall is the steepest mountain cliff in the Cairngorms. Its summer climbs are highly prized, but rarely climbed because they are almost always wet. In winter, the wall had only been climbed five times by four separate routes, but all this changed on 11 January when four new winter routes were added. The crack team of Guy Robertson and Greg Boswell were first to arrive and climb the plum line of *Defence of The Realm* (VII,7) which continues straight up a spectacular inverted staircase of hanging ice smears above the first pitch of the summer E1 *Falkenhorst*. A little to the right, Iain Small and Simon Richardson climbed *Hustle*, a thinly iced VII,7 to the left of *The Sting* (VII,6), the only existing route on this part of the wall, and first climbed by Doug

Hawthorn and Dougie Dinwoodie way back in January 1993. Between these two routes, Will Sim and Nick Bullock scooped *The Cure* (VIII,8), the most difficult new route of the trio. The sight of three of the finest Scottish winter climbers (namely Robertson, Sim and Small) leading new routes in parallel on one of the most revered cliffs in the Highlands was an extraordinary sight, and the uniqueness of the day was emphasised by the young pair of Uisdean Hawthorn and Callum Johnson making the first ascent of *Take The Throne* (VII,6), the thinly iced rib left of *Sword of Damocles*.

The weather remained cold and stable over the next three days. *Defence of The Realm* and *Take The Throne* both saw repeats, and Robin Clothier and Richard Bentley made an ascent of *The Last Oasis* (VI,6), which was first climbed in 1980 by Andy Nisbet and Neil Spinks and had only been repeated once in the following 30 years. Alongside this spectacular run of successes, there were also failures on *The Giant, Sword of Damocles* and *The Sting*, which highlighted both the difficulty of these routes, and the exacting conditions required for success. In light of this, the record of the Hawthorn team (two major new routes, and three second ascents) was remarkable. Their ability to predict conditions and be in the right place at the right time (a key Scottish winter skill) was particularly impressive.

Away from Creag an Dubh Loch, the major event in the Cairngorms was Greg Boswell's first winter ascent of *The Demon* (IX,9) in Coire an Lochain in the Northern Corries. Greg followed the E2 summer line, as opposed to the alternative line of *Demon Direct* first climbed by Alan Mullin and Steve Paget in 2001. Of particular note was the style of Greg's ascent and *The Demon* joins a very select group of Grade IX routes that have had on sight first ascents. Elsewhere in the massif, Andy Nisbet took advantage of the unique conditions of heavy snow to make the first ascent of *Scarebear* (VI,5) with Heike Puchan on **Stacan Dubha** in the Loch Avon Basin. This prominent line, with a pronounced overhang at half-height, was one of the last unclimbed gully lines in the Cairngorms.

Stob Coire nan Lochan

The week after the Dubh Loch Broad Terrace Wall ascents, the focus turned to the other side of the country and Glen Coe. Will Sim and Greg Boswell set the ball rolling with the second and third on sight ascents of *The Tempest* in Stob Coire nan Lochan. This touchstone route was first climbed by Neil Gresham in 2001 after climbing it as an M9 winter sports route by pre-placing the gear. Also that day, Guy Robertson and Nick Bullock climbed the icy groove left of East Face Route before continuing up the series of icy corners above. It is likely that *Slenderhead* (VIII,8) shares its first pitch with a route called *Boomshanka* that was first climbed by the late Mark Miller in the 1980s, but was left unreported at the time. Unfortunately, it is not known whether Mark finished his route and continued to the top of the crag, but Robertson was quick to point out that the first pitch is the crux of the route, so full credit to Mark for leading a modern Grade VIII pitch over 25 years ago using Chacals and Foot Fangs.

Olov Isaksson, FA of *Eggäschpili* (IX,9), left wall of SC Gully, Stob Coire nan Lochan. *(Karin Zgraggen)*

The next big event in Stob Coire nan Lochan took place a few days later when Iain Small and Tony Stone made the first winter ascent of *Scansor* (IX,9). This summer E2 takes the prominent pillar to the right of *Unicorn* and had seen at least four attempts in recent seasons including one by the first ascent pair. All parties had ground to a halt on the thin and exposed second pitch, but this time Iain found a devious line to gain the crucial traverse ledge.

In late January, Small followed up on his ascent of *Scansor* with *Year of The Horse* (IX,9) together with Blair Fyffe. This steep technical mixed route takes the soaring V-groove capped with a double overhang on the imposing wall to the left of *East Face Route*. A month later, Olov Isaksson from Sweden and Karin Zgraggen made an enterprising weekend trip from Switzerland to add *Eggäschpili* (IX,9). This outstanding mixed line takes a series of slim corners on the left wall of SC Gully, and is one of the most difficult Scottish winter first ascents ever climbed by an overseas team. It was spotted by Isaksson when he climbed *Slenderhead* during the International Meet.

Coire Mhic Fearchair

The south-easterly gales during January and February prompted many teams to visit the high north-facing cliffs of Coire Mhic Fearchair on Beinn Eighe. On the third day of the BMC International Meet, Will Sim and

Guy Robertson following the bold second pitch of *One Step Beyond* (IX,9), Beinn Eighe, during the FA. *(Pete Macpherson)*

Michelle Kadatz (Canada) made the fourth ascent of the fabled *West Central Gully* (VII,8), arguably the most difficult gully climb in Scotland. Andy Inglis and Martin Zumer (Slovenia) made the third ascent of *Hydroconicum* (VIII,8), and Dave Almond and Michal Sabovcik (Slovakia) climbed the now classic *Blood, Sweat and Frozen Tears* (VIII,8).

The following day, the pace stepped up another notch when Nick Bullock, Jon Walsh and Greg Boswell made the first ascent of *Making The Cut* (VIII,8), a major new line taking the soaring crack-line left of *West Central Gully*. Will Sim and Olov Isaksson (Sweden) also added *Crazy Eyes* (VII,9), the left-facing corner, roof crack and offwidth corner above *Hydro-*

Murdoch Jamieson nearing the top of *Minus One Superdirect* (VII,6), Ben Nevis. *(Iain Small)*

ponicum, and Andy Inglis made a return visit with Piotr Sulowski (Poland) to climb the brilliant *Sundance* (VIII,8).

The highlight of the exceptionally busy season on Beinn Eighe was the first ascent of *One Step Beyond* (IX,9) by Pete Macpherson and Guy Robertson on the Far East Wall. The route is based on an unusual hanging ice smear that oozes from a seep half way up the wall left of *King of The*

Swingers, and is a contender for the hardest new route of the season. The first winter ascent of the very steep summer E2 *The Root of All Evil* (IX,8) by Murdoch Jamieson and John Orr was another challenging addition, as was Nick Bullock and Tim Neill's *Crème de Violette* (IX,9) on West Central Wall. The latter was an attempt to repeat Ian Parnell's *Bruised Violet*, however a route finding error meant they followed a largely independent line. Also of note was the second ascent of *Vishnu* (VII,7) on the Far East Wall by Small and Jamieson – a Nisbet-Cunningham creation that had waited over 25 years for a repeat!

The Minus Face

New route activity in the Central Highlands was remarkably quiet, although the first winter ascent of *Turkish* (VII,7) on Number Five Gully Buttress on Ben Nevis in early January was a notable coup by Malcolm Bass, Simon Yearsley and Helen Rennard. Also in January, Donald King, Mike Pescod and Andy Nelson made the first ascent of *Angels* (VIII,9). This excellent new mixed route on the front face of Church Door Buttress on Bidean nam Bian in Glen Coe was climbed in rare good conditions of light winds, well rimed rock and usable ice. On Ben Nevis, Dave MacLeod made the first winter ascent of *Orient Express* (IX,9) in February with Adam Hughes. This tenuous looking winter line follows the summer E2 on the First Platform of North-East Buttress – a good venue for very snowy conditions.

With a huge amount of snow lying on the Minus Face for most of the season, Ben Nevis regulars knew that when it consolidated then conditions would be exceptional. A swift thaw in early March followed by a brief high pressure was the perfect recipe to transform the mountain into a Christmas cake of rock-hard frozen snow. Iain Small and Uisdean Hawthorn were quickly on the scene to add *Dark Star* (VI,5), the much-eyed line of grooves on the left side of *Astronomy*, and the following day they joined up with Murdoch Jamieson to climb *Minus One Superdirect* (VII,6). This archetypical Nevis thin face climb links together the 1977 and 2010 routes and is the first winter route to climb the very crest of the much sought after Minus One Buttress. The star performers however were French guide Remi Thivel and Laurence Girard who had an outstanding two days when they climbed four routes including the second ascent of *Shooting Star* (VI,6) – the longest route on the Orion Face, and an early repeat of *Point Blank* (VII,6). Their highlights were the first ascent of *Total Kheops* (VI,6), the impressive hanging groove cutting into the left flank on Minus One Buttress, and Remi's solo of *Urban Spaceman* (VII,7) in a mind-boggling 40 minutes.

A deep thaw meant that these once in a lifetime conditions only lasted three days, but a heavy snowfall two weeks later brought the mixed routes on Carn Dearg Buttress into condition. Guy Robertson and Nick Bullock nipped in for a new VIII,7 direct finish to *The Shield Direct*, and Iain Small and Simon Richardson climbed *From The Jaws of Defeat* (VIII,8), a direct line up to, and through, the triangular headwall on the adjacent North

Iain Small moves through a bulge on *From The Jaws of Defeat* (VIII,8), Carn Dearg, Ben Nevis. *(Simon Richardson)*

Wall of Carn Dearg. Soon afterwards a slow thaw set in, and by early April, the pristine white snows of Ben Nevis were rapidly disappearing into the raging Allt a'Mhuilinn *en route* to Loch Linnhe and the sea.

LINDSAY GRIFFIN

Afghanistan 2013

The Qara Jilga group from the north showing the line of the attempted route. Three of the four summits are visible, the fourth hidden in cloud on the left. The highest (6094m) is the visible summit furthest back. *(Alan Halewood)*

Only two mountaineering expeditions are known to have operated in the Hindu Kush during the summer of 2013. There is an increasingly widespread feeling that when NATO troops are withdrawn from the country in 2014, climbing in the Wakhan will quickly become untenable for foreigners. This could be the last mountaineering report from Afghanistan for a while. Hopefully not.

Alan Halewood returned to the mountains of the Pamir, this time with Richmond MacIntyre and Rich Parker. Halewood had climbed north-east of the Qara Jilga massif in 2010 and now wanted to attempt one of these summits. The team took the usual approach through Tajikistan, crossing into Afghanistan at Ishkashim, and driving east up the Wakhan Corridor to the roadhead at Sarhad-e-Boroghil. From here, they walked for seven days to a base camp at 4815m on the north side of the Qara Jilga. They acclimatized by checking out a couloir leading to the north ridge of the main top, climbing to the crest of this ridge at c. 5400m, and then descending prior to a summit attempt the following day. On the way down rockfall struck MacIntyre on the head, splitting his helmet and rendering him temporarily unconscious. He recovered enough for the others to assist him down and then, with an improvised neck collar, altered vision and great assistance from excellent Wakhi staff, was able to reach the road head on horseback and eventually return home with no permanent damage.

Dylan Taylor was also returning to the Wakhan for a second time. In 2012 he had made several ski descents above the Issik valley in the Pamir and this time, with fellow Americans Mick Follari and Aidan Loehr, planned rock routes on granite 'not dissimilar to Chamonix'. But they found September days cold, and instead opted for ice/mixed ascents. They made the first ascent of an unnamed peak of **5965m** (Austrian Map) between Koh-e-Seh

Aspe Safad and Koh-e-Helal, climbing the south face at AI4+ M5. GPS on the summit recorded an altitude of 6060m, and descent required 18 consecutive rappels from Abalakovs.

They then made two attempts on **Peak 5842m**, a couple of kilometres east of Koh-e-Seh Aspe Safad, but retreated from half-height on the northeast face, having climbed difficulties up to AI5 M6. Approaching nightfall and complete lack of bivouac gear made it prudent to descend. The

Richmond MacIntyre with the split helmet, head, and a rock of similar size to the one that hit him. *(Alan Halewood)*

team notes that, ominously, skirmishes between Taliban and the Afghan National Army had now reached within a few hours of Ishkashim. Exiting the country, Loehr discovered that he had only a single-entry visa to Tajikistan, and as this had already been used, his eventual escape from Afghanistan took almost one month and a considerable amount of cash.

During the winter following these two trips a Polish expedition attempted to repeat Tadeusz Piotrowski and Andrzej Zawada's historic February 1973 ascent of **Noshaq** (7492m), the first winter ascent of any peak above 7000m. Unfortunately, they were forced to give up relatively low on the mountain.

JOHN TOWN

China & Tibet

The situation in Tibet continues to be very difficult with permits for unclimbed peaks seemingly impossible to obtain and travel outside the central area heavily restricted. The neighbouring provinces of Xinjiang, Chinghai, Sichuan and Yunnan present greater opportunities although activity has continued to be concentrated in the relatively accessible Qonglai, Daxue and Litang Plateau areas of Sichuan. The latter, which includes the Chola, Shaluli and Gonkala ranges is not without its own issues. There has been strong and consistent hostility to climbing on holy mountains in certain valleys. One wonders whether, in accordance with local wishes, some areas may yet be set aside for the gods to roam the summits undisturbed?

Min Shan

The Min Shan is the most north-easterly massif in Sichuan, situated directly north of Chengdu. In May 2012, Karim Adouane (France), Jon Otto, and Su Ronqin made the first known ascent of **Xiao (Little) Xuebaoding** (5440m) by the north-east ridge.

Qonglai Shan

The rock walls and peaks of the Qonglai mountains continue to attract attention, particularly those accessible from the Shuangqiao valley. In 2010 Kazuyoshi Uematsu led a three-man team that made the first ascent via the south-east face of the ultra prominent **Niuxin Shan (Ox Heart mountain)** (4942m) at the northern end of the valley. They were closely followed by the local team of Tashi, Yangxinyong and Yao Liu, who climbed a new route on the south face. In September, after two earlier attempts, Chad Kellogg and Dylan Johnson finally succeeded in making the first ascent of **Seerdengpu** (5592m), whose 1500m walls dominate the heads of the Shuangqiao and Changping valleys. A few days later, with John Dickey, they nearly made the first ascent of the granite 'shark's fin' of **Peak 5086m**, being stopped by a blank section immediately below the summit. Chinese climbers Gong Xiaorui, He Chuan, and Wu Peng suffered similar disappointment in October having approached from the opposite (south) face. He Chuan returned in 2011 and climbed the south face to a point on the east ridge about 50m below the summit. His party also made the possible first ascent of **Peak 4970m**.

In July and August of 2012 Hiroo Yonezawa and his team made the first ascents of **Mountain Hermit** (5062m) via the north-west ridge, **Beauty Peak** (c.5360m) via the south-east ridge and **Chibu II** (c.5400m) via the west ridge. In late October Jerome Para and Damien Tomasi made the first ascent of the 700m north-west face of **Daogou** (5466m). Yonezawa returned in 2013 to make the first ascent of **Central Pillar** (5380m), just south of Potala Shan and in August of that year another Japanese team from the Keio University Alpine Club made first ascents of **Shizi Peak** (5057m), **Fenghuang Peak** (4984m) and **Xiao Peak** (4785m).

From the nearby Changping Valley, in July 2012, Ye Feng, Zhang Yunping, and He Chuan climbed a new line up the south-west face and south-south-west ridge of **Celestial Peak (Mount Pomiu)** (5413m). Two months later Zheng Chaohui and Li Yuan made an ascent via the south-south-west ridge. In the cold of November, Christophe Dumarest and Thomas Vialletet made the probable first ascent of **Pt. c.5600m** at the end of the south-west ridge of Chang-gou (Lara Peak) (5700m), immediately north of Siguniang North.

Goromity (Riyucaibao) (5609m), towards the southern end of the Siguniang Shan, remains the highest unclimbed mountain in the Qonglai Shan. Attempts by Luo Biao and Zhou Peng in 2010 via the south-west ridge and Hitoshi Onodera and Takeo Ohe in August 2011 were both unsuccessful.

Daxue Shan

The Dangling Range in the northern part of the Daxue Shan is an interesting and less visited region than the Minya Konka area. In April and May 2010 a 4-man Japanese Alpine Club expedition led by Chiharu Yoshimura visited the area. Hiroshi Matsushima and Ken Sato made the first ascent of the attractive **Xiaqiangla** (5470m) via the north-east face.

In the Minya Konka range a recent first was a ski descent of the west ridge of **Reddomain** (6112m) in 2009 by Jimmy Chin, Giulia Monego, Kasha Rigby, and Ingrid Backstrom. In 2010 a 23 member Korean team made a new route on the south-south-west face of **Ruiche Gongga** (5928m) with 9 members making the summit. The same year Tim Church (New Zealand) and Yvonne Pfluger made what they thought was the first ascent of **Dogonomba** (5960m) via the west ridge, only to find that it had been climbed in 2008 by Aidan Loehr in a solo ascent via a similar route.

Mount Edgar (6618m) continues to provide challenges at the highest level. Kyle Dempster and Bruce Normand climbed the east face and south ridge in 2010, encountering sustained difficulties over an eight-day round trip. In September and October of that year Alexander Novikov and Vladimir Belousov explored the west and north faces but their subsequent attempt in 2011 failed because of bad weather on their summit day.

Youthful achievements in 2011 included the first ascent of the east face and second ascent overall of **Daddomain** (6380m) by the Giri-Giri boys – Fumitaka Ichimura, Ryo Masumoto, and Takaaki Nagato – and the first ascent of **Melcyr Shan** (5910m), just north of Jiazi, by a group of young climbers from the *Deutscher Alpen Verein* led by David Göttler.

In the Tachenliu massif near Kangding, **Baihaizishan** (5924m) remains unclimbed, despite an attempt on the north-west ridge by Simon Moore,

Rimon Than, Alex Tomaczynski, and Duncan Francis in 2012. They were, however, successful in making a very cold ascent of **Wupingfeng** (5672m), reaching the summit on 3 December.

Gonkala Shan

Climbers have so far failed to make much of an acquaintance with the impressive peaks in this area, which lie about 30km south-east of Garze (Ganzi), with at least three planned trips being turned back by local opposition. **Kawarori I** (5992m) and **II** (5928m) continue to be admired, but only from a distance. Hitoshi Onodera and Takeo Ohe gained a permit in 2011 from the Sichuan Mountaineering Association for Kawarori but were refused access by the Deputy Director of the Sports Administrative Department, a senior official in the Ganzi Tibet Autonomous Region, on the grounds that the mountains were holy to the local people. In September 2005 a British expedition were ordered off the mountain by a party of 40 monks from the Khur Chong monastery with equipment lost and violence threatened.

Shaluli Shan

Similar problems were experienced in 2011 in the **Xiangqiuqieke Massif** where the village elders asked Tim Church (New Zealand) and Yvonne Pfluger to leave after several days of reconnaissance, indicating that the range was a holy one. They then tried to explore **Asa** and **Hari**, south of Haga La, but encountered resistance by locals who, in the light of recent mineral exploration, were sensitive to strangers.

Other parties had more success in 2012. Szuting Yi, Eric Salazar, and Dave Anderson made the first ascent of **Crown Mountain** (5609m) via its north-west face and west ridge. The peak lies in the northern part of the range, about 10 km south-east of Xiashe. Yi and Anderson went on to make the first ascent of the impressive granite tower of **Kemailong** (5873m) in the Genyen massif via the 1000m south ridge.

Tom Nakamura and two companions made a reconnaissance of the **Gangga Massif**, just south of Garze. Most of the peaks are between 5300m and 5500m, with **Gangga I** reaching 5688m. More detail and photos are available in Tom's article in the 2013 *Japanese Alpine News*.

In 2011 Sergi Ricart made an extended solo trip to Qinghai, Sichuan, and Yunnan, near the Tibet border, spending time with local inhabitants and exploring unclimbed mountains. On the north side of the Sichuan-Tibet Highway, east of the Chola Shan Pass (a.k.a. Tro La, 4910m), and directly north of the Chola Shan, is a small cirque of peaks. Exploring them from both the northern and southern sides he made first ascents of **Acha La Ri** (5000m), by the south-west spur, and **Ru Chen Gangri** (5350m), by the north and east faces. In the Daxue Shan, he climbed two small rocky peaks, **Tso Chong Ri** and **Tso Chen Ri** (5100m), which lie towards the end of the long north-west ridge of Reddomain, before it terminates at the Ruichi Haniya.

Kemailong (5870m). First ascent route follows the south ridge, seen in profile on the left. *(Tomas Obtulovic)*

Chola Shan

Hitoshi Onodera and Takeo Ohe also visited the northern end of the Chola Shan on their 2011 trip. They had information that there was an unclimbed massif called **Polujab**, south of Zhogchen Monastery. Locals explained that the highest peak was named Sejong. They took photos of peaks and concluded that 'the highest peak was **Sejong I** (5816m+ not marked on the Chinese map), the second highest **Sejong II** (5816m), southwest of Sejong I and marked on the map, the third highest **Nobuyugya** (5594m), north of Sejong I, also marked on map, and the fourth **Polujab** (5472m), west of Sejong II , marked on Chinese map.'

Yunnan, Yulong Xueshan

Over the winter of 2010/2011 Darryl Kralovic and Mike Dobie were active in the Yulong Shan which sit in the bend of the Yangtse River above Lijiang. In December they climbed the **unnamed peak** (c.5000m) situated at the southern end of the group and during February they attempted the prominent **unnamed easternmost peak** (5321m) in the northern half of the massif.

Yunnan, Hengduan Mountains

The Baimang Xueshan massif is situated in Deqen County, not far to the south of Meili Xueshan (Kawa Karpo, 6740m). It lies close to and west of the Yunnan-Tibet Highway, where it runs north-west from Zhongdian to Deqen. In October 2012 Sun Bin and a party from the Summit Outdoor School made five first ascents: **Duochubomubadeng** (5466m), **Unnamed Peak** (5288m), **Unnamed Peak** (5295m), **Unnamed Peak** (5250 m) and **Zhalaqueni South Summit** (5420m). In January 2013 Li Yuan, Zhang Xiaohui, and Zheng Chao Hui made the first official ascent of the north summit of **Zhalaqueni** (5429m) after three and a half days on the east face.

The 2013 *Japanese Alpine News* contains an interesting article by Tom Nakamura on **Damyon** (6324m) and other peaks of the Taniantaweng

East face of a c.5500m peak in the Chola Shan, north of the highway. *(Tamotsu Nakamura)*

Shan. These are situated within the TAR on the Salween-Mekong divide, south of the Sichuan-Tibet Highway. Permits have so far proved elusive.

Kangri Karpo

Though access is impossible at the present time, the 2011 *Japanese Alpine News* 2011 has an enticing article by Tatsuo (Tim) Inoue on the '47 six-thousanders in the Kangri Garpo Mountains'.

Qilian Shan

In August 2010 a 14 member Korean team made an ascent of **Gradiska** (5254m) via the south-west face and first ascents of **Peak 4722m** and **Peak 4880m**.

Tibetan Plateau

At the far eastern end of the plateau, on the border of Qinghai and Sichuan, is the Bayan Har Shan. A Chinese party made the first ascent of the highest peak, **Nyainbo Yuzi** (5369m) in July 2011. A second ascent was made in 2013.

With the restrictions on travel in the Tibetan Autonomous Region and elsewhere, the only way to climb in some areas is if you happen to have a permit for some other activity or, as in the 19th Century you penetrate the formidable barrier of the Kun Lun to the north. Understandably, accounts tend to appear rather later than normal, when campaigns have drawn to a close and the protagonists have moved on to greener pastures, both literally and metaphorically.

In 2004 Paul Knapp and another member of the University of Arizona Geosciences team climbed an **unnamed 6258m summit** in the **Muggar Kangri Range**, to the north of the Dagze Tso. The next year they climbed an obscure and **unnamed 5781m peak** in the **Ayi Shan** near the main road that leads west across the Ayi Shan into the Zhada basin. During the 2005 field season, while in the Kailas region they investigated the long gorge leading from the south shore of Lake Manasarovar into the **Gurla Mandhata massif** and climbed an unnamed **6085m peak**. Most recently, in 2012, Barbara Carrapa, Ryan Leary and one other visited the **Linzhou Range**, in the group of peaks immediately north-east of the Loinbo Kangri Range and designated on the Russian 1:200,000 topographic map of the region as the **Kanchun Kangri**. On June 26th they climbed an **unnamed 6164m summit** via the west face.

Kun Lun

In the 2010/11 *Alpine Journal* we recorded the extensive journeys across the plateau of a Swedish cyclist and climber. Janne Corax continued his exploration in 2010 with a formidable journey with Lars B. over the northern Kun Lun and through a series of remote ranges in the **Altyn-Tagh**. Their first target was **Aleke Tag** (Akato, Yusupu Aleketage 6080m). Having climbed this they moved on to the **Qimantag Shan**, on the shores of the Ayakkum Tso, where they made an ascent of **Peak 5551m**. They then turned west, reaching and climbing **Fujian Feng (5866m),** before heading towards the Ayalik Range, where they made ascents of **Ayalik East (5952m)** and **Ayalik (6167m)**.

Perhaps the most impressive achievement came in 2012 when Corax set off again across the main chain of the Kun Lun, aiming to reach the remote Ak Tag range. Details are sparse but, after his companion turned back, he reports approaching from the south to make the first ascent of **Ak Tag** (6758m).

Tien Shan

In July 2011 the Slovenian team of Ales Holc, Igor Kremser, and Peter Juvan made the first ascent of the last unclimbed peak of the main Xuelian Group, **Xuelian North-east** (6231m) via the 2400m west ridge. This had previously been attempted in 2009 by Jed Brown and Bruce Normand. During their acclimatisation period they also climbed **Yi-ge Feng** (4420m), south face; **Kundi Feng** (4601m), north face and north-west ridge; and **Huang Jin Feng** (4708m) via the south-west face and south ridge.

On 9 July 2012 the Chinese climber Yan Dongdong was killed in a crevasse fall in the Chulebos Massif of the Central Tien Shan. Yan was the first of a new generation of Chinese alpinists, climbing new routes at the highest level and epitomising a new spirit of adventure and exploration.

Further information and photos of many of these climbs are contained in the **Japanese Alpine News** *and* **American Alpine Journal**.

IAN WALL

Nepal

I would like to extend my gratitude to Liz Hawley and to those climbers mentioned for their permission to use their images and expedition report extracts in the following notes. – I.W.

Tragedy Strikes Khumbu

The risk to human life posed by climbing on the Himayalan giants was brought into brutal focus at 06.30 on 18 April 2014 when a house-sized piece of ice calved from a glacier on the west face of Everest and struck the Popcorn Field area of the Khumbu Icefall, where a group of some 50 Sherpa guides and high altitude Nepali support staff were waiting to ascend fixed ladders.

Sixteen Nepalese Sherpa guides were killed, three of whom remain unaccounted for. The dead and missing are officially listed as: Mingma Nuru Sherpa, Dorji Sherpa, Ang Tshiri Sherpa, Nima Sherpa, Tenzing Chottar Sherpa (missing), Phurba Ongyal Sherpa, Lakpa Tenjing Sherpa, Chhering Ongchu Sherpa, Dorjee Khatri, Then Dorjee Sherpa, Phur Temba Sherpa, Aankaji Sherpa, Pem Tenji Sherpa (missing), Aash Bahadur Gurung (missing), Pasang Karma Sherpa and Asman Tamang.

Spring Season 2013

In 1973 the Italian Everest Expedition led by Guido Monzino arrived in Nepal and was joined by a young Nepali support climber, Shambhu Tamang. Tamang, 16 years old at that time went on to summit on 5 May 1973 and in doing so became the youngest Everest Summiteer and unwittingly started the trend of record setting on the mountain.

This trend seems to be pursued with vigour even today with many 'firsts' being claimed and entered into record books. During the 2013 spring season **Yuichiro Miura** (80) from Japan, became the oldest man to climb Everest. His daughter, Emiri, reported that the climb cost ¥150 million. A Nepalese climber, Min

Chhurim Sherpa. *(Ian Wall)*

Bahadur Sherchan (81) was also making an attempt, but had to turn back due to poor weather conditions. Prior to the final outcome Miura had said that should Sherchan succeed he, Miura, was unlikely to make another summit attempt!

Another record set during the 2013 spring season was that of **Chhurim Sherpa**, (29) from the Tapeljung district of eastern Nepal. She climbed Everest twice in a week from Base Camp and became the first female climber to do so. After summiting on 12 May Chhurim had a two-day rest at Base Camp before setting off again for the summit for the second time which she attained on 29 May and, at her own admission, for no other reason than to achieve something that had not been done before.

The *Himalayan Times* announced on 2 March 2014 that the Peak Permit fees will be reduced from US $25,000 to US $11,000 per climber in January 2015. For Nepali climbers the Permit Fee will remain unchanged at NR60,000. Nepal's mountaineering revenue covers more than 4% of the GDP, (nearly US $3 million per year from Everest alone).

In a bid to increase this revenue the Cabinet is seeking permission to open another 104 peaks to climbing, which will increase the number of peaks open to mountaineering activities to 414.

During May 2013, **Everest** (8848m) predictably tops the league table of spring season ascents – 539 by 22 nationalities (409 climbers reached the summit in 2012); **Everest** (North) 119 by 21 nationalities (138 in 2012); **Lhotse** (8414m) 76 by 24 nationalities; **Makalu** (8468m) 9 by 6 nationalities; **Cho Oyu** (8188m) 16 ascents on 13, 21 and 22 May by climbers from Nepal, Estonia, UK, USA, and Switzerland; **Kangchenjunga** (8598m) 15, all on 20 May by 7 nationalities.

Other spring ascents include the FA of **Gandarbha Chuli** (6248m) located in the Annapurna Sanctuary (between Annapurna III and Machapuchari) by two Romanians, Cosmin Andron and Cristina Pogacean with the support of Purna Tamang, Hasta Magar, Sohit, Sukram Tamang, Dawa Tamang, Ram Shresta, Wanchu Sherpa and Lok Bahadur Gurung. The Romanian Route was established between 2 and 6 May 2013 and climbs a mixed line of moderate difficulty to the south-west ridge; this in turn joins the west and summit ridge.

Base camp was established near the confluence of the Modi Khola and the tributary running south from the Annapurna III Sanctuary and Advance Base Camp was established at 4448m just below the glacier. On 4 May bad weather set in causing slow progress and forcing the pair to bivouac below the SW ridge and then again on the ridge but by 6 May the storm had cleared and progress resumed. On the west ridge the climbers continued unroped until it became knife-edged and covered in a thin and unstable layer of snow. Easier terrain followed, but the final 30 metre summit section increased in severity with the angle varying between 55° and 65°.

Out of respect for local beliefs and following discussion with the Nepalese staff the climbers decided not to set foot on the actual summit. Instead they began their descent back down the route from their high point a few metres below the top. However the climbers maintain that in the official documentation for this peak it appears only as unclimbed and not 'sacred' or 'forbidden'. Andron described the route as a combination of the *Swiss*

The north face of Talung (7349m), showing Czech route. *(Marek Holeček / Zdeněk Hrubý)*

Route on the Courtes and the *Cosmiques Arête*, but bigger.

Himlung Himal (7126m) was climbed on 14 May 2013 by a Nepalese and French climber. Located in the Manaslu region north-east of the Annapurna range, Himlung Himal lies close to the Tibetan border in a remote northern corner of Nepal. It was first climbed in 1992 by a Japanese climber but due to its remoteness it receives little attention and by 2013 it had only had two British ascents.

Putha Hiunchuli (7246m) is situated in the Dhaulagiri range and is the westernmost peak in this Himal. It is also sometimes referred to as Dhaulagiri VI. It was ascended via the north-east face on 21 May by the Swiss climber Erwin Jaconet and German climbers Günther Dannecker and Peter Ulrich accompanied by a Nepalese climber.

Talung North Face (7349m), remotely situated on the Nepalese-Sikkim border immediately south of Kangchenjunga, has only had three previous ascents. From 15-19 May 2013 the accomplished Czech mountaineers Marek Holecek and Zdenek Hrubý made the first ascent of the difficult north face alpine style, descending the west face on 20 May. The pair established their base camp at 5100m in the Yalung Valley after a 16-day trek in. From BC they set about acclimatizing and carrying out reconnaissance trips to the mountain.

Initially they planned to climb the north-north-west pillar but a dry lower third made this impractical. Settling on a line on the face to the left of the *North West Pillar* the pair had four bivouacs before reaching the summit and then another on the descent in poor visibility and deteriorating weather conditions. The route consisted of steep hard water-ice, a series of gullies up

South Face of Annapurna showing line taken by Ueli Steck (solo) and later Stéphane Benoist and Yannick Graziani. *(Ian Wall)*

the headwall and a final ice slope and dièdre escaping through the summit rock band. Approximately 2500m in length, it took the pair a total of five days base camp to base camp. They named the route *Thumba Party* and graded it W16 and M6+ with the crux section being in the upper headwall.

Ama Dablam (6812m) had 13 recorded ascents from between 10-18 May representing Nepal, Russia and Austria. A photo was taken in April 2012 by Freddie Wilkinson of Ueli Steck negotiating a web of fixed lines on the summit. The proliferation of fixed rope and waste on popular routes in the Himalaya is a complicated issue. There have been noble efforts over the years to clean up this route, but the expedition debris keeps building up.

Baruntse (7152m), in the Khumbu district, had two ascents via the south-east ridge by German climbers, Christoph Descher and Olev Rick, summiting on 3 May 2013.

Dragmorpa Ri (6185m), situated in upper Langtang, is a recently opened peak. The first ascent was made on 30 May by Russian climber Roman Gretzky. Details of the ascent are sketchy but the permit details show he made his ascent on the south-east side.

Autumn Season 2013

On 10 October Ueli Steck completed a fast ascent of a new line on the **South Face of Annapurna** to the right of the route first ascended by Chris Bonington's team in 1970. The route was initially tried in 1992 by Pierre Béghin and Jean-Christophe Lafaille. Climbing without supplementary oxygen and completely alone, Ueli left his Advanced Base Camp at 5000m, crossed the bergschrund at 5650m and reached the summit in 18hrs 30mins. He spent just a couple of minutes on the summit before descending to his ABC via the same route, completing both the ascent and descent in a total of 28 hours.

Directly following Steck's ascent, French guides Stéphane Benoist and Yannick Graziani repeated the route alpine style over 10 days from 16-26 October. They, however, were pinned down for a significant period by bad weather high on the face. Benoist subsequently suffering severe frostbite injuries [see article page 24].

Bamongo (6400m), situated on the Tibetan/Nepalese border in the Rolwaling Himal, received its first ascent on 29 October 2013 by a Chinese and Nepalese team. The route follows the pillar feature on the steep southwest face leading to the south-west ridge which in turn was followed to the summit. Liu Yong, Mingma Gyalje and Pema Tshering Sherpa climbed to their first bivouac at 5440m. The next day leaving at 05.00 they reached the summit at 14.25 and had returned to base camp at 4800m by 21.30. The final upper ridge had been of soft snow preventing any real protection for five pitches followed by another hour of insecure climbing to the summit. The team climbed tied in to one 60m rope on the initial 40-60° slope which then reared up steeply in the final 30m to the summit.

Himlung (7126m) is situated in the Manaslu region and is increasingly being used to provide opportunities for 7000m+ ascents. Himlung is not technically difficult, but interestingly, during the autumn 2013 season, the peak received a visit from a huge 72-member medical research group and 25 climbing Sherpas. Led by the Swiss physician Urs Hefti the team employed 5000m of fixed rope along the route to the summit. Initially 30 members and 17 sherpas ascended the south-west ridge from their third and high camp to summit between 10.00 and 16.00 on 22 October, the remaining 33 members failing to go beyond their second camp at 6950m.

Ama Dablam (6812m) got off to a poor autumn season start with a late monsoon storm being blown back into Nepal as a result of the typhoon that hit India. This caused a considerable amount of snow to be deposited particularly in the central and western Nepalese Himalaya. Ama Dablam got more than its fair share of new and heavy snow causing a big back-log of expeditions building up at base camp which in turn resulted in 20 teams retreating from around 6350m. Their retreat was blamed on the lack of fixed ropes and none of the teams had mountain staff with rope fixing experience. It was not until 15 November that ropes were finally fixed to the summit; clients then reached the top on 16 November 2013.

MARCELO SCANU

Argentine Andes 2013

It has been a good year for climbing and exploration in Argentina. From the Northern and Central Andes to the far south, many summits remain unexplored and there is scope for many new routes. This report deals mainly with significant ascents in 2013.

Peinado (5741m). *(Marcelo Scanu)*

Northern Andes

Antofalla (6409m) volcano is the second highest summit of the barren high mountain desert of Puna. It was (and actually still is) a sacred mountain – the Incas erected a large stone circle on the summit. Christian Vitry, a well known high mountain archaeologist visited the area with Sebastián Cura and Diego Sberna. They had some difficulties reaching the first camp (4400m 25° 24' 34.80"S, 67° 54' 13.40"W) because rain had destroyed part of the track. Next day they continued 15km south and erected a second camp (5100m, 25° 31' 12.50"S, 67° 53' 17.49"W). That same day, 20 February, they climbed a virgin summit due north of Antofalla that they named **Colorado de Antofalla** (5787m 25° 31' 57.98"S, 67°53'56.48"W). Some days later they also climbed Antofalla itself.

Volcán Peinado (The Combed One) is a new, nicely shaped volcano,

Bolinder from the south-west with route marked.
(Guillermo Almaraz)

also climbed by the Incas. Legend has it that Peinado is unclimbable and that the summit is guarded by a bull with golden horns. The first non-Inca ascent was from the north (*Inca Route*) by Austrian Mathias Rebitsch and Argentine Sergio Domicelj. In 1996 Marcelo Scanu and party made the second modern ascent and the first by the *South Route*. This route subsequently received three more ascents. The summit, (approx. 26° 37' 30"S, 68° 07'W) is officially put at 5741m but many other summits in the area look to be higher (between 5800m and 5840m).

On 1 January, Brazilians Waldemar and Pedro Hauck climbed a new route on Peinado from the north, starting in a labyrinth of rocky, ash filled volcanic valleys, then climbing a rough face of large volcanic boulders before gaining a summit crater complete with turquoise lagoon. The descent was difficult, the party regaining their camp at 10pm. I must point out that an Argentine party has claimed this route but the report and the photos shown to me do not give any proof of it.

In November, on nearby **Volcán Bertrand** (5207m), an Argentine group descended to the bottom of the crater (some 400m below the summit) and from there made a new route to the north (5188m) summit. The first descent to Bertrand's crater was made in 2008 by Scanu and Querlico.

Various first ascents have been made in honour of Walther Penck (1888-1923), in the **Paso de San Francisco** region. Penck was a young German scientist who worked for the Argentine government producing maps. He climbed many mountains in 1912 and 1913, most of them awaiting a second ascent until recently. He wrote that he didn't think anyone would retrace his steps. Some Argentine climbers, knowing this, visited these mountains in the high desert between November 2012 and December 2013. Guillermo Almaraz repeated many of Penck's routes, variously with Eduardo Namur, Daniel Pontin, Lelio de Crocci, Pablo Coria or Pantaleón.

The group also climbed many virgin peaks in the **Cordillera de San Buenaventura**: **Loma Larga** (5200m) (26° 43' 51.5"S, 68° 10' 36.2"W) by its west face and south-west ridge, **Volcán Bolinder** (5597m) and his twin

Loma Larga with
Peinado behind.
*(Guillermo
Almaraz)*

Volcán Zacarías (5520m) (26° 44' 44.8"S, 68° 05" 44.1'W). Many other minor summits were also ascended.

In September, during the southern winter, Argentines Marcelo Casilli and Marcelo Scanu also made an ascent in honour of Penck's centennial in the **Sierra de Narvaez**. They left the Las Peladas hut at midday on 5 September in dust and salt laden winds up to 100 kph. At 16.30 they erected camp at 4500m in a creek beneath a 5000m peak. They set out at 09.00 next day, reaching the 5032m summit, with a little cairn but no documents, via the south-west ridge. They continued north with a condor overhead for company and reached the highest 5047m summit at 13.30. There they found a huge destroyed cairn, surely made by Penck a hundred years before and also surveyors' markings from c.1950. The pair descended to camp and then on to Las Peladas the same day.

On 20 December, Guillermo Almaraz and Pablo Bertoni established a new route on the south face of **Cerro Nacimiento**, reaching the highest summit – Nacimiento North-west or Nacimiento I, (6460m 27° 16' 51.5"S, 68° 31' 28"W). This summit has received only seven ascents and many climbers, including Almaraz, consider it to be the highest although Nacimiento II or North-east is shown on the Argentine map as the highest at 6436m. Regarded as the highest for many years, it has received 15 ascents overall. The other summits are Nacimiento III or South-east (6391m) and Nacimiento IV or South-west with (6322m). This high mountain region remains one of the least explored and little known in the world.

On 19 November, Argentines Glauco Muratti and Adrián Petrocelli ascended **Río Salado**, a virgin 6350m volcano in the Ojos del Salado Region.

They slept with their vehicle at 4700m in Cañada Cazadero Oeste and next day continued on foot to camp at 5200m next to some penitentes, which provided the only available water in this desert. On day three the pair continued through complex terrain to reach the col adjoining **Volcán Huayco** in strong winds. The rock here has strange surface channels carved

Rio Saldo massif with Muratti/Petrocelli line marked. *(Glauco Muratti)*

by thousands of years of wind erosion.

Leaving their sacs at 6100m the pair attempted the summit but had to retreat to the base of the west glacier of **Cerro Huayco** at 5900m where there was water and some shelter from the wind. On summit day they reached a 6150m col, descended a long way to a rare turquoise lagoon, continued up a lava flow to reach the north ridge and summit, an old crater rim, at midday before returning to base camp the same day. They named the mountain **Cerro Rìo Salado** after a nearby river.

The summit of **Volcán Veladero** (6436m) in La Rioja is home to the world's third highest ruins – a ceremonial Inca platform. The mountain received its first 'modern' ascent in 1986, but contemporary maps recorded it as a minor summit more than 1000m lower than the real height. Basque resident in Argentina Arkaitz Ibarra and Argentine Gerardo Cano climbed a new route, via the rocky north ridge, during 14-20 October from a base camp at 5000m.

Central Andes

Cerro Olivares del Límite lies on the border with Chile in San Juan Province and must not be confused with Olivares (6266m) located nearby but entirely in Argentine territory. **Olivares del Límite** (6220m) had only been climbed previously from Chile, the route facilitated by the lack of glaciers on that side, but in the last days of 2012, Máximo Kausch, an Argentine resident in Brazil, summited Olivares del Límite from Argentina. From a camp at c.4900m near Portezuelo de Olivares he climbed the north-east glacier (AD+/D-, 700m) taking in the lower, virgin North Summit (6105m).

Panorama of the world's highest volcanoes from the summit of Cerro Mesada. *(Marcelo Scanu)*

In the Precordillera, the limestone peak **Cerro Pachaco** (c.3200m) received a new route from Willi Luhmann and Gabriel Fava. *Pijchu* (1100m of which 600m climbing and 12 pitches were new, F6b+) finishes on the East Summit. The first three pitches are a variation of the *Canal de la Guasa*. The route then takes slabs on the East Face, followed by four big dihedrals to connect with the normal route, before more slabs lead right of the final spur.

There are now five routes on Pachaco: the original first ascent by Kummel, Altrichter and Leuzzi on 5 April 1958, IV with some V on the final section; *Canal de la Y* (Fritz Altrichter, Oscar Kummel, José Miní and Domingo Vega, 28 March, 1959), 800m IV; the *Central Spur* – few details are available about this route but it takes a similar line to the first ascent finishing on the highest East Summit by a grade V pitch; finally *Canal de la Guasa* (Roberto Piriz, Aníbal Maturano, July 2012) a short 200m F6a route not gaining the summit.

In the **Ansilta Range**, Argentines Sebastián Aguiar and Fabrizio Oieni put up *Tracción a Sangre* on the unclimbed south-east face of **Pico Número 3**, aka **Teniente Francisco Ibáñez** (5550m) on 15 November. *Tracción* is graded PD, 45° with sections of 60°, some pitches of Grade II rock and 1600m of altitude gain from base camp. In the **Cordillera de la Totora**, a nearly unexplored range north of Ansilta, there have been many ascents since 2012 including: **Cerro de los Dragones** (5615m), **Cerro Calingasta** (5330m), **Pico Maida del Calingasta** (5291m), **Cerro Alfil** (5130m), **Cerro Cabeza de León** (5045m), plus minor summits.

Aconcagua Massif

Cerro Tolosa (5432m) was first ascended in 1903 by Countess Nadine Lougonine Von Meyendorff and Alois Pollinger. On 28 October, Pablo Busso and Gabriel Fava climbed the west face from a camp at 5000m to

the slightly lower North Summit. The pair named the route *Por los huevos del hombre Cojo*, (1000m/65°/IV/M2).

Tierra del Fuego

During the dry winter of 2013 Argentines José Bonacalza, Ian Schwer and Julián Fehrmann were active putting up new routes. On 14 July they climbed *Eslabón de Lujo* (190m, M5), a new route on the south face of the well known **Monte Olivia** (1318m). The start involves 15 metres of M3, 120 metres of 50/60° and finally 50 metres of exposed M5 before a short traverse to the summit by the normal route.

On July 21 they made the first ascent of **Monte Toun**, naming the route *Castorcitis*. A 40° approach leads to 250 metres of mixed M4/M5. On 24 July they climbed a new line on the east face of **Cerro Cinco Hermanos** (1280m). *Pinguinos Voladores* (150m, M5) comprises: 25m 60°; 55m M4 and 60m M5 linking the dihedral route to the summit. Finally on 29 July they climbed *Viaje Completo* (230m, 50°, M3) a new route on the south-west face of **Torre del Pingui** (Torres del Rino group).

CALUM MUSKETT

Patagonia 2013-14

The 2013-14 summer season in Patagonia has once again seen a huge surge in popularity, with alpinists travelling from across the world to climb in this stunning area. With exceptionally good weather conditions over the previous three summer seasons it was beginning to look like global warming was having a positive effect on the climate in the notorious Roaring Forties; so much so that I booked two trips out to this area in an aim to further its effect. Unfortunately, it seems that climbers were premature in hailing this new phenomenon called 'good weather' as a reliable meteorological pattern because the storm-clouds and high winds have returned with a vengeance this year, chastising optimistic mountaineers and allowing for plenty of rest days down in El Chalten. Nevertheless, plenty of new routes have been climbed this year as well as repeats of some of the area's most classic routes and summits.

The news of the season so far appears to be Alex Honnold and Tommy Caldwell's traverse of the **FitzRoy** group, a line envisaged for quite some time now. The climb covers over five kilometres of ridgeline taking in around 4000m of vertical gain covering seven major Patagonian summits – chapeau boys!

Back in late October I headed out with Mike (Twid) Turner, Jerry Gore and Raphael Jochaud to attempt the impressive unclimbed south face of the **South Tower of Paine**. We were battered by bad weather from start to finish and despite reaching the top of the wall, we failed to make the final 200m or so of scrambling to the summit due to strong winds and blizzards. We dubbed our efforts *Wall of Paine* (900m A3+ E5). It's worth taking note that this line would go free given some good weather and would certainly be worth the effort... [*see article page 145*].

On **Cerro Domo Blanco** a US team consisting of Mikey Schaefer, Joel and Neil Kauffman made the first ascent of what is already considered to be a modern classic ice route called *Superdomo* (WI5 M5/6). This route saw rapid repeats from two British teams including Ben Silvestre, Pete Graham, James McHaffie and Tim Neill. Also on Cerro Domo Blanco another Brit, Dave Gladwin teamed up with Ben Erdmann and Kim Ladiges to make the first ascent of a rock pillar which they called *d'Artagnan* (400m, F7a, C1, M6).

Dave Macleod and I tackled the unclimbed wall to the right of the classic Amy-Vidailhet couloir on **Aguja Guillaumet** which was choked with snow and ice after recent storms. Although unplanned, this proved to be an excellent and sustained mixed climb of Scottish VIII, 8 and roughly 250m in length. On the same day Ally Swinton and Ben Winston climbed a new

Above: east face of Mermoz showing MacLeod and Muskett's high point. *(Calum Muskett)*

Right: Line of Macleod and Muskett's new route on Guillaumet. *(Calum Muskett)*

line directly opposite us at grade V 6. Dave and I also got painfully close to making the first ascent of what I'm sure will some day be a fantastic mixed line on the east face of the **Mermoz**; with difficulties of Scottish VIII, 9 up to our high point, it will be no push-over to complete.

With hundreds of new routes and free ascents still to be made in Patagonia, as well as a new guidebook to *Torres del Paine* in the pipeline, I'm sure we will be hearing an awful lot more about this incredible alpine area for many years to come.

DAMIEN GILDEA

Antarctica 2013-14

Ellsworth Mountains
Sentinel Range, Vinson Massif
Numbers were down slightly on Antarctica's highest mountain in 2013-14, with 111 climbers reaching the summit of **Mount Vinson** (4892m) and five of those also climbing **Mount Shinn** (4660m).

First East-West Traverse of Vinson
Although previously unreported, in January 2012 ALE guides Maria Paz 'Pachi' Ibarra (Chile) and Rob Smith (UK) were landed on the Crosswell Glacier to the north-east of Vinson and ascended the ridge of the 2008 *Australian Route* to reach Goodge Col. From here they joined the normal route near High Camp, summitted and descended the normal route to Low Camp on the upper Branscomb Glacier, thus making the first east-to-west traverse of the Vinson Massif.

During 2013 it became apparent that the 1985 second ascent of **Mount Shinn** had been misreported in the intervening years. Yvon Chouinard and Doug Tompkins climbed the striking, broad couloir splitting the west face of Shinn, in plain sight of the old Vinson Base Camp, and not a line on the southern face as had been noted elsewhere.

Heritage Range, Soholt Peaks
UK-based climber Ralf Laier returned for his third trip to the area,

Looking west to the Soholt peaks from Schanz Glacier. *(Ralf Laier)*

this time to attempt an alpine-style traverse of the **Soholt Peaks**. This is a string of summits on the western edge of the Heritage Range, just north from the Union Glacier base camp of Antarctic Logistics & Expeditions (ALE). Laier climbed with ALE guides Maria Paz 'Pachi' Ibarra and Seth Timpano and accessed the northern end of the peaks by Sno-Cat along the Schanz Glacier.

Starting west of **Hessler Peak** on the 19th December, they made the first ascent of the northernmost of the Soholt Peaks, traversed over the summit, then descended west to a col. From there they climbed the northern slope of **Eley Peak** (2280m), which they also traversed and descended to the next col and a camp site at 2100m.

The next day they continued south along the narrow crest, climbing knife-edges over a number of small tops and one 2300m peak they named **Lillywhite Peak**. After some tricky mixed climbing over gendarmes in high winds, they descended to camp on a glacier, intending to continue their traverse the next day, however forecasts of even higher winds forced a return and rest at Union Glacier.

On 26 December they returned to resume their traverse and attempted the next peak south along their line, which they named **Cerro Catedral**, but turned back 40m from the summit after finding loose 5.7 rock above an icy couloir.

Moving over to the west they made the second ascent of **Macalester Peak**, one of the highest of the Soholt Peaks, by the north-west ridge, but considered it too difficult to traverse so descended their line of ascent, before traversing further south on the western side. Poor weather prevented an attempt on **Bursik Peak** so the trio finished by descending an icefall

West face of Mount Shinn (4660m), Ellsworth Mountains. *(Damien Gildea)*

back to the eastern side of the range for a pickup on the Schanz Glacier.

Though this area had been visited in the 1960s and 1970s, the first recorded climbs were by geologising New Zealanders Paul Fitzgerald and Charlie Hobbs, in 1992. In 1994 British Antarctic Survey personnel Mike Curtis and Brian Hull made a number of ascents in the region, including on the Soholt Peaks, where they made the first ascents of Macalester Peak and Eley Peak.

Marie Byrd Land
Executive Committee Range, Mount Sidley

Antarctica's highest volcano once again drew Russian climbers, with Ilya Bykov, Liana Chabdarova and Andrey Filkov making the seventh ascent of **Mount Sidley** (4285m), utilising an ALE flight from Union Glacier.

Antarctic Peninsula
Mount Walker, Peak 1712 and Traverse

A French-Canadian team aboard *Spirit of Sydney* made the first known ascent of **Mount Walker** (2350m), one of the highest peaks along the Peninsula mainland. They also claimed the first ascent of another 1712m peak above the Montgolfier Glacier and completed a south-to-north ski traverse through The Catwalk, a narrow section of the Peninsula's spine that connects the Herbert Plateau to the Detroit Plateau.

Various Ascents

British climber Phil Wickens returned to the area on *Spirit of Sydney*, cementing his position as the most prolific Peninsula mountaineer of modern times. Unlike previous seasons when he bagged a number of large peaks, this season, with a variety of partners he climbed many shorter routes on Cuverville Island and Lemaire Island, **Dallmeyer Peak**, **Mount Hoegh**, an unnamed peak near Brialmont Cove and a ten-pitch couloir of Scottish II near Skontorp Cove.

Queen Maud Land –Ulvetanna

In January 2013, Leo Houlding, Sean 'Stanley' Leary, Jason Pickles, Chris Rabone and Alastair Lee (David Reeves ground support) climbed and filmed the first ascent of the north-east ridge of **Ulvetanna**, (E6 6b, 5.12a, A2, 33 pitches, 1750m), (See article page 129).

In mid December 2013 Andy Kirkpatrick (UK) with Kjerski Eide, Espen Fadnes, Ingerborg Jackobson, Jonas Langseth and Alexander Gamme (Norway) spent over 50 days living on the ice, making several first ascents and first BASE descents. The two stand-out climbs of the trip were a new route on **Holstinnd** (*Zardoz* A4 650m) and **Ulvetanna** (*South Ridge* A1+), this being one of the 'last great gems' of the range, having been tried by three strong teams already.

Ulvetanna: south ridge (L) *(Andy Kirkpatrick)* & north-east ridge. *(Alastair Lee)*

Mount Everest Foundation Expedition Reports

SUMMARISED BY BILL RUTHVEN

The Mount Everest Foundation [**www.mef.org.uk**] was set up as a Registered Charity following the first successful ascent of Everest in 1953 and was initially financed from the surplus funds and subsequent royalties of that expedition. It is a continuing initiative between the Alpine Club and the Royal Geographical Society (with the Institute of British Geographers).

Surprisingly, the word 'mountaineering' does not appear anywhere in its Memorandum and Articles, the prime object being the promotion of 'exploration' in mountain areas: this is mainly geographic, but also includes the application of other exploratory disciplines in these areas, such as geology, botany and zoology.

It has now distributed well over £1 million to more than 1700 British and New Zealand expeditions planning such exploration, mostly to ambitious young climbers.

In return for supporting an expedition, all that the MEF asks is a comprehensive report. Once received, copies are lodged in the Alpine Club Library, the Royal Geographical Society, the British Mountaineering Council and the Alan Rouse Memorial Collection in Sheffield Central Library.

Donations to assist the work of the MEF are more welcome than ever, so if you have previously benefited from MEF grants, why not include a bequest to the Foundation in your will?

2013 was the sixtieth anniversary of the first ascent of Mount Everest, and this milestone was celebrated with a major event in the Royal Geographical Society on the actual anniversary day, at which we were honoured with the presence of HM The Queen and HRH The Duke of Edinburgh, (the MEF Patron).

The following notes summarise reports from the expeditions supported during 2013, and are divided into geographical areas.

AMERICA – NORTH & CENTRAL

San Agustin 2013 (Mexico) Chris Jewell with Richard Hudson, Mirek Kopertowski, Jon Lillestolen & Jason Mallinson (all cave divers) plus a strong support team of more than 40 cavers from the UK, Canada, USA and Mexico (February-March 2013).

During previous visits to the Sistema Huautla in the remote Santo

Domingo Canyon, 55m-deep Sump 7 had been explored for 150m, but this team hoped to penetrate further. This necessitated using the latest cutting-edge cave diving equipment, including cylinders filled with tri-mix (a mixture of helium, oxygen & nitrogen) as well as re-breathers and cylinders of specially mixed decompression gases. Entering the system via one of the lower entrances (Sotano San Agustin) they hoped to descend to a depth of 840m below it. Within a week the cave was rigged to Sump 1, and (underground) Camp 3 established at c700m. From here the divers conducted exploratory trips, including dives to 440m in Sump 9. 1774m of dry passages were surveyed but no by-pass discovered to Sump 9. In total, the expedition surveyed 2.7km of cave to a depth of 1545m, which means that Sistema Huautla is once again the deepest known cave in the Western Hemisphere. MEF Ref 13/05

Bearly Adventures 2013 (USA) Dave Gladwin and Mike (Twid) Turner (April-May 2013)

The main aim of this duo was to attempt a line on the left hand side of the NE Face of the Bear's Tooth (3070m) – a 1400m steep mixed/ice line with sections of 'big wall'. Unfortunately, the day before they flew onto the Buckskin Glacier, there was a 50cm dump of fresh snow, which made the face very dangerous. While they were waiting for conditions to improve, an American team attempted a nearby route, but retreated for fear of being knocked off the face by the continuous snowfall. Eventually they decided to attempt a line on the Bear's Tooth, but as they approached the face a sérac collapsed engulfing them in avalanche dust. Unsure how long it would take for the northern side of the mountain to come into condition, they moved round to the south side, where conditions were good, and they climbed *Shaken Not Stirred*, a 1000m ice and mixed route on the Moose's Tooth. MEF Ref 13/07

British St Elias 2013 (Canada) Simon Yates and Paul Schweizer (April-May 2013)

The Wrangell St Elias range of mountains lies on the border between the USA and Canada, and although this team approached their objective from Alaska, their plan to make the first ascent of the North Spur of Mount St Elias (5010m) meant that the actual climbing would be on the Canadian side of the border. After being flown in to the Columbus Glacier they established a base camp at 2200m below the North Spur of St Elias, but soon realised that in this position they would receive little sunshine, so they moved it to a spot further to the west which received significantly more rays. From here, they made a reconnaissance up the glacier to look at their preferred descent line. For the next four days they were tent-bound by a terrific storm with unseasonably cold conditions, which made them realise that being exposed on the extremely long ridge was likely to result in serious frostbite. Reluctantly they therefore abandoned the expedition and headed for home. MEF Ref 13/15

Mount Augusta 2013 (USA) Dr Paul Knott and Dr Derek Buckle (April-May 2013)

Mount Augusta (aka Boundary Peak 183, 4289m) was first climbed in 1952 by its north ridge, a route followed by this leader in 1993 when making the fourth ascent. In 1993 he made an attempt to climb the east ridge (MEF Reference 93/29), but a badly corniced section on the approach spur from the north put paid to the attempt. In 2013 he returned, hoping that by approaching from the south, he would gain the ridge via long but relatively straightforward snow slopes. The flight into the range was delayed for a week by storms and record precipitation, so once on the Seward Glacier with a limited weather window they abandoned plans for Augusta, and concentrated on summiting Mt Eaton (3336m), an unclimbed summit on the east ridge. This they achieved in two days, and immediately started to reverse the route. On reaching their previous high camp, they decided to rest overnight before continuing the descent. But the weather was against them, and with only one day's food they were trapped there for the next eight days, as an estimated six metres of snow fell. Each day they had to dig out the tent and re-pitch on top of the snow pack. Eventually, they called for help, and in a welcome break in the weather, a rescue helicopter was able to land nearby to ferry them back to safety. MEF Ref 13/28

AMERICA – SOUTH & ANTARCTICA

Alpine Club Antarctic 2013 Dr Phil Wickens with Ms Hannah Baker, Dr Derek Buckle, Jamie Goodhart & Mike Pinney from UK plus Stefan Jachmich from Germany & Bjorn Riis-Johannessen from Norway (January 2013)

Very few people have landed in the Beascochea Bay and Leroux Bay on the Antarctic Peninsula, so the area is largely unexplored and hence ideal for an MEF supported expedition. Sailing from Ushuaia on *Spirit of Sydney*, the team cleared paperwork and other formalities at Puerto Williams and sailed east then south into the Drake Passage in relatively calm conditions to land at Clapp Point in Collins Bay, at the southern end of the Trooz Glacier. Two camps were established on the Belgica Glacier, from which first ascents were made of six mountains between 616m and 2270m by routes up to AD. Plans to attempt further peaks had to be abandoned when the forecast of strengthening westerly winds threatened to pack ice into the bays, and make crossing the Drake Passage and rounding Cape Horn potentially dangerous, so the decision was made to leave Antarctica as soon as possible. This expedition also received a grant from the AC Climbing Fund. MEF Ref 13/01

British Ulvetanna Big Wall 2012/13 (Antarctica) Leo Houlding with Alastair Lee, Jason Pickles & Chris Rabone from UK plus Sean Leary from USA & David Reeves from South Africa (December 2012–January 2013)

Ulvetanna (Norwegian for *Wolf's Tooth,* 2931m) in the Fenriskjetften

Range of Queen Maud Land had received four previous ascents, but this was the first team to attempt its 1750m NE Ridge: they also planned to make a high quality film of the climb. Although the weather was mostly good, they experienced two storms while on the wall, with 30 cm of snow, 35 knot winds and temperature (with wind-chill) of -35° C – so cold that several team members experienced problems with dental fillings and crowns falling out! They graded the route VI, E6 6b, A2+. The film, entitled *The Last Great Climb*, was released in November 2013, since when it has won prizes at Kendal and Banff. MEF Ref 13/04

Welsh Patagonia 2013 (Argentina) Tom Ripley with Ollie Burrows plus Phil Wesseler from USA (November-December 2013)

The publication of Rolo Garibotti's Guide Book has led to an increase in climbers visiting the FitzRoy group, particularly as there were reports that there had been a noticeable improvement in Patagonian weather in recent years. Ripley and Burrows hoped to climb one or more new rock routes in the area and teamed up with Wesseler who they had met previously. However, they discovered that conditions were far too cold for rock-climbing, so they had to be satisfied with repeats of the *Whillans-Cochrane Route* on Aguja Poincenot (3036m) and the *Amy-Vidailhet Route* on Aguja Guillaumet (aka 'La Guillo', 2579m). MEF Ref 13/08

Wall of Paine 2013 (Chile) Jerry Gore with Calum Muskett and Mike (Twid) Turner plus Raphael Jochaud from France (October-November 2013).

The main objective of this team was to climb the S Face of the South Tower of Paine, the biggest unclimbed 'big wall' in Patagonia. Unfortunately the local weather dictated otherwise, and after being trapped in the valley for eight days due to high winds, they decided to try and complete the line on the right edge of the face started by McAleese and Turner in 2006 (MEF Ref 06/13). Despite three weeks of bad weather, they eventually completed the route but a ferocious storm (with winds up to 150 kph) prevented them from reaching the summit, although only 100m of easy climbing remained. MEF Ref 13/13

British Darwin Range 2013 (Chile) Simon Yates and Andy Cave (September 2013) The Cordillera Darwin Range of mountains lies in Tierra del Fuego, and is noted for its poor weather – and hence many unclimbed peaks. After flying to Ushuaia, this team boarded Marcel de Letter's yacht *Iorana* to sail into the Fjord Senor Pia. Their first climbing attempt had to be abandoned due to dramatic changes in the glacier since the leader's visit in 2007. Moving further east to Caleta Olla, they made an attempt on the South Face of unclimbed Roncagli III (2019m), but were stopped short of the summit by a huge crevasse that split the whole face. It was filled with ice debris and overhung on its far side, and they could find no way to overcome it. Bad weather prevented any further climbing. MEF Ref 13/16

British South Georgia 2013 (Antarctica) Julian Freeman-Attwood and Ed Douglas (October-November 2013). This team sailed 1300km from Port Stanley to King Haakon Bay on *Pelagic Australis*, to act as unpaid guides to 5 non-climbers hoping to repeat the 'Shackleton Traverse' of 1916. They then planned to attempt the first ascent of one of the Trident Peaks in the Allardyce Range. The start of the traverse was delayed by several days because of the weather, but when they eventually set off, in continuing bad weather, they realised that the potential risk of wind slab avalanche during the descent from the Trident with an inexperienced team would be unacceptable. They therefore decided to omit this part of the traverse, and arranged to be picked up by *Pelagic Australis* in Cook Bay. After relocating to Fortuna Bay, they continued the traverse to Stromness Bay. But by now, so much time had been lost that there was insufficient left to attempt any of the Trident Peaks, so they had to be satisfied with an ascent of Mt Hodges (605m), near Grytviken. MEF Ref 13/18

GREENLAND & ARCTIC

Eagle Ski Club Liverpool Land Dave Wynne-Jones with Dr Philippa Cockman, Stuart Gallagher, Adele Long, Dr Declan Phelan, Howard Pollitt and John Russell plus Blackie – a dog taken as 'polar bear alert/ deterrent'. (April-May 2013)

This team planned to explore the coastal mountains of the Himmerland Peninsular in Liverpool Land (East Greenland) and make as many first ascents as possible on ski. From the head of Narratfjord (adjacent to some hot springs) they explored to east and west, making 4 first ascents. Moving south to Frydendal, they then climbed an unnamed 825m peak to the west. Further south still they climbed an 1100m peak to the east of Mariager Fjord, before evacuating to Scoresbyssund by snowmobile. MEF Ref 13/12

Oxford West Greenland Tom Codrington with Jacob Cook, Ian Faulkner and Peter Hill plus boat crew Angela Lilienthal & Clive Woodman (16 Jun-20 Aug 2013)

Although neither had any previous sailing experience, Codrington & Hill planned to emulate Bill Tilman and commence their expedition by sailing to Greenland. They therefore arranged to meet the owners of the 11.5 metre fibreglass 'Cosmic Dancer V' in Canada. After a brief introduction to the basics of off-shore sailing, they embarked on a hectic 4-week passage across a gale ridden Labrador Sea *en route* for Greenland. The less said about that the better, but eventually they met up with the rest of the team in Aasiaat. The object of the expedition was to explore the potential for new routes and first ascents of big walls around Ummannaq Fjord. In this they were successful, achieving five major big wall routes, including two on the huge Horn of Upernivik and three on previously unknown cliffs rising more than 800m out of the sea. MEF Ref 13/29

HIMALAYA – INDIA

Indian-British Exploration Expedition 2013 Victor Saunders with Dr Susan Jensen and Andy Parkin from UK plus Divyesh & Vineeta Muni from Mumbai (July-August 2013)

Access to the Saser group of peaks in the Indian Karakoram is only permitted to foreigners if accompanied by Indian climbers, so this team planned to explore and make first ascents, hopefully of Plateau Peak (7300m) and/or Chamshen (7017m).

In approaching the area, they made the first crossing of the very technical Sakang Col (6150m) from North Shukpa Kunchang Glacier to a valley between Saser Kangri II and Saser Kangri III. After a reconnaissance of the area, the British team members headed back to re-provision, and late one night, while they were camped on the N Shukpa Kunchang Glacier approximately 1.5km away from Saser Kangri II, a massive avalanche swept its N face. Although the debris did not reach them, the blast from the avalanche lifted Parkin's tent and deposited it – plus occupant, still in his sleeping bag – some 20m down a deep crevasse. The other tent, (together with Saunders and Jensen) was bowled along to rest on the lip of the same crevasse.

With limited equipment at their disposal, it took several hours before they could rescue Parkin from the crevasse, and as he had injured his back, the priority was to evacuate him to civilisation. Although strictly 'illegal', thankfully the team was equipped with a satellite phone, with which they arranged for him to be rescued by helicopter and flown to Leh.

Back in the mountains, the remaining team members were able to make the first ascent of Chamshen via its west ridge (PD-) before packing up and returning to face court proceedings (and a fine) for carrying the satellite phone. It is understood that Parkin has since made a complete recovery from his injuries.

Note: Dr Susan Jensen was awarded the Alison Chadwick Memorial Grant for 2013 for her participation in this and in 13/17. MEF Ref 13/11

Scottish Himachal Pradesh 2013 (India) Andy Nisbet with Robert Adams, Bob Hamilton, Dr Susan Jensen & Steve Kennedy (May-July 2013)

Summits in the Darcha Valley of Himachal Pradesh region were only officially opened to climbers a few years ago, thus offering scope for exploration and first ascents of peaks over 6000m. The prime objective of this team was Peak G22 on the border of Ladakh (Zanskar), which Jensen had previously attempted from the north/east (MEF Ref 12/18A). However, reconnaissance missions revealed that its approach from this side would test the hardiest siege tactics, so the team decided to attempt Peak 6080m instead. On this they achieved the first ascent, and named it 'Goat Peak'. The peak to its south had an attractive summit reminiscent of the Inaccessible Pinnacle on Skye, so this was the next one to be attempted. Although they reached the summit ridge at 5710m, worsening snow conditions and lack of time prevented them from reaching the summit. On the other side of the valley, they completed the first traverse of a ridge ('Para Handy Ridge') connect 4 peaks, which they named (N to S) 'McPhail's', 'Dougie', 'Sunny Jim' & 'Vital Spark'. MEF Ref 13/17

British Kishtwar Kailash 2013 Mick Fowler with Mike Morrison, Paul Ramsden & Rob Smith (September-October 2013)

Although Kailash (6451m) is the last major peak in the eastern sector of the Kishtwar Himalaya, there was no record of it ever being attempted before the arrival of this team. To avoid the troubles in Kashmir, their approach was via the Rhotang Pass and down the Chenab Gorge. Base Camp was established at c4000m, a few hours short of Kishtwar Kailash. Climbing as two separate pairs, Fowler and Ramsden were successful in making the first ascent of the peak via a challenging line on its West Face. The ascent took 5½ days with another 1½ to descend to base camp: the highest technical difficulties encountered were ED and Scottish VI. Meanwhile, Morrison & Smith undertook a reconnaissance of the peaks surrounding the Chomochior Glacier. MEF Ref 13/19A

HIMALAYA – NEPAL

NZ Anidesha Chuli 2013 Rob Frost with Ben Dare, Andrei van Dusschoten & Scott Blackford Scheele (April-May 2013)

Anidesha Chuli (aka 'White Wave', 6808m) lies in a 'Restricted Area' in remote far eastern Nepal, and prior to this team, there is no record of any previous attempt to climb it. However, it is one of the very few unclimbed peaks above 6800m which are on the NMT's permitted list. After establishing an interim base camp at 4600m in Ghunsa valley, they approached via the little visited Ramtang Glacier, setting up further camps at 4800m, 5100m, 5500m and 6000m. From here Dare and Scheele set out up the East Ridge hoping to set up one further camp from which to make a summit bid. When out of sight of his companion at 6500m, Scheele fell 85m sustaining serious head injuries: his companions managed to get him down to Camp 2 from where he was evacuated by helicopter a few days later. Dusschoten and Frost made one further unsuccessful summit attempt, before aborting. However, they think that they know of a less technical route to the summit which they would recommend to future expeditions. MEF Ref 13/02

British Chandi Himal (Nepal) Guy Wilson with David Chapman and Neil Warren (October-November 2013)

Inspired by the British Far West Nepal Expedition 2011 (MEF Ref 11/01), this team planned to visit the same area (Changla Himal) to explore and hopefully make the first ascent of Gave Ding (6571m). However, due to permit restrictions, they had to relocate to the largely unexplored Chandi Himal Range, with Chandi Himal (6069m) as their main objective. From a high camp at 5400m, they reached a col at 5950m where they dumped their technical equipment and proceeded unroped. Unfortunately, at 6000m the easy ground was replaced by a pillar of loose rock which formed the summit itself, and which brought them to a halt. Retreating to the col, they saved the day with an ascent of a subsidiary snow dome of 6024m on the other side of the col from Chandi Himal. As they recovered back at base camp, the weather took a dramatic turn with heavy snowfall putting a stop to further climbing: all efforts were now directed to getting themselves and all their gear safely back to civilisation. After a few days with little progress, their agent offered to arrange helicopter evacuation, which under the circumstances, they were happy to accept. MEF Ref 13/22

PAKISTAN

British Charakusa 2013 (Pakistan) Jon Griffith and Andy Houseman (July-September 2013)
Although the Charakusa valley is much frequented, there are still some unclimbed peaks in the area, The main objective of this duo was the first ascent of Link Sar (7041m), a very complex peak which has foiled several strong climbers in the past. They made a couple of recce runs on K6 (aka Baltistan Peak, 7282m) to introduce Houseman to the area, and to check out the current condition of the faces. The line on Link Sar that they hoped to climb starts on the north face and is huge and complex, and will require vertical and overhanging dry tooling to reach the rocky summit. Unfortunately, very hot weather did not bode well for north faces or even for acclimatising on lower peaks, as they were dangerously falling apart. Griffith is already planning a return visit.
This expedition received the Nick Estcourt Award for 2013. MEF Ref 13/24

CHINA AND TIBET

Haba Xue Shan 2013 (Caving) Gavin Lowe with Nick Edwards, Kayleigh Gilkes, Steve Macnamara, Steve Cullagh, Jock Read and Ed Whelan (August-September 2013)
Having examined the North side of Haba Xue Shan (5396m) in 2010, this team planned to prospect for caves on the SE Ridge of this peak in Yunnan Province, and carry out initial exploration if resources permit. The mountain is situated above the Jinsha Jiang (Yangtse River) which was thought to be the site of resurgences, and as the river is at 1600m there is potential for cave depths of well over 3000m. With almost continuous rain and low cloud while they were in the area, visibility was limited, but they managed to do a thorough search from valley level up to a ridge at 4600m. Unfortunately, they discovered that the rock in the area was very thinly bedded and shattered, so that the four small caves that they discovered soon became too tight for further exploration. MEF Ref 13/34

MISCELLANEOUS

Shan Plateau 2013 (Caving) Dr Peter Talling with Tim Guilford, Fleur Loveridge, Lou Maurice & Ben Wright from UK plus Prof Liu Hong from China (December 2012-January 2013). This was the fourth caving expedition to visit the Shan State of Myanmar (Burma) since access to foreign visitors was allowed in 2010. The prime aim of this trip was to continue the exploration of caves near the town of Ywangan, including extending the longest and deepest known system in the country (Kyauk Khaung or 'Stone Cave'). In this they were highly successful, extending the length from 2.3km to 4.8km. Exploration was curtailed at a depth of 148m when they ran out of rope at the bottom of a 30m pitch. The team also investigated 2 major resurgences, which if linked to Kyauk Khaung would indicate a major system with an elevation range in excess of 300m. They also collected and preserved samples of previously unknown cave-adapted fish, for study in the Universities of Oxford, Kunming and Mandalay. MEF Ref 13/03

British West Mustabbes 2013 (Kyrgyzstan) Paul Josse with Steve Brown, Phil Morgan, & John Venier from UK plus Terje Lokken from Norway (August-September 2013). Although British climbers have visited the Eastern Glacier of the Mustabbes river in the At Bashi range of Kyrgyzstan, the Western Glacier remains largely unexplored, so was an ideal location for this exploratory expedition. After flying to Bishkek, an eventful journey in a 6wd vehicle enabled them to establish a base camp at c3600m on the right-hand branch of the Mustabbes River. From here and an advanced base camp on the central glacier, they carried out a thorough exploration of the area, achieving first ascents of eight peaks ranging from 4430m to 4640m, with grades of F to PD+, giving each of them a unique name. This expedition also received a grant from the Alpine Climbing Fund. MEF Ref 13/09

'The Silk Road' Tajikistan 2013 Struan Chisholm with Leonard Horstmeyer, Max Jamilly, Sam Newmark, Calum Nicoll, & Theo Scott, (July-September 2013). After a 2-week drive from UK to Tajikistan, this team of university students started their walk-in to the mountains surrounding the Rog Valley, but when a rucksack containing a passport rolled down a hillside to disappear in a raging torrent, they were forced to return to Dushanbe to arrange for the British Embassy to issue a replacement. This wasted a whole week, leaving insufficient time to reach the area where they had intended to place their base camp. They therefore drove east up the Zerafshan Valley to approach the mountains from the north, establishing a camp at c4000m. From here, over the next 2 weeks they made ascents of Mt. Christopher Ward (4922m) and Mullach Siseal Scott (4492m) plus 3 minor tops, with difficulties up to TD. The drive back to UK was delayed due to changes in Russian visa legislation, and necessitated a more circuitous southern route. MEF Ref 13/20

University of Bristol Djangart 2013 (Kyrgyzstan) Ross Davidson with Harry Bloxham, George Cave, Clay Conlon, Al Docherty & Harry Kingston (July-August 2013)
The objective of this team was to explore the glaciated valleys in the Tien Shan that run into the Djangart valley, making first ascents of as many peaks as possible. Unfortunately just before leaving home they learned that one of their main objectives – Pik 5318m – had just received its first ascent by an American team. Undeterred, they concentrated on others, and climbing as pairs achieved first ascents of seven peaks ranging from 4822m to 5100m via routes which they graded AD- to D-. The team has proposed names for each of them, but still awaits the approval of the Kyrgyzstan Mountaineering Federation. MEF Ref 13/21

Scottish-South African Wakhan 2013 (Afghanistan) Alan Halewood and Richard Parker from UK plus Richmond MacIntyre from South Africa (July-August 2013)
Until fairly recently, the Little Pamir range of the Wakhan Corridor lay within a restricted area, and hence Qara Jilga (6094m) (aka Qara Jeelga), remained as one of the last unclimbed 6000m peaks in the country. On a previous trip to the area (MEF Ref 10/15) the leader had made a reconnaissance of the approaches to the peak, so hoped that the present trip would result in its first ascent. Unfortunately, while descending from the North Ridge of the main summit during an acclimatisation climb, MacIntyre was struck on the head by a falling sharp-edged rock which rendered him unconscious. After being lowered some 300m, he was able to walk with support, but reported neck pain and altered vision in one eye. It was obvious that he needed professional attention, so after a day's rest, evacuation continued to Dushanbe and early flights home. It is understood that MacIntyre has since made a full recovery, with no permanent damage. MEF Ref 13/25

Anglo-New Zealand Djangart 2013 (Kyrgyzstan) Tom Bell with Timothy Elson, Max Folkett, Reg Measures, Hugh Thomas & Neil Thomas (August 2013)
This team (mainly from the Universities of Leeds & Sheffield) decided that in view of its relatively easy access and lack of bureaucracy, the Djangart Range would be a good choice for a first expedition to the greater ranges. In particular, they hoped to make first ascents of several 5000m peaks in the Sauktor area, but unfortunately, the helicopter flying them in from Maida Adyr actually dropped them some 10km away from their intended base camp. Undeterred, they split into 2 groups of 3 and, between spells of bad weather, were successful in making the first ascents of Pt 4871 (Peak Fotheringham), Pt 4950 (Peak Kinmundy), Pt 5051 (Pk Macmillan) and Pt 5168 (Pk Vinton-Boot). They also made the first traverse of the Djanghorn Ridge, which included first ascents of 2 more peaks, and second ascents of 2 others. MEF Ref 13/27

Reviews

Dent du Géant, oil on canvas, 40x50cm. *(Tim Pollard)*

Reviews

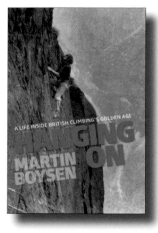

Hanging On
Martin Boysen
Vertebrate Publishing, 2014, pp288, £20

The dull cover and uninspiring title suggested to me that this was yet another boring climbing autobiography and sure enough it charts Martin's climbing career from humble beginnings on southern sandstone to becoming a member of the glitterati holding his own amongst the world's best. However, it is a very well written account with a natural easy-going style (just like the author's climbing) that draws you into the story.

It starts quite dramatically with the drone of Lancaster bombers flying over the home near Aachen where he spent his very early years with his Anglo-German family before moving to Kent at the end of the war. Here he discovered his natural talent for rock-climbing as well as his love for the natural world and very soon we are introduced to characters such as 'Richard' McHardy and Paul Nunn who were to become household names in climbing of that period. In fact, the appearance of so many of the stars makes the book read like a *Who's Who* of British climbing. A major strength is the brief but convincing pen-pictures of these characters that the author draws adding to the impression of authenticity.

An early high point was being asked to join Joe Brown on a new route on Cloggy when Doug Verity, his second had failed to follow. 'I was still walking on air for weeks afterwards.' Strangely, the name of the route, *Woubits Left Hand*, is not mentioned when many, many less important (to his story) are listed. At times this becomes a little tedious or it certainly would be for anybody not familiar with them.

I think that the book would have been improved by some pruning of the material and a good dose of proof-reading. On a first reading quite a few mistakes jumped out at the reviewer. There is no *Chequers Direct* at Curbar, nor is there an *Eliminate* on Castle Rock of Triermain (there are several routes that have 'Eliminate' in their title); I was thrown when Jeff Allison suddenly became Geoff and annoyed that Ynws Ettws was moved from the Llanberis Pass to Llanberis.

However, these are carping criticisms and pale alongside the book's undoubted strengths. The prose develops a certain long-term rhythm as we follow the ups and downs (no pun intended) of Martin's life as he describes triumphs and accidents both on and off the crags.

Climbing in the Alps leads to expeditions to the Himalaya and Patagonia, interspersed with a near-fatal car accident, various illnesses and attempts (eventually successful) to establish a career as a teacher. In and amongst these he becomes a major force as a rock-climber with first ascents of routes such as *The Skull* and *Capital Punishment*. Moreover, he and Baz Ingle made the staggering discovery of Craig Gogarth, one of our finest and most special crags.

What really shines through is his enduring love for his wife Maggie which his chosen life-style must have sorely tested. We also get an insight into his vulnerability, seen early on when he is first making his way in the climbing scene and still there when Chris Bonington tells him that he will not be in the K2 team. 'This sudden rejection hit me hard. I felt a deep disappointment and the pain of a long friendship betrayed. I had always loved Chris…' In fact this release from the really high-profile expeditions allowed him to take part in a series of what can be described as anarchic trips, more suited to his strengths, not least of which was the successful ascent of the Trango Tower with Joe himself. Whilst on this expedition news reached them of the death on K2 of Martin's close friend Nick Estcourt; it fell to Bill Barker to point out that maybe he was lucky to have missed out on K2. Other adventures come and go including doubling for Clint Eastwood in the making of *The Eiger Sanction* but eventually a greater sense of responsibility leads to the decision to give up expeditions and settle down as a family man and a rock-climber.

The book fades away (in the nicest possible way) with Martin, still happily married, a contented grandfather who is still active as a rock-climber – more often than not with his best friend Rab Carrington.

Mike Mortimer

Mont Blanc
The Finest Routes: Rock, Snow, Ice and Mixed
Philippe Batoux
Edition Glénat, 2012
English Edition – Vertebrate Publishing, 2013, pp216, £35

Stuff Napoleon! To alpinists of my generation, Gaston Rébuffat was the greatest Frenchman ever. A superb mountaineer, a celebrated guide, an AC member and a gentleman, as well as something of an entrepreneur, his books and his lectures inspired us to great things, especially on the Massif du Mont Blanc. His 1973 tome – *Mont Blanc, The 100 Finest Routes* – not published in English until January '75, was justifiably prized for its sensible route descriptions, clear diagrams and come-hither photographs, and became the ultimate Chamonix tick list, responsible for an unprecedented influx of new members to the then flourishing ACG.

Scroll forward forty years and a successor volume has now appeared, this time compiled by Philippe Batoux, also a guide and ENSA instructor,

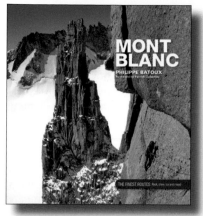

with the collaboration of his friend Patrick Gabarrou, using a similar treatment: excellent topos and even more magnificent photographs, many of them credited to Pascal Tournaire. It is refreshingly obvious that the unknown translator was familiar with the subject and the translation is idiomatic and seems impeccable. At 266 x 292mm and 1.5kg this is a most desirable tome.

In his lengthy and comprehensive introduction, Batoux explains the objective of the book: first to present one hundred of the finest itineraries in the Massif, bearing in mind that quality is subjective, that popularity demands consideration and unacceptable objective danger must be excluded. Secondly to introduce new climbs as well as worthwhile yet often forgotten classics, in locations spread throughout the Massif, meanwhile demonstrating the diversity of modern alpinism which embraces fully bolted summer lines besides great mixed routes in winter. In all these objectives he has surely succeeded.

Adding one for luck, Batoux has detailed 101 routes, all of which he's climbed – a *tour de force* indeed – although I should add that as a mere elderly British alpinist I've managed a dozen of them in my time, while being familiar with very many of the rest. Thirty five of Rébuffat's routes are included, as are several classics that Rébuffat omitted, while the remainder are modern climbs that have been put up since 1973. Here are short climbs and long ones, icicles and ice-hung gullies, bolted rock-jock routes and serious two-day epics, literally something for everyone. Unlike Rébuffat, Batoux has arranged his routes logically in an approximate progression of ability and difficulty, thus experience gained on one route is likely to be found useful for the next – a sort of learning curve. Route 1, for instance, is an Introduction to Ice Climbing and Moulin Exploring on the Mer de Glace, (the Bossons is now considered too dangerous). By Route 5 we've progressed to the *Cosmiques* on the Midi, by Route 49 to the Frendo Spur, while Route 93 is the Central Pillar of Frêney itself, to select a few of the old favourites. Route 101 will remain a secret.

Batoux introduces fashionable new winter locations such as the icicle climbs on the Argentière Glacier Right and Left Banks (Routes 12 and 51 respectively) and includes a number of intriguing short modern rock routes. Typical is that on the Petit Clocher du Portalet – Route 80, its foot accessible in under 2 hours from the Champex chairlift. Nevertheless it is disconcerting to find that many routes known by time-honoured names are now named after their first ascentionists. The Frontier Ridge of Mont Maudit, for instance, is now the *Kuffner Ridge*, the Dru North Face is the *Allain-Leininger* and the Charmoz North Face becomes the *Merkl-Welzen-*

bach. No doubt this is due to the proliferation of new routes on almost every rib and facet of almost every ridge or face, so it helps to know your history and I'd certainly encourage that.

Grading has always been a controversial subject, particularly on alpine routes where so many variables come into play. We always felt that the Vallot system was adequate with its grades covering overall seriousness as well as technical difficulty – mountaineering had to include an element of exploration, there had to be unknowns and surprises in a proper adventure. But Batoux devotes no less than 35 column-inches to explaining his comprehensive and complex system. Rather than waste our own column-inches explaining it, let us consider the Vl 5 M6 A3 6a grading for Route 100 – Batoux's own route *Little Big Men*, climbed in 2006 on the East Face of the Pointe Walker, off to the left of the Hirondelles Ridge. Vl means it's very serious, 5 covers the ice difficulty, M the difficulty of the mixed ground, A is the aid difficulty while 6a means British E1 on the rock pitches. Confusing – but no doubt extremely succinct?

In addition he recommends a gear rack for each route, a selection frequently as specific as quick-draws and cams of certain sizes, but then Rébuffat did likewise with the rather more simple requirements of his day. My eyebrows rise at the great frequency with which bolts are noted. Some seem to be in place on the majority of the climbs; doubtless they are all part of the game these days, though I cannot forget the times when every self-respecting British alpinist would complete a climb with more ironware than that with which he started.

Indeed, much has happened in forty years. Not just to the climbers and their gear – not just to the development of innovative tools, techniques, safety gadgets and climbing walls and the consequent explosive rise in technical climbing standards, especially on ice – but also to the mountains themselves. The so-called Little Ice Age is now long gone, winters are less harsh and summers warmer than in Rébuffat's day. In recent years the 0° isotherm has risen above 4000 metres during the summer, everywhere permafrost has melted, glaciers have retreated, séracs have become unstable and rockfall has increased. Batoux points out that throughout the massif many of the summits are merely huge granite blocks frozen into a matrix of ice, and reminds readers that even the western face of the Dru has collapsed on no less than three occasions since 2003, indeed in 2005 the entire 600 metres of the *Bonatti Pillar* self-destructed. Those superb Brenva Face lines – *Sentinel, Major* and *Pear* – are now shunned as suicidal, as are several of the classic Argentière routes such as the Triolet North Face. Such celebrated classics now considered too dangerous to attempt are excluded from this selection. In fact Batoux recommends a particular season for each route, suggesting that as a general rule snow and ice routes should be climbed in winter, rock routes in summer and except for those high on Mont Blanc, mixed routes in spring or late autumn. Bang goes the Brit's customary three weeks of route bagging in August!

I can find only one mistake in the book, and that on a route that demonstrates my provenance: Route 81 – the *American Route* on the Fou – i.e. the South Face. Stuart Fulton was a Scot, not an American. But seriously, this is an excellent book which should inspire both current Chamonix aficionados, aspirant alpinists planning their first ventures in the Mont Blanc Massif and those now past it who ponder what delights might have been. Its treatment is practical, its content is stimulating and its quality is worthy of anyone's library. I'm sure Rébuffat would approve.

But a photocopier may be useful.

John Cleare

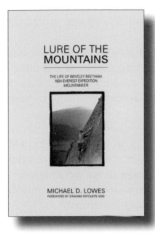

Lure of The Mountains
Michael D. Lowes.
Vertebrate Publishing, 2014, pp156, £12.99

No name appears more regularly in the early series of rock climbing guides to Borrowdale than that of Bentley Beetham. Once in his stride, the number of routes on the valley's crags increased ten-fold. Few have become classics, many are mildly difficult lines on well hidden, little-visited cliffs taking routes that wander artificially, causing later generations of compilers to dismiss them as shambling or poor, little recognising the prodigious effort that Beetham put into his explorations.

Some Beetham routes have however survived to achieve fame, among them *Little Chamonix* on Shepherd's Crag and *Corvus* on Raven, where polished holds testify to popularity and the passage of generations of boots. But Beetham achieved wider fame as a member of the ill-fated 1924 British attempt on Everest which ended with the disappearance of Mallory and Irvine. His selection and recognition as a leading mountaineer of his day made him a likely candidate for the summit but it was not to be.

This excellent, well illustrated biography by the late Michael Lowes, an old boy of Barnard Castle School where Beetham taught and introduced many boys to rock climbing and a deeper appreciation of the natural world, gives a valuable glimpse of history. A bachelor and son of a local bank manager, Beetham developed a passion for ornithology and photographing birds which led in turn to a love of climbing and for the solitude of open countryside. After leaving Barnard Castle School as a pupil and developing his drawing skills working for an architect, he returned to the school as a teacher, spending holidays climbing in the Lake District and the Alps with some of the era's leading mountaineers. It was his record of climbing 35 summits in six weeks with Noel Odell that qualified him for the Everest attempt, despite lacking the usual credentials of a public school and university education.

His skill as a bird photographer and publication of his first book, The Home-Life of the Spoonbill, the Stork and Some Herons led to an invitation to join the 1911 expedition to Jan Mayen Island which, as described by Lowes, would rival the ascent of Rum Doodle as a doomed enterprise. Their ship almost ran out of coal, navigation lacked a chronometer and was so haphazard that examining the chart showed the vessel had been sailing for miles over dry land. The multinational make-up of the party led to fierce disputes and when eventually they reached Jan Mayen Island the shoreline was so inhospitable it was impossible for the party to land. They retreated having achieved nothing. On arrival back in Newcastle the ship rammed the quayside and in a riot of striking dockworkers the champagne intended for celebrating their landfall on Jan Mayen Island was lost along with some personal belongings.

Beetham failed to reach stardom on Everest although his camera work has left a fine legacy of still photographs. After suffering a bout of dysentery and an acute attack of sciatica, Beetham refused to obey doctor's orders and insisted on climbing to Camp Three, only to be ordered back to base by the expedition leader.

He returned to teaching at Barnard Castle School where, after his part in yet another glorious British failure in the world of exploration, he was held in fear and awe. A good teacher and housemaster, he was also a strict disciplinarian. Lowes reflects that in the days when beatings were regarded as legitimate punishment, Beetham might have been described as a sadist. Nevertheless, this is a enthralling portrait of an exceptional man.

Ronald Faux

From The Edge: Selected Poems
Dennis Gray
Flux Gallery Press, 2012, pp72, £8.95

As you'd expect from a climber of the Arthur Dolphin era, there is a lot to look back on in the reflective and often playful poems in this selection from a long climbing life. Just check out the poem *Watching* to see the number of famous climbers and famous ascents witnessed by Dennis Gray, often on the other end of the rope.

Some of the wittiest poems here would have become classic performance pieces if we still entertained each other in huts on winter nights: *A Hymn to Harnesses, A Yorkshire Bouldering Rhyme, Sport Haiku, Spoorts Climbing, Watch the Bloody Rope* and *Sleeping Bags I Have Known*. On the other hand, a few poems do suffer from appearing to be thinking aloud, untroubled by poetic devices. At his best Dennis Gray can hit just the right note of humour and wisdom. *The Tao of Climbing* ends: 'An inferior climber heard about the Tao / And rejected it laughing loudly. // If it had not provoked such laughter / It would not have been the Tao.'

Gray's commitment to poetry and his sense of the strong tradition of mountaineering poetry has led to his orchestrating two participatory evenings for the AC in London and in Bristol in 2013. Both were a combination of the moving and the hilarious, rather like his own poems *From The Edge*.

Terry Gifford

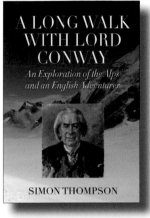

A Long Walk With Lord Conway
Simon Thompson
Signal Books, 2014, pp320, £16.99

Lord Conway, the first Baron Conway of Allington, art critic, author, politician, cartographer and mountaineer, emerges from this excellent biography as a man one might hold in awe, but at arm's length. Ruthlessly ambitious, a dealer in dubious shares, prone to cheating and exaggeration and careless about the feelings of those close to him, this multitasking pillar *manqué* of the Victorian establishment had few equals when it came to walking. He was a redoubtable walker, in 1894 the first man to stride the entire length of the Alps, 1000 miles from the Col de Tende in Italy to the Ankogel in Austria. It was this feat that Thompson repeated 120 years later as a platform to rediscover the life of an extraordinary man.

Restlessly curious, determined and multi-talented, Conway pursued many fields but according to Thompson failed to achieve real distinction in any single one, being unable to sustain concentration for long enough. Even so, what he did achieve through great personal charm and a network of famous names in the artistic and intellectual world, would have granted him celebrity status in today's society.

Beyond pioneering exploration of the Himalaya, Spitzbergen, the Andes and Patagonia he also became Professor of Art at University College, Liverpool, and then Slade Professor of Fine Art at Cambridge University and the first director general of the Imperial War Museum. As Martin Conway he entered politics in pursuit of a knighthood and a barony and achieved both. Seventeen books on art and travel along with innumerable magazine and newspaper articles written in his grandiloquent prose echoed the Victorian and Edwardian age. He lived in grand style, restoring Allington Castle in Kent, but remained permanently short of funds, spending his younger years living off his mother, his middle years off his wife's family and old age off his daughter. Aged 68 he had an affair with his 24-year-old secretary and after his wife's death married a wealthy American widow, who was happy to receive a grand title but reluctant to part with any of her wealth.

This is hardly an affectionate tribute, but Simon Thompson has done a most thorough job in presenting Conway the man and the age in which he lived, reflecting on the social and physical changes that have happened over that 120-year gap between their two walking expeditions. Conway did the walk in one season accompanied by two guides and two soldiers, 'borrowed' from a Gurkha regiment, who had served him in the Himalaya. They had the worst of the experience, carrying all the loads, cutting steps, forging a path through snow drifts, eating strange food in a strange land and living under the poorest shelter. Thompson spent two seasons covering the route, travelling mostly alone with one rucksack and a busy notebook.

Ronald Faux

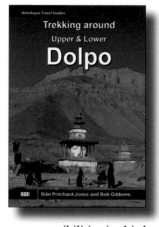

Trekking around Upper & Lower Dolpo
Siân Pritchard-Jones and Bob Gibbons
Himalayan Map House, 2014, pp 245, £16.50

Blanks on the map have shrunk to the smallest pockets; now it is blanks in guidebook coverage that provide havens in the mountains. But these spaces of mystery too are vanishing.

The publication of this trekking guide to Dolpo, tucked up against the border of Tibet, north of Dhaulagiri in Nepal, gives me mixed feelings. First, I have written about Dolpo myself so I can hardly take a purist line, and second, authors Siân Pritchard-Jones and Bob Gibbons have highlighted possibilities in this land of bare hills and huge skies that I was unaware of, including a ski ascent of Putha Hiunchuli (7246m). Anyone interested?

Politically Dolpo has been a part of Nepal since the second half of the 18th century. But it does not look or feel like the Nepal of the Kathmandu valley or even of the Khumbu-Everest region. Culturally and economically, until recent times, its closest ties have been with Tibet. Indeed since the Chinese occupation of Tibet in the 1950s Dolpo has been one of the last relatively undisturbed remnants of an authentic Tibetan culture, and also a redoubt of the little understood Bon religion, elements of which predate Buddhism. Until now, the only English guidebook to Dolpo has been a slim volume by Kev Reynolds published by Pilgrims Book House in Kathmandu, with routes venturing no further into the upper heart of Dolpo than Shey Gompa and Dho Tarap. Siân and Bob, who edited Kev's guide, have here detailed possibilities right up to the border with Tibet, coupled with a wealth of supporting 'how to do it' information and sections on the culture and natural wonders of the region.

There are also a couple of pages on mountaineering possibilities, translated from information supplied by Paulo Grobel. If this seems meagre encouragement for a 'climber' to buy the guide, remember that 90 per cent of your time in Dolpo will be spent trekking, not climbing. Anyway I imagine that even for climbers a large part of the lure of Dolpo has to be the cultural experience.

Siân and Bob are insatiable travellers with a deep love of Nepal and its people that permeates this guidebook: informal in style, informative and inspiring. The pair are devotees of Peter Matthiessen whose *Snow Leopard* remains the classic text for Dolpo romantics. Matthiessen quotes pepper their guidebook. The following recalls for me cresting the Kang La and looking north beyond the Crystal Mountain:

'Confronted with this emptiness, it is not hard to imagine that somewhere down among those peaks... the centre of the world, Shambala, might exist.'

Stephen Goodwin

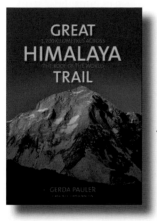

Great Himalaya Trail
Gerda Pauler
Bâton Wicks, 2013, pp 218, £12.99

In 2012 Gerda Pauler walked the length of Nepal, east to west, along the Himalayan chain. This is an account of that 1700km journey. A slender woman in her mid-fifties, Gerda would shy away from calling herself a 'mountaineer' yet in the course of her four-month walk she crossed passes of five and six thousand metres and experienced more of 'mountainous' Nepal than most climbers on summit dashes ever do.

More pertinent perhaps was her immersion in the life of the hill people. This book will give you a better picture of the day-to-day life, worries and beliefs of Nepalis beyond Kathmandu than any guidebook, Lonely or Rough, or chest-beating narrative of peak bagging. Gerda's daily diary entries, recording her conversations with sad-eyed child labourers, disillusion over failing aid projects, and ponderings on the mixed blessings of new roads and the rightness of Buddhists eating meat, build into a fine piece of simply-told reportage.

Though you can research the GHT on the internet and buy the map, it's a very different matter to walk the talk. When Gerda reached the Khumbu and sat down in a Dingboche café to satisfy her craving for a cappuccino, she saw more trekkers pass by in one hour than she'd seen in the previous 39 days from Taplejung, south of Kangchenjunga. She and her small crew had, in previous days, crossed Sherpani Col (6180m), West Col (6190m) and the Amphu Labsta (5845m) – surely mountaineering by any measure. Gerda had deliberately left Kangchenjunga Base Camp on 2 April 2012, the United Nation's 'Autism Awareness Day'. She estimates there are some 30,000 autism suffers in Nepal, the majority without any form of professional help whatever. Hopefully her long walk will have made a difference, raising not just awareness, but also US$ 9,000 for Autism Care Nepal – enough to train two Nepali specialists.

The GHT is no Pennine Way with comforting acorn signs at key junctions: it is network of existing trails between villages and over passes that together form one of the longest and highest walking routes in the world. Only where it joins popular areas such as the Khumbu, Langtang and Annapurna are there lodges; elsewhere a tent and crew was a necessity for Gerda who is fulsome in her praise for her guide, Temba Bhotia.

Gerda Pauler was born near Munich and lives in Norway, though one might suspect she is just as likely to be found in the garden of the Kathmandu Guest House. She has been visiting Nepal for 25 years, gaining a perspective on its people and their changing lives that informs this gem of a book. Gerda's vicissitudes along the trail included insect bites, heat stroke, sore throat, a persistently drunken crew member, and an occasional, though seemingly not frequent, faltering of the will to go on. Reading this book, one is grateful she persevered.

Stephen Goodwin

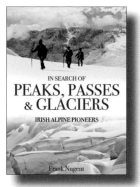

In Search of Peaks, Passes and Glaciers
Irish Alpine Pioneers
Frank Nugent
The Collins Press, Cork, 2014, pp310, £29.99

They were pioneers from the 'golden age' of Alpinism, determined and often successful in their first ascents of unclimbed summits, and they were Irish. Although they did not trumpet this incidental fact, the historical record rather overlooks it and in this account, which borrows the title of the first *Alpine Journal*, author Frank Nugent aims to set the record straight. The history and record of some 18 Irish climbers is covered, a relatively small number set against the importance of what they achieved. They were often well-to-do individuals, some of them on the Grand Tour, and their individual experiences reflect the confusing milieu that was Irish society in the 19th century. John Ball, born in Dublin but educated in England, was among the first pioneers of the Alps from 1840, mixing an active mountaineering life with a significant political career. A Poor Law commissioner during the Great Famine, he was elected MP for County Carlow in 1852 and only two years later made a legendary ascent of Mount Pelmo in the Dolomites. The following year he was elected the Alpine Club's first president, his most significant work being his editorship of the first series of Alpine guidebooks, updated by the club ever since.

John Tyndall, born in County Carlow two years after Ball, became an eminent research physicist professionally and a competitor with Edward Whymper to be first up the Matterhorn. He made two unsuccessful attempts in 1860 and 1862 and, after the tragic first ascent in 1865 three years later achieved the first completed traverse of the mountain from Breuil to Zermatt.

This is a scholarly and carefully researched account of the high place Irish climbers hold in the wider history of Alpinism, at a time when improved travel, a long period of European peace and a growing band of professional guides made the high mountains an attainable goal. Anthony Adams-Reilly, born in County Westmeath, made first ascents of Mount Dolent, Aiguille de Trélatête and Aiguille d'Argentière with Michel Croz and Whymper a year before the fatal accident on the Matterhorn. Adams-Reilly climbed Mont Blanc by seven different routes but his chief work was to produce the first correct map of the Mont Blanc chain and the Monte Rosa district.

Among this colourful list of characters was Elizabeth Hawkins-Whitshed whose great aunt ordered that she should be stopped from climbing mountains 'because she is scandalising London and looks like a Red Indian'. Elizabeth, daughter of a baronet and brought up in County Wicklow, visited the Engadine in 1880 to recover her health after her son's birth and made a fast recovery.

She returned a year later to climb Mont Blanc twice and make two winter ascents of Chamonix Aiguilles. She preferred mountaineering in autumn because she disliked tourists. Her keenness for mountain climbing survived the death of her husband, a colonel in the Royal Horse Guards, lost in an abortive attempt to rescue General Gordon at Khartoum. After remarrying and in a 20-year period from 1882 to 1903 she made some 130 major tours, including climbing the Weisshorn in four hours and crossing the Zinalrothorn twice in the same day. By the time of her third husband Elizabeth had won a reputation as a mountaineer who recorded her adventures in word and camera, firmly declaring that women should climb. She was appointed first president of the Ladies' Alpine Club.

And so the list in this fascinating story goes on with Charles Barrington, born in County Wicklow, a lover of steeplechasing, hunting and yachting, who on a Grand Tour and with no previous mountaineering experience first climbed the Jungfrau and two days later made the first ascent of the Eiger, achieving, at a stroke, international mountaineering immortality. This is a handsomely produced and valuable gathering together of one thread in a wider history of mountaineering that reaches the 20th century with Charles Howard-Bury, son of an Irish heiress, a soldier who survived the First World War to lead the first British attempt on Everest in 1921, mapping the approaches to the mountain and reaching the North Col.

Ronald Faux

Bridget Collier on the magnificent *Direct Route* (Hard Severe 4c), on the main cliff of Glyder Fach. A 1907 creation from KM Ward and HB Gibson, this route remains one of the most popular on the cliff.
Photo by Mark Glaister from the new *North Wales Climbs* (Rockfax) selective guide. (*See review page 356*)

**Heights of Reflection: Mountains in the German Imagination from the
Middle Ages to the Twenty-First Century**
Sean Ireton and Caroline Schaumann (eds)
Camden House, 2012, pp 396, £50.00

This book might be seen as a German counterpart to the proceedings of a
2007 conference in France published as *Mountains Figured and Disfigured
in the English-Speaking World* edited by Françoise Besson (reviewed in *AJ*

115). Here eighteen essays in English are assembled in historical order, mostly concerned with German literary texts, music (Richard Strauss's *Eine Alpensinfonie*) and films, since the editors are aware of the 'voluminous' illustrated book on mountains in German fine art by Bettina Hausler, *Der Berg: Schrecken und Faszination* (Hirmer, 2008).

So, from a text composed around 1170 to Christophe Ransmayr's postmodern novel of 2006 *Der Fliegende Berg* and Werner Herzog's mountain climbing films, the contributors to this volume try hard to challenge assumptions and develop appropriate theories to provide new insights into the essential enigma of mountains as they mirror the needs and fascinations of human culture. The assumption, for example, that Johann Jacob Scheuchzer's 1723 famous illustrations of sightings of dragons in the mountains typifies pre-Romantic attitudes is confounded by the attraction of mountains to medieval hunters in Emperor Maximilian's Theuerdank of 1517. The editors cleverly point out that the 1991 discovery of a Neolithic traveller with his framed rucksack circa 3300 BC at 3210m in the Ötztal Alps, was not the only person around at that height, as testified by the arrowhead buried in his shoulder that led to his death.

But the attractions of mountain climbing peculiar to Germans in the twentieth century are heavily indebted, as elsewhere, to cultural conditions. Wilfried Wilms argues that Arnold Franck's *Bergfilm* of the 1920s 'perform rituals of mobilization and restoration for an excited German audience bogged down by defeat and massive loss of life in the Great War. The films provide codes of conduct for a society in poor health' (269). Contemporary variations of the genre of *Bergfilm* manage to give an 'anti-Nazi spin' (16) to both a pre-war attempt on the Eiger (*Nordwand*, 2008) and a postwar attempt on a Himalayan peak (Nanga Parbat, 2010). The editors even suggest that the German obsession with Nanga Parbat might be linked to a kind of postcolonial Aryan myth: 'Even though Germany had no colonial presence in India, nationalists traced their ethnic history back to Indo-European origins and a mythic Aryan homeland' (14). Indeed, Harald Höbusch's chapter on this obsession concludes that Hans Ertl's film *Nanga Parbat 1953* 'sees nothing wrong with perpetuating fascist ideas into a democratic future' (298).

Between the medieval and the twentieth century, essays range from the mountains of tropical Polynesia, the myth of von Humbolt's ascent of Chimborazo, Thomas Mann's *Der Zauberberg*, to W.G. Sebald's *Magic Mountains*. Novelist Christof Hamann relates how, in researching his novel *Usambara* (2007), he found a fascinating fictional and non-fictional history of the Mountains of The Moon and Kilimanjaro. In a brilliant ecocritical essay *Heather I.* Sullivan reconsiders Faust's mountains in the light of Goethe's interest in climate science. Goethe's studies of the water cycle lend an irony, for Sullivan, to the fact that Faust 'succumbs, unwittingly [...] to the very forces against which he dedicates his final battle against the sea' (127). Sullivan produces a convincing conclusion that 'Faust resists and then succumbs to the modern human fate: he believes that he can move beyond matter, but he remains, of course, fully within environmental materiality, no matter how poetically garbed that realm may appear' (131). Three caveats are needed. After noting in the Introduction the first recorded female ascent of an Alpine peak in 1552 by Regina von Brandis and her daughter, the editors then ignore women's ascents and neglect a potential gendered dimension to this book – which calls for another one. Second, also neglected is the body of mountaineering poetry and song which exists not far under the surface of all mountaineering cultures. Third, amazingly, the editors ignore the long tradition of German mountaineering litera-ture, the literary and cultural qualities of which might have the subject of a chapter here. Nevertheless this is an invaluable and intellectually lively contribution to a growing international scholarship on the cultural signifi-cance of mountains.

Terry Gifford

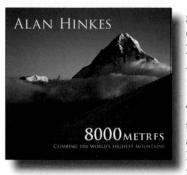

8000 Metres
Climbing the World's Highest
Mountains
Alan Hinkes
Cicerone Press, 2013, pp192, £25

This book celebrates a rare achievement, that of its author reaching the summit of all fourteen 8000 metre peaks, the first British mountaineer– and only the 13th mountaineer ever – to do so. Many of the ascents were made in alpine style, and many required several attempts before reaching his final summit, Kangchenjunga, solo, in 2005. To accom-plish this feat demanded 18 years of dedicated effort, great skill, incredible physical fitness and mental stamina, the surviving of many epics and not least a generous helping of good luck. It surely places Alan Hinkes among the ranks of the world's leading athletes – and great adventurers to boot. If any achievement warrants an Olympic Gold, it is climbing these four-teen mountains, but unlike athletics, mountaineering is not – thankfully – a popular entertainment.

Nevertheless, many of us regret that even the mountaineering establish-ment itself has not properly recognised Hinkes's achievement. Indeed it is a sad reflection on modern society that many self-styled 'explorers' are lionised as 'celebs', having achieved little beyond inflated publicity, while the real doers, who quietly persevere and finally achieve, remain unsung. Knowing Hinkes, I think he's not particularly concerned, nevertheless he is very proud to have been nominated twice as Yorkshire Man of the Year. But I'm not alone in feeling that if any mountaineer has earned a 'K', – the ultimate national recognition – it is Mr Hinkes. Credit where credit is due. This book also marks another achievement, different but worthy in its own way, that of Cicerone Press, internationally known as a publisher of myriad guide books, who deserve to be congratulated on their first foray into large format, glossy coffee-table-type publishing. I'm assured that this doesn't mark a change of tack, merely that an excellent combination of subject, illustration and text is worth publishing properly. And excellent it is.

Alan Hinkes is a big, blunt Yorkshireman. He's a grandfather, a professional mountain guide and a dab hand with a camera, who gives up much of his time, freely, to good causes such as the Duke of Edinburgh's Award. Once the face of Berghaus, he's long been operating on his own with no sponsor, PR agent or lecture tour manager. He's canny, obviously lucky and an experienced masochist who has surprisingly managed to retain all his fingers and toes.

Essentially this book is a record not only of his fourteen climbs, but also of a similar number of failed attempts. It is a large format picture book, broken into fourteen chapters, arranged in the chronological order of their ascent, and buttressed with the usual front and end-matter. The text of each chapter is quite short – that for the longest, K2, occupies some 3700 words – and is an interesting, honest, matter-of-fact account of the mountain and his experience in climbing it, though now and then where appropriate, Hinkes can be quite introspective. One detects a structural formula throughout, a certain sameness in the way each attempt, and thus its recounting, is handled, but then that's the way expeditions unfold. A short, interesting essay follows each chapter and covers a relevant subject such as The Death Zone for the K2 chapter, Jerzy Kukuczka & the Polish Climbers for Shisha Pangma and Photography & Filming for Lhotse. While obviously aware of what he's achieved, Hinkes doesn't hide his light under a bushel (or is it down a crevasse?) but neither does he boast about it, and though hardly great literature, the book is very readable.

Hinkes makes no mention of the Cho Oyu controversy which he has dismissed as tittle-tattle but which cannot fail to annoy him. Cho Oyu is the most straightforward of the 8K peaks and its summit a mere point on a wide, featureless snow plateau. Essentially Hinkes was a member of a heavily-sponsored French expedition on a public relations exercise. The summit party turned back on encountering thick hill fog on the plateau, but being British and thus being adept at navigating accurately in such conditions, Hinkes continued to the summit by dead reckoning. No big deal for a Scottish trained UIAGM mountain guide. The expedition itself failed and one cannot but feel that sour grapes entered the food chain at some juncture. Of all fourteen, Cho Oyu would have been the easiest peak to re-ascend should he have been unsure; he did, after all, make several attempts on other far more committing and dangerous peaks on which he had found himself high up but alone, and thus could easily have claimed.

However, the pictures are the *raison d'être* of the book. It is a fantastic and probably unique collection, given that they were taken at all. I know only too well how difficult it is to combine serious photography with serious climbing – try too hard and it becomes an easy way to die. Yet Hinkes has been assiduous in his photography and survived. He has an excellent eye, a talent rarely given to high altitude mountaineers, and he has gone out of his way to use it. Thus most of his shots are well composed pictures rather than merely grabbed snaps in impressive situations, and where possible he includes the small figures of other climbers, giving both scale and a suggestion of personal involvement to the viewer. No less than 68 of the pictures are used full page or more to great effect, with numerous portrait-format pictures where appropriate and with many detail images set in the text. My favourite is the unusual frontispiece depicting a tangle of seracs and crevasses on Kangchenjunga's Great Shelf shrouded in mist. Spread over two pages, it is an all but abstract composition of surreal grey shapes through which two roped climbers warily thread their way. A photographer's picture! Another superb image is that of the final 600 metres of K2 seen looking upwards from the Shoulder; three tiny figures plod upwards towards the Bottleneck under that rearing, frightening ice wall – the summit so near and yet so far, an extremely telling illustration. The double-spread panorama at dusk from high on Broad Peak over the sea of alpenglow-tipped Karakoram peaks is impressive too, a stark contrast to the intriguing Mess Tent interior at Cho Oyu Base Camp where one must wonder exactly what did the French have for supper?

In so many of these pictures I recognise the futile-seeming loneliness of the climber amid this hostile world of savage beauty. Likewise I can recall the comradeship of camp, tent and the rope. Such images say more about the ethos of high altitude mountaineering than words can tell. Indeed, I am especially struck how useful this book would be as a guide book for any high altitude mountaineer, whether actual, aspirant or arm-chair. Several of the pictures are among the most descriptive I've seen of a particular mountain, such as those of the northern side of Everest. Thus although detracting from the picture, a dotted line and some annotation would have been both explanatory and informative. Other photographs give an indication of some of the terrain encountered – 600 metres of steep, technical rock climbing on Manaslu's South Face for instance, and a corniced knife-edge to the summit of Makalu – while the text itself fills in some of the gaps. These days extensive research is prerequisite to any attempt to climb a great mountain, and planners of any expedition to the Fourteen could learn much from this book.

John Cleare

Fast and Free – Pete Livesey
Stories of a Rock Climbing Legend
Compiled and produced by John Sheard and Mark Radtke
2QT Publishing, 2014, pp342, £20

This collection of essays by Livesey's friends, colleagues, one or two of his protagonists and Pete himself serves as a biography covering the period in his life most interesting to climbers. Contributors include John Long,

Nico Mailänder and Martin Berzins as well as his 'boss' at Bingley College, Tom Price, and the essays range from straight accounts of climbs, through appraisals of Livesey's ability and character to a 'Eulogy on Orienteering'. The first thing to say is that this a great read and, for me, much more interesting than most climbing books. With such a wide variety of topics it is suitable for dipping into as suits one's moods and I found some of the essays quite riveting, including those by Pete who comes over as a much better writer than I remembered him to be. It is particularly interesting to read different view-points about him, although in some cases the authors

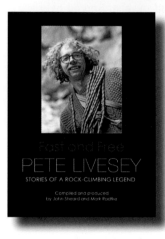

PETE LIVESEY
STORIES OF A ROCK-CLIMBING LEGEND

Compiled and produced
by John Sheard and Mark Radtke

take the opportunity to slip in their own personal bullshit, and the main point of Jill Lawrence's excellent contribution is that her climbing really took off when she split up from Pete.

The quality of the writing is quite variable and in some places editorial intervention would have been appropriate. For instance, several times in the book it is said that he made the first ascent of *Nagasaki Grooves*, whereas it was the first free ascent. I read the Mailänder article on free-climbing in the Dolomites with anticipation but found it confused and confusing, switching back and forth as it does between ascents of the *Lacedelli* on the Cima Scotoni and the *Hasse-Brandler* on the south-west wall of the Rotwand. Tom Price had died before John Inverdale made his famous remark about Marion Bartoli, but should an educationist have written: 'A female climber very different from Jill Lawrence and Gill Price was Bonny Masson. . .good looking, personable and self-assured,'? Some essays make a very strong case for Livesey being an exceptional sportsman, for example Dennis Gray says that he was 'the most outstanding all-round outdoor pursuit performer of his, or any other generation' and it would be very difficult to argue against this given his prowess in orienteering, fell-running and canoeing and caving, not to mention rock-climbing. His influence on climbing both in the UK and abroad was profound and long-lasting with some of his tactics, though controversial at the time, becoming the norm. The advance in standards that he was mainly responsible for was the result of applying training methods adapted from athletics, something almost unknown or even an anathema to most climbers at the time. Of course his strong competitive drive played a part in this but it did lead to what, even in this book, is referred to as his 'ruthless' approach.

His veniality is mainly glossed over but here and there some of the peccadilloes for which he was infamous are hinted at and I was amazed that Pete Gomersall was quite open about their activities in a piece entitled 'The Turd Mincer.'

I did feel that an exploration of the darker side of his character might have given a more complete picture of Livesey but in a book mainly of contributions from his friends this is probably asking too much. Overall this is a fascinating account of the life of a major figure in the development of rock-climbing which I cannot recommend too highly.

Mike Mortimer

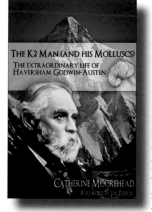

The K2 Man and his Molluscs (the extraordinary life of Haversham Godwin-Austen)
Catherine Moorehead
Inn Pin, 2014, pp279, £24.99

Haversham Godwin-Austen was pre-eminent among the explorers, surveyors and map makers who were the cutting edge of British imperialism. Sir George Everest, as head of the Great Trigonometric Survey of India, may have had his resounding name attached to the world's highest summit but as this biography makes clear, Godwin-Austen's achievements were far more memorable. His discovery and surveying of the Baltoro, Hispar and Biafo glaciers, the greatest group of valley glaciers in the world, and of fixing, with great accuracy, the position and heights of many of the giant peaks of the Karakoram, including K2, was a truly historic achievement. Sir George perhaps never clapped eyes on Everest and, though K2 may occasionally be known as Mount Godwin-Austen, only the glacier now bears his name on the map.

This excellent and meticulously researched biography makes no comparison between the two characters but presents Godwin-Austen alone as a tool of the British Raj, establishing boundaries between countries and fiefdoms that preferred not to have them, a pawn in a much bigger political and diplomatic picture. The artistic talent he developed so skilfully began under military training with an ulterior purpose; paintings that could disclose secrets, maps that would reveal the best route for an army to take. His five expeditions between 1860 and 1865 were the highest achievement by any British mountain explorer at that time and for years to come. Simply 'carrying out orders' opened for Godwin-Austen a much wider scope for exploration and developing his talent for natural science. A fascination with Indian molluscs, for example, was sparked when he spotted a small wading bird with one foot trapped in the clamped jaws of a mollusc. An interest became unparalleled knowledge of the subject and an admiration of Indian molluscs for their beauty of form and variety.

Catherine Moorhead lays out Godwin-Austen's life in some fine detail with a wealth of information added in copious footnotes. She admires his achievements in a life complicated by three marriages and an illegitimate son by an Afghan lover, which rather dented his credentials as a member of an ancient, noble family. Like Lord Conway, his contemporary among mountain explorers, he suffered severe financial problems and in the Great Agricultural Depression of the late 18th century he was declared bankrupt. He was a tough and determined mountain explorer who set new altitude records and survived all that hostile nature and hostile local communities could throw at him, a polymath among polymaths, an adventurer respected among adventurers. Indeed Moorhead suggests that the shrewdness and experience behind some of Godwin-Austen's advice would almost certainly have led to an earlier British success and saved lives on Everest: 'possibly sparing us the endless and largely fatuous controversy about the deaths of Mallory and Irvine,' she declares. And who would want that?

Ronald Faux

The Sunlit Summit
The Life of W. H. Murray
Robin Lloyd-Jones
Sandstone Press, 2013, pp384, £19.99

Rumours, rumours... Shortly before his death in 1996, Bill Murray was seen burning letters and diaries on a bonfire in his garden on the shores of Loch Goil. This at least is according to 'several reports' that reached the author and former tutor in creative writing Robin Lloyd-Jones.

How painful it must have been for Lloyd-Jones to learn of all that potentially valuable source material going up in smoke. But think too of the pain of that man stood by his bonfire, so distressed at the idea of his personal life and thoughts being paraded in biography that he would rather burn the evidence.

Lloyd-Jones does not name the witnesses to this conflagration (they must have been close to know that Murray was burning letters and diaries, and not old phone bills) but he does concede it was 'most probably the act of a man protecting his privacy'.

To this end, Murray has been supported loyally by his widow who declined to share any material with Lloyd-Jones. Anne Murray did not want a biography written about her husband, the author explains: 'He was such a private man,' she said, 'and he would have hated the idea.'

But would Bill Murray really have hated this book? Murray's output as a writer, together with his mystical philosophy, has been treated with such sensitivity by Lloyd-Jones it is hard to imagine what the gentle Scot, even in his later-life reclusion, could have found intrusive. Of course one might argue that the book would have been different had Lloyd-Jones had access to the diaries that allegedly went up flames. But even so, such is Lloyd-Jones's reverent feeling towards Murray that the outcome would always have been sympathetic.

No other person had filled him with such a strong desire to write about them, Lloyd-Jones says. 'I feel that I have at least a few things in common with Bill Murray – as a lover of mountains, and of wild places, as a fellow writer, both of wilderness topics and of fiction, and as someone who, as did he, daily meditates.'

In the mid-1960s, Lloyd-Jones, like so many of his generation and mine, had read Murray's *Mountaineering in Scotland* and been entranced. Nearly 70 years after its first publication it is still *Mountaineering in Scotland* that comes closest to capturing the rumbustiousness and joy of winter climbing with good friends in the Highlands. This may be less so now for those on the near-roadside routes of the Northern Corries or set gimlet-eyed on some super-hard testpiece. But for most, I suspect, a day on, say, Liathach or seeking out the Upper Couloir on Stob Ghabhar, where Murray and his pals taught themselves step-cutting, is still a Murray-esque experience.

Mountaineering in Scotland (1947) and its sequel *Undiscovered Scotland* (1951) were acclaimed by Robin Campbell in his obituary of Murray in the 1997 *Alpine Journal* as the *Iliad* and *Odyssey* of Scottish mountain writing – though the former, the first draft of which was famously written while Murray was a Prisoner of War, is the superior of the two books. It seems the author thought so too. Lloyd-Jones notes that Murray says not a single word about *Undiscovered Scotland* in his autobiography *The Evidence of Things Not Seen* (Bâton Wicks, 2002), pieced together by Anne Murray and Ken Wilson.

Murray wrote more than 20 books, including novels and guidebooks, and numerous articles; his passion was Scotland's mountain landscape, and in its cause he devoted countless hours – 'years' might be more accurate – of voluntary work to bodies such as the National Trust for Scotland and the Countryside Commission for Scotland. Yet how well do we really know him?

Lloyd-Jones says that a proper understanding of Murray's life and work requires we appreciate four things: his driving force was his quest to achieve inner purification that would lead him to oneness with Trust and Beauty; from this stemmed his denial of self which translated into a life of service to others; his lifelong love of mountains and exploration; and his abhorrence of boasting and any form of self-promotion or publicity seeking.

About a third of *The Sunlit Summit* deals with Murray as writer. For anyone interested in mountain literature, or the craft of writing in general, this is an absorbing analysis. Murray was a 'supreme craftsman' whose work needs to be re-evaluated, beyond the Scottish dimension into a British, European and worldwide context, concludes Lloyd-Jones. 'In the fields of mountaineering literature, wilderness writing and landscape description, he would hold his own with the best.'

This claim would hold up all the better if the inspirational magic of *Mountaineering in Scotland* had carried over to more of Murray's subsequent work. Why didn't it? The answer may lie in two of those four things that Lloyd-Jones bids us appreciate: Murray's modesty (he never used or spoke of his OBE) and his mystical philosophy. Lloyd-Jones deals with the origins of the latter in some depth, but unfortunately in later writing Murray largely withdrew from deeper engagement in philosophical thought.

In a perceptive review of *The Evidence of Things Not Seen*, quoted by Lloyd-Jones, Dave Hewitt, writing for *The Angry Corrie*, lamented Murray's 'unwillingness or inability to fully portray himself': formal modesty did not make for good autobiography... Murray was being 'too humble for his own good'.

The Sunlit Summit goes a long way to filling in the gaps and smoothing out the unsatisfactory portrait painted in *The Evidence of Things Not Seen*; Lloyd-Jones has done a valuable service with this insightful biography; however one is left with the thought that the means to a full understanding of W. H. Murray may have gone up in smoke on that bonfire by Loch Goil. (And who are we to protest if that is what his conscience bid?)

Stephen Goodwin

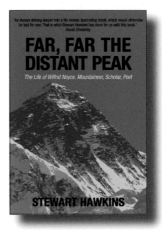

Far, Far The Distant Peak
The Life of Wilfrid Noyce, Mountaineer, Scholar, Poet
Stewart Hawkins
Curbans Books, 2014, pp368, £25

Wilf Noyce was a seminal figure in the lives of many people, including the author of this biography Stewart Hawkins. A long time member of the Climbers' Club, Hawkins was introduced to rock climbing and hill walking by Noyce, his Scoutmaster at Charterhouse. The huge amount of research he has undertaken and new material he has unearthed about the life of his subject is truly impressive and it is obvious that, from a personal perspective, he feels he owes Wilf's memory such respect.

Noyce was born in India in 1917 and his father Sir Frank was a major figure in the Indian Civil Service based at Simla. Typical of a child of the Raj he was sent back to England for schooling, first at a preparatory then Charterhouse public school. Through his mother, Enid, he had climbing connections for she was a Kirkus, and Guy and Colin were his cousins. The family had a summer home at Ffestiniog and it was there that Noyce caught the mountain bug and started wandering up the nearby hills, leading on to a desire to start rock climbing which he did first with Guy Kirkus as his teacher, then with Colin.

He was still a schoolboy when he met the leading climber of that era Menlove Edwards, an older man, with whom he started to climb and who became a major influence on his young life. The author deals with this relationship, and it's homosexual possibilities reasonably frankly, noting that Noyce was bereft of the influence of any father figure, his own being away abroad whilst he was growing up.

With Edwards, Noyce undertook the first of his guidebook works, *Tryfan* in 1937 and *Lliwedd* in 1939. These were masterworks for their day, setting the standard for following volumes, and in later years Noyce became guidebook editor for both the Climbers' Club and the Alpine Club.

At Cambridge Noyce began to show his leadership qualities, being a 'main man' in the CUMC, taking on such roles as Treasurer, journal Editor, instructor on its beginners' meets, and finally President.

At the outbreak of WW II Noyce joined the Friends Ambulance Unit, but after Dunkirk his pacifism melted away and he joined the Army, eventually serving as an intelligence officer based in New Delhi. Somehow, despite this arduous posting, he managed to get away to climb in the Garhwal Himalaya in 1943 and 1944 and Sikkim in 1945 where he managed to climb Paunhunri (7127m). These were small lightweight trips, on the latter he being the only European, accompanied by two Sherpas, Angtharkay and Namgar.

Returning to Britain after the war Noyce was rather lost for a while, wondering about what his career would be, before finally settling on a career as a schoolmaster, teaching classics and modern languages first at Malvern College then at his old school Charterhouse.

In 1953 he was invited by John Hunt to join the Everest expedition and *Far, Far The Distant Peak* goes very thoroughly into the ascent and the crucial part he played on the expedition – finally opening the route to the South Col.

After Everest Noyce settled back into teaching and family life. He went with a small group of friends to Nepal, attempting Machapuchare (6993m) in 1957, getting to within 150 feet of the summit of this most iconic mountain with David Cox, and Trivor (7577m) in 1960, summiting with the American Jack Sadler.

It was around that date I got to know Wilf. He became the President of the Alpine Climbing Group and I was its Secretary. In order for him to take office, being over 40 years old we had to change the constitution to allow this. At one ACG meet in Derbyshire Noyce, climbing with Martin Boysen, surprised us all by seconding *Right Eliminate* on Curbar, at that time an acknowledged difficult climb.

Ending, the book covers the controversial events of the ill-fated 1962 Pamirs Expedition, during which Noyce and Robin Smith were killed. *Far, Far The Distant Peak* deals with the aftermath of these events with sensitivity but leaves one ruminating on what might have been if Noyce had survived into old age? He had recently resigned from teaching before the Pamirs expedition, to concentrate on his writing. Some of his books, *The Springs of Adventure, They Survived, Mountains and Men* and his translation, with John Hunt, of Rébuffat's *Starlight and Storm* had a great impact on many climbers of my generation.

On reading *Far, Far The Distant Peak* someone like myself might envy Noyce's privileged background, but cannot blame him in any way for that.

He was so lucky, but he used every opportunity in his life to use his good fortune to the best of his ability, and in so doing helped many others to achieve their goals providing inspiration by a life so well lived.

Far, Far The Distant Peak is an outstanding biography of an outstanding man.

Dennis Gray

PS There is one serious typo in the book, Charles Evans did not marry Nea Morin, it was of course Denise her daughter with whom he tied the nuptial knot.

Mountain Geography
Physical and Human Dimensions
Edited by Martin F. Price, Alton C. Byers, Donald A. Friend, Thomas Kohler and Larry W. Price
University of California Press, 2013, pp 396, £65

As the title suggests, *Mountain Geography* is an academic textbook, and as such is likely to be of little attraction to those whose sole interest in mountains is in new routes or peak bagging. If your concern for the mountains and their inhabitants goes wider (and your pocket is sufficiently deep) then this hefty tome gives a comprehensive overview of the processes at work in the world's mountains and their impact on culture and society.

Aimed primarily at American undergraduates, *Mountain Geography* constitutes a major revision of Larry Price's book *Mountains and Man* published in 1981. Since then much has been learnt and unlearnt – not least that the Himalaya are not, after all, on the brink of environmental catastrophe. In 1979, the World Bank had predicted that Nepal would be denuded of forest cover by the year 2000: as anyone who has trekked or climbed there recently will have seen, even along popular trails such as the Langtang there is still plenty of cover for tribes of langur monkeys and laughing thrushes.

Thankfully, subsistence hill farmers are no longer seen as the problem – ignorant peasants undermining the life support of hundreds of millions of people on the plains – but in academic circles at least, as part of the solution: that is an environmentally sustainable future. And as academic understanding of mountains has progressed so too has a better public appreciation of the importance of mountains to the wellbeing of society at large.

A good deal of the credit for this goes to the editors of this book and academic colleagues, who, through a plethora of international bodies and over many years, have been endeavouring to push mountain issues up the international policy agenda. (Does that sound a Sisyphean task?) Martin Price will be familiar to *AJ* readers as Professor of Mountain Studies at the University of the Highlands and Islands, Perth, and an AC member. Alton Byers, Director of Science and Exploration at the Mountain Institute, in the USA, took part in the AC's 'Summits of Learning' seminar in 2007 and has written for the AJ on conservation in Nepal.

Though not all like to admit it, mountaineers have been in the vanguard of tourism in the mountains; in the wake of climbers, pioneering in the Alps and Himalaya, have come columns of trekkers, skiers, mountain bikers and so on. As this book points out, tourism has been a major force of change in mountain areas. Tourism has become one of the largest and fastest-growing economic sectors in the world, with particularly strong growth in emerging and developing countries; 15 to 20 per cent of this, or US$128-170 billion a year, is associated with travel to mountain areas. But it can be a mixed blessing: negative impacts include loss of farmland, air and water pollution and an erosion of indigenous cultures and communities.

Reflecting the fresh thinking since *Mountains and Man*, there are new chapters on mountain people and on sustainable mountain development. And Edwin Bernbaum, the American scholar-mountaineer and author of *Sacred Mountains of The World*, has contributed, together with Larry Price, an informative overview of 'Attitudes towards Mountains' from pre-history to the present. It concludes: 'Mountains are considered the embodiment of the good, the beautiful, and the sublime.' Perhaps in that emotional, rather than scientific response, lies their salvation.

Stephen Goodwin

Reading the Gaelic Landscape
John Murray
Whittles Publishing, 2014, pp240, £16.99

In the pre-dawn one June many years ago, four of us slogged up from Glen Brittle to a peak we called 'Guard's Van'. We were set on the Cuillin ridge; Gars-bheinn (910m) is its southernmost eminence, but such a name was for us unpronounceable (including for our Scottish comrade) and so, mocking our own ignorance, we dubbed it Guard's Van – and trudged on.

There is a mischievous suspicion that the mountains of the Highlands of Scotland were named in such a way as to confuse English climbers, except that most Scottish climbers are similarly lost among the toponyms of the *Gàidhealtachd*. The district guides of the Scottish Mountaineering Club include helpful translations (eg Sgurr a'Choire Bhig = peak of the little corrie, when you might have guessed 'big') while SMT's *Scottish Hill Names* has long provided enlightenment; Peter Drummond's 2007 revision remains both absorbing and accessible, enabling the reader to see the hills as the Gaels and Scots saw them.

And now comes further insight. John Murray's *Reading The Gaelic Landscape* takes a more academic approach and could well become a popular textbook for students of Gaelic, certainly in respect of interpreting the landscape. Murray goes beyond hill names to the valleys and fields, covering land use, ecology and culture. A specific theme explores how poets like Sorley MacLean and Duncan Bàn MacIntyre used their homeland symbolically in their work.

Murray is director of landscape architecture at the University of Edinburgh. His aim with this absorbing book is to appeal to 'serious enthusiasts' who seek a deeper understanding of what they study and enjoy in the Highlands. 'What is being attempted is a semantic reclamation of a lost domain,' he says. 'An attempt to recapture a poetry of place, enshrined in the identifying labels which have been given to the landscape by Gaelic-speakers.'

That last clause is worth mountaineers bearing in mind. Murray's exclusive focus is the *Gàidhealtachd* – the Highlands and Islands. Murray's Hill Names cover the whole of Scotland; Gaelic is most widespread of the languages used, but there are also hills with names in Scots, Norse, Cumbric, and just a few in English (notably on Skye).

As for 'Guard's Van', neither Murray nor Drummond is particularly helpful. However the SMC's *The Islands of Scotland* states that the name translates as 'possibly echoing mountain' (bheinn = mountain) while a paper on the University of the Highlands and Islands website gives the pronunciation as 'Garsven'. In our ignorance, 'Guard's Van' wasn't so far out after all.

Stephen Goodwin

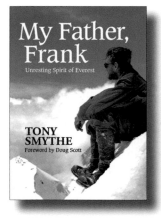

My Father, Frank
Tony Smythe
Bâton Wicks, 2013, pp324, £20

Frank Smythe was, by any conceivable measure, a remarkable man: author, photographer, botanist, but above all, a pioneering mountaineer, who broke boundaries not only at altitude but also in his writing career. In this biography – and it is assuredly that, with no trace of hagiography – his son Tony seeks not only to know and understand the father who was often absent from his life, but to frame him within the ethos of the emerging pre-Second World War climbing scene. Further, in so successfully offering vivid recreations of mountaineering exploits, poised as they are on the extremes of existence, he has given readers an opportunity to examine the place of ambition – and its consequences – in their own lives.

Smythe enjoyed little success during his school years in England, feeling rather that they should be simply endured. In desperation, his mother took him to Switzerland to continue his education and it was during the long, tedious train journey that he caught his first sight of high mountains:

'It was as though God had chosen to manifest Himself by raising earth to sky and making of it a single step to Heaven.'

The sense of spirituality and singularity which remote peaks engendered possessed him throughout his short life and it was this, not the desire for self-publicity or financial gain of which he was later accused by the more reactionary members of the Alpine Club, which fuelled his remarkable mountaineering achievements. At 26, with two failed careers behind him and no employment, he devoted himself to that which he subsequently excelled at – mountaineering: first in the Alps, often soloing exacting routes, and later the Himalaya.

Tony Smythe's descriptions of his father's most notable climbs are cinematic in their detail and immediacy – a skilful blend of the minutiae of the rhythm and restriction of progress on crumbling rock, slick ice and thigh-deep snow, set against the broad sweep of ambition, often realised. Smythe ascended Jonsong Peak in 1930 and Kamet in 1931 – both the highest-ever climbs at the time – and then in 1933 came within 250 metres of the summit of Everest as Eric Shipton lay ill in Camp 6, unable to accompany him. Frank's own account of this astonishing feat is both powerful and terrifying and demonstrates how his skill as a writer enthralled both climbers and non-climbers alike.

Here, too, there were forays into new territory. Victor Gollanz recognised Smythe's potential and encouraged him in his desire to fund his expeditions both through his writing and his mountaineering photography. This kind of financial arrangement was, hitherto, unknown – of course, at that time, one simply wrote for fellow climbers in journals and publications which they alone would read. When Gollanz had the audacity to advertise The Kangchenjunga Adventure Sir Arnold Lunn's observation; 'foul bad taste' perfectly illustrates both the tenor of the times and Tony Smythe's wry humour.

However, whilst Smythe senior was enjoying success both as an author and a mountaineer, his personal life was in disarray. He had married in 1931, something which his son comments on perceptively;
'I got the feeling that Frank saw marriage at this stage of his life as simply a Good Idea.'

He admired Kathleen, Tony's mother and felt that he did not want to lose her. His all-important expedition to Kamet loomed large so the deed had best be done before he left, three months hence. The marriage lasted only seven years and when it ended with his attachment to Nona Guthrie he confessed to Francis Younghusband that he had 'married the wrong woman' for whom he felt only 'a sort of unfeeling indifference.'

Frank's self-sufficiency, imperviousness to home comforts and social rituals and his awkwardness in polite company served him well in the mountains but did little to create a happy marriage. Tony Smythe is scrupulous in his analysis of his father's personal life, rife with difficulty as it often was and this open-handed and courageous account fully reveals a complex and sometimes troubled man to both author and reader:
'He had plenty of self-assurance on the heights, whereas at sea-level he was either shy or over-assertive.'

He tackles the famous and enduring rift between his father and Graham Brown in the same even-handed way, employing a combination of vivid descriptions of the difficulties and eventual triumph on the Route Major and painstaking research into the details of the controversy which ensued and which caused an irreparable rift between the two men, despite Smythe's later attempts at reconciliation.

Frank Smythe's untimely death from cerebral malaria at 48 came at a time when his domestic life with Nona was harmonious, his mountaineering skills had been recognised internationally and he had the luxury of choosing from a variety of climbing trips which had been offered to him. Despite all these obvious signs of success, his restlessness was never subdued, his desire to escape into the high places in which he felt most comfortable never quelled.

Clearly, Tony Smythe inherited his father's questing spirit and this highly readable and authoritative biography celebrates his great success in not only discovering the father he never really knew but also bringing him to a wider audience, new and old.

Val Randall

The Summits of Modern Man: Mountaineering after the Enlightenment
Peter H. Hansen
Harvard University Press, 2013, pp 380, £25.95

Let us begin with the acknowledgements, lest we forget the world importance of our own library and archives and the voluntary guidance generously offered by Glyn Hughes and Jerry Lovatt to scholars such as Peter H. Hansen, who will have been demanding and has left no document unturned. This is a scholarly book that also references – in English, French, German, Italian and Swiss sources (yes, Hansen even speaks Swiss, Scots and, with disastrous results in the opening sentence, his native American). It could be argued that his need to follow up references sends the book off course, but more of this later.

The title and first chapter of this book might create the wrong impression, not to mention that opening sentence, again: "On belay!' calls a climber after tying to the rope'. If he's just tied on, surely his partner is standing beside him. This gives the unfortunate impression of an academic historian of mountaineering who is going to make embarrassing blunders about the practice of climbing mountains. The endnote reference to a Sierra Club Bulletin article titled *Belaying the Leader* dated 1946 actually makes Hansen's point that nautical terms were adopted by the military and used by demobbed climbers in America post-war, in a phrase which must translate as the Whillanesque fag-in-mouth 'Have you got me, youth?'.

The book's title is even more deceptive. This book is mainly concerned with the summit of Mont Blanc and the reception of its first ascent(s). Mont

Ventoux and Mont Aiguille are mere precursors and the Matterhorn and
Everest are discussed as comparisons – all in terms of the political contexts
of the time, the changed identities and relationships of the first ascentionists, and the subsequent shifting of the 'facts' of the ascents. Running
throughout the book are discussions of modernity and masculinity,
although in the latter case less discussion and more unreflective assertion
– apart from Marie Paradis's and Henriette d'Angeville's ascents of Mont
Blanc, *The Summits of Modern Man* deals only with 'muscular' men. Finally,
'after the Enlightenment' might suggest an interest in Romanticism, but
this book not only argues for the continuation of the Enlightenment in
mountaineering into the nineteenth century, it is itself a kind of Enlightenment project – to record all the versions and meanings of a handful of first
ascents, impeccably referenced.

If they can get past the first chapter of historian-speak (which concludes,
'Thus, the perennial rediscovery of beginnings must lead, necessarily, to
a multiplicity of modernities'), the readers of this journal will find a fascinating wealth of detail about the local, regional and national positions of
not only the main players in the early history of Mont Blanc, but of the
people who reported and debated the early ascents. The chapter 'Ascent
and Enfranchisement' weaves a fascinating argument for linking the end of
feudal obligations in Chamonix in 1786 with the first ascent of Mont Blanc
by the peasant Balmat and the village's first doctor Paccard, the crystal
hunter and the plant hunter, the guide and the scientist, the seeker after de
Saussure's reward for the first to the summit and the seeker after de Saussure's respect for the first summit recordings.

During the French Revolution the government in Paris 'incorporated Mont
Blanc into the new regime of festivals and practices that constituted the
revolution'. But who would have thought that Marie Paradis's dragged-to-
the-top ascent, 'whether demonstrating female courage, enacting Marian
veneration, lampooning Napoleonic festivals, or acting as an intervention in local politics [...] had seditious potential on July 14, 1808'? Or that
Balmat's repeated attempts as disenfranchised peasant would be echoed
by Whymper's persistence on the Matterhorn, which Hansen links to the
fact that 'unlike almost all other members of the Alpine Club, Whymper
remained disenfranchised in England, unable to vote until after the second
Reform Act of 1867'?

Indeed, Hansen's interest in parallels to the reception of the first ascent
of Mont Blanc leads him to consider the Everest first ascent. 'Multiple
parallels between the two events appeared obvious at the time: proposals
to rename the peak, subscriptions to reward the poor guide, and notarized
certificates to settle the question of who was first'. Official and journalistic
celebrations in Nepal, India, England and New Zealand provide the historian with a veritable snakes and ladders of parallels and interpretations.
Then, the day after the state reception for the British Everest expedition,
Graham Brown and Gavin de Beer wrote to the AC to propose a book
about the first ascent of Mont Blanc. Their book, which appeared in 1957,

'credited Paccard with discovery of the route, leadership of the climb, and he alone was 'the prime cause of the first ascent of Mont Blanc'', accompanied only by 'a single porter'. Hansen claims that 'the first ascent of Mount Everest changed the 'facts' of the first ascent of Mont Blanc'.

The book's final chapter, 'Bodies of Ice', which some may think a mistake, moves towards considering the 'facts' of the discovery in 1991 of Ötzi, the mummified Neolithic man. This seems partly to be an excuse to consider the Italian side of Mont Blanc, partly to discuss its current role in providing data for climate change (having mentioned the Anthropocene – an informal geological epoch of human influence – Hansen needs to recount and reference the evolution of the term), and partly a chance to return to the instability of 'facts', 'modern man' and the way 'the verticality of the mountains locates us in a continuum of past and present and future'. But, for all its academic play with grand ideas, this is a thoroughly researched and thought-provoking account of the cultural history of the stories told about the first ascents of Mont Blanc, their contexts and their reverberations. It exemplifies the idea that the narratives of the ascent of shining mountains mirror the tensions in the cultures below them. And obviously still do so.

Terry Gifford

Langdale
Max Biden
The Fell and Rock Climbing Club, 2013, pp 492, £25

Scafell & Wasdale
Al Phizacklea and Ron Kenyon
The Fell and Rock Climbing Club, 2014, pp 348, £25

'A new ascent was made today on the Central Buttress of Scawfell...
The first section is difficult and involves an 80 foot run out for the leader...'

'The extraordinary nature of the difficulty of this climb can hardly be over expressed. The safe ascent of the crack was rendered possible only by the most daring combined tactics on the part of the Leader and Second. The work of the Second in threading the rope and afterwards giving a shoulder at the most exposed part was only less remarkable than actual leading of the crack.'

The quotes above are from the Wasdale Climbing Book and dated 20 and 21 April 1914, recording the first ascent of what Al Phizacklea, among many others, believes 'can justifiably claim to be the most famous rock climb in the country'.

One hundred years to the day, six climbers repeated Sansom, Herford and Holland's landmark route on Scafell Crag, watched by a host of others. All then retired to Brackenclose, the Fell and Rock's hut at the head of Wast Water, to celebrate publication of the FRCC's latest guide to Scafell and

Wasdale – the CB Centenary Edition.

Phizacklea has again authored the Scafell section – his third updating of the area in 30 years, but as he says, done without boredom or apathy 'because the crags around Scafell are the best in England.' Meanwhile, day after day, Ron Kenyon was trailing family members and Penrith pals all the way round to the west coast to check out the diverse crags of Wasdale. The results of their labours are impressive.

The Scafell guide comes close on the heels of a new guide to Langdale authored, once again, by Max Biden. The two guidebooks follow a change of FRCC series editor, Steve Scott taking over from the long-serving Stephen Reid. And with a new editor comes, perhaps inevitably, a change in the appearance of the FRCC guides, quite a dramatic change in fact. I have sung the praises of Reid's editorship in past reviews for the AJ, finding volumes such as *Gable & Pillar* and *Buttermere & St Bees* to be gems of the guidebook art, clear and concise for doing the job at the crag, yet a trove of fascinating historical and other detail for poring over in idle hours.

So what of the new look? Well the word 'gems' seems no longer appropriate. Scott has adopted a larger format – too large, in fact, to fit into my guidebook pouch. Pocket-sized, these are not. With bigger size comes more weight; no problem if the guide-book is left at the foot of the crag, but if you're multi-pitching and take the Langdale guide with you, that's more than half a kilo extra to bear.

What is taking up the extra space? There are new routes of course – Dave Birkett is the stand-out star with such as *Another Lonely Day* (E8 6c) on Scafell's East Buttress. He says it's 'simply the best traditional route in the country.' But so far nobody has been able to repeat the route to verify this. However neither of these guides is definitive: due to what are described as 'changed attitudes to conservation', poor or overgrown routes and in some cases whole crags have been omitted and descriptions placed in the archive section of the FRCC website.

The bigger page size of course means photo-diagrams can be even clearer, as are the maps. What is really bulking out these two books though are photographs, both action and purely landscape. While many of these are excellent in themselves, is, say, a double page spread of Yewbarrow from Overbeck really earning its keep? A few of the action shots are truly inspiring, but many could have been omitted at no detriment to the utility of the guidebook, utility surely being the principle yardstick of such publications (and utility includes portability).

Another change with these two guidebooks is the cover material. Yes, I know you can't judge a book by its cover, but for a book that will get some rough handling (and no longer fits a pouch) the casing matters. The change is from tough plastic (that wrinkled a bit on some volumes) to a sort of plasticized card that is creasing already as I leaf though the book at my desk.

Hopefully I will get over these quibbles and come to love the new look FRCC guidebooks as I loved those of the Reid era. There's no doubting the work that has gone into them by Al, Ron, Max, Steve Scott and a good many others on the guidebooks team; so much great climbing laid out for our delectation. Many thanks.

Stephen Goodwin

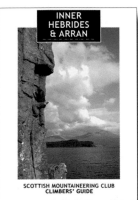

Inner Hebrides & Arran
Scottish Mountaineering Club Climbers' Guide
Colin Moody and Graham Little
Scottish Mountaineering Trust, 2014, pp 320, £25

Clean rock, friction like Velcro, sun on your back and somewhere below your feet the sound of wavelets lapping lazily on to a white sand beach. A climber's cliché of paradise perhaps. Yet in the Inner Hebrides this earthly paradise really exists. OK, it is not an every day experience, but fine weather and dry rock is not as rare on these islands as you might think; Tiree is allegedly one of the sunniest places in the UK.

New routing in the Inner Hebrides, notably around the bays and islets of the Ross of Mull, has been prolific since publication of *Skye and The Hebrides Volume 2* in 1996. This latest offering does not include the Outer Hebrides or Skye, instead Canna, Muck, Coll, Tiree, Islay, Jura and Cara appear in a guidebook for the first time. And then there's Arran added on with its wealth of trad climbing.

More than 2500 routes are included in the guidebook, a large number of them put up by its authors, Colin Moody and Graham Little. The first ascents list at the back of the book is testimony to the pair's insatiable appetite for exploring sea cliffs and surely also to patience with fickle island weather and disrupted timetables of Calmac ferries.

To make an appreciable inroad into routes over such a wide and watery area would take a huge investment of time and travelling. Yet even a few good days on the cliffs at Erraid, Kintra or on Iona would more than repay the ferry journey from Oban to Mull and the purchase of this well-produced guide.

Mike Hutton relishing *Sentinel* (HVS 5a), Erraid, Mull. *(Mike Hutton, selfie)*

Elsewhere in this journal's review section, I have had a gripe about the Topsy syndrome in recent guidebooks – they just grow and grow. However with the exception of Arran, most of the routes in this book are not multi-pitch and therefore portability is of less importance. What a pity that Arran could not be dealt with in a slim volume of its own.

The coastlines and inland cliffs of the Inner Hebrides are so vast and often difficult of access that this already compendious guidebook is likely nowhere near the end of the story. I have climbed on outcrops on Mull's Ardmeanach peninsula that do not appear in this book, yet I've been only an irregular visitor. I suspect there are unrecorded routes aplenty throughout the islands, but does that matter? I wouldn't want to dissuade you from buying *Inner Hebrides & Arran* – Moody and Little have done a superb job in pulling together so much climbing and useful crag detail – but climbing on the short sea cliffs that are the real lure of the Inner Hebrides is an easy-going holiday affair; pick the most inviting lines, once the tide has washed any footprints from the beach it all looks and feels like new ground.

Stephen Goodwin

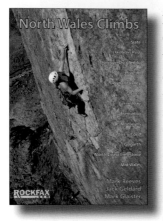

North Wales Climbs
Jack Geldard, Mark Glaister, Mark Reeves
Rockfax, 2013, pp400, £29.95

To re-phase that old adage about buses, you wait years for a selected guide and then three appear in relatively short succession. In 1970 we saw Ron James's *Rock Climbing in Wales*, 200 selected climbs and possibly the first North Wales guide to use the now common, entertaining one liners. Twenty years later came the incomparable Mr Paul Williams and *Rock Climbing in Snowdonia*, which increased the selection to around 500 and, despite its age, still remains relevant. In 2009 Simon Panton and Ground Up brought us *North Wales Rock*, a feast of 675 climbs, though none further south than the Lleyn. The following year Jack Gelgard and Rockfax produced the little pocket guide *North Wales Classics*. Although highly limited, with some errors, but including a winter section, it is useful in its own way. However, it was simply a forerunner, a taster, of what was to come.

Mark Reeves, Gelgard and Mark Glaister, three men who know a thing or two about climbing in North Wales, have come together to produce *North Wales Climbs*: over 1000 routes from Diff to E7 and F4 to F9a. Actually, the title is wrong; it should be North and Mid-Wales climbs. But more significant is that this is not a 'selected climbs', it is a 'selected crags', and in that sense a more commercial production.

The authors have chosen 56 different crags and for each included a reasonable spread of routes; Lower Pen Trwyn, for instance, is almost comprehensive, with 49 routes described. This more inclusive approach leads to a few climbs described as 'a rather scrappy line', or 'rather contrived'. It also leads to the omission of the single route on a crag. Those wanting a description of classic mountaineering excursions like *Reade's Route* on Crib Goch or *Adam Rib* on Craig Cwm Du, those wanting to taste the wonderful adventure climbing (read sometimes scary at the grade) of *Angel Pavement* on Craig y Bera or *Fantan B* on the Lleyn, will need to look in previous selected (or definitive) guides. Indeed, all climbing on the Lleyn was obviously thought inappropriate for this guide.

As we have come to expect from a Rockfax production the layout is superb, navigation throughout excellent, and the crag diagrams are simply wonderful. There can be no longer any excuse for not finding the chosen route, and a larger format makes it arguably the clearest guide to North Wales.

Action photos are less consistent. There are marvellous shots but also a number that are grim and grubby, scarcely showing North Wales in its best light. But then best light is often hard to come by in North Wales. To single out just one example, there is the strange inclusion of the upper section of the three-star E4 *Resurrection*, which makes it look relatively gentle, so much so that it needs the qualifying statement in the caption, 'don't be deceived by the camera angle, this is definitely not a slab'. Given that good shots of *Resurrection* are nearly 10 a penny, and that the front cover boasts a magnificent and sensational image of adjacent *Left Wall*, you do wonder at its inclusion.

Rockfax continues to develop its modern approach and plans to have a fully functioning smart phone app version of the guide available by 2015. Parking locations for all crags are displayed with GPS coordinates. Plug them into your Satnav, and indeed into your phone, so you can find your way back to the car from the crag. Maybe in the future we'll find crag coordinates, or even route coordinates, particularly useful when locating the top of that elusive sea cliff climb that requires a rappel to access. These coordinates can be quite difficult to enter onto a smart phone, so the authors have also supplied Quick Response Codes, which can be scanned and read with the appropriate app. There are also useful codes for webcams, weather, tides etc. At 750g the book is obviously too bulky to take with you on a climb: either scan and print the section, or photograph it with your phone.

People will argue for ever about grades. I'm not going to bother. The authors have to their advantage the Rockfax/UKC database, where users can log opinions on star rating and grades: is this a hard, VS, or an easy HVS? Is it hard for 4c or closer to 5a? Can I do it, or can't I? The consensus has no doubt proved vital in compiling the guide. In fact it is hard to find any information missing in getting you to, from, up and off the route. Oh, alright, there is one small thing that bothers me. Climbs are given no overall length; instead just individual pitch lengths on a multi-pitch route. That's fine, but single pitch routes have no indicated length, the best you get is a small box atop part of the crag, giving the vertical height at that point. Whilst this will do nicely for routes in that vicinity, a bit of guesswork is needed for others. As I said, this is a minor difference from other guides.

For the real tickers there is the Top50 symbol, a list of, well actually, 78 trad routes and eight sport climbs considered the best of their kind in the whole of North and Mid-Wales, with a full grade spread from *Cyfrwy Arête* to *Strawberries*. Included in this is the former Gist Ddu classic *Aardvark*. I say former because whilst I've wanted to do it, I've been put off by the number of friends who have tried and bailed on reaching impenetrable vegetation, and rap slings. Maybe, it's been unearthed: perhaps I should go and check. If you already have a selected guide then you'll seriously want to think twice before buying another. If you've not, then I would suggest this is the one. In the introduction the authors start their description of North Wales by saying 'nowhere in the UK is there such a concentration of classic traditional rock climbs of all grades and such variety'. A few lines further down it has slightly improved to be 'perhaps the UK's finest climbing area'. A few lines later it has become 'truly one of the best climbing areas in the world'. It's hard not to succumb to such sales talk.

Lindsay Griffin

Spain: Costa Blanca
Chris Craggs and Alan James
Rockfax, 2013, pp456, £29.95

The Costa Blanca Rockfax guidebook keeps getting bigger and better. There is no doubt that this third edition is the premier guidebook to the area in terms of design, coverage, accuracy and access details. Apart from the sport climbing, there are long multi-pitch trad adventures to be had (my current favourite is *Via Gene* on Cabezon de Oro, now downgraded to F4+) and one of my best days ever in the mountains was the complete traverse of the Bernia Ridge with Jim Fotheringham on a blue-sky day in February. This guidebook now includes four ridges that are serious undertakings, but as spectacular as anything the area has to offer.

Some rather scrappy and far-flung crags have been dropped at Sierra de Magdelena, Ibi, Alcoi and Baranc de l'Avern. Expat activist Al Evans will be disappointed that the long crag he developed at Segaria has been dropped, but a 25 minute uphill walk has apparently proved too much, unless it's the lack of bolts up there.

The gains, however, are significant: the most important crag to be developed in the area for some time, especially for those operating in the mid-grades, is the magnificent Guadalest, home to nearly 160 routes. The steep main wall is of perfect dark grey limestone, littered with sharp, incut holds and extremely well equipped.

Some improvements are still possible. For some time it has been possible to abseil back down *Espolon Pertemba* without having to go up to find the descent ramp across the Divino face. It's useful to know that there are more abseil points along the Bernia ridge than are described – at the top of every steep downclimb, in fact – and that red dots are the key to the winding route-finding on the ridge. Also that if you approach from the south you can begin at the East Peak and make a complete traverse. Worth knowing, too, that at the end of pitch 7 in this description it is possible to escape the ridge to the north side.

It has to be said that all this information comes at a price. The new-routing Spanish climbers I've spoken to resent the colonialist nature of the Rockfax enterprise that puts nothing back into the Spanish climbing scene. They (mostly) offer their information and admire the end result, but are privately bitter about the commercial ethics of the whole business. There are ways of easing this situation and a bolt fund would be a good start, perhaps. The Spanish economy needs all the help it can get and the possible contribution of visiting climbers to local rural tourism by way of using village shops, bars and accommodation could be one benefit from this guidebook. It used to be the driest winter rock in Europe, although climate change has unsettled this claim a little. But it's still a magnificently varied climbing location for most of the year. Only the Norwegians come in August, seeking north-facing walls.

Terry Gifford

The Great Encyclopaedia of Mountains and Mountaineering
Eds: Malgorzata Kielkowska, Jan Kielkowski
Stapis, Katowice, Poland, 2013

The biography section of *The Great Encyclo-paedia of Mountains and Mountaineering* was published in September 2013. The volume, entitled *Mountain People*, is a veritable Who's Who of the mountaineering world. It covers alpinists, modern climbers, explorers, discov-erers, scientists, artists – all whose work helped allow greater accessibility and led to a deeper understanding of the mountains.

The tome also contains biographies of high achievers in mountain water sports, canoeing, ski-alpinism and many more and we are introduced to those who organise expeditions to the furthest corners of the world and those who manage and contribute to club life in various countries. Not to mention the hard working alpine historians, authors, publishers and editors of climbing and mountaineering magazines!

All in all, the publication contains some 6000 entries including many biog-raphies of British and international mountaineers and mountain celebrities. This book is the sixth out of a total of seven volumes of *The Great Ency-clopaedia of Mountains and Mountaineering* which, at this point, contains a total of 4366 pages, over 22,000 entries, over 800 maps drawn or sourced exclusively for this publication and hundreds of illustrations. All volumes have been published in Polish.

Volume I – Introduction contains general information about the moun-tains (geology, fauna, topographic and geographic terminology) and about the different types of mountain-related activity, with a focus on mountain-eering. Lots of room is given to the history of mountaineering, the ideology, techniques, equipment as well as related scientific research, artistic activi-ties, journalism, collections and organisational aspects.

The four following volumes: Mountains of Asia, Mountains of Europe, Mountains of America and Mountains of Africa, Antarctic, Australia and Oceania describe all the Earth's mountain ranges and the more prominent massifs, mountains, peaks, valleys and glaciers, giving an overview of their geography and topography and a synopsis of explorations and ascents. The seventh and final (as yet, unpublished) volume will contain, amongst other things, comprehensive index and dictionary.

Ola Hudowska

Itching To Climb
Barbara James
Bâton Wicks, 2014, pp 204, £9.99

Itching to Climb has now been reprinted. Described by Val Randall in her review in the 2012 *AJ*: '*Itching To Climb* provides readers with meticulously detailed descriptions of the development of outdoor education, unquenchable enthusiasm for conveying knowledge and understanding of mountaineering history'. Of her condition Barbara says: 'I am one of the statistics ... today 1:5 children & 1:12 adults have this very life affecting health problem. All monies I raise from book sales goes to the National Eczema Society. *(BCN)*

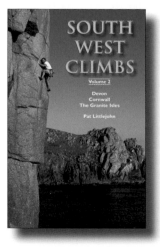

South West Climbs Vol. 2
Devon, Cornwall, The Granite Isles
Pat Littlejohn
Climbers' Club, 2014, pp416, £25

Pat Littlejohn's essential selective *South-West Climbs* was first published in 1979 by Ken Wilson and has gone from strength to strength though two subsequent editions. It was a winning formula: get one of Britain's finest and prolific adventure climbers to choose and describe a selection of the country's best adventure climbs and illustrate them with a collection of the finest sea cliff climbing action photographs.

This latest incarnation has been split into two volumes and produced by the Climbers' Club – that bastion of definitive guidebook production, who are now spreading their wings a bit. The first volume (2012) covers the Avon, Wye Valley and Dorset cliffs and was written by a team of local activists, but Vol. 2 is the work of the Master himself.

It's difficult not to gush about this guide: it is gorgeously illustrated – I couldn't find an action photo that didn't inspire. The crag photo-diagrams have been brought firmly into the 21st Century and are second-to-none for clarity and ease of use, ditto the maps, augmented on occasion by remarkable aerial shots of the coast. I cheered when, turning to the Bosigran section, I found the routes described from right to left – as you come to them – gasp! Now I don't have to approach the crag from a boat. . .

Sea cliff climbing in the far south-west is very, very special and this selective guide has done it proud.

Bernard Newman

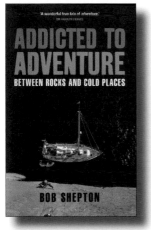

Addicted to Adventure
Bob Shepton
Adlard Coles, pp244, £12.99

'It was a dark and stormy night. . .' and the Rev Bob Shepton, the Tilman of our time, would yet again be somewhere in the wild North Atlantic in his Westerly 33 fibreglass hulled yacht, *Dodo's Delight*, on his way to Greenland, the land of icebergs, icecaps, fog and stupendous rock walls.

Bob's new book, *Addicted to Adventure*, is an all too brief account of his life so far. The fact that he is now in his late seventies means that he has a lot to get through in the 204 pages of this book. The first half of the book details his early life and his subsequent pastoral and teaching career which gives the reader an idea of his old-school British background and the Corinthian attitude that he absorbed from his upbringing. His approach to modern life has similarities to the famously dyspeptic Tilman although Bob is more relaxed and accommodating in his appreciation of modern sailing technology. His sailing career has flourished in more recent times, when technology (i.e. GPS) has become somewhat more reliable and genuinely helpful.

This book is both a sailing and a climbing record of an extraordinary man. With so few pages it is hard to give the sort of detail that technical specialists from each activity would like. Personally I would like to see more detailed maps to show where they were all the time and the maps and photos to be positioned nearer the relevant pages in the manuscript.

However, whilst Bob will never receive awards for his writing style, his enthusiasm, energy, commitment, humour and personal kindness come across in spades. Not only has he sailed on a variety of boats on most of the world's seas he has now crossed the 'storm channel' of the North Atlantic passage to Greenland more than 14 times, overwintered in Greenland (with spectacular results!) and has become the conduit of choice for top adventure climbers to the big seawalls in the spectacular fjords of West Greenland.

In 2012 he and the 'Wild Bunch' (a group of trad climbers from Belgium) were awarded the prestigious Piolet d'Or for the style of their brilliant ascent from Bob's boat of the huge 850m E7 route, the Impossible Wall in Sortehul Fjord in West Greenland.

Not content with this fantastic achievement, in 2013 Bob went on to navigate the infamous North West Passage, sailing from Scotland to Greenland with a group of South African climbers who put up some spectacular big wall routes in Greenland. Then aboard *Dodo's Delight* they threaded their way across the top of North America for 3000 miles through ice-bound channels and wild weather to Nome in Alaska. This was the first crossing of the North West Passage by a small fibreglass yacht, a level of commitment that few would contemplate! For this and his lifetime achievement and activity he was awarded the yachting journalists 'Yachtsman of the Year' Award. Not bad to have top awards for his two great passions, climbing and sailing.

Bob's story is a lesson on what can be done with commitment and drive. All you need to keep it going for a lifetime is character and Cap'n Bob has enough of that for two lifetimes! *(Thanks to* Climb *magazine for permission to re-publish this review.)*

Dick Turnbull

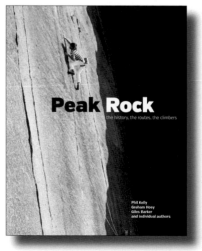

Peak Rock
Phil Kelly, Graham Hoey, Giles Barker *et al*
Vertebrate Publishing 2013, pp396, £37.95

Wow! This is some book! No, not a book, rather a tome or volume, one that commands respect and, to be fair, is somewhat daunting! To start with you need to have at least E3 shoulders and hands to handle a book that weighs in at approx 5lbs – and it is not a good bedtime read unless you have an upper body like Arni.

The first thing to say is that this is a magnificent production. Vertebrate Graphics have gone to town to make sure that the book physically matches the content. The front cover is Bernard Newman's stunning black and white photo of Andy Pollitt leading Ron Fawcett's seemingly impossible (in 1982) *Scritto's Republic* on Millstone. Inside, the high quality 128gsm silk finish FSC (Forest Stewardship Council) approved paper gives a good base for the hundreds of photos and the massive script of over 200,000 words – the equivalent of two extensive biographies!

The photos in themselves form a fantastic visual record of Peak climbing – more than a few are iconic images that will remind many climbers of their youth! My only grouse is that I would like the year that the pictures were taken to have been incorporated in the photo captions. As someone who has been selling rock boots/shoes for 40 years I can date photos from the rock shoes alone but I don't expect the average reader to know anything about rock boot lineage apart from the great divide between the old era of EB's and the arrival of modern times with the ground breaking sticky rubber of Boreal's *Firés* in 1983.

The text throughout the book is somewhat controversially arranged to incorporate quotes from activists and contemporary sources (i.e. first ascentionists, comment articles from magazines etc.) which appear in a lighter typeface than the main text. This device gives the book a tremendous sense of immediacy and veracity which allows you both a reflective and considered historical view as well as seeing the climbs from the climbers' point of view at the time.

As a reference volume *Peak Rock* is a significant work, a real *tour de force* of historical research, authoritatively chronicling the entire known history of Peak climbing from 1885 to the present day. It seeks to unravel many of the well-known controversial incidents – for example the section on the first ascents of *Fern Hill*, *Boot Hill* etc on Cratcliffe provides a masterful and illuminating analysis of what probably happened. However, it is difficult to find specific incidents, routes, etc as there is no index!

The authors have a right to be proud of what they have achieved both literally and visually, but *Peak Rock* achieves more than that – it evokes the vibrant spirit of Peak climbing through the ages and underlines its importance as a major forcing ground of British climbing.

Every climber interested in the development of rock climbing in the Peak and the people who made it happen should have a copy of this superb 'tome' to dip into, especially on those cold winter nights, when all you can remember is your latest trip to the climbing wall!

Dick Turnbull

Obituaries

NE Buttress, Ben Nevis, acrylic on canvas, 51x61cm. *(Tim Pollard)*

In Memoriam

As usual, the Editor will be pleased to receive obituaries for any of those above not included in the following pages.

George Bintley 1932 - 2013

With the death of George Bintley in April 2013, the British climbing world has lost one of its most active, best-known and popular characters. For nearly 60 years – apart from an interlude for sailing adventure during the 1980s – his cheerful and friendly face could be found almost every weekend in one or other of the barns, bothies, club huts or pubs in which climbers congregate. He seemed to know everyone; yet he was no extrovert, he never put up a new route, he wasn't a writer, he had no connection with education or administration. He was just a thoroughly nice guy who loved the mountains.

George Bintley. *(Ben Stroude)*

George began his climbing career in the 1950s with that slightly controversial Wirral-based club known to outsiders simply as 'the Wallasey'. This was one of those groups of townies – the Bradford Lads, the Creag Dhu and the Rock & Ice were better-known examples – who went to the hills to escape authority, to climb hard, to booze when funds allowed and to make merry. There are folk tales of what – depending on one's age and outlook – some called high spirits and others hooliganism, and in which George certainly played his part. Yet only a few years later he was invariably welcomed with open arms by two of the supposed 'victims', Sid Cross and Chris Briggs, of the ODG and Pen y Gwryd hotels respectively, and it's hard to believe much harm was done. It was in the Wallasey MC that he met Cora Baker, a climber whose good-natured tolerance helped to sustain a happy marriage which ended only with George's death.

In 1958 George traded up, with other ex-Wallasey refugees such as Roger Salisbury and Alan Minett, to the respectability of Merseyside's senior club, the Wayfarers. There, with a wider circle of climbing partners, particularly Allan Stuart, he climbed consistently at VS/HVS and occasionally harder (much more difficult to achieve then than now) and ticked off a long list of Welsh and Lakeland Classics. It was Allan who introduced him to the Alps, and although George invariably suffered from altitude sickness on the first route or two of each trip, they completed an impressive list of middle-grade routes, including the North Ridge of the Peigne, the traverse of the Drus and the Frontier Ridge of Mont Maudit.

I joined the Wayfarers in 1966, and George and I immediately clicked. He was a superb climbing partner, with a calm confidence and unflappability which more than made up for my nervousness. He was much the better rock-climber but, by chance, I was more confident on snow and ice, so that in the Alps we became quite a useful team and thoroughly enjoyed knocking off the classic mixed routes at Chamonix, the most boastworthy being the Route Major and the Innominata Route on Mont Blanc. However, while retreating from the East Face Direct on the Réquin in 1978, we stupidly slipped on the steep slope of afternoon slush below the rocks and, but for the good fortune of hitting an isolated boulder some 500 ft lower, would have undoubtedly ended up very dead on the Mer de Glace, a long way below. George, though much battered, very gallantly crawled to the hut to initiate my rescue.

That episode put an end to alpine climbing for a time, but George had long been an admirer of fellow-Wayfarer Bill Tilman. He sought, in admittedly pale imitation, to learn a new set of ropes so that, during most summers in the 1980s he was to be found more often at sea than in the hills. In pursuit of mountains near the sea we did once reach northern Spain but found that it just took too long. Home waters were more productive and in one memorable 6-week cruise from the Wirral to the Hebrides and back, George knocked off no fewer than 25 Munros/Corbetts as he went. The 'sea interlude' did not last but Munro-bagging did and he duly completed the list; a feat made the more impressive as he had never owned or driven a car, and consequently became an expert on Scottish public transport. Not that he had ever normally suffered from a lack of lifts; as an electrician at the local shipbuilders he had been known as 'the only Sparks at Lairds with six chauffeurs.'

Despite such distractions, rock-climbing was always George's first love, and as a summer evening habitué of Helsby crag – much more important as a training ground then than now, in these days of indoor walls – he had befriended some of the Climbers' Club 'Cheshire set', particularly Hugh Banner and Derek Walker. They introduced him to the CC and a yet wider circle of friends. Later, with a promiscuity which was really just a tribute to his popularity, George was induced, additionally, to join the Fell & Rock and the Merseyside CC. As he had long been an Alpine Club member as well, it can be seen how the word 'clubbable' might have been especially coined. Few men holding down a full-time job in industry, and with a close and loving family, can have used their weekends and limited holidays to better advantage. His life was full of action, adventure and kindness to others, and the climbing world is much the poorer for his passing.

Ben Stroude

Ray Colledge in 1952. *(Colledge archive/ Mark Harrison)*

Ray Colledge
1922 - 2014

Of all the climbers I have known from more than six decades of activity within the sport, Ray was the most unlikely looking 'hard man', for he was quiet, self effacing and unassuming. Of medium height and slim build with an almost cherubic face, he looked much younger than he was, but despite these misleading impressions he burnt with an inner fire that few other British mountaineers of his generation equalled.

Born in Coventry, Ray grew up on a farm outside the city and having left school as a teenager found work with an engineering company as a costing clerk. He was called up into the RAF during the War, serving with a mobile radar unit which went to Normandy immediately after D-Day. He saw action in France and Germany, and was there when the American and Russian forces met up outside Berlin.

Discharged from the RAF, Ray began to visit the hills and in 1946 at the Idwal YH met Dennis Davis. This was to be a life-changing event for Ray for their climbing partnership was to last many years, particularly in the Alps, where they climbed many Grandes Courses together over more than ten Alpine seasons, beginning in 1949. Today's climbers have little idea what alpine climbing entailed in those post-war years – rationing, travelling by train, and with limited finances due to exchange controls. But from the first they headed for the great classics, the Innominata, the Brenva Spur, the Diables Ridge. One particularly impressive feature of Ray's climbing was that he could only ever manage a two or three-week holiday throughout his whole career, saving these for Alpine forays.

Ray was a lifelong member of the Midland Association of Mountaineers, and was elected to the Alpine Club in 1951.

In 1952 he was invited to take part in Eric Shipton's controversial expedition to Cho Oyo (8201m). The trip was planned as a 'training expedition' for Everest 1953 and included many who would go on the successful expedition the following year: Hillary, Lowe, Evans, Gregory, Bourdillon, and Griffith Pugh the scientist.

Little has been written about this expedition for there were some conflicts about the outcome. It was felt the mountain was unclimbable from the

Ray Colledge on *Curving Crack*, Cloggy.
(Colledge archive/Mark Harrison)

south, and from the north it meant encroaching into Tibet, high on the mountain. Shipton refused to agree to this, for their permit was to attempt the mountain from Nepal and so, almost without any real serious attempt on the peak, the climb was called off, much to Ray's dismay, for he maintained that the approach on the mountain's north side was open, there were no border guards there, and the mountain was technically easy. He made his views known strongly about this, which probably cost him a place on the 1953 expedition, for unfairly he was branded a troublemaker!

On his return to the UK he confided to Dennis Davis that if he had been there with him, he was certain they could have climbed Cho Oyu. Which may not be too far-fetched, for the mountain is now agreed to be the easiest of the 8000m peaks.

After the abandonment of the attempt on Cho Oyu the climbers headed off in different directions to explore areas of the Rowaling Himalaya. In the Menlung area, Ray with Tom Bourdillon climbed Ripimo Shar (6705m). For this climb Griffith Pugh persuaded Colledge to test rates of oxygen flow. These data would prove crucial in determining the usage on Everest in 1953.

Harriet Tuckey, Pugh's daughter, told me that her father had the highest regard for Ray and considered him one of the few climbers in 1952 who understood how crucial his high altitude physiological work would prove to the successful ascent of Everest.

Despite the shortness of his holidays, through the 1950s into the 1960s Ray racked up a truly impressive list of ascents in the Alps, usually just two or three each season, but always major climbs: the North Face of the Triolet, the *Red Sentinel*, North Face Dent d'Hérens, the *Cassin Route* on the Piz Badile, South Ridge of the Aiguille Noire de Peuterey, the *Route Major*, and the North Face of the Grosshorn in the Bernese Oberland.

Only once during his many alpine climbs was Ray involved in an accident. This happened when climbing as two ropes of two, high on the Aiguille Blanche de Peuterey. Dennis Davis with a partner had climbed far ahead, and Ray with an American climber was bringing up the rear. At one point an abseil was required and Ray went down first. The American followed, bouncing heavily on the double ropes, at which point the anchor failed and he fell to his death. Ray was left on the mountain alone, without a rope and his other two companions too far ahead to be contacted. Somehow, he managed a solo descent of the mountain and raised the alarm.

I met Ray when I moved to work in Derby at the end of 1959. The town was then a hot-bed of climbing activity, and one of the presiding spirits was Nat Allen with whom I re-formed the Rock and Ice Club. Ray occasionally attended some of our meets and was happy to fall in and climb with our new recruits, including Gordon Smith, Dez Hadlum and Jimmy Fullalove (a.k.a Dan Boone).

In 1969 Ray managed to slot in three major routes into his

Ray Colledge on the *Cassin Route*, Piz Badile. *(Colledge archive/Mark Harrison)*

allotted two-week holiday. Having been let down as to a climbing partner he drove out to Chamonix on the off-chance, and teamed up with Dan Boone. Their first route was the Walker Spur, which posed little difficulty despite their lack of acclimatisation. Next up was the *Pear Buttress* of Mont Blanc, which is now rarely climbed due to its difficult and dangerous approach, and finishing off with the North Face of the Eiger (one of Ray's keenest ambitions). This was the third British ascent, and was not achieved without some alarms. Dan climbing up the edge of one of the ice fields decided to layback on the edge of the ice, which broke off and he fell 120 feet. Ray stopped him by whipping the rope around a spike. In the Exit Cracks on the third day they were overtaken by a violent storm, and when it eased Dan's rock climbing skills came to the fore and they finally gained the summit. Ray had just a few hours sleep in the valley before he had to head for home and back to work. Few climbers aged 47 can have covered so much ground in just a two week holiday.

Ray was always amiable and I enjoyed several climbs with Ray in the UK perhaps the most outstanding being the *Western Gully* of the Black Ladders in winter with Dennis Davis, Derrick Burgess and Ray Handley. On one occasion, during a lecture about his 1969 season, Ray was engrossed in an animated account of crossing a huge bergschrund to reach the Pear Buttress, all the while walking backwards across the stage. He was so gripped at re-living the story he fell off the stage into the laps of the front row of the audience.

I guess Ray Colledge was an unsung hero of British climbing, for unlike today's fame-seekers who report their every move on the social media, he kept his own counsel and climbed for the sheer love of the sport and the outdoors. He kept active, skiing and walking into his old age, and few have enjoyed such a wealth of mountain experiences. He never married, and noted that none of his climbing friends who were, with families, were keen to climb routes like the Eigerwand with him because of the perceived danger. But together during the long period he was mountaineering with Dennis Davis, they must have made one of the strongest ropes in the history of British alpinism.

Dennis Gray

Dennis Davis writes: I first met Ray Colledge at Idwal Cottage Youth Hostel in North Wales. Ray was a forceful character, when it came to mountains. He would always plan the routes he wanted to do in Alps.

I was once invited to his home in Spondon near Derby, but on arrival I realized I had forgotten the number of his house. I stopped to ask a young lady walking by whether she knew him. I explained he was single and had a green MGB sports car. She answered, 'No, but when you do find his address will you give it to me?'

We travelled to the Alps frequently together and on one occasion we took Ray's MGB. After I'd done a spell of driving he took over, but before setting off he meticulously wiped the steering wheel, and put on white driving gloves.

Over time we did many Alpine routes together, among them the Macugnaga Face of Monte Rosa, and the North Face of Aiguille de Bionnassay, (along the ice ridge which appeared to overhang on both sides! Then up to the Vallot hut to traverse Mont Blanc, Mont Maudit, Mont Blanc de Tacul and down to Montenvers and Chamonix). In the course of one holiday we did the Cassin Route on the Badile and the first British ascent of the North Face of the Grosshorn.

I shall never forget the happy times with Ray and the pleasure he gave us. He will not be forgotten.

Ted Dance 1927 - 2013

Ted Dance was one of the finest hill and mountain athletes of his generation – and all this without training, or so it seemed. He often said he didn't need to train and would argue you to a standstill on the point. Within his range of activities, argument was one of his preferred sports. You could at least be sure of good conversation along the way, and best tempted out of him while you were going uphill, breathless, but making the occasional contentious provocation in order to keep him within sight. He would argue even if you agreed with him. No matter, there was no malice in him.

Ted was born in Bangalore, India, in 1927, the first of three brothers and a sister. His father's work as a chemist in textiles had taken him and his mother from the UK. The children began school as boarders in the Nilgiri hills. When Ted was nine, the family moved back to live in Sale, Cheshire, where his father took on a newsagents shop.

He met Geoff Eglinton at Sale Grammar School and they became life-long friends. Geoff went on to Manchester University, and Ted

Ted Dance, 2011. *(Geoff Eglinton)*

started his working life in ICI at Blackley, Manchester, studying externally for his Chemistry degree. He stayed with ICI for the whole of his working life, retiring early in the 1980s.

Geoff introduced Ted to the outdoors, and to the Manchester University Mountaineering Club, the pair writing a rock climbing guide to Quellyn, published by the MUMC in 1954. Ted was a bold rock climber – on one inspired day he soloed all the VSs on Kern Knotts, up one, down the next, in little more than an hour.

Ted joined the Rucksack Club in 1951 (age 24) and was soon breaking long distance walking records (Marsden – Edale in 4hrs 29 mins) and in 1953 with Neil Mather repeated the the Tan Hill – Cat and Fiddle in just over 54 hours. In the early 1960s orienteering caught his imagination; and he was a founder member and later President of the Manchester and District Orienteering Club (1966 – 1969).

From these beginnings Gerry Charnley evolved the idea of a two-day mountain marathon, now the KIMM. The first two, of 1968 and 1969, were won by Ted and Bob Astles.

Ted's Alpinism also began with the Rucksack Club. In 1953 he was with a strong party which climbed the Dent Blanche and attempted the west-north-west face of the Dent d'Hérens. This mountain required four attempts until success in 1992 by the route from the Aosta side. Later he went on to climb the *Couturier Couloir* on the Aiguille Verte with Ron Moseley.

It was the route itself that mattered most in his earlier Alpinism (e.g. successes on the Aiguille du Chardonnet by the Forbes Arête, the SW Ridge of the Moine, the Charmoz-Grépon traverse, the traverse of Les Courtes, to name but a few). Parsimony was a hallmark of Ted's attitude to equipment – he used the same crampons for 50 years; they had very short spikes towards the end!

Commitment, determination, strength, fitness, stamina – all these enabled Ted to join the Rucksack Club expedition to Masherbrum in 1957

Ted Dance on the Pointe de Cenastre. *(Tom Gerrard)*

led by Joe Walmsley. This turned out to be a tough proposition, the summit not reached after weeks of graft. Unhappily, Bob Downes died of pulmonary oedema and the team struggled indefatigably and successfully to get his body down.

Joe wrote recently that Ted was among the best; worked tirelessly pulled his weight to the utmost to reach 25,000 feet following a distressing and arduous descent to recover the body.

News travelled slowly and was not always properly checked, it was reported that Ted had died, not Bob. The *Manchester Guardian* and *Evening News* printed Ted's obituary, and for want of detail the *Evening News* based theirs on the colourful memories supplied by his landlady!

Ted married Kath in 1960, with daughters, Janet, Catherine and Ruth to follow. They had started married life in Atherton, near Bolton, Lancashire, but moved to an old farmhouse, Martinside, above Chapel-en-le-Frith in the Peak District. Ted commuted a daily round trip of about 50 miles by bicycle.

With a boundless enthusiasm for new challenges, in 1968 Ted completed a circuit of the 2500ft summits of the Lake District, along with John Eastwood and Stan Bradshaw, assisted by Dennis Weir, a walk that covered 105 miles with 43,065ft of ascent in 70 hours.

Perhaps the boldest of Ted's pioneering walks was the North Wales Horseshoe, almost certainly a result of a map reading error. He had spotted the line on the quarter inch map of Wales, and mistaken it for a map of twice that scale. The route covers some 140 miles with 40,000ft of ascent and became the Holy Grail for that generation of ultra-distance walkers. Originally to start at Prestatyn and heading for Barmouth via Cader Idris, in 1979 a threesome of Ted, Geoff Bell and Mike Cudahy set out in the reverse direction from Aber via the Welsh Threes, Moelwyns and Rhinogs to Barmouth where Ted was forced to retire with sore feet.

Ted took early retirement from ICI in the 1980s and in later years became keen to complete the 4000m summits. Between us we climbed all of the

Bernese, Zermatt and Saas 4000m peaks, and a number of the Chamonix, Courmayeur and outlying giants. If Ted had begun the 4000m list earlier in life, there is little doubt that he would have completed them.

In his seventies, with Tom Gerrard, one of his oldest and long supporting friends, Ted traversed from the Midi téléphèrique station over Mont Blanc du Tacul, Mont Maudit, and Mont Blanc, descending over the Dôme du Goûter to the valley via the Goûter hut in one long day.

Innovator, pioneer, motivator, this spare of frame athlete was climber, mountaineer, harrier, orienteer, record breaker, alpinist, tour guide and family man. It has been a privilege to know him and we extend our condolences to Kath and Ted's three daughters.

John Allen and Tom Gerrard

Karl Lugmayer
1926 - 2013

Karl Lugmayer, born 1926 in Upper Austria, was just 18 years old when he was taken prisoner and spent the rest of the war in a British prisoner of war camp. Returning home in 1946, he threw himself into mountaineering. It was the start of one of the most impressive of Austrian mountaineering careers. Climbing with Allen Steck from Berkeley,

Erich Vanis, Karl Lugmayer and Hans Ratay after making the ninth ascent of the North Face of the Eiger, August 1952. *(Lugmayer archive)*

California, he climbed all the big walls of the Eastern and Western Alps: the north wall of the Grosse Zinne, the north-west wall of the Civetta (5th ascent of the Comici's direttissima), the Grossglockner north wall and the Däumling east ridge. Shortly afterwards, he soloed the north wall of the Dent d'Hérens.

In August 1952 Lugmayer, Hans Ratay and Erich Vanis made the ninth ascent of the Eiger Nordwand. Setting out on 6 August, they had a cold first bivouac and woke to an icy morning with 25cm of new snow. Missing the route, they lost a day and returned to the bivouac for a second night. At last, on the third day they had better conditions and crossed the Traverse of The Gods and climbed quickly through the White Spider where Lugmayer was hit by a stone. Nevertheless, in the evening of the third day, in the light of the setting sun, they climbed along the summit ridge to the top. Throughout the climb Lugmayer had suffered acute toothache.

In 1954 on the Austrian Alpine Club Andes Expedition Lugmayer made five first ascents including Navado Sorapo (6143m), in the Cordillera Huayhuash in Peru. In 1961 he climbed Kilimanjaro and in 1965 he crossed the Andes by bicycle, on the way making a solo ascent of Aconcagua (6961m).

His account of the first winter ascent of the North Face of the Schermberg was published in the *Alpine Journal* (**LXX**, Nov 1965, No.311 pp286-293).

Reinhold Messner was to remark 'Lugmayer was my role model.'

Karl is survived by his wife, Elisabeth and his five children, Barbara, Ilga, Karl, Elisabeth and Theresia.

John Fairley

Allen Steck writes: I was studying in Switzerland when I got a letter from a friend in California saying I should contact Karl in Vienna as he was interested in a summer climbing trip.

Karl Lugmayer in the Dolomites in 2012, NW face of the Civetta in the background. *(Allen Steck)*

We met in Vienna, liked each other and made plans for a long bicycle trip from his home in Wolfern, upper Austria, all the way to Mont Blanc. By the time we left Wolfern, we had already climbed the two super-routes on the Fleishbank, the east and south-east routes. One of the next stops was the north face of the Cima Grande, where Karl took a long fall when a pin pulled. Luckily he was unhurt. Moving on, we climbed the Civetta, then the north face of the Grossglockner. Karl was good at finding us lodging in various small places with haylofts or we slept in cornfields.

We didn't do much in the Mont Blanc region…just a traverse of the Aiguille du Diable. We'd hoped for a major route but a sore ankle prevented it.

We last met in Genoa when I was about to board a ship for the voyage home. We discussed our war experiences. He told me how he was sent to the front in Flanders in 1944 where his unit was surprised by heavy British artillery. One morning at dawn he looked up from his foxhole and saw a British personal carrier approaching. As it passed his position he jumped up and leapt into the vehicle, parting the rifle barrels. He spent the next two years in a POW camp in England.

'Mac' Ian McNaught-Davis
1929 - 2014

With the death of Mac our little world has lost a giant; its clown prince of British climbing. He was a man of many parts; a leading Alpinist in the 1950s with a string of British firsts, and with Joe Brown, Tom Patey and John Hartog, making the first ascent of the 'impossible' Mustagh Tower in the Karakoram. In the 1960s he became a TV personality taking part in most, if not all, of the BBC's Outside Broadcasts including the biggest and best one, the Old Man of Hoy, where he provided light relief to Brown's laconic understatement and Bonington's earnest professionalism. He later found a different kind of fame, fronting television programmes on computing, then in its infancy and later still he became President of the BMC and then the UIAA where he was a thorn in the flesh of the arch-conservative Swiss.

Mac. *(Jim Curran)*

Above all Mac was an action man, a fun-loving, gregarious extrovert who lived life to the full. He loved mountains and climbing and managed to remain active well into his 70s. I was lucky enough to climb with him for the last 30 years of his life and we had unforgettable adventures in Wales, the Alps, Spain, Kenya, South Africa, the States and Chile. It was an unlikely partnership. Both of us were tolerated by the glitterati of British climbers for our humour and, in Mac's case, his ability. To our surprise we hit it off immediately when we realised we both had the ability to make each other laugh. This carried on almost to the end of his life and, as Mac said, got us out of some serious situations.

Another potential problem was that Mac was seriously wealthy and I wasn't. Mac's solution was simple: 'I'll pay the big bills and you pay the small ones.' It worked throughout our partnership, though on occasion the small ones weren't that small.

Mac had an endless fund of stories about his illustrious past, with Arthur Dolphin, Tom Patey, Al Alvarez and, of course, his oldest friend, Joe Brown, with whom he made many new routes on Gogarth. I always felt that many people imagined Joe hauling him up on a tight rope, but Mac had immense strength and natural ability. At Harrison's he could still climb the classic 5cs well into his 60s. Though he usually preferred me to lead, I was

Mac on the Mustagh Tower expedition, June
– July 1956. *(Joe Brown coll.)*

under no illusion that when push came to shove Mac would rise to the occasion. This was epitomised on the last iced-up pitch on Mount Kenya, though it remains the only time I ever saw Mac seriously tired on the descent. But a week later, climbing the Arrow Glacier on Kilimanjaro he was undoubtedly faster and fitter than I was. Sadly the last three years were painful as Mac suffered from Alzheimer's Disease. He was lovingly cared for by his wife Loreto and even occasionally managed a flash of his old humour.

Mac, climber, writer, speaker and wit has left us but I will never forget the most generous and big-hearted companion I have ever had the privilege to know.

Jim Curran

John Cleare writes: A doughty climber and irrepressible companion, beneath Mac's larger-than-life exterior lurked a remarkably kindly and generous fellow. It was in February '61 that first we met after a CUMC Annual Dinner at which I was a guest and he was the guest speaker. Next day, very much the worse for wear, I'd just started breakfast in an Indian restaurant when in staggered Mac, also in search of a curry cure-all. Recognising a fellow-suffer, he joined me, soon discovering that I was a photographer on a glossy fashion magazine, and more to the point, I had a decent alpine record. As he was a keen photographer we had much in common.

'Are you in the AC?', he demanded. 'Why not?'

'Are you in the CC? Why not?'

'We must see about fixing that!'

It was Mac who proposed me for both these august bodies and thus in due course I found myself part of the mountaineering establishment.

We would often meet for lunch and climbing talk at a curry house between Fleet Street and his office in Southampton Row, and that summer we climbed together in the Lakes – not my usual stamping ground – where Mac introduced me to his favourite classics such as Troutdale Pinnacle, White Ghyll Wall and so on, as well as to prominent Lakeland climbers.

I'm not quite sure how Mac became a BBC celeb, though his outgoing personality and myriad connections obviously had much to do with it. He'd spent time working in Paris, climbing regularly at Fontainebleau with the local hot-shots, and was thus able to involve a token Frenchman, his

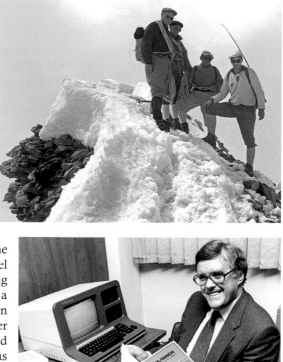

Mac (right), live on the summit of the Matterhorn during the Centenary broadcast, July 1961. Heini Taugwalder on left and two members of the Carrel family.
(John Cleare / Mountain Camera Picture Library)

Mac – a pioneering entrepreneur of computing.

chum Paragot, on the first BBC Live TV climb in 1963. This took place on dank, mist-shrouded Cloggy and – as they say – there were lessons to be learned. Consequently Mac had been the token Brit on RTF's Eiffel Tower climb the following Easter, so he was already a seasoned TV climber when the Beeb scheduled another go. By now they'd realised that live TV climbing was as much circus as climb and Mac suggested the great roof at Kilnsey as the 'big top' for the July '64 broadcast. Not only was the Wharfedale weather fairly reliable and there was road access to the foot of the crag, but an evening finale, with floodlights on the white limestone, promised to be a right spectacle.

'Just your line of country!' said Mac. 'They need a proper climbing cameraman. I'll get you involved.' And so I was co-opted into the BBC Climbing Circus, a great team of technicians and climbers for which Mac was an inspirational catalyst. The series of BBC climbs, televised live throughout the '60s, are now history: the Matterhorn ('65) and Old Man of Hoy ('67) were merely the famous ones and did much to introduce our game to the general public. Mac The Telly was the constant star, usually climbing with his chum Joe Brown – the perfect foil – and so guaranteeing a lively flow of witty commentary.

Those introductions of Mac's opened a whole series of new doors for me, and looking back I can see but for that hung-over breakfast curry, I might have spent the ensuing forty years shooting fashion models and tasteless cookery books.

Sidney Edward Payn Nowill OBE (1921-2013)

Sidney Nowill was what that now defunct periodical Readers Digest would have styled as 'the most remarkable personality I ever knew'. Scholar, author, economist, political analyst, painter, photographer, art connoisseur, gourmet, wine buff, raconteur and compulsive traveller, Sidney was above all a passionate mountaineer.

That his extraordinary life well exceeded three score years and ten and that his formidable mind remained unsullied to the end, is testament to his determination to live life to the full, notwithstanding that his early years were dogged by ill health. Intimations of mortality might have induced Sidney to write the first volume of his autobiography *The Mountains of My Life* at the precocious age of 33. Published by Blackwoods – whose literary magazine became his vehicle to record his more memorable mountaineering adventures – this rare book not only describes his early climbs in Turkey and Alps, but also his Arcadian upbringing at Bournabat, the family's country retreat above Smyrna. The writing has a haunting, lyrical quality which perhaps gets closer to Sidney's inner psyche than anything he wrote or said about himself in later years.

For it was from Bournabat that, as a sickly child, he would gaze longingly towards the snow-clad Nimph Dag, his first 'mountain love' and the one that sowed the seeds of what became a lifelong passion. His Turkish upbringing also shaped much of his complex personality and cosmopolitan outlook. His family were part of the great British mercantile dynasty in the Levant that made Smyrna the commercial jewel of the Ottoman Empire until its catastrophic destruction in 1922. Sidney's great-uncle had originally come out to Istanbul from England in 1865 to make his fortune. His grandmother was the redoubtable matriarch Magdalen Whittall who left 256 direct descendents.

Sidney was born in Istanbul in 1921 but educated in England travelling to and from school on the old Orient Express which not infrequently became snow-bound on the Balkan Plain. As a scholar at Rugby, he had intended to read modern languages at Trinity College, Cambridge, but the severe illnesses that had blighted his childhood frustrated that ambition.

Returning to Istanbul on the eve of the Second World War, he was recruited to work for British Intelligence as his father had done during the First World War. His boss was the notorious traitor Kim Philby who, in Sidney's own words, he 'cordially loathed'.

After the war, Sidney began full-time work with MI6 in London, but had to retire prematurely after failing the medical. The imprint of clandestine work always remained with him and in his writings he adopted Ashenden as his nom de plume after Somerset Maughan's First World War Secret Service hero. After this early career hiccup Sidney joined his father's import business in Istanbul and thereafter, until his eventual retirement to England, his working life was Turkish based.

His business acumen, highly-tuned political antennae and fluency in

Sidney Nowill on the Ala Dagh Taurus trip, Turkey, December 1961. *(John Harding)*

Turkish and several other languages made him an authority on the country's commercial and political scene. He ran a Turkish public company Catalkaya and for forty-years was prominent in the affairs of the British Chamber of Commerce in Turkey. With his access to influential Turks, his insider advice was much valued by a line of British Ambassadors. In 1971 he was appointed External Economic Adviser to Shell with whose chairmen, particularly Peter Holmes, he established very close friendships. A former US ambassador to Turkey's tribute: 'Your insight into the political process and economic development of Turkey is unmatched' was more economically matched by HMG's award of an OBE.

Early setbacks and traumas can be the making of a mountaineer. Sidney's youthful ill-health acted as a spur, though living in Turkey gave him few opportunities to meet fellow climbers. Only when he was 28 did he enter the Alpine lists and then proceeded to climb the Matterhorn during his first season.

In his approach to mountaineering Sidney was essentially a traditionalist whose circumstances initially steered him towards the company of professional guides with whom he formed lasting friendships. In the five years prior to his election to the Alpine Club in 1955, his three seasons of classic routes in the Pennine Alps were done with Alfons Franzen and his three in the Dolomites with Celso Degasper.

Ever ambitious to tackle the best classic alpine routes, his most notable included the Zmutt ridge, the Marinelli Couloir and a three-day epic on the Peuterey Ridge with Elizabeth Parry.

Sidney was a compulsive mountain traveller, a family trait inherited by his two sons Julian and Edward to their father's great satisfaction. His numerous visits to remoter ranges were usually with his imperturbable wife Hilary whether in sickness or in health with blithe disregard for each other's physical or other frailties. These including the Yemen, Iran, Lahul, the Karakoram, the Rockies, Zanskar, the Himalaya, the Andes, Patagonia or wherever wanderlust took him. Yet the mountains dearest to his heart were those of Turkey for which he became the acknowledged expert. Having first cut his climbing teeth on the Ulu Dag above Bursa, his many Turkish expeditions took in Ergiyas Dag in Central Anatolia, the Ala Dag Taurus, Hakkiari in Turkish Kurdistan and the Kackar Dag above the Black Sea.

Sidney was in his element in these remote ranges where his preference was to climb with glamorous oreads such as Elizabeth Parry, Nigella Hall (née Blandy) and his cousin Phillipa Treadwell. On one particularly successful expedition to the Ala Dag in 1963, his modest boast was to have shared twenty-nine successive bivouacs with this gorgeous harem. The same visit also enabled him to make the second British ascent of his old adversary the Demirkazek, the 'Iron Stake', by the eponymous couloir pioneered by Robin Hodgkin and Edward Peck in 1943. It was particularly appropriate that Ted Peck should have been Sidney's proposer for his AC membership.

I first climbed with Sidney and Nigella Blandy in 1961 when we brushed with the Ulu Dag, Erciyas and the Ala Dag. In 1965, Sidney, Hilary and I were the first British party into Hakkiari since Weir and Scott's 1957 foray. His May 1986 Ala Dag expedition, when it snowed solidly for a fortnight, effectively closed his serious climbing days. All these were revelatory visits in which Sidney's fluency in Turkish and his unrivalled knowledge of the country and its peoples added a wholly different dimension to the experience.

Sidney's idiosyncratic personality, intellectual acuity and honesty manifested itself in robust and cogently expressed views on politics and economics, and a tendency to revert to litigation when he considered this appropriate. This was strong meat to some as was his disinclination to bear either fools or rogues gladly. Yet this unusually gifted man possessed a deep humanity and his particular gifts of friendship, loyalty and unstinting generosity will never be forgotten by those who had the privilege of knowing him.

John Harding

Mike Pinney 1951 - 2014

Born in Solihull, Warwickshire, on 21 July 1951, Mike did not take long to embrace a lifelong interest in the outdoors; an interest fine-tuned during his time with the Scouts. With strengths in maths and physics it seemed natural that Mike would develop these talents and in 1973 he graduated from Southampton University with a BSc in mechanical engineering after serving as a university apprentice at Lucas Gas Turbine Equipment.

After gaining his degree Mike spent the rest of his professional life as an aeronautical engineer with Westland Helicopters, becoming an active member of the Royal Aeronautical Society and eventually specialising in computing and data acquisition.

As a young man Mike developed his interest in hill-walking, camping and canoeing, which inevitably progressed to his commitment and enthusiasm for climbing and mountaineering. His first Alpine season was in 1974 after which he was smitten. But Mike did not simply climb; as with his work he contributed considerably to every organisation of which he subsequently became a member. He was an active founder member and President of the Yeovil Mountaineering Club, a member of the Climbers' Club and of the Association of British Members of the Swiss Alpine Club (ABMSAC), of which he was a past President. He retained a

Mike Pinney. *(Marion Parsons)*

life-long commitment to the Britannia Hut. He joined the Alpine Club in 1982 and following his retirement in 2011 joined the committee to become the Honorary Treasurer until his untimely death in 2014.

Mike ran the joint Alpine meets for longer than most people can remember, but certainly for several decades, and he followed these with Alps reunion meets at the George Starkey Hut in Patterdale. This, of course, gave him ample opportunity to indulge his passion for the 4000m peaks, which he completed in 2007.

Retirement provided further opportunities to explore regions further afield and he jumped at the chance to visit the mountains of Nepal, India, Antarctica and Canada. Although I had known Mike for many years through ski-touring and ice climbing trips to the Alps, it was on expeditions to the greater ranges where our all too short deeper friendship developed. Sharing a tent with Mike in the Indian Himalaya in 2012 led me to fully appreciate his many qualities. Quiet and shy by nature he enthusiastically endorsed any reasonable climbing objectives, adding sound constructive comments and good judgement. In contrast to many climbers he also knew when to be silent.

It was soon evident that the impressive north-west face of Barmal (5879m), our primary objective in 2012, was unsuitable but we still had plenty of alternative objectives such as Oti-ka-danda (5782m) and the plethora of unclimbed peaks at the head of the Sematoli cirque. We began with Kagbhusandi Parbat (5301m) and continued with Peak 5515 before Mike climbed Peak 5120 with Stuart Worsfold in his enthusiasm to get the most out of the expedition – so typical of Mike when in the mountain environment.

Later that year we were again together, this time on the AC expedition to

Mike approaching the summit of Peak 5515, Semartoli Valley, India, 2012. *(Derek Buckle)*

the Antarctic Peninsula. Like the others, Mike endured the long Drake Passage crossing from Ushuaia to become entranced by whales, dolphins, penguins and Antarctica's other abundant wild-life. But exploratory mountaineering was the raison d'être of the expedition and this did not disappoint. Exploration of the Belgica Glacier leading to first ascents of Alencar Peak (1592m), Peak 1333, Peak 2032 (Belgica Dome), Peak 1475 and Lancaster Hill were all added to Mike's tally. While poor weather prevented further exploration we did get the opportunity to visit the Darwin Range in Chile before returning to the UK.

With his increasing free time Mike and I planned a private expedition to the Zanskar region of India with Tony Westcott and Chris Storie in the Autumn of 2013. Our plan was to explore the Pensilungpa Valley where we had identified a number of unclimbed 5000m peaks. It was to be another highly successful expedition where we managed the first ascents of Peak 5802 (Hidden Peak) and Peak 5825 (Twin Peak). We narrowly failed on Peak 5641 when time, distance and increasing difficulty forced a retreat, but safety was always our first concern.

2014 was to have been a bumper year. Mike and I had spent considerable energy organising the Alpine Club expedition to the Cordillera Blanca in the Peruvian Andes and over last Christmas we refined our plans with other team members. Mike's tragic death following a fall in Snowdonia on 9 March left a huge hole in the team that was impossible to fill. We had also planned a private expedition to the Spiti Valley in the Indian Himalaya where more exploratory mountaineering was involved. The Peruvian expedition has already taken place, and that to India will go ahead, but there is little doubt that Mike's memory will continue to be foremost in our thoughts as we explore these more distant regions.

Mike's companionship, generosity, enthusiasm, self-effacement and compatibility will be sorely missed by his many friends, as too will be his contribution to the organisation and smooth running of those clubs and organisations to which he dedicated considerable time and energy.

Derek Buckle

Alpine Club Notes

Great End, oil on canvas, 40x50cm. *(Tim Pollard)*

OFFICERS AND COMMITTEE FOR 2014

MICK FOWLER

President's Valedictory Address

Read before the Alpine Club on 4 December 2013

I was introduced to mountaineering by my father, George. He was widowed when I was three and had a superficial interest in mountaineering before I was born with a highlight being failing to reach the Bertol hut by going up the wrong valley and spending a night bivouacking in the rain. As far as I know his only summit from those early days was the Allalinhorn which he employed a guide to take him and my mother up in 1947 on their honeymoon.

The seed of enthusiasm must have been sewn and by the time I was 13 he decided that the time had come to do something about it. That something was to book us both on a two-week mountaineering course in Austria run by the AAC. I remember that I was under the minimum age requirement but somehow he persuaded them to take me. We were not well off and I realise now that the trip must have been a huge expense for him.

After the course he decided that we would start to take annual trips to the Alps. We would go out by train from London and spend three weeks each year climbing routes up to about PD standard. Because we climbed from hut to hut and took all our equipment with us we had to leave home travelling light. I still vividly recall the embarrassment I felt leaving our suburban home dressed in climbing breeches and boots and hoping against hope that we would not bump into any of my school friends.

After a few years of these trips I rebelled as older teenagers do. Then, when I was 18 or so, I developed a liking for rock climbing and by the age of 20, in 1976, felt the urge to return to the Alps with friends that I had met climbing at the southern sandstone outcrops. One of these friends was Mike Morrison who I have just spent four weeks with in the Indian Himalaya. I spent two months in Chamonix in 1976 and 1977 doing classic routes with Mike and others on a shoestring budget.

Returning home in 1977 I ended up back at George's house in London. He was clearly becoming concerned at his son's focus on climbing as opposed to a career and thrust various job advertisements under my nose. The tax office paid the most, they proved appropriately flexible and I have been working there full-time for 36 years.

In 1979 I joined the AC, well the ACG actually, and in 1980 I climbed the North Face of The Eiger with Mike Morrison. That was the last climb that I had on my early alpine tick list and I started to look further afield.

It was through meeting Al Rouse at an ACG event that I ended up climbing in Peru in 1982. It was my first time flying and my first time outside Europe. Chris Watts and I had a great time climbing a route on Taulliraju but just as important for me was the eye-opening insight into a completely different culture from that which I was used to in my suburban UK existence.

It was perhaps inevitable that a trip to the Himalaya would follow and in 1984 I visited Pakistan on a trip led by Victor Saunders. There were seven of us on the trip and we tried to climb a (then) unclimbed mountain called Bojohagur Duonasir which apparently means 'boldly go where only the Devil's horse may go.' It would seem we were not the Devil's horses and the end result was a dismal failure accompanied by a remarkable number of mishaps, including a dropped boot, a cracked vertebra, lost food dumps and a broken abseil sling. To add insult to injury a Japanese walking club team joined our line from the far side of the mountain and walked very efficiently to the summit, albeit using a reported 5000m of fixed rope. If this latter point was true it was quite an achievement on a 7300m peak. On returning to Britain I wrote an article about the trip and then received a letter from a Club member which basically told me that we were an embarrassment to British climbing.

I wondered whether I would ever return to the Himalaya but three years later Victor persuaded me back to Pakistan. This time we tried a more technical line on Spantik (7027m) which turned out to be much more to our liking. I experienced for the first time the addictive and enduring sense of retrospective pleasure that goes with Himalayan success. I knew then that I was hooked.

Since then, for over 25 years now, I have climbed in the greater ranges at least every other year and have been lucky enough to enjoy successes with a wide variety of talented mountaineers: Taweche with Pat Littlejohn, Mugu Chuli with Dave Turnbull, Mount Kennedy with Andy Cave, Kajaqiao with Chris Watts, Cerro Kishtwar, Changabang, Arwa Tower with Steve Sustad and, over the last 10 years or so Manamcho, Siguniang, Shiva and just six weeks ago Kishtwar Kailash with Paul Ramsden. But sadly amongst all the pleasures there will always be the memory of Brendan Murphy being swept away by an avalanche on Changabang.

Throughout all of this I have never really viewed myself as being a clubby kind of person. I am not a paid-up member of any other club, I never stay in huts and thus far I have never been on any climbing meets. So how, you might well ask did I end up joining the AC and becoming President.

Well, the reason is that I viewed the AC as being different from any other club. I joined because it appeared to me to be a vibrant focal point of British mountaineering and it looked to offer the kind of motivational environment that I craved for. And I must admit that I joined too because I was vaguely aware of links between the AC and the MEF and felt joining might enhance my chances of grant support. As that was 34 years ago it would seem that what I found has been to my satisfaction. It has been a privilege to serve first as Vice President and then as President.

Special scones for
the President at
Kailash base camp.
(Paul Ramsden)

The last three years has been an incredibly busy time as I have sought to balance a full-time job with family responsibilities whilst at the same time doing my best to carry out the intentions that I set out to the AGM in 2010, namely to ensure the future health of the Club by increasing the membership and particularly bringing in more young members.

I think the six action points that resulted from the 2012 survey remain the key challenges for the Club and I would like to give you a summary of what we have done and, based on my experience over the last 3 years, what I think we should be aiming to do in the years ahead.

1. Actively seek to increase membership and specifically consider ways to make the Club more attractive to young mountaineers and leading mountaineers. Specifically reach out to members across the country, particularly in Scotland and work further on ensuring that the club is not perceived as old-fashioned.

As I have already mentioned the AC's lecture programme has been extended and now includes Edinburgh and the Lake District in addition to our long standing venues of London, Bristol and the Peak District. Giving a lecture for the Club is a condition of receiving a Climbing Fund grant so we have significantly more lecturers available than used to be the case. I see arranging face to face gatherings of mountaineers as being a key aim of the Club and the arrangements with the Climbing Fund and lecturers look to be a win-win situation all round. It seems pretty obvious to me that we should continue pushing both the Climbing Fund grants and the lecture programme.

To tackle the perception that the Club is old-fashioned we have taken steps to be more professional about our communication strategy. Laetitia Sterling has been appointed as Communications Officer and efforts have been made to increase our profile on social media sites. Our Twitter presence has been a notable success. When I last checked earlier this month the AC had about 25,000 followers, compared to 15,000 for the BMC and 3000 for the Climbers' Club. Our website front page was improved a couple of years ago and plans are afoot to make further improvements both to the appearance and functionality of the site. A bright, attractive and up to date website sends a positive signal and is something I consider very important.

It would be great if we could somehow persuade younger members to get involved with the running of the Club. But that's a lot easier said than done. Your Committee has discussed this on a number of occasions over the last three years but has found it difficult to overcome the fact that the posts are unpaid and most of those prepared to take them on are either retired or have risen to senior positions which give them a degree of flexibility. And most of the people in these categories tend to have quite a lot of grey hair. Part of the answer must be to employ more administrative resource but I think too that we should be bolder about spending some of our not insignificant reserves on specific projects.

As to making the Club more attractive (to young, active mountaineers in particular) I think awareness of the Alpine Climbing Fund is crucial. Over the last year we have raised awareness via an article in *Climb* magazine, flyers at lectures and a programme of emails to non-members applying for Mount Everest Foundation grants and the annual Nick Estcourt Award. Most of these non-members immediately join when made aware that the Club is an active supporter of expeditions like theirs. Even now though there seem to be many young mountaineers who are unaware of the Fund. We have found the money to invest in mountaineering in this way and somehow we need to spread awareness further to maximise the take up.

2. Maximise membership benefits and opportunities for networking. In particular bottom out the mountaineering insurance issue, be more proactive in giving advice to those undertaking self-mounted expeditions and increase awareness of resources such as digital maps and climbs databases.

Firstly, all ideas for improving membership benefits are very welcome. Do keep them coming. This year we have maintained a very full meets programme, arranged a very successful Symposium and extended the lecture programme. Insurance issues are moving forward slowly and meetings have been held with the insurance broker that arranges insurance for the British Mountain Guides. The aim is to arrange very basic rescue/repatriation cover with further cover as necessary on an itemised basis. As part of the process we recently sought claims information via *Alpinet* and we are now waiting to see the best set of premiums that the broker can secure. Keep your fingers crossed on this one.

In the meantime the various insurance options available to members are detailed in the Expedition Information Centre document publication of which has been held up for computing reasons but which will shortly be available on our website.

Modern technology allows easier communication from remote ranges and, thanks to a generous gesture by our member James Bingham, the Club has recently acquired two GPS spot trackers. These are available on loan on a first come, first served basis and will shortly be joined by a satellite telephone which will be available on the same basis. There is now a range of expensive high tech devices that mountaineers are reluctant to buy for one-off trips and I see building up a stock of these for loan as an obvious service that the Club can provide. Again it means finding the resource to review the market and oversee the loan arrangements.

At this point I would like to say something about administration and the organisation of the Club and Committee. Three years ago we restructured the Committee and moved away from a model of communal responsibility to one where specific officers are responsible for specific issues. I felt this created a more efficient structure, but increasing membership numbers and more demands from the main Committee have created a heavy workload on the Club's administrative resources such that they are now stretched beyond capacity. The pressure on the Honorary Secretary position, in particular has become difficult to sustain. John Town, in his resignation email, (John is standing down on 31st March) cited 'unrelenting pressure' as one of the reasons he did not want to continue in the post.

A structure involving more remunerated assistance is likely to be agreed in the near future but the workload shouldered by the key Committee members looks likely to remain an issue that is difficult to resolve. I will give some statistics later but the general picture shows no sign of a let-up in strongly growing membership numbers. The more members we have the greater the subscription income, the healthier the Club and the greater the need for good, efficient administration. I can offer no easy solution but as a growing Club with significant liquid assets we need to make sure we manage ourselves in a professional way and this is an issue which I think calls for close scrutiny going forward. It is not going to be solved completely by employing limited extra resource in the office.

An initiative that I am really pleased about is the Expedition Information Centre which will shortly be available on our website. This is a document which contains just about every bit of information that anyone visiting any of the greater ranges might ever want to know. The intention is that it will be a living document updated by users. It fits well with the spirit of the Climbing Fund and I would like to see it built up to become a flagship document recognised as offering the best possible all-round advice for any mountaineer intending to arrange a trip to the greater ranges.

I have often said that I see arranging events where mountaineers can share experiences face to face as an essential service to the mountaineering community and something that should be a key aim of the Club. Continuing with the annual symposia and organising further events such as the 'Evening with the Alpine Club' that was arranged at the Keswick Mountain Festival look to be very much the way to go and I hope we will continue to dig deep so that we can carry on with such events.

3. Review and agree plans to improve the accommodation at Charlotte Road so that it is of maximum benefit to the membership.

A sub-committee was set up under Roger James and much time and effort has been spent looking at the feasibility and cost of various options. The subject was debated at the AGM and the Committee will be now be considering the way forward in light of the opinions expressed at the AGM and by old and new Committee members.

All I will say on that subject now is that I think the Committee has to be decisive on such issues and not allow them to fester. The last thing that I would want is for issues to cause deep rifts and dominate Committee discussion over a lengthy period to the detriment of other important issues.

The Club does have a bit of a history of re-inventing the wheel and we really do need to try and avoid that in the future.

4. Set up a sub-committee and make recommendations about the Club's future policy on guidebooks.

Matters have moved rather slowly here. A sub-committee has been set up under the chairmanship of Craig Cook but this is an area that will have to be taken forward further next year.

And it is an area where close consideration must be given to our future policy. It is all very nice for members to indicate that they very much like the AC producing guidebooks but the days when the AC produced just about the only English written guidebooks to the Alps are now long gone. Even British rock climbing clubs which have, in relative terms, a closed market are finding that sales are significantly down and it is increasingly difficult to make a financial case for publishing comprehensive guidebooks.

Personally I hope that the AC will be able to find a way forward through selected routes guides and bespoke publications such as big format books which provide ideal showpieces for the Club and the remarkable photographs in our archives and those taken by many of our members.

Whatever we publish, though, we must introduce a procedure whereby publications are approached in a more structured manner with a business case being prepared and approved for every publication. If we are going to invest in a publication that might cost the club money we at least need a structured assessment of the likely cost.

5. Maximise opportunities to show and conserve the Club's collections and make all reasonable efforts to secure Lottery funds to help with costs.

This year was the 60th anniversary of the first ascent of Everest so it is perhaps unsurprising that there has been a focus on displaying items linked to Everest this year.

The Queen and Prince Philip (not to mention 500 or so others) viewed items from the AC collections at an RGS event in May and a comprehensive display of material from nine Everest exhibitions was wonderfully displayed at Charlotte Road in June, in the Outside Café in the Peak District in November and is now here in Buxton.

Away from Everest memorabilia, Frank Tucket's collection (Tucket was a contemporary of Whymper and a former Vice President) along with exhibits from the AC archives attracted over 600 visitors to the Frenchay Village Museum (near Bristol) between January and March. And in a similar vein Peter Berg has continued to wow audiences with his modern presentation of Edward Whymper's *Scrambles in the Alps* lantern slide show, all proceeds of which have been generously gifted to the Club. All this is of course is in addition to the regular exhibitions of paintings that continue in the Charlotte Road lecture theatre.

The rich heritage of the Club helps to build its current standing. Looking forward, plans are being hatched for a major showing of AC collection items in the UK, Chamonix and Zermatt in 2015 which is the 150th anniversary year of major first ascents such as the Matterhorn and Brenva Spur.

On a less positive note, extra restrictions imposed by the Heritage Lottery Fund led to a decision to call a halt to efforts to secure Lottery funding to restore and digitise our photographic collection. This was a major blow after a tremendous amount of work had been put in. Further options are currently being considered but whatever the outcome we clearly need to make sure that our valuable collections are maintained in good condition and made available as widely as possible.

6. Consider how best to make the Alpine Club a louder voice in influencing events in the mountaineering community and on mountain ethical issues.

Here a more structured programme of attendance at important mountaineering events has been introduced with AC representation at events such as the UIAA General Assembly, the EU Mountaineering Forum and the *Piolet d'Or* steering group. Also, the Club has lent support to various initiatives aimed at protecting the alpine environment, including the UIAA's 'Preservation of natural rock for adventure climbing' policy document. Representation is sometimes not cheap and I think this is an area that needs to be monitored closely going forwards.

Achievements

Three years ago I said that I wanted to increase membership numbers and particularly the number of young members. The latest statistics show:

• There are now over 1500 members, which is 20% more than 3 years ago.
• c25% of current members have joined in the last 3 years.
• Most pleasingly we have over four times as many members under the age of 30 as we had 3 years ago.
• About 8% of our members are now under the age of 30 (compared to about 3% under 30 in a certain major British rock climbing club).
• After a tightening up of subscriptions collection the number of paid-up members is now 35% higher than it was 3 years ago.

The above is of course just a brief summary of what has been achieved by the combined efforts of a large number of people. When I look back over the last three years I am proud that so much has been achieved by the remarkable people who work tirelessly for this Club on a completely voluntary basis.

On that note I would like to thank those Committee members who have moved on during the year or whose terms end at the end of 2103: Andy Cave, Jamie Goodhart, Steve Goodwin, Pete Holden, Anna Seale and Stuart Worsfold. For 2014 I would like to welcome to the Committee Lindsay Griffin as your new President, Amanda Beddows, Charles Burbridge, Susan Jensen, Kimball Morrison, Bernard Newman, Victor Saunders and Jonathan White. And I would like to extend a special personal thank-you to John Town who I was lucky enough to have as Honorary Secretary throughout the duration of my presidency. John has served a very full three years and achieved a tremendous amount during his tenure. He intends to stand down on 31st March and will be a very difficult act to follow.

And of course I too have served three years and will be handing over to Lindsay Griffin. Not only is Lindsay a popular figure and all-round good chap, he also knows more about mountaineering and has more influential mountaineering contacts than just about anyone else in the mountain world.

I hand over having no doubt that the leadership of the Club will be in safe hands.

2014 Piolet d'Or winners (l-r) Ueli Steck, Ian Welsted and Raphael Slawinski on stage in Courmayeur with their 2014 awards *(Pascal Tournaire)*

The 2014 Piolets d'Or

At the 22nd Piolets d'Or, held at the end of March in Chamonix and Courmayeur, a six-person jury selected two very different ascents to represent the spirit of modern mountaineering and the various aspects of the ethical charter that forms the basis of these awards. Prior to the event the technical committee had provided over 70 significant ascents from 2013 that more or less met the Piolets d'Or criteria. The committee and the jury then spent many days choosing the most representative, finally deciding to make five nominations and one Special Mention.

The nominated climbs were: the first ascent of Kungyang Chhish East (7400m), formerly one of the highest virgin summits in Pakistan, climbed via the 2700m south-west face by Simon Anthamatten (Switzerland), Hansjorg and Matthias Auer (Austria); the first ascent of K6 West (7040m), also in Pakistan, by Canadians Raphael Slawinski and Ian Welsted, via the north-west face and west ridge, a 2700m rise from base camp; the first ascent of the 2000m north face and descent of the west face of Talung (7349m), a summit situated in Nepal immediately south of Kangchenjunga, by Czechs Marek Holecek and Zdenek Hruby (the latter sadly killed on Gasherbrum I a few months later); a new route on the 2700m south face of Annapurna (8091m) by the 'Swiss Machine' Ueli Steck; and the first ascent of the north-east buttress and north ridge of Mt. Laurens (3052m) in Alaska by Mark Allen (USA) and Graham Zimmerman (New Zealand/

USA). Whilst this year no British were nominated, a tenuous link is that Welsted has a Welsh mother still living in Cardiff!

This year's jury was a diverse group, ably presided over by George Lowe (first ascents of the Kangshung Face of Everest, *Infinite Spur* on Foraker amongst many others, and part of the well-known Lowe dynasty). Other members were Kazakh high altitude specialist Denis Urubko, Catherine Destivelle, a well-known Italian author Erri de Luca, German alpinist and author Karen Steinbach, and Lim Sung-muk, a mountaineer and editor of the Korean magazine *Man and Mountain* (one of the organizers of *Piolets d'Or Asia*).

Diverse as they are in personality and mountaineering background, the six jury members were also completely different in their opinions of which ascent, or ascents, should receive an award. Consequently, a consensus was not possible, deliberations took several hours, and the final decision a democratic compromise, awards being made to Annapurna and K6 West.

The two ascents chosen represented different forms of exploration (a much climbed face on a well-known mountain as against an unclimbed peak), and extremes in the management of risk. Steck knew he was accepting great danger, and is very conscious that he will probably not put himself in a similar situation again: the Canadians timed their ascent perfectly, minimized exposure to rockfall, and planned days to get enough rest at each bivouac. The jury also noted that as regular visitors to Pakistan, these two decided to continue with their expedition immediately after the Nanga Parbat massacre, realizing the need to show their support for the local people, and as encouragement to other mountaineers not to paint all Pakistanis with the same brush.

Uncontested were the Sixth Piolets d'Or Lifetime Achievement Award, presented to the legendary American mountaineer John Roskelly, and a Special Mention made of the second ascent of Steck's route on Annapurna by Stéphane Benoist and Yannick Graziani. This endeavour was cited as a wonderful example of 'brotherhood of the rope'. Benoist suffered from a lung infection high on the face, making the descent very taxing, and he has since undergone severe amputations to both fingers and toes. However, the fact that they managed to return alive demonstrated that there are occasions where a partnership can be greater than the sum of its components.

Over and above the general subjectivity of giving these awards, this year there was added controversy: did Steck really solo the south face of Annapurna? There is considerable belief, largely centred in the Austro-German quarter, that he did not.

Whilst there is still no definitive proof that Steck went above the base of the rock band, there is absolutely no evidence that he did not. Is his ascent a plausible scenario? Some argue that the times simply don't add up, failing to accept the fact that Steck may have reached the performance level of a world-class Olympic athlete. Graziani, a superbly fit, active guide, and one of France's top mountaineers, knows Steck well and says he is simply in a completely different class.

Patricia Jolly, a journalist with *Le Monde*, and one who takes her work seriously, went to Nepal, hired an interpreter, and sought out the two Sherpas who were at Advanced Base during the night Steck was on the mountain. One stated categorically that he saw the light from Steck's headtorch 'about 200m below the summit'. Did he dream it? Could this be a giant conspiracy? Remember that earlier in the year Steck had alienated himself from many Sherpas due to an incident on Everest. Benoist has chatted extensively with Steck about their various lines through the rock band, which Steck was able to describe in some detail, giving the impression that at the very least, the Swiss Machine got high on this section of the wall.

Steck set off up the face with little or no intention of climbing it: his partner had declined to follow at the bergschrund, but as the weather was good, Steck decided to climb to below the rock band for further acclimatization. It was only there, when he realized the exceptional nature of the conditions, that he elected to continue, but only as long as he felt able to climb down. Once above, on the easy summit slopes, he also knew he had to move fast; when the sun hit the wall the névé-covered passages

Ueli Steck. *(Bernard Newman)*

on the rock band would likely melt, making descent very difficult. In the end he made eight rappels from Abalakovs, threading his light, 60m rope directly through the holes.

People cite obvious parallels with Cesen, but when the Slovenian claimed the south face of Lhotse more than 20 years ago, it was a huge leap into the future, probably more so than Bob Beaman's 1968 Mexico long jump. Whilst not denying that Steck's ascent took mountaineering to a new level, a number of alpinists, including Benoist and Graziani, agree that the time was right; we were almost waiting for something like this to take place.

The 22nd edition might be the last of this genre of Piolets d'Or, as the event tries to move more towards being a celebration of alpinism, rather than being seen as some sort of 'Oscars' of the climbing world. It may have a different format, it may have different partners, but the charter will remain the same, though no doubt, given the current world of mountaineering professionals, with the requirement for some form of proof and transparency for each ascent.

Lindsay Griffin

The Godfathers of American climbing literature: Steve Roper and Allen Steck.
(Terry Gifford)

Lunch With Steck and Roper

'We don't climb outdoors anymore,' Roper had emailed me. But when I was arranging a visit for lunch at Steck's house with my host and their friend Larry Giacomino I had to avoid Tuesdays and Thursdays because on those days they went to the Berkeley climbing gym. Steve Roper (73), wrote the first guidebook to Yosemite and the history of climbing in the Valley, *Camp Four*, and Allen Steck (88), is co-author of the famous *Steck-Salathé* route on Yosemite's Sentinel Rock in 1950 and of the still-unrepeated *Hummingbird Ridge* on Mount Logan, Alaska, in 1965 which Roper and Steck included in their 1979 book *Fifty Classic Climbs of North America*.

Steck came to door, slightly stooped, but still with the wild silver hair and sparkling eyes. 'Allen Steck, you're still alive! And held together with duct-tape!' I pointed down to the silver taped toe of his left slipper. 'Come on in and I'll get you a glass. I've already started.' Steck picked up his wine glass from the mantelpiece above the open fire on which he'd cooked salmon last time I was here. We wandered through to the kitchen. From this kitchen Steck and Roper edited 14 editions of the best climbing writing in the English-speaking world for 32 years until they ran out of steam in 1999 and the glossy magazines were paying writers more than they could.

'Do you still have your own wine with the *Ascent* label for those long editorial lunches with Roper?'

'Here's the last unopened bottle, probably undrinkable now.'

Incubus Hills, the label says, with the famous image of bodies falling in the Matterhorn disaster. The name celebrates the title of an article first published in *Ascent* written by Ed Ward-Drummond.

'Drummond used to mix three metaphors in one sentence, the Sierra Club publishing editor used to complain. We liked them and kept them

Allen Steck with the *Hummingbird Ridge* secret weapon. *(Terry Gifford)*

in. One of the best writers we ever published. *Rock and Ice* magazine bought the title of *Ascent* from us and paid us $2000 each to agree not to publish another issue. We were never going to edit another issue anyway. Here's Roper with the comestibles.'

Roper came bustling through the door with the lunch, saying, 'You know it's 18 years since we stayed at Larry's cabin and climbed together in the Valley on *Overhang Bypass*. Then we went back to Steck's 70th birthday party here in this house.'

What a day that had been. I was amazed that a two-star route of only 5.7 could be found winding up to the rim of the Valley left of Bridalveil Falls, with a distinctive pitch called the 'Hog Trough' – 'clean and exposed' – giving it a memorable character. The steep descent down Gunsight Gully to the sound of a peregrine was equally memorable. Then there was the party in the garden at Steck's house with the golden age of Yosemite climbing in attendance. I remember Steck's older brother George, who pioneered long hiking routes in the Grand Canyon and wrote the guidebooks to them, being concerned that I was helping the champagne disappear a little too swiftly.

Steck was still musing on Drummond. 'He once said to me, "Allen, will you be my father?" He knew he needed someone to look after him and that was before the onset of his Parkinson's.'

Talk turned to the *Hummingbird Ridge* and I asked if they included it in their book *Fifty Classic Climbs of North America* as the equivalent of *The Scoop* on Sron Ulladale in Wilson's *Hard Rock* – the stopper route that would prevent people from ticking the complete list too easily. Roper was animated.

'Not at all. We definitely didn't do that. We included it because it was a classic route, an elegant ridge. We expected that it would be repeated within the next five years.'

Steck said that it would be repeated this summer. Not one, but two teams had contacted him about it.

'Did you remind them to take a shovel?'

'Of course. That granulated snow was taking forever to cut steps in it with an axe. I had insisted on taking a garden shovel along and that solved the problem. Do you want to see it?'

Steck shuffled off to his basement and came back with the biggest, heaviest agricultural implement Uncle Sam had ever produced. But its blade was cunningly full of holes.

'What were the hardest routes in Yosemite when you started climbing there?'

'*Lost Arrow Chimney*', said Roper, 'was probably the hardest climb in the world in its day.'

'*Higher Spire*,' chipped in Steck, the elder and earlier pioneer.

'Allen, what's the story I've heard about you getting benighted on your own route?'

'It was the fiftieth anniversary ascent, when I was 73. All went well until at the Narrows I ran out of steam. I simply could not climb it. This has only ever happened to me twice before in my life. So we were benighted. There was nowhere to lie down and my head kept falling off my arms folded over the rock. It was a horrible night. In the morning my partner rigged a pulley system and hauled me up. It was the end of my annual anniversary ascents of that route.'

The last time I had seen Steck was at Stanage a decade ago when he'd arranged to meet Ken Wilson and Dick Turnbull for an ascent of *Right Unconquerable*, an old favourite of his. It was raining heavily and Steck approached the crag with an umbrella and street shoes. It was clear that climbing was not on for a Californian in his 70s, although Dick did actually lead the route in the rain. But Roper remembered their first visit to Stanage when Steck was leading the route.

'He was close to the top when suddenly there was an almighty scream. He'd taken a fall onto a number four Friend. And I was only using a hip belay. Californians of a certain generation, like us, were slow to adopt the Sticht plate from Europe.'

Steck was grinning at the memory of this story told against himself. It was time to leave.

'End of an era,' mumbled Steck as we walked out the door.

A few days later Larry took me into the Valley again to climb a three pitch 5.6 called *Munginella* to the left of Yosemite Falls. There was snow on the top of Half Dome and the Falls gave their famous display of rainbows in the sun as we gained height above the trees. There was no-one above or below us on the route. We took time to linger and chat on the stances. The rock offered its bright granular friction and perfect jams. This, I was forcefully reminded, is what I like doing. And 67 is no age at all these days. I decided to give up alcohol for a month again, stick to Larry's high fat/ low carb diet and get fit for a long classic route in Scotland this spring with my son.

'Rock!' shouted Larry on the lead. A rock the size of a haggis fell at speed between us. A raven flew away above us with a stick for its nest. I know, I know. I should have been wearing more than a Californian bandana.

Et in Arcadia Ego. It could have been the end of an era.

Terry Gifford

ALPINE CLUB LIBRARY ANNUAL REPORT 2013

Hywel Lloyd, Chairman of the Council of Trustees of the Alpine Club Library writes: This has been the year of the 'Road Shows'; the Library initiative to bring out some 'Treasures of the Alpine Club' from the basements of Charlotte Road, and show them to our members.

We started in January with a small exhibition in the Frenchay Museum, near Bristol. The main theme celebrated the centenary of the death of Frank Fox Tuckett, a Frenchay man, pioneer alpinist and our Vice-President 1866-1868. The Chairman of South Gloucester Council, Janet Biggin, opened the show.

In the summer, we staged an exhibition at Charlotte Road to recount the stories of the Nine AC Expeditions – 1921 to 1953 – that led to the summit of Everest 60 years ago. During four weeks, we were able to exhibit many books, paintings,

Members and guests at the opening of 'Everest 1921 to 1953 – the nine AC expeditions leading to the summit'. *(Hywel Lloyd)*

artefacts, and original photographs. We also showed a compilation of historic photos on a large screen at the Pen y Gwryd Hotel in Snowdonia over the anniversary of the ascent. Next, we took a selection of the exhibition (to keep extra insurance costs sensible) to Hathersage in the Peak District, also for four weeks. Finally, the show moved to Buxton for the weekend of the Club AGM and Dinner. In all, a total of over 2,500 members, guests, and public visitors viewed these shows during the year.

Janet Biggin, Chairman of South Gloucester Council, opened the AC exhibition brandishing Frank Fox Tuckett's hefty 1850s ice axe, while Hywel judiciously retreats. *(Hywel Lloyd)*

Now to report on the plan to scan the many thousands of historic photographs held in the Library; new rules published by the Heritage Lottery Fund in spring 2013 gave us some advantages but also several significant disadvantages. After careful consideration, the Library and the Club felt we could not proceed with pursuing this possible line of funding. Thus,

Discussing methods and achievements of the 1922 Everest Expedition at the 'Everest 1921 to 1953 – the nine AC expeditions leading to the summit' show. *(Hywel Lloyd)*

The Library Team examining donated books for items to fill gaps, or allocate to back-up loan stock: L to R: Tadeusz Hudowski, our Librarian; Glyn Hughes, the Hon Archivist; Barbara Grigor-Taylor, Library Trustee; Jerry Lovatt, the Hon Librarian. *(Hywel Lloyd)* Below: Sandy Irvine's ice axe, lost when he disappeared in 1922; found in 1933. *(Hywel Lloyd)*

we are now moving ahead with a modest project, funded by the Club with some additional funds from the Library and the BMC, and volunteer work by the Photo Library team. Already, we have reproduced many historic photos to exhibit at the road shows.

Looking ahead, 2014 will be the celebration of the climax of 'The Golden Age of Alpinism', the period of achievement of many alpine summits by British alpinists, virtually all members of the AC. We are working with the Chamonix Museum to stage a significant exhibition of our archives, paintings and artefacts, which will be open for many months. Before and after this major show, we will take smaller shows to several locations in the UK. Dates and locations are not yet final, but 'watch this space'.

All this involves a great deal of effort and I am privileged to be working with the strong, keen and knowledgeable team of Library volunteers that is making this all happen. Our thanks are due to each of them.

Contributors

DEREK BUCKLE is a retired medicinal chemist now acting part-time as a consultant to the pharmaceutical industry. With plenty of free time he spends much of this rock-climbing, ski-touring and mountaineering in various parts of the world. Despite climbing, his greatest challenges are finding time to accompany his wife on more traditional holidays and the filling of his passport with exotic and expensive visas.

JOHN CLEARE has been a freelance professional photographer for over 50 years but a climber for rather longer. Business and many expeditions have taken him all over the world, while he has several dozen books, several films and live TV broadcasts, more than a few new routes and several virgin summits to his credit. An ex-vice president of the AC and an ex-president of the Alpine Ski Club, he lives in remote Wiltshire.

KATHARINA CONRADIN is the managing director of Mountain Wilderness, board member of the International Commission on the Protection of the Alps (CIPRA) and herself an active mountaineer, though her current job doesn't leave her as much time in the mountains as she would like to.

KELLY CORDES Aside from being short, having a low IQ and a girl's name, Kelly Cordes is a climber and writer resident in Colorado, USA. He's climbed throughout the world including the Greater Ranges, though a series of injuries has relegated him primarily to the crags rather than the mountains; a reality he'd long secretly desired. He was formerly Senior Editor of the *American Alpine Journal* and now survives as a freelance writer.

EVELIO ECHEVARRIA is a professor of international literature, now retired, and has been an AC member since 1959. His mountaineering record includes many obscure peaks in South and North America. He specializes in the history and chronicaling of Andean mountain ascents.

PETER FOSTER is a recently retired hospital physician and is researching the life of T. Graham Brown. He has been a member of the Alpine Club since 1975.

MICK FOWLER works for Her Majesty's Revenue and Customs and, by way of contrast, likes to inject as much memorable adventure and excitement into his climbing ventures. He has climbed extensively in the UK and has regularly led expeditions to the greater ranges for more than 26 years. He has written two books, *Vertical Pleasure* (1995) and *On Thin Ice* (2005). Mick served as president of the Alpine Club from 2010-13.

DAMIEN GILDEA, an Australian, has led a number of expeditions to the high mountains of Antarctica that have resulted in many new routes and first ascents. He is the author of *Mountaineering In Antarctica: Climbing In The Frozen South*, has produced two topographical maps for Antarctic mountain areas and is the Antarctic correspondent for the *AAJ* and *Alpinist* magazine. Damien has also undertaken climbing trips to the Karakoram, Himalaya and Andes.

STEPHEN GOODWIN renounced daily newspaper journalism on *The Independent* for a freelance existence in Cumbria, mixing writing and climbing with a ten-year stint as Hon Editor of the *Alpine Journal*, stepping down after publication of the 2013 edition.

YANNICK GRAZIANI is one of France's leading Guides. He was born on the Côte d'Azure near Nice in 1973 and discovered rock climbing in Chamonix at the age of 17. His horizons soon expanded to embrace the high mountains including the Himalaya and as he puts it, 'entering this magical world naturally made me push at the doors of the highest peaks.' He returns to the Himalaya almost every year.

DENNIS DILLON GRAY started climbing on Yorkshire Gritstone in 1947 aged 11. Secretary of the ACG, first National Officer, then General Secretary of the BMC, Dennis has visited over 60 countries and, following early retirement from the BMC, enjoyed several trips to the Himalaya. More recently Dennis has travelled widely in China and undertaken three research projects, two of which involved spells in Xinjiang. He's written two autobiographies, two books of stories/anecdotes, a novel and a volume of poems. Plays the banjolele and sings, equally badly, on three CDs of climbing/mountain themed songs.

JIM GREGSON has climbed widely in the Alps since 1972. He is also a telemark ski mountaineer who makes regular trips to Norway. He first visited the Arctic in 1991 and has returned many times, often as an expedition leader. His book Exploring Greenland documents many of his trips and showcases his photography. He hopes to return to Greenland again – and again. . .

TERRY GIFFORD was Director of the annual International Festival of Mountaineering Literature for 21 years. Former Chair of the Mountain Heritage Trust, he is the author of *The Joy of Climbing* (Whittles, 2004) and *Al Otro Lado del Aguilar* (Oversteps Books, 2011). Visiting Professor at Bath Spa University's Centre for Writing and Environment and Profesor Honorifico at the University of Alicante, Spain, in his 51st year of rock-climbing he is struggling up long easy routes in Scotland, Ireland, Yosemite and the Avon Gorge.

LINDSAY GRIFFIN lives in North Wales, from where he continues to report on the developments in world mountaineering. An enthusiastic mind still tries to coax a less than enthusiastic body up pleasant bits of rock and ice, both at home and abroad. He is currently serving as AC President.

LEO HOULDING (*culled from his website*) Based in the Lake District, Leo is one of Britain's top climbers and among the best in the world. He is the veteran of a score of epic ascents, including Everest, is an experienced BASE jumper but specialises in free climbing the most technical peaks and biggest walls in the world.

GARETH JONES was Professor, Cambridge Clinical School, UK. He has published *The Hypoxia Hilton*, which describes attempting to induce pulmonary oedema by acute exposure to altitude. Also *Aviat Space Environ Med* 2008;**79**:81 – 6, *T Graham Brown, Behind the Scenes at the Cardiff Physiology Institute and The Brenva Feud*.

ALASTAIR LEE Film maker and climber Alastair Lee has spent the past 20 years grafting his way to the top of his game. His genuine passion for the mountain environment is expressed through innovative filming and superb cinematography. Alastair has climbed in all seven of the world's continents producing over a dozen adventure films, three TV commercials and is an author of seven books.

CALUM MUSKETT (20) was born and brought up on the edge of the Carneddau, and started climbing aged 13. Since his first outing on the Idwal Slabs Calum was hooked by the adventurous traditional rock climbs of Snowdonia, putting up new routes to E8. Between his varied work as a cleaner, writer, speaker, MIA & WML instructor, Calum has travelled the world seeking out difficult alpine routes as well as free climbing big walls such from Yosemite to Patagonia.

TAMOTSU NAKAMURA has been climbing new routes in the greater ranges since his first successes in the Cordillera Blanca of Peru in 1961. He has lived in Pakistan, Mexico, New Zealand and Hong Kong and has made more than 30 trips exploring the 'Alps of Tibet'. In 2010 he retired as editor of the *Japanese Alpine News* but continues as contributing editor. He received the RGS Busk Medal in 2008 and more recently the 4th Japan Sports Prize.

BERNARD NEWMAN started climbing the day England won the World Cup, so you'd think he'd be better at it by now. He joined the Leeds University Union Climbing Club in 1968 when Mike Mortimer was president, and was closely associated with that exceptional group of rock climbers and super-alpinists which included Syrett, MacIntyre, Baxter-Jones, Porter and Hall, without any of their talent rubbing off. One-time geologist, editor of *Mountain* and *Climber*, Bernard is now a 'freelance' writer, editor and photographer and current Hon. Editor of the *Alpine Journal*.

TED NORRISH read classics at Brasenose College, Oxford, where he enjoyed three Alpine seasons, an expedition to Arctic Norway in 1955, and, in 1958, organised and part led the Oxford Chitral expedition.
A classics master at KH VIII school in Coventry for 30 years, Ted has climbed in the Taurus, Carpathians, Elburz and Hindu Kush and spent time as a volunteer ranger in four US National Parks, including the Grand Canyon for three months in mid winter.

TIM POLLARD is an Art teacher and climbing instructor (MIC) who began climbing in the early seventies on Yorkshire grit and limestone. Winter climbing in the Lakes and Scotland soon followed. Alpine rock and ice came next and is still a necessary fix. His main passion at the moment is ice climbing, although friends are still trying to convert him to mixed. Tim started mountain painting twelve years ago and it remains a significant and vital part of his life.

SIMON RICHARDSON is a petroleum engineer based in Aberdeen. Experience gained in the Alps, Andes, Patagonia, Canada, the Himalaya, Caucasus, Alaska and the Yukon is put to good use most winter weekends whilst exploring and climbing in the Scottish Highlands.

DES RUBENS has retired after 35 years in teaching and is therefore having the rest of his life off. Thus, his best years are yet to come. He still gets very excited about climbing in the Alps and Scotland. Recent visits to Canada and Peru have rounded out a CV based around the Indian sub-continent, to which he still aspires to return.

C A RUSSELL, who formerly worked with a City bank, devotes much of his time to mountaineering and related activities. He has climbed in many regions of the Alps, in the Pyrenees, East Africa, North America and the Himalaya.

BILL RUTHVEN was made an honorary member of the Alpine Club in 2004 for his service to mountaineering as honorary secretary of the Mount Everest Foundation. Before being confined to a wheelchair, he had built up more than half a century of mountaineering experience, which proved invaluable to him in his MEF work. However, this will be his last compilation of MEF reports – after 29 years in this post he has now retired and handed over the reins to Glyn Hughes.

MARCELO SCANU is an Argentine climber who lives in Buenos Aires. He specialises in ascending virgin mountains and volcanoes in the Central Andes. His articles and photographs about alpinism, trekking, and mountain history, archaeology and ecology appear in prominent magazines in Europe and America. When not climbing, he works for a workers' union.

MIKE SEARLE has been on over 30 expeditions, starting in Patagonia, Peru and Ecuador, and progressing to the Himalaya in Ladakh, Zanskar, Garhwal and throughout Nepal and Bhutan. In the Karakoram he has climbed on K2, Masherbrum, Biale, Trango, and on granite spires in the Baltoro, Biafo and Hushe regions. He has also rock climbed in Jordan and Oman and is now Professor of Earth Sciences at the University of Oxford.

DOMINIK SIEGRIST is president of the International Commission on the Protection of the Alps (CIPRA) which campaigns to protect the environment of the Alps and is a board member of the King Albert I Memorial Foundation.

PAUL SCHWEIZER started rock climbing in California in 1973. He was active in establishing new routes in Joshua Tree in the 1980s, and has climbed in big mountains the world over, from Alaska to Pakistan, Nepal, Kazakhstan, the Andes, Tajikistan and India, along with the Alps and Scotland in winter.

PIOTR SZAWARSKI was born and brought up in Poland. Having initially pursued a career in internal medicine and gaining MRCP and MSc in Infectious Diseases, he then moved into anaesthetics and is an FRCA, holds a European Diploma in Intensive Care and is part of the faculty for the Diploma in Mountain Medicine. He was on a successful expedition to Cho Oyu in 2005 and worked for the Himalayan Rescue Association in Pheriche, Khumbu in 2007.

MARK THOMAS was born and brought up amongst the surf and sea cliffs of North Pembrokeshire. Having climbed since childhood he ventured into the Alps for the first time thirteen years ago, finding himself strapped to a very snowy and cold West Face of the Dru for three days on his first route. That rather intense introduction caused him to instantly fall in love with Alpine climbing and eventually became a fully qualified International Mountain Guide. He is director of Elite Mountain Guides.

JOHN TOWN is a retired University Registrar and, until recently, AC Honorary Secretary. He has climbed in the Alps, Caucasus, Altai, Andes, Turkey and Kamchatka and explored little-known mountain areas of Mongolia, Yunnan, Xinjiang and Tibet. He is old enough to remember the days before satellite phones and GPS.

MATT TRAVER is a British-American filmmaker originally from Hong Kong. He has previously organised climbing expeditions and adventurous film projects to Central Asia, Greenland, Mongolia and Malaysia. He's most interested in exploring little-known corners of the world and returning to share his stories with others through his photography and films.

DICK TURNBULL started climbing in 1970 at Surrey University. His Alpine experience has been gained mainly in winter, due to family summer commitments, and includes winter ascents of the north faces of the Eiger, Matterhorn, Dru, Droites, Walker Spur, (95% of Croz Spur!). Many trips to other areas including one to Gangotri in 1985. For many years Dick has owned and run the outdoor retailer *Outside*. Dick currently edits the *Alpine Club Newsletter*, and is still climbing.

IAN WALL worked at Plas-y-Brenin in the 60s, where his friendship with 'Jacko' and leading climbers of that period shaped his future. Ian has climbed extensively throughout the UK, Alps and in Norway, leading treks in Africa, Ladakh, Tibet and Nepal where he now lives. Ian keeps busy acting as an advisor to the Kathmandu International Mountain Film Festival, the Kathmandu Environmental Education Project and in developing and training the Nepal Mountain Leader programme, working closely with the Nepal Mountaineering Association. In his spare time he's out exploring his 'back-yard' of Nepal... but he still retains his CC membership!

NOTES FOR CONTRIBUTORS

The *Alpine Journal* records all aspects of mountains and mountaineering, including expeditions, adventure, art, literature, geography, history, geology, medicine, ethics and the mountain environment.

Articles Contributions in English are invited. They should be sent to the Hon Editor *The Alpine Journal*, Alpine Club, 55 Charlotte Road, London EC2A 3QF, UK. (**admin@alpine-club.org.uk**) Articles, including images, should be sent on a disk or memory stick (with accompanying hard copy as appropriate, e.g. sketch maps) or as an email attachment. With files created in Microsoft Word please confine any extra formatting to italics and bold and set the language to English UK. Length should not exceed 3000 words without prior approval of the editor **and may be edited or shortened at their discretion**.

It is regretted that the *Alpine Journal* is unable to offer a fee for articles published, but authors who are not AC members receive a complimentary copy of the issue of the *Journal* in which their article appears.

Preferably, articles and book reviews should not have been published in substantially the same form by any other publication.

Maps and diagrams These should be well researched, accurate, and show the most important place-names mentioned in the text. It is the author's responsibility to get their maps redrawn if necessary. If submitted electronically, maps should be originated as CMYK via Adobe Illustrator, Freehand or similar and submitted as pdfs with any embedded images at 300dpi resolution and CMYK. Hard copy should be scanned as a Photoshop compatible 300dpi tiff at A4 finished size. This can be arranged through the production editor if required.

Photographs Colour transparencies should be originals (not copies) in 35mm format or larger. Prints (any size) should be numbered (in pencil) on the back and accompanied by a separate list of captions (see below). Pre-scanned images should be Greyscale or RGB, 300dpi tiffs or Maximum Quality jpegs at A4 final size or larger. Images from digital cameras should be Large jpegs, tiffs or RAW files at the maximum file size (quality) the camera can produce.

Captions All image files (also any slides and prints) should have **short**, unique names/serial numbers **that correspond to a list of captions** appended your article as a word processing document, or in an email. Captions should be reasonably detailed and include the photographer's name.

Copyright It is the author's responsibility to obtain copyright clearance for text, photographs, digital images and maps, to pay any fees involved and to ensure that acknowledgements are in the form required by the copyright owner.

Summaries A brief summary, listing dates, team members, objectives attempted and/or achieved, should be included at the end of articles where appropriate.

Biographies Authors are asked to provide a short biography, in about 50 words, listing the most noteworthy items in their climbing career and anything else they wish to mention.

Deadline Copy and photographs should reach the editor by 1 February of the year of publication.

Index 2014

'Realise your potential.
Achieve your dreams.
Live for Adventure.'

berghaus®

LIVE FOR ADVENTURE®

Discover our adventures at www.berghaus.com

#liveforadventure

MOUNTAIN
EQUIPMENT

mountain-equipment.co.uk

NEW GORE-TEX® PRO
LHOTSE JACKET
FULL FUNCTION, 4-SEASON PROTECTION

Climb gear of the year 2013

TRAIL MAGAZINE
BEST IN TEST
NOVEMBER 2013

Featuring a new Alpine fit, award-winning HC hood, YKK® Aquaguard® zips and the new generation GORE-TEX® Pro fabric.

Mountain Equipment
Pro-Partner Nick Bullock puts
the Lhotse through it's paces
on an alpine gear test,
Rive Gauche, Chamonix.

📷 Lukasz Warzecha

GORE-TEX

Engineered with GORE-TEX® Pro product technology
Built for maximised ruggedness and are ideal for extreme
and extended use.

"...it's only when you wear the new
Mountain Equipment Lhotse jacket
that you appreciate just how good
the new Alpine Fit really is."

Jon Doran, outdoorsmagic.com

"...excellent arm-lift movement without
coming untucked from your harness,
and the hood works really well with
or without a helmet."

Tom Richardson, Climb, August 2013

"...GORE-TEX® Pro fabric and the
Lhotse jacket have both received
superb upgrades" Test Rating: 5/5

Graham Thompson, Trail, August 2013

Ice
Snow
Rock
Climb
Ski

All seasons, all games

ATTACK

The Alpine Attack is the perfect companion for the modern alpinist: Lightweight, durable and packed with functional features - A flawless pack for all your alpine adventures.

LOWEALPINE.COM

THERE WHEN YOU NEED US MOST

BMC ACTIVITY INSURANCE
thebmc.co.uk 0161 445 6111

LIGHTEN YOUR LOAD.
GO CARBON.

Still on aluminium sticks?
Then it's time to rethink!

3 YEAR guarantee
„NO QUESTIONS ASKED"

MOSER
climbing Couloir
Cortina d'Ampezzo

Hardwear Expert Circle.

On a sheer rock face, every detail needs to be just right.
Mammut dealers from all over the world came together
in Ticino, Switzerland, to test the design, ergonomics
and quality of the new Mammut hardwear. The experts
all agreed: exceptional functionality, thanks to a clear
focus on the essentials. To find your new hardwear, visit:
www.mammut.ch